The Climate Casino

The Climate Casino

Risk, Uncertainty,
and Economics for a
Warming World

William Nordhaus

Yale UNIVERSITY PRESS

NEW HAVEN & LONDON

Yale University Press books may be purchased in quantity for educational,
business, or promotional use. For information, please e-mail sales.press@
yale.edu (U.S. office) or sales@yaleup.co.uk (U.K. office).

Set in 10.5/17 Meridien type by Westchester Publishing Services.

Printed in the United States of America.

The Library of Congress has cataloged the hardcover edition as follows:

Nordhaus, William D.
  The climate casino : risk, uncertainty, and economics for a warming
world / William Nordhaus.
        pages cm
  Includes bibliographical references and index.
  ISBN 978-0-300-18977-3 (cloth : alk. paper) 1. Climatic changes—
Effect of human beings on.   2. Climatic changes—Environmental aspects.
3. Climatic changes—Social aspects.   4. Environmental policy.   I. Title.
  QC903.N8545 2013
  363.738'74—dc23
                                                              2013010722

ISBN 978-0-300-21264-8 (pbk.)

A catalogue record for this book is available from the British Library.

10 9 8 7 6 5 4 3 2 1

To Annabel, Margot, and Alexandra

CONTENTS

ACKNOWLEDGMENTS

The author wishes to highlight the distinguished contributions to energy modeling by the late Stanford economist Alan Manne, who pioneered research in this field with both methods and empirical modeling. Others who have participated in advancing the field and made generous suggestions and critiques to the present work include George Akerlof, Lint Barrage, Scott Barrett, Joseph Boyer, William Brainard, William Cline, Noah Diffenbach, Jae Edmonds, Alan Gerber, Ken Gillingham, Jennifer Hochschild, Robert Keohane, Charles Kolstad, Tom Lovejoy, David Mayhew, Robert Mendelsohn, Nebojsa Nakicenovic, David Popp, John Reilly, Richard Richels, John Roemer, Tom Rutherford, Jeffrey Sachs, Herbert Scarf, Robert Stavins, Nick Stern, Richard Tol, David Victor, Martin Weitzman, John Weyant, Zili Yang, Janet Yellen, and Gary Yohe, as well as many anonymous referees and reviewers.

This book has reached its elegant final form through the skilled and tireless efforts of the staff at Yale University Press here in New Haven. They have guided the author and made countless suggestions for improving both its form and substance. Particular thanks go to the Executive Editor, Jean Thomson Black, who saw it through from e-scribbles to published book and beyond. Editorial assistant Sara Hoover served as skilled problem solver. Similarly helpful were manuscript editor Mary Pasti, designer Lindsey Voskowsky, and production manager Maureen Noonan. Bill Nelson drew the art. Debbie Masi and Westchester Publishing Services moved it from electronic files to handsome printed pages. The art of book publishing is another reminder of Adam Smith's observation that the "greatest improvement in the productive powers of labor [are] the effects of the division of labor."

I especially salute the memory of my teachers and sometime collaborators who pioneered in fields that were critical to development of climate-change economics, especially Tjalling Koopmans, Robert Solow, James Tobin, and Paul Samuelson. The research underlying this book has been generously supported by Yale University, the U.S. National Science Foundation, the U.S. Department of Energy, and the Glaser Foundation. This book is intended as a survey of the field rather than an original research monograph. Many of its chapters have appeared in technical form in earlier publications. However, most of the explanations, diagrams, and tables have been designed expressly for this book.

NOTE TO READERS

There are two electronic editions of this book. One is identical to the print edition and is available on various e-readers and platforms. The other is an enhanced edition that provides access to more web references, examples for further study, and interactive material that elucidates key ideas and concepts. The enhanced edition is available through Inkling.com. More details on the DICE model used in this book are available at dicemodel.net.

PART I

THE GENESIS OF CLIMATE CHANGE

Risk varies inversely with knowledge.
—*Irving Fisher*

1 FIRST ENCOUNTERS IN THE CLIMATE CASINO

If you read the newspaper, listen to the radio, or scan the daily blogs, you are virtually certain to encounter stories about global warming. Here is a sample from a variety of sources:

> The last decade was the warmest on record.
> The most inconvenient fact is the lack of global warming for well over 10 years now.
> Polar bears could disappear within a century.
> Global warming claims are a hoax.
> The Greenland ice sheet has experienced record melting.[1]

Clearly, global warming is getting a lot of attention today. And just as clearly, people disagree about whether it is real, whether it is important, and what it means for human societies. What should the interested citizen conclude from these conflicting stories? And if the answer is that global warming is real, how much does it matter? Where should our concerns about global warming rank among the other issues we face, such as persistent unemployment, a soaring public debt, low-intensity wars, and nuclear proliferation?

The short answer is that global warming is a major threat to humans and the natural world. I will use the metaphor that we are entering the Climate Casino. By this, I mean that economic growth is producing unintended but perilous changes in the climate and earth systems. These changes will lead to unforeseeable and probably dangerous consequences. We are rolling the climatic dice, the outcome will produce surprises,

we're gambling w/ our futures

and some of them are likely to be perilous. But we have just entered the Climate Casino, and there is time to turn around and walk back out. This book describes the science, economics, and politics involved—and the steps necessary to undo what we are doing.

A ROAD MAP OF THE TERRAIN AHEAD

Global warming is one of the defining issues of our time. It ranks along with violent conflicts and economic depressions as a force that will shape the human and natural landscapes for the indefinite future. Global warming is also a complex subject. It spans disciplines from basic climate science, ecology, and engineering to economics, politics, and international relations, and the result is a book with many chapters. Before embarking on an extended journey, readers may find it useful to look at a map of what lies ahead. Here are the major themes discussed in the five parts that follow.

Part I surveys the science of global warming. Climate science is a dynamic field, but the essential elements have been developed by earth scientists over the last century and are well established.

The ultimate source of global warming is the burning of fossil (or carbon-based) fuels such as coal, oil, and natural gas, which leads to emissions of carbon dioxide (CO_2). Gases such as CO_2 are called greenhouse gases (GHGs). They accumulate in the atmosphere and stay there for a long time. Higher atmospheric concentrations of GHGs lead to surface warming of the land and oceans. The initial warming effects are amplified through feedback effects in the atmosphere, oceans, ice sheets, and biological systems. The resulting impacts include changes in temperatures as well as impacts on temperature extremes, precipitation patterns, storm location and frequency, snow packs, river runoff, water availability, and ice sheets. Each of these will have profound impacts on biological and human activities that are sensitive to the climate.

Past climates—varying from ice-free to snowball earth—were driven by natural sources. Current climate change is increasingly caused by human activities. The major driver of global warming is the emissions of CO_2 from the burning of fossil fuels. CO_2 concentrations in the atmosphere were 280 parts per million (ppm) in 1750 and have reached

390 ppm today. Models project that, unless forceful steps are taken to reduce fossil fuel use, they will reach 700–900 ppm by 2100. According to climate models, this will lead to a warming averaged over the globe in the range of 3–5°C by 2100, with significant further warming after that. So unless there is either a major slowdown in economic growth or strong steps to curb CO_2 emissions sharply, we can expect continued accumulations of CO_2 emissions in the atmosphere—and the resulting global warming with all its consequences.

links s/on + climate

Part II analyzes the impacts of climate change. The major concerns are not temperature per se but the effects on human and natural systems. A central concept in analyzing impacts is whether a system can be managed. The nonagricultural sectors of high-income countries are highly managed, and this feature will allow these sectors to adapt to climate change at relatively low cost for at least a few decades.

However, many human and natural systems are unmanaged or unmanageable and are highly vulnerable to future climate change. While some sectors or countries may benefit from climate change, there are likely to be significant disruptions in areas that are closely tied to climate-sensitive physical systems. The potential damages are likely to be most heavily concentrated in low-income and tropical regions such as tropical Africa, Latin America, coastal states, and the Indian subcontinent. Vulnerable systems include rain-fed agriculture, seasonal snow packs, coastal communities, river runoffs, and natural ecosystems. There is potential for serious impacts in these areas.

Scientists are particularly concerned about "tipping points" in the earth's systems. These involve processes in which sudden or irreversible changes occur as systems cross thresholds. Many of them operate at such a large scale that they are effectively unmanageable by humans with existing technologies. Four important global tipping points are the rapid melting of large ice sheets (such as Greenland), large-scale changes in ocean circulation such as the Gulf Stream, feedback processes where warming produces more warming, and enhanced warming over the long run. These tipping points are particularly dangerous because they are not easily reversed once they are triggered.

Part III discusses the economic aspects of strategies to slow climate change. There are several potential strategies for slowing climate change, but the most promising is "mitigation," or reducing emissions of CO_2 and other GHGs. Unfortunately, this approach is expensive. Studies indicate that it will cost in the range of 1–2 percent of world income ($600–1,200 billion annually at today's level) to attain international climate targets, even if this is undertaken in an efficient manner. While some miraculous technological breakthroughs might conceivably be discovered that can reduce the costs dramatically, experts do not see them arriving in the near future.

The economics of climate change is straightforward. When we burn fossil fuels, we inadvertently emit CO_2 into the atmosphere, and this leads to many potentially harmful impacts. Such a process is an "externality," which occurs because those who produce the emissions do not pay for that privilege, and those who are harmed are not compensated. One major lesson from economics is that unregulated markets cannot efficiently deal with harmful externalities. Here, unregulated markets will produce too much CO_2 because there is a zero price on the external damages of CO_2 emissions. Global warming is a particularly thorny externality because it is global and extends for many decades into the future.

Economics points to one inconvenient truth about climate-change policy: For any policy to be effective, it must raise the market price of CO_2 and other GHG emissions. Putting a price on emissions corrects for the underpricing of the externality in the marketplace. Prices can be raised by putting a regulatory tradable limit on amount of allowable emissions ("cap and trade") or by levying a tax on carbon emissions (a "carbon tax"). A central lesson of economic history is the power of incentives. To slow climate change, the incentive must be for everyone—millions of firms and billions of people spending trillions of dollars—to increasingly replace their current fossil-fuel-driven consumption with low-carbon activities. The most effective incentive is a high price for carbon.

Raising the price on carbon will achieve four goals. First, it will provide signals to consumers about which goods and services are carbon intensive and should therefore be used more sparingly. Second, it will provide signals to producers about which inputs are carbon intensive (such as coal and oil) and which use less or no carbon (such as natural gas or wind power), thereby inducing firms to move to low-carbon technologies. Third, it will give market incentives for inventors, innovators, and investment bankers to invent, fund, develop, and introduce new low-carbon products and processes. Finally, a carbon price will economize on the information that is required to undertake all these tasks.

Part IV examines the central questions of climate-change policy: How sharply should countries reduce CO_2 and other GHG emissions? What should be the time profile of emissions reductions? How should the reductions be distributed across industries and countries? What policy tools—taxes, market-based emissions caps, regulations, or subsidies— are most effective?

It is tempting to set climate objectives as hard targets based on climate history or ecological principles. The simple target approach is unworkable because it ignores the costs of attaining the goals. Economists advocate an approach known as cost-benefit analysis, in which targets are chosen by balancing costs and benefits.

Because the mechanisms involved in climate change and impacts are so complex, economists and scientists rely on computerized integrated assessment models to project trends, assess policies, and calculate costs and benefits. One major finding of integrated assessment models is that policies to slow emissions should be introduced as soon as possible. The most effective policies are ones that equalize the incremental or marginal costs of reducing emissions in every sector and every country. Effective policies should have the highest possible "participation"; that is, the maximum number of countries and sectors should be on board as soon as possible. Free riding should be discouraged. Moreover, an effective policy is one that ramps up gradually over time—both to give people time to adapt to a high-carbon-price world and to tighten the screws increasingly on carbon emissions.

While all approaches agree on the three central principles—universal participation, equalizing marginal costs in all uses in a given year, and increasing stringency over time—there are big differences among analysts on the stringency of policies. Our analysis suggests that policy should aim for limiting temperature to a range between 2°C and 3°C above preindustrial levels (here taken to be the 1900 temperature) depending upon costs, participation rates, and discounting. The lower target is appropriate if costs are low, participation rates are high, and the discount rate on future economic impacts is low. A higher target would apply for high costs, low participation rates, and high discounting.

An effective policy must necessarily be global in scope. Earlier treaties (such as the Kyoto Protocol) were ineffective because they provided no incentives to encourage participation. Countries have strong incentives to free ride on the efforts of others because emissions reductions are local and costly while the benefits are diffuse and distant over space and time. An effective global arrangement will need an effective mechanism to encourage participation and discourage free riding. The most promising approach is to impose import tariffs on the products and services of nonparticipants. This will be sufficiently burdensome that it will encourage most countries to participate in an international climate regime.

As Part V discusses, a realistic appraisal must recognize the high hurdles on the road to effective policies to slow global warming. Even though climate scientists have made great strides in understanding the basic trends, it has proven difficult to implement policies to slow climate change.

One major reason for the slow progress is the nationalist dilemma, which leads to free riding. Countries that do not participate in a global agreement to reduce emissions get a free ride on the costly abatement undertaken by other countries. This incentive leads to a noncooperative free-riding equilibrium in which few countries undertake strong climate-change policies—a situation that closely resembles the current international policy environment. They speak loudly but carry no stick at all. A link whereby nonparticipants are penalized through international trade tariffs would help alleviate the free-riding syndrome.

Additionally, there is a tendency for the current generation to ride free by pushing the costs of dealing with climate change onto future generations. Generational free riding occurs because most of the benefits of emissions reductions today would accrue many decades in the future.

The double free-riding difficulties are aggravated by interest groups that muddy the water by providing misleading analyses of climate science and economic costs. Contrarians highlight anomalies and unresolved scientific questions while ignoring the strong evidence supporting the underlying science and current projections of climate change. The need to introduce effective policies has been particularly difficult in the United States, where ideological opposition has hardened even as the scientific concerns have become increasingly grave.

THREE STEPS FOR TODAY

Concerned citizens naturally wonder what we should do right now to slow the trajectory of global warming. This is a complex process involving the public, the economy, and technology. I would emphasize three specific items to focus on.

- First, people around the world need to understand and accept the gravity of the impacts of global warming on the human and natural world. Scientists must continue intensive research on every aspect from science to ecology to economics to international relations. People should be alert to the trumped-up claims of contrarians who find a thousand reasons to wait for decades to take the appropriate steps.
- Second, nations must establish policies that raise the price of CO_2 and other greenhouse-gas emissions. While such steps meet resistance—like our aversion to taking foul-tasting medicine—they are essential elements for curbing emissions, promoting low-carbon technologies, and thereby inoculating our globe against the threat of unchecked warming. Moreover, we need to ensure that actions are global and not just national. While politics may be local, and the opposition to strong steps to slow warming comes from nationalistic attitudes, slowing climate change requires coordinated global action.
- Third, it is clear that rapid technological change in the energy sector is central to the transition to a low-carbon economy. Current low-carbon technologies cannot substitute for fossil fuels without

a substantial economic penalty on carbon emissions. Developing economical low-carbon technologies will lower the cost of achieving our climate goals. Moreover, if other policies fail, low-carbon technologies are the last refuge for achieving our climate goals. Therefore, governments and the private sector must intensively pursue low-carbon, zero-carbon, and even negative-carbon technologies.

These three themes will run through this entire book: increased public awareness, pricing of carbon and other greenhouse-gas emissions, and accelerating research on technologies to decarbonize our economies.

THE CIRCULAR FLOW OF CLIMATE CHANGE, IMPACTS, AND POLICY

We can visualize the discussion in this book in Figure 1, which displays the logical circular flow from emissions to impacts and finally back to emissions, closing the circle.

It is worthwhile to spend a minute examining the logic of Figure 1. The global warming problem starts at the upper-left box where economic

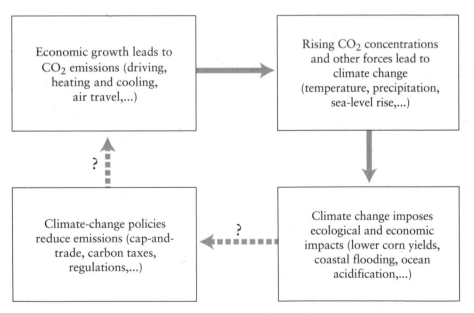

Figure 1. The circular flow of global warming science, impacts, and policy.

growth and distorted price signals from the market lead to rapidly rising emissions of CO_2 into the atmosphere. The arrow then moves to the box at the upper right, where the CO_2 concentrations and other forces lead to major changes in the climate system.

The changing climate then produces impacts on human and natural systems in the box on the lower right. Finally, the box on the lower left shows societal responses to the threat of climate change.

The arrows in Figure 1 represent the linkages between the different parts of the economy-climate-impacts-politics-economy nexus. However, the last two arrows are dashed with question marks. These links do not yet exist. As of 2013, there are no effective international agreements to limit the emissions of CO_2 and other greenhouse gases. If we continue along our current path of virtually no policies, then the dashed arrows will fade away, and the globe will continue on the dangerous path of unrestrained global warming.

2 A TALE OF TWO LAKES

Although our world is huge and seems impervious to human insults, life on earth is in fact a fragile system. It is full of organisms, linked together in a complex web of relationships, all of which are made possible by the warmth of the sun and the protection of the atmosphere. We need only look at our moon, which receives about the same amount of solar radiation each year as the earth, to recognize the contingency of our earth's systems. There on the moon, but for the grace of our atmosphere, would we go. Perhaps living systems have evolved elsewhere in the universe. But it seems highly unlikely that the living systems of our earth—our plants, animals, humans, and human civilizations—are found anywhere else. The drama that is life on earth will play only once.[1]

I can illustrate the fragility of life on earth with a tale of two lakes. The first is a small string of salt ponds in southern New England, where I love to visit in the summer.[2] Twenty thousand years ago, during the last ice age, New England was buried under a mountain of glacial ice. The ponds were coastal estuaries left behind as the glaciers retreated. Today, they are home or way station for piping plovers, least terns, horseshoe crabs, and multicolored jellyfish. On the ocean side of the ponds are long barrier beaches.

The ponds are vulnerable spots, subject to abuse from many quarters. Developers, hurricanes, and motorboats all beat upon the fragile coastline. Conservationists, ecologists, and environmental agencies fight back. In recent years, there has been a standoff between the forces of preservation and those of degradation.

What will these ponds look like in a century? The answer depends on our actions over the coming years. If we succeed in stopping climate change, in 100 years they may be as beautiful as they are today. However, if CO_2 emissions continue unchecked, the combination of warming, changes in ocean chemistry, and sea-level rise may turn them into dead salt marshes.

Death is already approaching a second lake. The Aral Sea in Central Asia was once the fourth-largest lake in the world. But over the last half century, it has shrunk from 26,000 square miles to about one-tenth that size (roughly akin to New York State shrinking to the size of Connecticut).[3] What caused this? It was nothing dramatic like a hurricane or war or ruthless exploitation under runaway capitalism. The cause was primarily bad economic planning driven by perverse incentives: The centrally planned "socialist" Soviet Union decided to divert the rivers that feed the lake for irrigation of marginal lands.[4] Like a child starved of nutrition, the lake is slowly dying.

This tale of two lakes tells the story of this book in the simplest way. We humans control the future of our planet, with its lakes, forests, and oceans brimming with life. Our living earth has many enemies—global warming is our focus, but it takes place alongside unchecked market forces, war, political woodenheadedness, and poverty. We first need to understand the destructive forces at work. Then, through a combination of scientific analysis, careful planning, good institutions, and appropriate channeling of market forces, we can preserve the unique heritage around us.

This book examines but one of the issues that we must address to preserve our world—global warming. Humans have been contributing to a warmer globe on a small scale for centuries. But the present century is a critical period in which we must curb the unchecked growth in greenhouse gases, particularly those that come from fossil fuels. If we have not largely reduced the impact of these gases by this century's end, the environmental future of the earth is grim.

A PERSONAL PERSPECTIVE

The purpose of this book is to put global warming in perspective so that concerned citizens can understand and come to an informed judgment about it. In these pages, I discuss the problem from start to finish—from the beginning where warming originates in our personal energy use, to the end where societies take steps to reduce the dangers of warming.

This book will be interesting primarily for readers who want to learn what science and economics have to say about global warming. An open mind will help here. If you are already convinced that global warming is just a vast left-wing conspiracy launched by people trying to micromanage our lives, it is unlikely to change your view. At the other pole, if you have already concluded that the world is headed toward climatic Armageddon, you may dismiss this book as underestimating the seriousness of the threat.

But most people's views are somewhere in between. They are pulled in different directions by the competing arguments and may view the debate like a courtroom argument between lawyers. What this book does is listen to both sides, review the evidence in as fair and unbiased a manner as possible, and present the best that science and economics have to offer.

Notice that I called this section "A Personal Perspective." As with any subject of scientific inquiry, there are solid facts. But each of us inevitably views these facts from a different vantage point. By studying the subject at hand carefully, from our own perspective, and merging our observations with different ones, we can arrive at a more complete understanding.

What is my perspective? I am an economist working at a research and teaching university. I have taught and written in many areas of economics, particularly environmental economics and macroeconomics. I am the coauthor of a textbook in introductory economics that is now in its nineteenth edition, and that experience has given me a special appreciation for people who are struggling with new ideas.

I have also studied and written on the economics of global warming for more than three decades. I have participated in many studies sponsored by the U.S. National Academy of Sciences since warming first became a serious issue. I have written three books as well as several dozen specialized journal articles on the economics of global warming. I teach the economics of energy and global warming to undergraduates. Moreover the rhetorical wars about global warming are familiar territory because I have witnessed similar battles in different areas of economics and national budget policy. My experience tells me that we need to cool down the rhetoric so that we can understand the underlying issues.

You might be asking yourself whether we really need another book on global warming. If so, why read a book about global warming by an economist? Isn't this really a scientific issue?

Yes, the natural sciences are essential to understand why climate change occurs, as well as to determine the pace and regional dimensions of change. Clearly, we cannot hope to understand the problems of warming without studying the basic findings of earth scientists.

But global warming begins and ends with human activities. It begins as the unintended side effect of economic activities—growing food, heating our homes, and even going to school. To understand the linkage between economic activity and climate change requires an analysis of our social systems, which are the subjects of the social sciences, such as economics.

Moreover, designing effective measures to slow or prevent climate change requires understanding not only the physical laws that carbon dioxide obeys, but also the more fluid laws of economics and politics—those that involve human behavior. Our policies must be well grounded scientifically. But the best science in the world will not by itself change the way people spend their incomes or heat their homes. It will take policies based on a sound understanding of human behavior to change the direction of economic growth toward a low-carbon world. So getting the science right is the first step in mapping the way humans are changing our future climate, but understanding the economic and political dimensions is essential for designing ways to fix the problem.

I wrote this book particularly for young people, and I dedicate it to my grandchildren. They and their generation will inherit this world and are likely to live through the twenty-first century. The globe at century's end will be vastly different than it is today. The condition of our planet will depend on the steps we take in the interim, but those to slow global warming are perhaps the most momentous for the natural world. I hope that our grandchildren can look back in the years ahead and say that this generation had the resolve to reverse the dangerous course we are currently on.

3 THE ECONOMIC ORIGINS OF CLIMATE CHANGE

Most people think that global warming is a question for the natural sciences, that it primarily involves heat waves, melting ice sheets, droughts, and storms. True, scientific controversies have been central to public debates about global warming. However, in reality the ultimate source — and the solutions—lies in the realm of the social sciences.

WHY IS CLIMATE CHANGE AN ECONOMIC PROBLEM?

Begin by stepping back and asking a basic question. Why is global warming such a special problem? Why is it a global problem and not a national problem or a household problem? Why is it such a persistent problem?

The economics of climate change is straightforward. Virtually everything we do involves, directly or indirectly, the combustion of fossil fuels, which results in emissions of carbon dioxide (CO_2) into the atmosphere. The CO_2 accumulates over many decades, changes the earth's climate, and leads to many potentially harmful impacts.

The problem is that those who produce the emissions do not pay for that privilege, and those who are harmed are not compensated. When you buy a head of lettuce, you pay for the costs of producing it, and the farmers and retailers are compensated for their efforts.

But when producing the lettuce requires the combustion of fossil fuel—to pump the water that irrigated the lettuce field or to fuel the truck that delivered the lettuce—one important cost is not covered: the damage caused by the CO_2 that is emitted. Economists call such costs externalities because they are external to (i.e., not reflected in) the market transactions. An externality is a by-product of economic activity that causes damages to innocent bystanders. (These are also called public goods in the economics literature, but the term externality is more intuitive and will be used here.)

Life is full of externalities. Some are harmful, such as when someone dumps arsenic into a river and kills the fish. Others are beneficial, such as when a researcher discovers a polio vaccine. But global warming is the Goliath of all externalities because it involves so many activities; it affects the entire planet; it does so for decades and even centuries; and, most of all, because none of us acting individually can do anything to slow the changes.

Global warming is a particularly thorny externality because it is global. Many critical issues facing humanity today—global warming and ozone depletion, financial crises and cyber warfare, oil price shocks and nuclear proliferation—are similarly global in effect and resist the control of both markets and national governments. Such global externalities, whose impacts are indivisibly spread around the entire world, are not entirely new phenomena, but they are becoming more important because of rapid technological change and the process of globalization.

So global warming is a special problem for two central reasons: It is a global externality caused by people around the world in their everyday activities of using fossil fuels and other climate-affecting measures; and it casts a long shadow into the future, affecting the globe and its people and natural systems for decades and even centuries into the future.

Economics teaches one major lesson about externalities: Markets do not automatically solve the problems they generate. In the case of harmful externalities like CO_2, unregulated markets produce too much because markets do not put a price on the external damages from CO_2 emissions. The market price of jet fuel does not include the cost of the CO_2 emissions, and so we fly too much.

Economists talk about an "invisible hand" of markets that set prices to balance costs and desires. However, the unregulated invisible hand sets the prices incorrectly when there are important externalities. Therefore, governments must step in and regulate or tax activities with significant harmful externalities. Global warming is no different from other externalities; it requires affirmative governmental actions to reduce harmful spillovers.

Global externalities pose special difficulties because there is no workable market or governmental mechanism to deal with them. There is no world government that can require everyone around the globe to participate in the solution. The absence of a world government makes it difficult to stop the overfishing of whales, rein in dangerous nuclear technologies, and slow global warming.

The fact that climate change is both external to markets and global is the central hurdle that policymakers must overcome if they are to slow the pace and avoid the dangers of climate change in the coming years.

WHY ARE CARBON DIOXIDE EMISSIONS RISING?

Discussions of global warming usually begin with the emissions and accumulation of CO_2 and other greenhouse gases (GHGs) in the atmosphere. However, the real starting point is with humans and their daily lives. I will use my own experience as an American living in a midsized city, but one could equally well talk about a Nigerian oil worker, a German brewer, or an Indonesian weaver.

Suppose I am invited to give a talk at the University of Connecticut, about 50 miles from my home in New Haven. The most convenient way to get there is to drive my car up and back. The round trip is about 100 miles, and taking into account sitting in traffic and city driving, my car will get about 20 miles per gallon, so I consume 5 gallons of gasoline. This will produce about 100 pounds of CO_2, which will come out of the tailpipe and go into the atmosphere. I can't see it or hear it or smell it, and I generally do not even think about it. If I am like most people, I will probably assume that my trip will have no effect on the world's climate, and so I will ignore the consequences.

But there are more than 7 billion people around the world making analogous decisions many times every day and every year. Suppose that everyone on earth consumed the equivalent in fossil fuel energy of my drive twice a week, for heating, lighting, cooking, and other activities. All this would add about 30 billion metric tons of CO_2 to the world's atmosphere each year, which is what global CO_2 emissions were in 2012. Virtually everything we do has some CO_2 buried in the process. You might think that riding your bicycle is carbon free. But a little carbon was emitted in making the bicycle, and quite a bit was involved in building the road or sidewalk.[1]

Why in the world do we use this vast quantity of fossil fuels? We use it to drive, to fly, to heat our houses and schools, to run our computers, and for everything we do. Almost 90 percent of the energy we use comes in the form of fossil fuels, and burning those fuels produces the CO_2 emissions.

Say we are shocked by how much energy we use and want to cut back. Why can't we simply stop using fossil fuels now that we know about global warming? I discuss this issue in Part III, but it is so central that a few words are useful here. It turns out that we cannot simply convert to other energy sources by flipping a switch, because those other sources are more expensive. It generally costs more to power our lives with renewable fuels (such as solar power). In some cases, using low-carbon fuels requires a completely different capital stock—new power plants and factories, different engines and furnaces—from what exists today, and this adds greatly to the expense.

Return to the example of my trip to the University of Connecticut for which I use my gasoline-powered car. I might decide to buy an electric car instead. It would not emit any CO_2. But it would probably use electricity fueled by natural gas, and generating the electricity emits CO_2. Similarly, my home furnace burns only natural gas. To convert it to run on solar power would require a major investment—not to mention that the sun does not always shine where I live, and it never shines at night.

So for now, like most Americans, I am for practical purposes hooked on fossil fuels. Moreover, I enjoy my current lifestyle. I like my car, my computer, and my cell phone. I prefer a warm house in the winter and a cool house in the summer. I definitely do not want to return to a caveman standard of living.

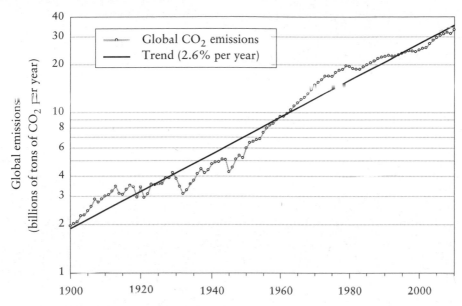

Figure 2. Global CO$_2$ emissions, 1900–2010.

The net effect of all these decisions around the world is shown in Figure 2, which displays the long-term trend in global CO$_2$ emissions over the period from 1900 to 2010.[2] There have been periods of fast growth and of slow growth, but on average, emissions grew at a rate of 2.6 percent per year. This upward trend is the source of our worry. These rising emissions are leading to rising CO$_2$ concentrations in the atmosphere, which is what produces climate change.

I note here one geeky detail about the figure: The vertical scale on the diagram, and on several others in this book, is a ratio scale. This is a diagram in which equal vertical distances have equal proportions; thus, for example, the vertical distance from 200 to 400 is the same as that from 400 to 800. Ratio scales are convenient because a straight line (one with a constant slope) has a constant rate of growth or decline. If you look at Figure 3, you see that a given percentage increase looks the same no matter where it occurs on the chart.

It will be useful to give the global totals here. Global CO$_2$ emissions have been growing because the global economy has been growing. The world's population has expanded from around 2 billion in 1900 to over

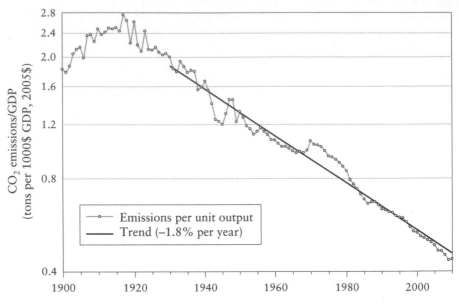

Figure 3. Carbon intensity of U.S. economy, 1900–2010.

7 billion in 2012. In most countries, output of goods and services (gross domestic product) per person has grown as well. Fortunately, world CO_2 emissions have not been growing as rapidly as world output because of what is called decarbonization. This means simply that over time we are using less CO_2-rich energy to produce a given amount of output. This is seen in the trend of the "carbon intensity" of economic activity, which is measured as the ratio of CO_2 emissions to output.

The reasons for decarbonization are many, but three factors explain most of it. One is that, for most products, we use less energy per unit of output today than in earlier years; this is true whether the output is a shirt or a gallon of milk or a telephone call. Another source of decarbonization is that our most rapidly growing economic sectors, such as electronics and health care, tend to use less energy per unit of output than sectors that are growing less rapidly or shrinking. In other words, our economic mix is shifting from industries and activities that are more energy intensive to ones that are less so. A final source of decarbonization has been the shift in energy sources away from the most carbon-intensive fuels (e.g., coal) toward less carbon-intensive fuels (e.g., natural gas) and to renewable and nonfossil sources (e.g., nuclear and wind).

Figure 3 illustrates the declining carbon intensity of economic activity for the United States, for which we have reasonably good data going back over a century. It is a fascinating picture. The figure shows that the carbon intensity of the U.S. economy increased until around 1910 (this period was the first age of coal). Since 1930, the CO_2-gross domestic product (GDP) ratio has fallen at an average rate of 1.8 percent per year.

While the carbon intensity of production is declining, it is not declining fast enough to reduce total CO_2 emissions, either for the world or for the United States. Over the last eight decades, real output in the United States has grown at an average rate of 3.4 percent per year, while carbon intensity has declined at 1.8 percent per year, which means that CO_2 emissions have grown at 1.6 percent (3.4 − 1.8) per year. Although high-quality data for the world as a whole are not available, the best estimates indicate that, over the last half century, global output grew at an average rate of 3.7 percent per year; the rate of decarbonization was 1.1 percent per year; and CO_2 emissions grew at 2.6 percent per year.

So here is the CO_2 problem in a nutshell: Countries around the world are growing rapidly (aside from some chronically poor performers, and putting aside recessions as painful but temporary setbacks). And they are using carbon-based resources such as coal and oil as the main fuel for their economic growth. The efficiency of energy use has improved over time, but the rate of improvement is insufficient to bend down the emissions curve. Hence, total CO_2 emissions continue to rise.

MODELS AS A TOOL FOR UNDERSTANDING

Let's step back a moment to review the terrain. We have seen that, because of economic growth and increased use of fossil fuels, humans are putting ever-larger quantities of CO_2 into the atmosphere. The growth of CO_2 concentrations is confirmed by scientific monitoring around the world. We need to know the consequences of rising GHG concentrations. Because we cannot calculate all these complicated formulas in our heads, we use computerized models to project the results of past and future economic growth on emissions, climate, and thence upon human and natural systems.

So how do economists and natural scientists project future climate change? It is necessarily a two-step procedure. The first step, explained in this chapter, is to estimate the future emissions of CO_2 and other important GHGs. The second step is to put those emissions estimates into climate and other geophysical models to project future change in CO_2 concentrations, temperature, and other important variables. This second step is discussed in Chapter 4. I begin by discussing an important element in modern natural and social sciences: the use of models.

A complete picture of future climate change requires projections of the economy, energy use, CO_2 and other emissions, and different climatic variables, along with the impacts in various sectors. A *projection* is a conditional or "if-then" statement. It states, "If a given set of input events take place, then we calculate that the following output events will occur." Economists often make this kind of projection, as in, "Given current fiscal and monetary policies and the impact of the Euro crisis, we expect real output to rise 2 percent next year." Similarly, scientists and economists use projections for future climate change. The main inputs we need are variables like the path of annual CO_2 and other GHG emissions. With these inputs and knowledge about the relevant physics, chemistry, biology, and geography, climate scientists can calculate the time paths for temperature and precipitation, sea level, sea ice, and many other variables.

Because humans cannot calculate such projections in our heads, they are all done with computerized models. What is a model? There are different kinds of models, from model trains to architectural models to scientific models. The basic idea is that a model is a simplified picture of a more complex reality. Economists represent the complex set of relationships that govern output, inflation, and financial markets using "macroeconomic models." These are mathematical and computerized engines that allow governments and businesses to project events for purposes such as planning the federal budget.

Climate models, similarly, use algebraic or numerical equations to represent the dynamics of the atmosphere, oceans, ice, and other related systems.[3] So just think of a climate model as a mathematical representation of the earth, with different layers of the atmosphere and oceans, running in short time steps of minutes to hours. They are very large models, deploying hundreds of thousands of lines of computer code that have been developed by dozens of teams of scientists in many countries. Many good descriptions of how models are developed are available in books and also online.[4]

You might wonder whether climate models are simplified. That is actually their purpose—to simplify, but not to oversimplify. After all, reality is enormously complex. The U.S. economy, for example, includes more than 300 million people, each making hundreds of decisions every day. There is no way to represent this system "accurately" in the sense of "literally." What we need for economic and climate modeling is to simplify the picture for the purpose at hand. We need the relevant details, not all the details.

Figure 4 illustrates the difference between a simplified model and the full reality. The left-hand side shows a photograph of a high-voltage transmission line that moves electricity from generators to customers. This is the "reality." The right-hand side shows the computer code in GAMS language for the energy system and the economy (actually, it is the DICE model discussed shortly). The model is a conceptual representation of the complex interactions of the electricity sector along with the rest of the energy system. Which do you prefer? An architect might choose the picture, while someone interested in dealing with climate change would prefer the computer program.

A good model, whether of a transmission tower, an economy, or the earth's climate, should capture the essence of the process without overwhelming the user with unnecessary clutter. In economics we build models of output and incomes, for example, to help the government forecast its revenues and spending and to provide an informed basis for

Figure 4. A comparison of a transmission line on the left with a computer model of the energy and economic system on the right. Each serves a useful function, but computerized models are crucial tools for understanding trends and the impacts of different policies.

determining what is happening to, say, government debt. A good model of the fiscal situation today does not need to contain any information on CO_2 emissions because that would have only a tiny effect on the current budget. To think about climate change, we build models to estimate future emissions of CO_2, the impact of those emissions on atmospheric concentrations of CO_2, and the changes in climate that result. The government deficit does not enter into climate models because it is a second-order or third-order influence on climate change.

```
parameters
** Economic parameters
        elasmu   Elasticity of marginal utility of consumption    /  1.45  /
        prstp    Initial rate of social time preference per year   / .015   /
        gama     Capital elasticity in production function          /.008   /
        pop0     Initial world population (millions)               /6838    /
        popadj   Growth rate to calibrate to 2050 pop projection   /0.134490/ ;
parameters
** Modeling parameters
        pbacktime(t) =pback*(1-gback)**(t.val-1);
        cost1(t) = pbacktime(t)*sigma(t)/expcost2/1000;

VARIABLES
        MIU(t)              Emission control rate for CO2
        TATM(t)             Increase atmospheric temperature (deg C from 1900)
        YGROSS(t)           World output (trillions 2005 USD per year)
        UTILITY             Welfare function;

EQUATIONS
        CCACCA(t)           Cumulative carbon emissions
        MMAT(t)             Atmospheric concentration equation
        TATMEQ(t)           Temperature-climate equation for atmosphere
        YGROSSEQ(t)         Output gross equation
        UTIL                Objective function ;

** Equations of the model
ccacca(t+1)..   CCA(t+1)        =E= CCA(t)+ EIND(t)*5/3.666;
mmat(t+1)..     MAT(t+1)        =E= MAT(t)*b11 + MU(t)*b21 + (E(t)*(5/3.666));
tatmeq(t+1)..   TATM(t+1)       =E= TATM(t)+c1*((FORC(t+1)-(fco22x/t2xco2)
                                      *TATM(t))-(c3*(TATM(t)-TOCEAN(t))));
ygrosseq(t)..   YGROSS(t)       =E= (al(t)*(L(t)/1000)**(1-GAMA))*(K(t)**GAMA);
util..          UTILITY         =E= tstep*scale1*sum(t,CEMUTOTPER(t))+scale2;

** Model definition and solution
model   CO2 /all/;
solve CO2 maximizing UTILITY using nlp ;
```

Figure 4. (continued)

Building good models is an art as well as a science. It is a science because you need accurate observations and reliable scientific theories. You could build a model based on the idea that earth and all life were created 10,000 years ago. But that theory would have deep trouble explaining the history of Long Island, because much of the island is debris left by ice ages more than 10,000 years ago. And you wouldn't know what to make of ice cores from Antarctica because they contain ice rings going back more than half a million years.

But modeling is also an art because you have to simplify to capture the essential details. Some models contain information on all the power plants and transmission links in the United States. But even such a huge enterprise cannot represent power generation in other countries, or international trade in electricity, or the interactions with the rest of the economy, or the carbon cycle. As Leonardo da Vinci is often cited, "Simplicity is the highest form of sophistication." The great formulas of physics are stunningly simple.

The central idea of climate change is also stunning in its simplicity. It is that the average temperature of the earth changes with the relative concentration of CO_2 in the atmosphere. A doubling of CO_2 concentrations is expected to lead to a rise in average temperature of around 3°C. Another doubling is expected to produce another 3°C of warming. Unfortunately, the parallel with the law of gravity breaks down at this point. To begin with, we don't know the exact rise in temperature per doubling of CO_2. Additionally, the effect may depend upon other factors, especially on the time scale over which the increase takes place.

Finally, just as maps are designed for different uses—for example, hiking versus sailing, or driving versus flying—models also are designed for different purposes. Many climate models are extremely detailed and require supercomputers to calculate the trajectories of the components they track. Other simplified models focus on projections of specific outcomes, such as impacts on agricultural output, sea level, or the geographic spread of malarial mosquitoes. Different problems require different models.

INTEGRATED ASSESSMENT MODELS

An important approach for analysis of climate change is a class of integrated assessment models (IAMs). These are comprehensive models that include not only climate but other aspects of the science and economics of climate change. IAMs combine in one package the end-to-end processes from economic growth through emissions and climate change to impacts on the economy and finally to the projected effects of policies for slowing climate change.

IAMs also contain highly simplified climate models. Like the computer code in Figure 4, they attempt to capture the linkage between emissions and climate change without including all the architectural nuts and bolts. The main advantage of IAMs is that they can represent the entire process from start to finish. The main disadvantage is that they simplify some of the processes that are analyzed in greater detail in the more complete models.

Many IAMs—large and small—have been developed by modeling teams around the world, and they have proven remarkably useful for understanding the implications of policies to slow climate change. Throughout this book, I rely extensively on IAMs in describing the economic aspects of climate change.

Additionally, I often refer to the results of models that have been developed at Yale University by me, students, and colleagues, known as the DICE family of models. DICE is short for Dynamic Integrated model of Climate and the Economy. There is also a more elaborate Regional version, known as the RICE model.[5]

The DICE model has a logical structure similar to the circular flow in Figure 1. An energy-economy module generates economic growth and CO_2 emissions in different regions over coming decades. Small carbon-cycle and climate modules generate global temperature trends. The DICE model includes damage calculations, where damages depend upon the size of the economy and on the temperature increase. Finally, there is a policy module, where countries can either limit emissions or put a price on CO_2 emissions, thereby bending down the emissions trajectory.

In the simplest global version, the model includes only a few equations and is relatively easy to understand. The more complete RICE model—with twelve major regions such as the United States, China, and India—contains thousands of lines of computer code and is more challenging to grasp. Readers who would like to examine the simple DICE model are encouraged to look at the online version (DICE-2012). You can change the parameters and assumptions (such as the long-run world population or the climate sensitivity) to get a feel for how integrated assessment models work as well as how sensitive they are to the underlying assumptions.[6]

PROJECTIONS: BASIC PRINCIPLES

Understanding future climate change begins with a set of projections for inputs into climate models. These are primarily the paths of emissions of CO_2 and other GHGs. To keep the discussion manageable, I focus primarily on CO_2 because it is the most important of the GHGs, but complete assessments include other gases as well. When looking at actual projections, I use CO_2 equivalent (CO_2-e), which adds together the contributions of all the GHGs and expresses them as the effect of an equivalent amount of CO_2.

How do statisticians and economists make projections? They begin by estimating statistical relationships using the historical data along with the underlying physical laws and economic relationships. With these results, a demographer or economist can then make a statistically based projection of future trends. The advantage of the statistical approach is that it can be reproduced and updated. That is, because each of the steps can be performed using publicly available data and computer software, the estimates can be checked or challenged by other scientists.

As I discuss above, total CO_2 emissions are driven by three components: population, GDP per capita, and the carbon intensity of GDP. Mathematically, the CO_2 growth rate is equal to the sum of the growth rates of each of the three components. Data for 2010 and projections for 2050 are shown for the United States and for the world in Table 1.[7] These projections for 2050 assume that countries make no policies to reduce emissions. The estimates come from the Yale DICE model, but they do not differ markedly from those found in other studies.

Look first at the top half for the United States. As Table 1 shows, population is projected to grow at 0.6 percent per year, per capita output to grow at 1.7 percent per year, and the CO_2 output ratio to decline at 1.6 percent per year. On the basis of these assumptions, CO_2 emissions would grow at 0.7 percent per year, increasing emissions by about one-third by midcentury.

Similar calculations can be made for different regions. Most economic models have modules for the different components. They might

Table 1. Projections of uncontrolled CO_2 emissions for the United States and the world, 2010–2050.

	2010	2050	Growth rate (% per year)
	United States		
GDP/Pop (2005 $/person)	42,300	83,700	1.7
CO_2/GDP (tons/$1,000,000)	432	226	−1.6
Population (millions)	309	399	0.6
Total CO_2 Emissions (million tons CO_2)	**5,640**	**7,550**	**0.7**
	Global		
GDP/Pop (2005 $/person)	9,780	22,400	2.1
CO_2/GDP (tons/$1,000,000)	522	278	−1.6
Population (millions)	6,410	9,170	0.9
Total CO_2 Emissions (million tons CO_2)	**34,900**	**57,600**	**1.3**

have elaborate energy-sector models to project the availability and use of different fuels. The output projections might take into account the capital in structures and equipment, software, technological change, and other factors. But the essential idea can be captured by this example.

The bottom half of Table 1 shows projections for the world (including CO_2 released by land-use changes as well as industrial emissions). If there are no policies to curb emissions, the global total of CO_2 emissions is projected to rise about 1.3 percent per year to midcentury. The difference between the top and bottom projections is primarily due to expectations that developing countries will grow more rapidly than the United States.

Table 1 suggests that there are three ways to reduce emissions: lower population growth, lower growth in living standards, and lower CO_2 intensity (decarbonization). People sometimes think that the CO_2 growth rates shown in Table 1 are ironclad laws that are unresponsive to economic policy, or, perhaps even more pessimistically, that we can only bend down the emissions trajectory by severely limiting growth in living standards or imposing draconian limits on population.

Such pessimistic conclusions are an incorrect reading of both history and policy. Societies can bend down the CO_2 growth curve by more rapid decarbonization, and if wisely undertaken that can be done with modest costs. There are many technologies that can produce goods and services with less carbon or even zero net carbon emissions. For example, electricity can be generated with low-carbon fuels (such as natural gas) or with noncarbon fuels (such as nuclear, solar, and wind power). We can develop more efficient appliances and cars. We can better insulate our houses. At some point, we may even be able to remove CO_2 from emissions streams or from the atmosphere inexpensively. So rather than focusing on painful limits to economic growth, economists tend to emphasize steering the economy toward low-carbon technologies.

Table 1 provides an illustration of a standard projection of CO_2 emissions and their determinants. An important starting point is the baseline or "no-policy" path of unconstrained CO_2 emissions. This provides a reference or starting point for policy—a look at how the world would evolve over the coming years with normal economic growth and unrestrained CO_2 emissions. Basically, this estimate combines a projection of economic growth along with the underlying trend toward decarbonization, discussed above, but with no limits on CO_2 emissions.

What do the different IAMs show? For this discussion, examine a group of IAMs surveyed under the aegis of the Energy Modeling Forum (EMF) at Stanford University.[8] The project is called EMF-22. It included modeling teams from around the world: six groups from Asia and Australia, eight from western Europe, and five from North America. Eleven of the modeling teams provided results for the baseline scenario of CO_2 emissions through 2100, and they are shown in Figure 5.

In addition, I have shown as two heavy lines the average of the EMF models along with the results of our Yale DICE model, which is used extensively in this book. It is useful to note that the DICE model predicts almost exactly the same growth rate for global CO_2 emissions over the next century as the average of the EMF-22 models.

The heavy line with triangles is the average of the eleven models surveyed in the EMF-22 project. The heavy line with the circles is from the Yale DICE model. The light lines are the individual EMF models.[9]

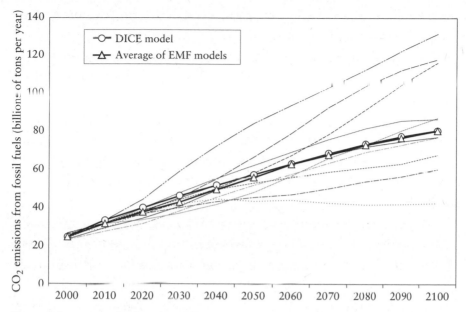

Figure 5. Projections for baseline CO_2 emissions.

UNCERTAIN CO_2 TRAJECTORIES IN THE CLIMATE CASINO

Figure 5 shows an example of the Climate Casino at play. A first point that emerges is that all models—every single one—project continued growth in CO_2 emissions. Growth rates range between 0.5 percent and 1.7 percent per year over the 2000–2100 period. Even though these rates look small, they add up to large cumulative changes due to the compounding effect over time. For example, the average growth rate of 1.2 percent per year means an increase of a factor of 3.3 over a century. These models represent the best efforts of economic and energy experts today, and they indicate that the CO_2 problem is not going to disappear or be magically solved by unrestrained market forces.

The second point concerns the uncertainty about future emissions. Because of the momentum of economic and technological systems, the near-term projections show few differences. However, the divergence among different projections splays out as we go further into the future. This is visualized in the spaghetti diagram of projections in Figure 5. Model projections of CO_2 emissions for 2100 range from 1.6 to 5.4 times higher than in 2000. The reasons for the divergence go back to the determinants of emissions growth and involve differing estimates about economic growth, technology, and energy use in the coming years.

Can we pin down the sources of the differences more precisely? A careful analysis finds that the biggest unknown arises from uncertainty about future growth of the world economy: Will the world enjoy robust economic growth like that from 1950 to 2005? Or will it stagnate, with slow technological change, recurrent financial crises and depressions, spreading pandemics, and occasional widespread wars? These are the most important questions behind the divergent estimates of CO_2 emissions.

The answers to these deep questions are at this point essentially unknowable—like the roll of the wheel in the Climate Casino. No one can reliably predict roulette wheels, the stock market, or future technologies. Remember that the recent deep recession was a complete surprise for virtually every professional forecaster. Because of the deep uncertainty about future economic growth, the divergence in emissions projections shown in Figure 5 is unlikely to narrow significantly in the next few years.

People will naturally wonder how to respond to these vast uncertainties when making climate-change policy. Isn't 100 years a long way off? One reaction is to postpone action—to assume that because life is uncertain, we should wait until we know more. Sometimes, if the stakes are low and we will soon learn the right answer, waiting until the wheel stops spinning is a reasonable approach.

But for climate change, waiting for the right answer is a perilous course. It is like driving 100 miles an hour with your headlights off on a foggy night and hoping there are no curves. We are unlikely to resolve the uncertainties soon. Waiting for many years to act is costly because of the delayed responsiveness of the economy and the climate system to our actions. It is less costly to spread our investments over time than to cram them all into a short time when the fog lifts and we see disaster right in our path.

Economic research on dealing with uncertainties leads to the following conclusion: Start with a best-guess scenario for output, population, emissions, and climate change. Take policies that will best deal with the costs and impacts in this best-guess case. Then consider the potential for low-probability but high-consequence outcomes in the Climate Casino. Take further steps to provide insurance against these dangerous outcomes. But definitely do not assume that the problems will just disappear.

4 FUTURE CLIMATE CHANGE

The first step to an understanding of the dangers of climate change is a solid grounding in climate science. Those who read only the popular press or listen to television debates might think it is the latest scientific fad—something dreamed up a few years ago by an entrepreneurial scientist. The truth is quite the opposite. The science behind CO_2-induced global warming is more than a century old. It is among the major accomplishments of modern earth sciences. For those who study the subject as scientists, looking at the wealth of studies and without an eye to the politics of the issue, it is an important and challenging scientific discipline.

I emphasize that this book is primarily about the societal aspects of climate change—concerning the economic roots, the economic costs and damages, policies to slow change, and international spillovers and bargaining. For those who wish a more complete treatment, there are many excellent books on the scientific aspects of global warming, and those who desire a full understanding should look there.[1] But before we deal with the social aspects, it is necessary to lay the groundwork for later chapters by laying out the scientific foundations of climate change.

THE SCIENCE OF CLIMATE CHANGE

Before settling in, I begin with a note about terminology. What exactly is meant by climate change? This capsule description is important at the outset:

Climate is usually defined as the statistical average and variability of temperature, wind, humidity, cloudiness, precipitation, and other quantities over a period of time ranging from months to thousands of years. *Climate change* is a change in these statistical properties when considered over long periods of time. Climate is distinguished from *weather,* which is the realization of the climatic process for a short period of time. The distinction between weather and climate can be seen because the climate is what you expect (such as cold winters) and weather is what you get (as in an occasional blizzard).

In this book, I generally use the terms "global warming" and "climate change" interchangeably. Accuracy would require a long and awkward phrase such as "the impacts of rising CO_2 and other related gases and factors." The term "climate change" is perhaps closer because the issues include much more than warming—for example, sea-level rise, droughts, increased storm intensity, and health impacts. But even climate change does not capture the impact of ocean carbonization. Some have proposed "global change," but that term is hopelessly vague. So I just use the two terms—global warming and climate change—with the understanding that these words represent a complex set of forces that are under way as a result of the buildup of CO_2 and other greenhouse gases.

I generally use the centigrade (°C) scale as that is the standard scientific convention. Americans usually hear about the Fahrenheit scale (°F). As a rough guide, you can multiply any °C change by 2 to get the °F change. If you want to be absolutely accurate, you should multiply by 9/5.

FROM EMISSIONS TO CONCENTRATIONS

Chapter 3 analyzed the emissions of CO_2, past and future. These emissions are not themselves the source of concern. If they were to quickly disappear or to be transformed into some innocuous rock, this book would not need to be written, and people could worry about other issues.

It is the concentrations of CO_2 and other GHGs in the atmosphere, not emissions, that are the concern of scientists. So there is an intermediate step from emissions to climate change in Chapter 4—the link between emissions and concentrations.

The process by which CO_2 emissions are distributed around the planet is called the "carbon cycle." This is an active area of research, and many carbon cycle scientists study how carbon moves among different carbon reservoirs. In studies done for the Intergovernmental Panel on Climate Change (IPCC), the models on average estimated that between 50 and 60 percent of carbon emitted during the twenty-first century would still be in the atmosphere at the end of the century. There were large differences across different models and depending upon the emissions growth.[2]

Before I begin the detailed discussion, let's start with a simple question: Can it really be possible that human activities are significant enough to change the global climate? After all, humans account for but a tiny part of global activity. To answer this question, I focus on the area that is both best documented and most important—the rising concentration of CO_2 in the atmosphere.

There is no question that atmospheric concentrations of CO_2 are rising. Thanks to the foresight of scientists who began monitoring atmospheric CO_2 in 1958 on the big island of Hawaii, we have measurements spanning more than fifty years. Figure 6 plots the monthly observations from the Mauna Loa Observatory through 2012. Over that half century, atmospheric CO_2 concentrations have risen 25 percent.[3]

Are we confident that rising CO_2 concentrations are due to human activity? Might they arise from natural variability? Both modeling and measurement of historical data strongly support the view that the increasing concentrations shown in Figure 6 are due to human activities. One interesting finding comes from ice cores. Using these, climate scientists estimate that CO_2 concentrations have ranged from 190 parts per million (ppm) to 280 ppm over the last million years. Since current concentrations are now over 390 ppm, the globe is well outside the range of concentrations experienced during the period that *Homo sapiens* emerged on earth.

I mentioned above that a little more than half of emissions are estimated to be in the atmosphere at century's end. What happens to the rest of the CO_2? Some of the additional CO_2 may go into the biosphere (such as trees and soils), which means that it is absorbed by plant life

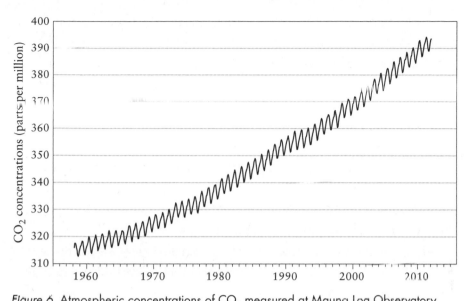

Figure 6. Atmospheric concentrations of CO_2 measured at Mauna Loa Observatory, Hawaii, 1958–2012.

around the world. Based on intensive measurements and modeling, scientists believe that most of the nonatmospheric CO_2 eventually goes into the oceans, where it spreads gradually into the depths. But that is a very slow process.

You can do an experiment yourself to picture slow ocean diffusion. Fill a clear glass with water. Then put a few drops of red food coloring at the top. Time how long it takes for a perceptible amount to get to the bottom of the glass, and also how long it takes for it to appear uniformly diffused. Now pretend that the glass is 6,000 feet deep. This will give you an idea of how long it takes CO_2 to be absorbed into the deep ocean.

The major result of these scientific findings is that CO_2 released into the atmosphere stays there for a long time. This has very important implications for how we think about climate change. The long residence time means that the effects of today's actions cast a long shadow into the future. They do not just wash away in a few days or months. In this sense, CO_2 and other GHGs are more akin to nuclear wastes than to normal pollution. This long residence time will come back to haunt us when we consider the problem of discounting costs and benefits.[4]

HOW RISING CO_2 CONCENTRATIONS CHANGE THE CLIMATE

Once we have projections of CO_2 concentrations along with other GHGs and other important input data, climatologists put these into climate models. Climate models are mathematical representations of the circulation of the atmosphere and oceans. These models start with some fundamental laws of physics and details of the earth's geography that are written into computer programs, but you can think of them as equations representing the dynamics of the atmosphere and oceans. So to understand climate models, we need to understand the basic science underlying the equations.

The heat that we feel from the sun is radiant energy, or radiation. If you turn your face to the sun, you will feel the warmth of the radiation hitting your skin. Radiation comes in waves of different lengths or frequencies. Most of the energy from the sun is visible as light, which is "hot" and has short wavelengths. About 30 percent of the hot radiation is reflected back to space. The atmosphere and surface of the earth absorb the rest of the energy, and this warms the earth. The energy coming in and going out are balanced, so the earth emits radiation back to space. But because the earth is warm rather than hot, the outgoing earth radiation has a longer wavelength than incoming solar radiation.

Here is the interesting part. Some gases in the atmosphere, such as CO_2 and methane, as well as water vapor, absorb more outgoing warm radiation than incoming hot radiation. This selective absorption acts like a blanket on a cold winter's night, which captures some of our body heat and keeps us warm. This is why the atmosphere is described as a natural "greenhouse"—because gases such as water and CO_2 trap the heat. Because radiation is retained near the earth, the equilibrium temperature of the earth rises. This is called the "natural greenhouse effect." Scientists have calculated that the natural greenhouse effect—that is, the result of gases that were in the atmosphere before humans started adding more—warms the earth about 33°C (60°F) above what its temperature would be with no atmosphere. In other words, if there were no GHGs, the earth's surface temperature would be −19°C, whereas the actual average temperature on earth is 14°C. Using this relationship, we can actually calculate temperatures on the moon, and these fit the lunar reality reasonably well.

The "enhanced greenhouse effect" is what happens when humans enter the picture and add more GHGs. The current stock of atmospheric GHGs absorbs some but not all of the outgoing long-wave radiation. As more and more gases are added, an increasing fraction of the outgoing long-wave radiation is absorbed by the atmosphere, and this in turn pushes the planetary temperature equilibrium higher. The process of CO_2-induced global warming means that humans are adding more "blankets" to the atmosphere in the form of additional CO_2, thereby increasing the average temperature on the earth's surface. Increasing the atmospheric concentration of CO_2 by what seems a tiny fraction (from about 280 to 560 ppm) is projected to increase average surface temperature of the planet by around 3°C (5½°F).

The enhanced greenhouse effect has diminishing returns, however. As CO_2 blocks more and more of the outgoing radiation, adding yet more CO_2 has a smaller impact. The capacity to absorb outgoing radiation gradually becomes saturated. Hence, doubling the amount of CO_2 in the atmosphere might raise the temperature by 3°C, but adding the same quantity again might lead to an increase of only 1.8°C.

The exact pace and extent of future CO_2-induced warming are highly uncertain, particularly beyond the next few decades. However, there is little scientific doubt that humans are causing major geophysical changes that are unprecedented for the last few thousand years. Scientists have detected the results of the changes in several areas. Emissions and atmospheric concentrations of GHGs are rising, as we just saw. The average surface temperature is also rising. Other "fingerprints" are also evident, including warming oceans, melting glaciers and ice sheets, enhanced polar warming, stratospheric cooling, and a shrinking ice cap in the Arctic Ocean.[5] Most of these are consistent with a warming that is induced by GHGs rather than natural variability.

The idea of sitting in a black car or a white car on a hot summer day makes a useful analogy to CO_2 warming. The white car will reflect more of the sunlight and remain relatively cool, while the black car will absorb more of the sunlight and become very hot. Adding CO_2 to the atmosphere is like having an invisible team of trolls slowly painting your car darker and darker. This analogy is also useful because it allows for the possibility that you might actually like a dark-colored car, for example, if you live in a wintry climate. However, if you live in a hot region like Arizona or India, you might find the idea of your car getting darker and hotter quite unattractive.[6]

PROJECTIONS OF FUTURE CLIMATE CHANGE

The previous section provided the basic intuition behind climate-change science. From a practical point of view, we need to know the magnitude and timing of warming along with other effects such as precipitation and sea-level rise. For a starting point, let us consider the impacts of doubling atmospheric CO_2. This question has been studied by climate scientists for more than a century and is a standard calculation. As it turns out, because of the complexities of the science, our current understanding is still incomplete.

Figure 7 shows a sketch of the estimated climate sensitivity found in recent climate model comparisons.[7] While the models are continually improved and refined, the calculated sensitivity of climate to CO_2 increases has changed little over the last three decades.[8] In a standard model comparison, such as that shown in this figure, several climate models were run with identical scenarios. They first ran the models with no increase of atmospheric CO_2. They then ran a scenario in which atmospheric CO_2 increases smoothly and doubles over seventy years, then holds steady at that doubled level for the indefinite future. This is an artificial situation, but it is useful for comparing models.

The models make two important calculations. They first estimate a "transient response," which is the temperature increase after seventy years, or at the time of CO_2 doubling. The curve to the left shows the distribution of transient responses, whose average was 1.8°C.

The models also calculated an "equilibrium response," which is the long-run temperature increase once all adjustments have taken place. The equilibrium results are shown by the distribution to the right in Figure 7. The average equilibrium or long-run temperature increase for

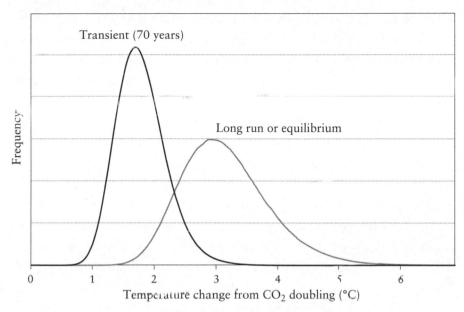

Figure 7. Temperature response of models in IPCC Fourth Assessment Report. The curves show a smoothed distribution of the calculated transient temperature (darker line, at left) and equilibrium temperature (lighter line, at right) increases from eighteen models.

all the models was a little above 3°C, which is not quite two times the short-run or transient response.

How do these idealized experiments compare with the projected concentrations of CO_2 and other gases? Most integrated economic-climate models suggest that CO_2-e (the CO_2 equivalent of all GHGs) will be two times preindustrial levels by around 2050. So the solid curve to the left in Figure 7 would be a rough estimate of the temperature response around 2050 according to the best-guess emissions paths. If we look at the economic models, they are close to the middle of the left-hand curve, showing an estimated temperature increase of 1.8°C for 2050.

We might also compare this estimate with what has actually occurred to date. The instrumental record indicates that the actual increase of global temperatures is around 0.8°C over the last 100 years. So the models suggest that temperature will warm another 1°C over the next four decades (but with substantial disagreement among models).

Now look at the light curve to the right in Figure 7, which shows the long-run or equilibrium temperature increase. The average long-run temperature increases predicted by the models is a little above 3°C, which is almost double the transient response. The transition to equilibrium proceeds slowly, over many centuries.[9] The long-run warming is so gradual because the deep oceans warm slowly. This great inertia contributes to the difficulty of projecting temperature increases and climate change. As with cigarette smoking, it may take a long time to see the effects. Luckily, this slow response has a happy side. If today's rising concentrations of CO_2 are reversed relatively quickly, then temperature will also come down because the deep oceans have not yet warmed.

Many nonscientists look at the divergence among climate models and wonder why these uncertainties cannot be resolved. There is a joke about economists: "If you ask five economists, you will get six answers." This is actually true here because some climate models get different answers as they are refined over time.

There are valid reasons for these differences. The basic greenhouse effect described above is well understood and has relatively little uncertainty. The major uncertainties about the magnitude of the temperature increase come when modelers include additional factors that can dampen or amplify the basic effect. For example, if a warmer earth melts snow and ice, this will expose more land and ocean surface, making the earth darker. The darker surface absorbs more sunlight, which then warms the surface and amplifies the greenhouse effect. This is known as the "albedo effect" and is exactly like the effect of your car becoming darker.

The most important amplifying factor is the greater evaporation of water with higher temperatures, which leads to increased water vapor in the atmosphere. Remember that water vapor is a powerful GHG. Clouds are another important contributor to uncertainty. Clouds are a headache for modelers because they can both cool and warm: Clouds can cool the globe when they reflect sunlight back into space or warm it when they trap heat radiating from the earth's surface. Modeling cloud formation is extremely challenging and produces a substantial amount of the difference among models.

Climatologists have estimated that if there were no feedback effects, the global warming from doubling CO_2 would be relatively small, about

1.2°C. But very strong amplifiers are at work in the climate-change process, and they can boost that temperature increase to the range of estimates shown in Figure 7.

TEMPERATURE PROJECTIONS FOR THE NEXT CENTURY

We now have the two basic building blocks for projecting future climate change. First, we saw how energy specialists project future CO_2 emissions, and how these are translated into future concentrations of CO_2 and other GHGs. Second, we described how climate modelers take these projected concentrations and compute the path of climatic variables such as temperature, precipitation, and sea-level rise in the decades ahead.

The next step is to integrate the two parts to develop projections of climate change. For these estimates, we calculate the path with no climate policy, or the baseline scenario. In other words, we examine what would happen if countries take no steps to slow the growth in CO_2 and other GHG emissions. While no one would recommend this as an appropriate policy, it provides an important reference to estimate the trajectory of climate variables, such as temperature, when countries sit back and roll the climatic dice.

It is useful to start with the instrumental temperature record. The basic trends in global temperature since the late nineteenth century, as recorded by thermometers and synthesized by three different research groups, are displayed in Figure 8.[10] The rising trend over this period is clear. However, the year-to-year movements are erratic and sometimes difficult to explain (like the stock market).

Now move to projections of future climate. One set of baseline projections uses the standardized IPCC-SRES scenarios. These scenarios are from a Special Report on Emissions Scenarios (SRES), which have been extensively used by climate modelers as a way of standardizing inputs into their analyses. These have been updated with a new set of IPCC reference scenarios that are developed from paths of GHG concentrations, but the projections have changed little over the last decade. Standardized scenarios may not be the most accurate projections, but they generate a range of emissions trajectories to test the models—like using a wind tunnel to test aircraft.

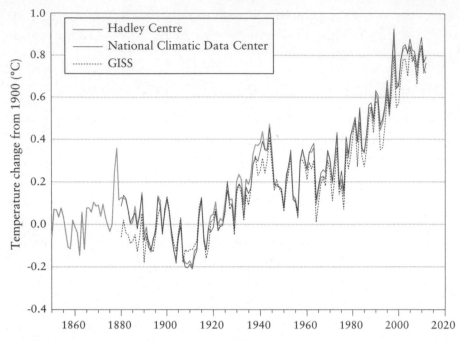

Figure 8. Global temperature trend as constructed by three research groups, 1850–2012.

The second approach applies integrated assessment models (IAMs), the economic models discussed in Chapter 3. These models combine population, technology, energy sectors, and economic growth as well as carbon cycles and climate models. They construct what might be called a combined best estimate of climate change over the coming years. For this calculation, I use the average of CO_2 concentrations from the different EMF-22 models shown in Figure 5.[11] For comparison, I also show the temperature projections from climate models reviewed by the IPCC using the stylized emissions scenarios.

Figure 9 shows the results of these estimates.[12] The two heavy lines in the middle indicate the average of the EMF-22 models (dashed line) and the results from the RICE model (heavy solid line). This picture provides a good overview of different future climate-change possibilities predicted by multiple modeling groups around the world.

Let's focus on the IAMs. Although the models have different assumptions about economic growth, population, the energy sector, new technologies, and the carbon cycle, they generate very similar tempera-

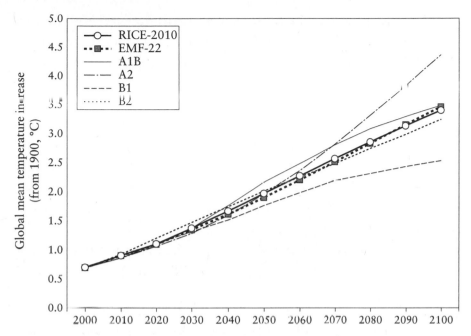

Figure 9. Global mean temperature increase as projected by IPCC scenarios and IAMs. The figure compares four projections using IPCC scenarios with those of the regional DICE (RICE) model and the average of the EMF-22 integrated economic models. The letters A1B, A2, B1, and B2 represent standardized emissions.

ture trajectories over the next century. The average increase in temperature in 2100 is projected to be 3½°C above the 1900 average, according to both the EMF and the DICE model estimates.

SOME IMPORTANT FINDINGS

Because climate models are extremely detailed, they produce a fascinating array of results, which can be assessed and used for studies of impacts. Here are some important results from the last full assessment, along with updates and the most recent scientific literature.

- Current concentrations of CO_2 far exceed the levels observed for at least 650,000 years.
- The best estimate of the global temperature increase from 1900 to 2100 is between 1.8 and 4.0°C (3½ and 7½°F) depending upon the scenario.

- The range of estimates of sea-level rise over the twenty-first century is between 18 and 60 centimeters (7–23 inches) depending upon the scenario but excluding the effects of the large ice sheets.
- Temperatures are expected to rise more rapidly over land and much more rapidly in the Arctic than the global average rise.
- The Arctic Ocean is expected to be largely ice free during the summer by the end of the twenty-first century, and it might occur much sooner.
- The intensity of hurricanes is expected to increase.
- Increasing atmospheric CO_2 concentrations will lead directly to acidification of the oceans.
- Many regions will see more hot days and fewer cold days, but the evidence on other extreme events is still unclear.
- Major uncertainties in many projections include the role and impact of small particles known as aerosols. They are expected to cool the climate, but the extent and regional dimensions of this cooling are difficult to determine.[13]

The different models provide different answers about the projected increases and regional impacts over the next century. However, even with the disagreement among models, we should not lose sight of the central finding, which is that all modeling groups project large climatic changes over the twenty-first century. These findings are at the cutting edge of modern climate science, and the basic message should not get lost in the differences.

Climate models can teach us much more, particularly regarding impacts, but that discussion will have to wait until later chapters.

THE CLIMATIC ROULETTE WHEEL

Figures 7 and 9 are warnings about the limitations of our knowledge of the climate system. In the most carefully studied part of all climate-change science—the response of the climate to a doubling of atmospheric CO_2 concentrations—major uncertainties remain about the way the system works.

The uncertainties about climate change were dramatized in a striking way by a group of MIT climate scientists. Instead of just publishing their results, they gave a press conference with a roulette wheel showing the possible outcomes. Their results indicated that global warming by 2100 would be almost half again as large as other estimates, with a central estimate of 5¼°C as compared to the 3½°C shown in Figure 9. While their results are an outlier among those of other modeling teams, they emphasize the great uncertainties that scientists confront in making projections.[14]

The bottom line is that if no policies are made to slow global warming, the central estimate is that the average global temperature by 2100 will be about 3½°C above the 1900 level. There is considerable uncertainty about this projection. But unless all the economic models and all the climate models are dead wrong, the pace of global warming will quicken over the decades to come and climate conditions will quickly pass beyond the range of recent historical experience.

5 TIPPING POINTS IN THE CLIMATE CASINO

People might wonder how concerned they should be about the temperature trends described thus far. A change of 2 or 3°C does not seem that alarming. After all, we often experience that much change in one hour in the morning. Moreover, the temperature changes envisioned are small relative to those that individuals and groups experience through migration. People today happily move from Snowbelt to Sunbelt to enjoy the warmer lifestyle. If you move from Minneapolis to Phoenix, you will be moving to a climate that is 13°C warmer.

But this description ignores the real risks. The problem is not a simple rise in average temperature but rather the accompanying physical, biological, and economic impacts of such a change—in particular, the thresholds and nonlinear responses that may be encountered. A rise in our body temperature from 98°F to 104 or 105°F does not sound like a large change, but it may signal a deadly infection.

The importance of thresholds is easily illustrated by the following example. Consider what happens when you are driving along on a wet road. The surface temperature changes from 1 degree above freezing to 1 degree below freezing. In an instant you go from slippery to potentially deadly conditions.

A less dramatic example is what happens every year to my outdoor basil plants. They happily produce leaves to have with pasta until one night in the late fall when the temperature drops below freezing. When I go out to gather some leaves, they have turned black and are ruined.

These simple examples from daily life are reflected on a global scale as well. Scientists are concerned about critical thresholds in earth systems that may be crossed because of climate change. But be warned: These processes are much less well understood than the sequence of events described so far. We now leave the realm of relatively well-understood systems and enter areas that are much more complex and poorly mapped. Although we see these systems through a clouded lens, these phenomena encompass some of the most dangerous and frightening potential effects of climate change.

THE VARIABILITY OF PAST CLIMATES

One of the triumphs of modern earth sciences is the development of techniques that map out the climatic history of our world. These techniques include taking core samples from ice sheets and measuring the width of tree rings. Using these proxy variables, scientists can construct estimates of past climates, sea levels, vegetation, and atmospheric gases.

The major conclusion drawn from this research is that past climates have differed dramatically from what we live with today. Studies show that the earth has experienced a sequence of cold and warm periods. In some periods, ice sheets may have covered virtually the entire planet, while at other times the earth was ice free. Many of the largest climatic changes were caused by changes in the earth's orbit. The reasons for the timing of short-run fluctuations are still unclear, but we do know they happened. Small changes in the energy balance of the earth can lead to vast changes in the distribution of ice, vegetation, animals, and living conditions.

A second and equally surprising finding is that our planet has experienced an unusually stable climate for about 7,000 years. There are many different methods to determine this, but one method calculates temperatures based on ice core samples from Greenland (see Figure 10). This reconstruction uses the quantity of an isotope of hydrogen called deuterium as a thermometer.[1]

Look at the last 7,000 years as shown in Figure 10 (time runs backward from right to left). Note how stable the temperature has been over

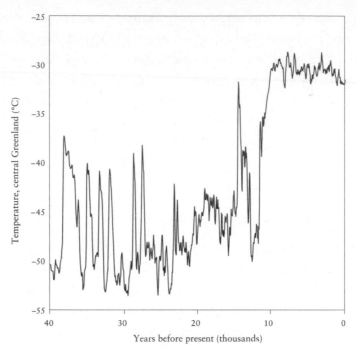

Figure 10. Historical proxy temperature estimates for Greenland.

this period. By contrast, the thirty-three millennia before that saw violent fluctuations in and out of ice ages. Other longer-term records indicate that the last 7,000 years have been the most stable climatic period in more than 100,000 years.

This is a sobering finding because this is also the period that has witnessed the emergence of written languages, cities, and human civilizations. Was climate stability a prerequisite for the emergence of farming and cities? Would the Sumerians have developed the first written language if they had been confronted with an unstable climate system? How would philosophy and literature have developed in Greece if the city-states were suddenly plunged into an ice age? We do not know, but many anthropologists believe that the stability of climates over the last seven millennia was an important contributor to the evolution of human societies as we know them today.

But the future is almost surely going to be different from the last 7,000 years. The CO_2 implications of larger populations, economic expansion, and new technologies are affecting the earth's climate. This will change ecosystems, land use, and water flows in ever-larger ways. Over the next century or so, human influences will almost certainly push global temperatures beyond the top of the scale shown in Figure 10. In doing so, we will probably alter the earth system beyond the biophysical limits within which human civilizations have developed and thrived.[2]

I have primarily discussed climate models up to this point. But the cutting-edge models in this area now include far more than the atmosphere. They integrate the oceans, terrestrial systems, and ice sheets. In addition to the large models surveyed previously, more detailed models examine the dynamics of large ice sheets, the genesis of hurricanes, patterns of river runoff, and similar features. All these studies taken together help inform scientists about not only temperature trends, but also precipitation, drought, snow packs, and potential tipping points in the earth system, to which I turn next.

TIPPY CANOE AND CLIMATE TOO

If you look at the jagged climate history shown in Figure 10, you might wonder why the earth moves so erratically from cold period to warm period and back again. Is the earth on some kind of slippery slope? Are we like skaters on a frozen pond who might break through if we unwittingly move onto thin ice?

This is the domain of tipping points—an analysis that examines whether climate change might trigger instabilities in the earth's systems. A tipping point comes when a system experiences a sharp discontinuity in its behavior. We are familiar with tipping points from our daily lives. For example, if you are sitting in a canoe and lean to one side, you eventually will pass the tipping point. The canoe will flip over and dump you into the water. On more than one embarrassing occasion, I have tipped over a canoe—but I am here to tell the tale because the outcome was not disastrous.

Financial specialists are familiar with tipping points as well. One well-studied example is the phenomenon of bank runs, which were endemic in early American history. If too many people lose confidence in a bank, they rush to the bank and attempt to withdraw their funds. Because banks typically have only a small fraction of their deposits on hand as cash (or gold and silver in the days of a metallic standard), they could not satisfy all their depositors. Once people think that there is likely to be a bank run, it becomes a self-fulfilling expectation. They run to the bank to get their funds before other people, who in turn are trying to get there before they do, and the bank quickly runs out of cash. If you watch the 1946 film *It's a Wonderful Life*, not only will you be entertained, you will also see a bank run on the silver screen.

For many years, bank runs existed only in courses in economic history. But they returned in the financial crises of 2007–2008 at the speed of electronic transfers. When lenders smelled trouble with investment banks Bear Stearns in March 2008 or Lehman Brothers in September 2008, they withdrew billions of dollars overnight. When distrust crossed a critical threshold, these firms were run out of business in a week, and the ensuing panic in financial markets contributed to the deep economic downturn that has haunted the United States since 2008. A similar phenomenon occurred in Greece in 2012 and in Cyprus in 2013. When people worried that their euros deposited in Greek or Cypriot banks might lose their value, they withdrew their euros and put them in a safe place.

One of the most important lessons from the recent financial crises is that no one understood how fragile the system was. No one anticipated how profound the economic costs of the financial panics would be. We should heed this lesson as we think about the tipping points that might be crossed as we alter the climate.

A STRANGE BOWL TO ILLUSTRATE TIPPY SYSTEMS

Figure 11 illustrates tipping points using a ball in a strange double-bottomed bowl. The vertical height of the bowl represents the health of the system. It might be a bank, an ecosystem, or the height of an ice sheet. In panel (a), the ball starts out in a good or desirable equilibrium. Then some kind of stress (warming in the climate system or fear in a

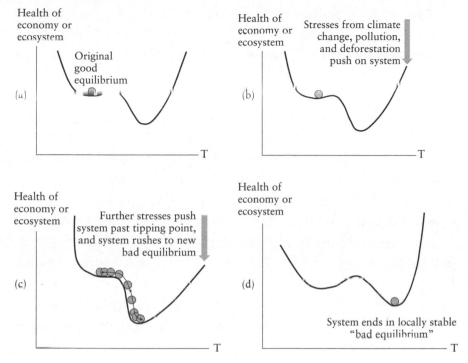

Figure 11. Tipping points: moving from a good to a bad equilibrium. The double-bottomed bowl illustrates how stresses can change a system slowly until a tipping point is reached, after which there are rapid and potentially catastrophic changes. Note that there are two equilibria—a good equilibrium in (a), and a bad equilibrium in (d).

financial system) pushes the right side of the bowl downward. If the stresses are mild, the ball moves only a little, and when the stresses stop, it rolls back to where it started, back to panel (a).

But if the stresses are only a little larger, the tipping point is reached, and the ball races to the bottom of the second curve, as shown in panel (c). This new position is a "bad equilibrium" because it has undesirable properties. The bad property might be ruined banks, nuclear meltdowns, or melted ice caps. The problem is that the ball stays in the bad equilibrium. Once the ball is in the bad equilibrium, even when the stresses are removed, the ball is stuck in the bad equilibrium shown in panel (d). This system turns out to have multiple locally stable equilibria.[3]

What causes this strange behavior? The basic cause is the nonlinear reaction to stresses, as shown by the curved double-bottomed bowl. When systems have this kind of nonlinear behavior, there is a possibility of tipping points and bad equilibria.

Tipping points have many interesting features. To begin with, they often have multiple outcomes or equilibria. For example, in the case of tippy canoes and bank runs, there are good outcomes (sitting in the canoe, and or having your money in solvent banks) and bad outcomes (swimming in the water, or left with worthless deposits).

A second feature is that systems can tip over into bad outcomes very quickly and unexpectedly. Indeed, abrupt climate change is sometimes defined as a change in the climate state that occurs much more quickly than the precipitating cause.[4] The brilliant economist Rudy Dornbusch remarked that financial crises take much longer to arrive than you think, and then they happen much faster than you could imagine. One of the most dangerous features of tipping points and abrupt events is their unpredictability.[5]

DANGEROUS CLIMATE-CHANGE TIPPING POINTS

What are the tippy canoes of climate change? I emphasize that, like financial crises, the exact timing and magnitude of such events are often impossible to predict. They may occur rapidly and unexpectedly—or they may not happen at all.

With that background, four global-scale tipping elements are of particular concern:

- The collapse of large ice sheets
- Large-scale changes in ocean circulation
- Feedback processes by which warming triggers more warming
- Enhanced warming over the long run

The first example is sea-level rise from abrupt melting or collapse of the major ice sheets of Greenland and West Antarctica. These events would have adverse consequences for the entire planet but particularly for coastal communities, often with large population centers. Sea level might rise in a gradual way without any abrupt events. But many specialists believe that the current models of glacier disintegration do not fully capture the dynamics, and that the rise may occur much more rapidly. Scientists are hard at work modeling these changes, and it seems likely that the pace and scope of ice sheet melting will be better understood in the coming years. I discuss this tipping point in more detail in the next section.

A second important singularity is change in ocean currents, particularly the Atlantic thermohaline circulation, popularly known as the Gulf Stream. In the present era, the Gulf Stream carries warm surface water to the North Atlantic. As a result, North Atlantic communities are much warmer than their latitude would indicate. For example, Scotland is at the same latitude as the peninsula of Kamchatka in far eastern Russia, but the average temperature in Scotland is about 12°C (22°F) warmer than in Kamchatka.

Although the Gulf Stream has been stable for several thousand years, it appears that large and rapid shifts occurred in earlier times, particularly during ice ages. The Gulf Stream has even switched direction on several occasions. A reversal of the Gulf Stream would lead to a steep temperature decline in the North Atlantic region as it would no longer bring a flow of warm water to the north.

Currently, as the warm surface waters of the Gulf Stream move north, they release their heat in the North Atlantic region, with the result that communities there are pleasant for humans and other living things. As the water flows north, it cools and becomes denser. At some point, the cooler dense water sinks, and then moves back south as if on a conveyor belt.

What would lead to a shift in the flow of the Gulf Stream? In a warmer world, the conveyor belt can get disrupted. This would happen because of increases in both temperature and (freshwater) precipitation at higher latitudes. These changes would make surface water less dense because salt water is denser than fresh water. The sinking process would weaken and reduce the speed of the conveyor belt—or might even cause it to stop and reverse. This process would tend to cool the North Atlantic relative to the rest of the world.

The most recent studies indicate that the Gulf Stream is likely to weaken over the next century. However, expert assessments indicate that it is unlikely to undergo an abrupt transition or collapse over the next century. Even in models that show a weakening of the Gulf Stream's circulation, northwestern Europe continues to warm because the cooling effect of the ocean current slowdown is smaller than the global warming effect itself.

A third concern is a set of positive or reinforcing feedback interactions between climate, the biosphere, and the carbon cycle. Some background on standard climate models will be helpful here. Many climate model experiments consider a given path of industrial emissions of CO_2 and other GHGs. The CO_2 is gradually distributed through different reservoirs, including the atmosphere, the oceans, and the biosphere (uptake by natural vegetation, crops, and soils). In standard scenarios, CO_2 is added only from human sources such as burning fossil fuels.

A warmer climate and higher CO_2 concentrations bring important feedback effects that may reinforce the effects of rising industrial emissions. One type of feedback comes from the oceans. As a result of some complicated ocean chemistry, the uptake of CO_2 by the oceans will be reduced as the globe warms and the ocean becomes saturated with carbon. This ocean-CO_2 feedback is estimated to increase atmospheric concentrations of CO_2 over the twenty-first century by about 20 percent relative to a no-feedback scenario.[7]

More reinforcing feedback is the impact of warming on the release of locked-up carbon and methane (CH_4). Methane is a powerful greenhouse gas that is gradually transformed into the stable compound CO_2. Vast quantities of methane are stored in the form of methane hydrates, which are methane molecules trapped in ice crystals. Most of the methane hydrates are stored in sediments in the oceans, while another large quantity is frozen in the ground in cold regions in permafrost. Scientists believe that warming would increase the releases of methane from both these sources into the atmosphere, which could intensify the global warming process; the timing of these releases is still an open question.

A fourth and final mechanism involves the difference between the medium-run and the very-long-run response of climate to human activities. Today's climate models are basically designed to calculate the "fast feedback processes"—those involving the direct effects of increasing concentrations of GHGs and the associated rapid feedback, such as changes in water vapor, clouds, and sea ice. These are slow by economists' standards, as they occur over a few hundred years rather than in a few minutes or months, but they are fast by the standards of earth scientists.

However, there are also likely to be "slow feedback processes" that would amplify the effects of global warming. The slow processes involve ice sheet disintegration, the migration of vegetation, and accelerated releases of GHGs (such as the frozen methane just discussed) from soils, tundra, and ocean sediments, as well as decomposing vegetation. For example, as glaciers and ice sheets melt, or as the spring snows melt earlier, the earth becomes darker. This leads to a lower albedo (reflectivity), which in turn further warms the earth.

Some model calculations suggest that, when the slow feedback processes are included, climate sensitivity may be twice as large as that calculated by the current suite of climate models. That is, the long-run sensitivity to CO_2 doubling might be as high as 6°C instead of the standard 3°C found in most models today.[8]

While this is a very frightening prospect, it has yet to be validated by multiple models. Furthermore, it applies over a time span of hundreds to thousands of years. We probably have time to understand and react to these slow feedback processes, so they may be less alarming than would appear at first blush. Careful modeling of the economic, emissions, and longer-term climate models will be necessary to determine how central these slow feedback processes are to decisions about climate policy.

The four global-scale tipping points discussed above are easily visualized and dramatized. Many marine scientists believe that a less dramatic but equally important tipping point has already been passed. The combination of rising CO_2 concentrations and warming is likely to cause catastrophic loss of coral reefs along with major impacts on the systems that depend upon them.

Although coral reefs represent a small fraction of the oceans, they are extremely productive in nourishing marine life. Scientists estimate that about one-fifth of the world's coral reefs have already been lost as a result of habitat destruction, pollution, overfishing, warming, and ocean acidification. The main threat to corals in coming decades is the increasing carbon concentration in the oceans caused by the rising CO_2 in the atmosphere. This is the phenomenon of ocean acidification (discussed in detail in Chapter 9).

At today's CO_2 concentrations, coral reefs will probably go into long-term decline. According to a report by a technical group of scientists from the U.K. Royal Society, when CO_2 concentrations reach 450 ppm (which is likely to occur within three decades), coral reefs "will be in rapid and terminal decline world-wide from both temperature-induced bleaching and ocean acidification."[9]

There have been a few systematic surveys of tipping points in earth systems. A particularly interesting one by Lenton and colleagues examined the important tipping elements and assessed their timing.[10] Their list includes the examples given above, plus shifts in monsoons, dieback of the Brazilian rain forest, and a few others. The most important tipping points, in their view, have a threshold temperature tipping value of 3°C or higher (such as the destruction of the Amazon rain forest) or have a time scale of at least 300 years (the Greenland Ice Sheet and the West Antarctic Ice Sheet). Their review finds no critical tipping elements with a time horizon less than 300 years until global temperatures have increased by at least 3°C. However, at 3°C, we encounter the danger zone for several important tipping elements. This conclusion is tentative, however, because of the inherent difficulty of assessing the danger and timing of tipping events. For those interested in pursuing this point, a detailed discussion is available in the endnotes.[11]

THE POTENTIAL MELTING OF THE GREENLAND ICE SHEET

It will be useful to analyze a specific tipping point, the Greenland Ice Sheet (GIS), to illustrate the mechanisms and why they are of great concern. This discussion provides a taste of what climate science is grappling with at the frontier of knowledge.

The GIS covers 1.7 million square kilometers—roughly the size of western Europe. It is the planet's second largest ice sheet, after the Antarctic Ice Sheet. It is on average 2,000 meters (1.2 miles) thick. If the entire volume of the ice sheet were to melt—all 2,900,000 cubic kilometers or 750,000,000,000,000,000 gallons—it would cause global sea level to rise by 7 meters (or 23 feet).[12]

Measurements of the GIS indicate that it was stable for most of the twentieth century but began to shrink during the last two decades. The current melt rate is estimated to be 0.75 mm (0.03 inch) per year of sea-level rise equivalent (SLRe). Recent estimates suggest that the GIS will contribute a small amount to SLRe over the next century; a central estimate is 7 centimeters (3 inches) in the case of rapid temperature increases. More detailed models indicate that very high temperature increases, such as those associated with the baseline runs in Figure 9, would lead to a SLRe of 1.5 meters (5 feet) in three centuries, and on the order of 3 meters (10 feet) over the next millennium, just from the melting of the GIS.[13]

Now we can see the tipping element. Global warming would cause the GIS to warm, melt, shrink, and drop in elevation. Temperatures increase with lower altitude, so a smaller ice sheet will be warmer at the top than the current ice sheet, and this higher temperature will further accelerate the melting. The ice sheet would also tend to be darker as it warms, absorbing more solar radiation, and warming even further. Once the ice sheet passes some threshold in a warmer world, most of its ice might melt away.

While this seems far in the future, some scientists worry that the GIS is an unstable system, like the bowl shown in Figure 11. There may be two distinct equilibria—one a cold, white, high-altitude ice sheet and the other being a warm, green, low-altitude and largely ice-free Greenland.[14]

Why might there be multiple equilibria for a given temperature? Suppose after centuries of warming, the remaining ice sheet is in the green, low-elevation equilibrium. Then the earth begins to warm up again. However, since the ice sheet is warmer and darker, it remains stuck in the low-elevation equilibrium. If there is a tipping point of this kind, a climate that is warmed for a sufficient period of time would lead to an irreversible melting of the GIS and an inevitable large sea-level rise.

Figure 12 uses a simple ice sheet model to show how the GIS might jump from a large to a small ice sheet.[15] This figure shows two sets of lines. The solid upper line shows the equilibrium volume of the sheet for different global temperatures, starting from today's temperature and ice sheet. You can follow the upper arrows to see the sequence of warming. If the world warms 1 degree, the GIS shrinks about 2 percent; at 2°C the shrinkage is 4 percent; up to 5°C, where the shrinkage is about 15 percent. When the globe warms just a little beyond the 5°C threshold, the unstable dynamics of warming, lowering of elevations, darkening, and melting enter a downward spiral, so that at 6°C the ice sheet melts completely. In other words, at a certain point, the equilibrium jumps down the steep slope to a new and drastically smaller size. If the jump occurs quickly, it might lead to several feet of sea-level rise in a short time.

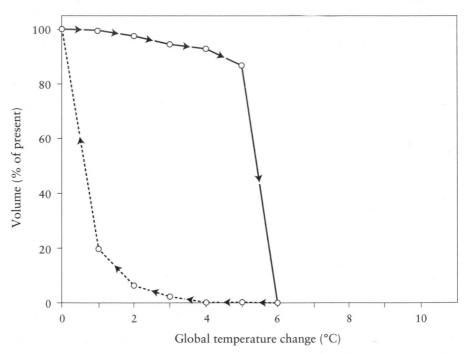

Figure 12. Illustration of a tipping point for the Greenland Ice Sheet. This figure shows a calculation from the GRANTISM model of the response of the Greenland Ice Sheet to different temperatures.

The interesting feature is that this model shows a "hysteresis loop," or what is sometimes called path dependence. The dashed lower line in Figure 12 shows an alternative set of stable ice sheet sizes. Starting from a low-elevation warm-world situation, the ice sheet responds differently as the globe warms. For this case, you can follow the lower set of arrows. Suppose the globe starts at an initial temperature of 6°C of warming or more with a small ice sheet. As the globe cools from 6°C to 5°C, the ice sheet hardly grows at all. Indeed, the ice sheet begins to recover only when temperature declines below 3°C. Even if the globe returns to today's temperature of around 1°C, the GIS grows to only one-fifth of its present volume. Finally, as the globe cools sufficiently, the ice sheet regains its current size.

Figure 12 is a striking example of the kind of instability that scientists worry about. It shows how complex dynamic systems can move into completely different states when they are pushed beyond some tipping point. The behavior is similar to that of a tippy canoe at super-slow motion—but much more frightening and consequential on a planetary scale.

I must emphasize that, while the picture in Figure 12 comes from a detailed computer model of the GIS, it is highly simplified. Other models show different patterns. Scientists do not know for sure if there are steep slopes like the one in Figure 12, or if the slippery slope is at 2 or 4 or 6°C, or if there might be many slippery slopes and many different solid and dashed lines. However, the worrisome finding is that the strange tipping behavior shown in Figures 11 and 12 has been found in different areas of the earth's systems.[16]

The example of the GIS illustrates several points. First, all the systems involved in the analysis of tipping points are perplexing because they involve poorly understood dynamics and nonlinear responses. We generally do not know exactly where a tipping point is, or when we will cross it, or whether we can climb back over the tipping point to the good equilibrium with a large enough effort. If we use the analogy of the little double-bottomed bowl in Figure 11, we need to understand exactly how steep the sides of the bowl are, how much the bowl is being tipped, and how deep the second bad equilibrium is. The fact is that we do not know these details for any of the major tipping elements involved in global warming.

Even if we understand the dynamics of earth systems, a further difficulty is to determine the gravity of the consequences. This can be demonstrated by continuing the analysis of the GIS and sea-level rise. We know the elevation of most places on earth and have reasonable estimates of how seriously different locations would be threatened by sea-level rise today.

But knowing the quantitative sea-level rise does not help us very much in understanding its economic and social impacts. It is difficult to estimate the consequences if the oceans rise two or three centuries from now because we don't know where people will be living, or whether they will have taken adaptive measures to protect their houses from sea-level rise if they know it is coming, or even what kind of houses people will be living in. If you think about the differences between modern houses and those of the eighteenth century, you can grasp how difficult it is to estimate the impact of future changes like sea-level rise on human societies two or three centuries from now. (I return to an assessment of sea-level rise in Part III.)

Other tipping points are even more difficult to assess. Scientists can estimate the scope and timing of melting of Arctic sea ice in the summer. But the impact of this melting on commerce, wildlife, and ecosystems is very difficult to measure. What will it mean for Russia or Canada if their northern ports are open to shipping six months of the year? Equally perplexing issues involve the impacts of large-scale changes in the Amazon rain forest or the Sahara region. We might suppose that any change is unwelcome because people have adapted to the world as it is today. But that does not help us understand how serious it would be if the Sahara turned green or if the Amazon rain forest were transformed into savannah.

The research on tipping points is in its infancy. Scientists have already found new potential tipping elements since the first draft of this book was written. We can take steps to reduce the chances of crossing these boundaries, which are covered later in this book. But the main point to emphasize is that potentially dangerous discontinuities can occur in complex systems. This is true of banks, frozen ponds, and global climate processes. Current research indicates that a number of sectors and earth systems may be threatened in the next century or so once the earth has warmed by 3°C or more.

You might be wondering whether I am making a mountain out of a bump in the road. Climate change is part of earth's history, from the warm periods of the dinosaurs to the cold periods when New England lay under a mountain of ice. Is this time really different?

It is true that large changes in climate have occurred in the past, some of them extremely rapidly. During a period known as the Younger Dryas, about 12,000 years ago, the earth apparently experienced one-third of an ice age in a few decades. In other words, one-third of the drastic cooling that buried much of North America under a giant ice sheet happened in a few decades of abrupt climate change. Similar abrupt climate changes occurred in earlier periods, although the reasons are not well understood.

But this time is different because of the pace of human-induced climate change over the next century and beyond. Climatologists have concluded that no climate changes of the speed and scope we are currently witnessing have occurred through the course of human civilization (roughly the last 5,000 years) While there are no reliable instrumental temperature records much before the twentieth century, proxy records can be gathered from sources such as ice cores, tree rings, ancient plant pollens, and boreholes in the ground. The best guess is that the rate of global climate change people will face over the next century will be about ten times as rapid as any change experienced by humanity during the last five millennia. So while perhaps not unprecedented on the scale of geological time, it is unprecedented during the era of human civilization.

This concludes the introduction to the broad concepts of climate change. We have seen how global warming has its wellspring in economic growth and technologies—particularly in the harnessing of fossil fuels to power our societies. Further, we observe how largely invisible greenhouse gases such as CO_2 are changing the energy balance of the earth. Climate scientists explain that this will lead to many predictable changes, such as global warming, higher and more variable precipitation, drying in midcontinental regions, acidification of the oceans, and amplification of warming at the poles.

But we also are likely to encounter surprises, and some of them will be nasty. Perhaps winters in the Northern Hemisphere will become much snowier. Perhaps hurricanes will intensify greatly and change their storm tracks. Perhaps the giant Greenland Ice Sheet will begin to melt rapidly. Perhaps the West Antarctic Ice Sheet, which sits on the seabed, might disintegrate rapidly and slide into the ocean.

Subsequent parts of this book examine the results of climate changes as they move downstream to affect human and natural systems; the potential steps to slow climate change; and the use of science and economics to produce an integrated analysis of policies to address the challenge.

Finally, we must also recognize that climate-change science and policies must extend beyond pure science. They involve winners and losers, burden sharing, and bargaining. Because these issues entail government actions—particularly cooperation among governments—they also engage people's deeply held political beliefs about the proper role and size of government. And all these are subject to the influence of money, results-oriented analysis, political action committees, and advocacy groups. Climate change is no longer just geophysics and ecology; it has become economics and politics. So in the very last part, I examine the narrative surrounding climate change, the critiques, and ultimately how a concerned citizen should view the contentious debates.

PART II
IMPACTS OF CLIMATE CHANGE ON HUMAN AND OTHER LIVING SYSTEMS

All the evidence shows that God was
actually quite a gambler, and the universe is
a great casino, where dice are thrown, and
roulette wheels spin on every occasion.
—*Stephen Hawking*

6 FROM CLIMATE CHANGE TO IMPACTS

Part I of this book recounted how scientists discovered that we are altering our global climate. Our daily activities—driving our cars, heating our homes, and cooking our pizzas—generate vast and long-lasting changes in the world around us. Part II maps out the impacts of those changes on human societies and natural systems.

The focus now shifts from determining geophysical changes to anticipating their impacts on human and other living systems. This subject might seem easier than the deep physics and chemistry of climate science because it is more familiar to us, but the opposite is true. In reality, this task—projecting impacts—is the most difficult and has the greatest uncertainties of all the processes associated with global warming.

What issues arise in impacts analysis? Look back to Figure 1, which shows the interactions among global warming, economics, and politics. Thus far, we have traveled from box 1 to box 2, from rising greenhouse-gas concentrations to a suite of geophysical changes.

In Part II we trace the consequences of these changes. How does climate change affect the economy and habitability of different regions? Will food become more expensive? And what are the consequences for the natural world? Will ecosystems be disrupted by the changing climate patterns? Will some species become extinct? What will happen to marine life as the oceans become more acidic?

On reading assessments of the harmful impacts of climate change, you can easily become overwhelmed by the scope of the problems. The latest assessment on impacts covered 976 information-rich pages. The major chapters included studies of freshwater resources; ecosystems; food, fiber, and forest products; coastal systems and low-lying areas; industry, settlements, and society; and human health. The report discusses potential problems in every region of the world, from tropical Africa to the icy poles.[1]

Clearly this book cannot deal with every one of these topics, but a few key questions can be addressed. Most people want to know what the important impacts are and how large they are relative to other problems facing humanity. How does global warming compare with the financial crisis, the long recession, and African poverty? And how will key natural systems fare in a warmer world?

The next chapters review some of the central concerns about climate change and also explore the difficulties in making predictions. Chapters 7 and 8 focus on two concerns that are central to human societies: agriculture and health. Each of these has been prominent in discussions about the potential impacts of climate change. They share a common feature: Each will be affected by rapid technological and societal changes over coming decades. Moreover, given the growing importance of human decisions and technologies, climate is likely to play an ever-smaller role over time in these sectors. The discussions will therefore emphasize the race between the forces of climate change and those of human adaptation.

In Chapters 9 through 11, the focus shifts to areas that are less manageable: rising sea levels, ocean acidification, hurricane intensification, and damage to wildlife and natural ecosystems. These are major problems because it will be more difficult for human adaptations and new technologies to slow or stop these.

I then pull the different strands together to summarize the overall impacts of climate change.

MANAGED VERSUS UNMANAGED SYSTEMS

A central principle in understanding the impacts of climate change is the difference between managed and unmanaged systems. The idea of management originates in the science of ecology but applies more generally to any complex system.

A *managed system* is one in which societies take steps to ensure the efficient and sustainable use of a resource. For example, a farmer may introduce a drip irrigation system to optimize soil moisture for vines. In another example that may surprise you, dairy farming has prospered in the deserts of Arizona. Farmers have found that designs that provide shade and water cooling in the hot summers make for productive cows. Some systems may suffer from harmful mismanagement. For example, if people clear mangrove forests for fuel, this might lead to a major drop in shrimp farming, which thrives among mangroves.

Indoor living is another example of a managed system. With the use of well-designed and engineered structures, equipment, and monitoring devices, humans have modified their indoor structures so that they can live in virtually every environment from Antarctica to the tropics to outer space.

By contrast, in our context an *unmanaged system* is one that operates largely without human intervention. It might be unmanaged because humans choose to leave it alone. An example would be a wildlife reserve. Or it might be unmanageable because the system is too large for humans to control. For instance, given current technologies, intense hurricanes and sea-level rise are unmanageable. Similarly, a human walking outside without any clothing is a good example of an unmanaged environment, which is not a good idea in most climates. The importance of a managed environment is shown by the fact that humans could not long survive in most parts of the planet if they were forced to live outdoors without clothes or shelter.

Another example—particularly important for the impacts of global warming—is the distinction between managed and unmanaged ecosystems. An ecosystem is a set of living organisms—microbes, fungi, plants, and animals—along with the physical environment in which they interact. One of the most important ecosystems for humans is agriculture. Some types of agriculture are heavily managed. For example, hydroponics is a method of growing plants using water and nutrients in a controlled environment without soil. Hydroponic establishments are essentially food factories. With the right materials and design, this ecosystem is resistant to heat and cold, drought and hail.

At the other extreme is the food system of hunting and gathering cultures, which were practiced by virtually all humans until about 10,000 years ago. This technology was highly dependent upon climatic patterns. The main way that management entered the picture was through mismanagement from deforestation, overfishing, or overhunting. Human history is full of civilizations that declined or disappeared because they depended upon unmanaged food supplies that dried up with drought, cold periods, or bad management of local resources.

A fascinating account of how past societies declined is found in Jared Diamond's 2005 book, *Collapse*.[2] He recounts the perils of deforestation, soil erosion, water mismanagement, overhunting, and overfishing by a range of human societies that include the Greenland Norse, Easter Islanders, Polynesians of Pitcairn Island, Anasazi of North America, and Maya of Central America. From an economic point of view, decline and collapse came from narrowly based economic structures, heavily dependent on unmanaged or mismanaged systems, with few trade linkages to enable provisioning from other regions. When most economic activity is based on local hunting and gathering of food, and the food supply dries up because of the interaction of climate and human activities, there is little resilience in the system, and the population must migrate, decline, or perish.

There are multiple strategies by which living organisms or human societies can manage themselves or their environment to increase their resilience in the face of shocks. One strategy is migration, by which birds and animals can follow their food supplies. Another management mechanism, of which humans are particularly fond, is developing technologies that enable them to adapt to local conditions. People build structures to warm or cool themselves and to provide shelter against storms, and they make devices to manipulate their environment. Few species have survived all the shocks that have occurred during the 4 billion years of life on earth, but it is remarkable how adaptive strategies have allowed so many species to adapt to a range of climates from hothouse periods to snowball earth.

We need to be careful to distinguish unmanaged systems from unmanageable ones. Hurricanes are currently unmanaged in part because they are unmanageable. But in the future, as technologies improve, countries might attempt to weaken hurricanes or deflect them to less damaging tracks. Indeed, Microsoft chief Bill Gates actually filed a patent application in 2008 for a technique to reduce hurricane intensity. Similarly, sea-level rise, which is one of the best-established results of climate change, might conceivably be managed by cloud seeding or even by some fantastic device that pumps water back onto the top of Antarctica. In the extreme, some have proposed "geoengineering" approaches that would offset global warming by increasing the reflectivity of the earth. The potential of such approaches is explored in Part III. One of the major advantages of human technologies is their ability to control microenvironments. Humans increasingly manage farming through the use of fertilizers and irrigation, forests through recycling wood and other forest products, and fisheries through new fish-farming techniques. One group has even made a hamburger in a factory. Many people dislike farmed fish, underground shopping malls, and genetically modified organisms, but these technologies should be viewed in part as a reaction to the riskiness of unmanaged systems.

The most consequential example of managing human affairs is the rise of modern medicine. As late as two centuries ago, illness and death were often thought to be visited upon people by evil spirits or the gods. If a child died at an early age, there were others waiting to sit at the table. Today, health care is the largest single sector of the American economy, constituting 16 percent of total U.S. output. While most of our bodies are natural in the sense that they are driven by complex biological mechanisms, we may find that our future bodies are increasingly made up of manufactured parts. All this sounds like some science fiction fantasy. But if you imagine how the modern world would look to a time traveler from 1,000 years ago, you can get an intuitive feel of how strange human societies are likely to appear a century from now.

Table 2. A spectrum of systems, from managed to unmanageable.

Extensively Managed Systems	Partially Managed Systems	Unmanageable Systems

Most economic sectors:
   Manufacturing
   Health care
Most human activities:
   Sleeping
   Surfing the Internet
	Vulnerable economic sectors:
	   Agriculture
	   Forestry
	Nonmarket systems:
	   Beaches and coastal
	     ecosystems
	   Wildfires
		Hurricanes
		Sea-level rise
		Wildlife
		Ocean acidification

Why is the distinction between managed and unmanaged systems so important for our topic? This distinction helps us identify those areas where climate change is of greatest concern by contrast with those areas where humans may be able to adapt to climate change.

Table 2 lists major areas, dividing them into extensively managed, partially managed, and unmanaged (or unmanageable).[3] Most of the economy falls into the extensively managed area and is likely to experience relatively little direct impact from climate change. At the other end of the spectrum are natural systems that are unmanaged or unmanageable with current technologies. One theme of this book is that major concerns stem from unmanaged sectors, while the managed sectors pose limited risks as long as societies use sensible adaptation strategies.

WEATHER VERSUS CLIMATE

Before discussing the impacts in different sectors, I need to issue one important warning about impacts analysis. Climate impacts need to be distinguished from the effects of weather. Recall that climate is the statistical mean and variability of temperature, precipitation, and other variables over a period of decades or more. Weather is the actual realization of the climatic process for a short period of time, for a particular day or year.

In estimating impacts, people often confuse weather and climate. A persuasive body of evidence shows that especially hot weather reduces farm yields in the United States. But studies show that a small climatic warming would probably increase farm yields in the United States. The difference is that farmers can adapt to the warmer climate by changing their management practices, but they cannot easily adapt to a severe and unexpected summer drought after all their planting decisions are made. So stories about "weather disasters" tell us nothing about the impacts of climate change. Of course, weather disasters like floods, hurricanes, and droughts bring adverse effects. But we need to know whether there will be more of these weather disasters in a warmer world and whether people can prepare for them.

The lesson here is that our analysis needs to be alert to examining climatic impacts, including the adaptations that take place, while separating these from the background variability of day-to-day weather events.

AN OVERVIEW OF IMPACTS ANALYSIS

When we consider the question of impacts, we are generally not concerned about climate change itself. The average surface temperature of the earth is by itself no more worrisome than the surface temperature of Jupiter. Rather, we are concerned about the effects of climate change on physical and biological systems and on human societies. This central point implies that sensible policies will depend upon our assessment of the ways, some obvious and some subtle, that climate changes affect the different human and natural systems.

A related important point concerns costs. Economists and engineers who have studied ways to slow climate change or reduce its damaging effects conclude that steps to slow global warming will impose costs. Put differently, if we want to reduce our CO_2 emissions so as to reduce impacts, it will require using costlier technologies and policies and therefore will reduce real incomes. For example, we might lower CO_2 emissions by improving automobile fuel economy. Current automotive technology can indeed improve fuel efficiency, but it will raise the cost of the car. A hybrid gas-electric car might reduce CO_2 emissions by 20 percent, but the batteries and other systems might add $3,000 to the cost. Similarly, energy consumption for heating and cooling buildings can be reduced with better insulation, but that requires some up-front investment for materials and installation. I discuss these issues in Part III, but the basic point is that reducing emissions will require sacrificing valuable goods and services today in order to reduce future climate damages.

A third and related point is more subtle. Sensible global warming policies will require some balancing of costs and benefits. This means that an economically desirable policy is one that reduces emissions in an optimal fashion—to a level beyond which further reductions in damages are not worth the additional abatement costs. This point is actually quite intuitive if we look at the extreme options. We could stop global warming in its tracks by banning all fossil fuels today. No one advocates this policy because it would be extraordinarily expensive (the "wreck the economy" approach). At the other pole, we could do nothing at all, forever, or at least for a long time. Some people actually do take this position, but that proposal appears to me to be a reckless gamble (the "wreck the world" approach).

By thinking of these extremes, we see that good policies must lie somewhere between wrecking the economy and wrecking the world. Current ideas about how to weigh the competing demands of economics and the environment are discussed later in this book, but for now, the basic point is that some kind of balancing is required.

The final consideration is whether, after we have balanced costs and benefits in a careful manner, a precise target for policy will emerge. I call this a "focal policy" because it would be an obvious policy that people can agree and focus on. Some areas have natural focal policies, such as eliminating AIDS, smallpox, financial collapses, or nuclear wars.

For climate change, there is a great temptation to find focal policy targets because that tremendously simplifies analysis and policy. Setting a firm target is sensible if there is a threshold beyond which important dangerous effects appear. Our review of tipping points in Chapter 5 suggests that serious tipping points will be encountered when global temperature increase passes 3°C. On the other hand, international meetings have agreed to a global maximum target of 2°C, and some scientists have argued strenuously that dangerous limits will be triggered if temperature increases surpass 1½°C.[4] One of the central questions, therefore, is whether we can find support for any of these focal points for policy on the basis of current knowledge.

7 THE FATE OF FARMING

We begin our review of economic impacts with farming. Of all major sectors, farming is the most sensitive to climate and is therefore most likely to feel the impacts of climate change. Most plants do not thrive in the Sahara Desert, and we would naturally want to know how much current farmland will turn to desert in a warmer world. Additionally, other impacts of climate change are connected to agriculture. Two of the major health impacts—malnourishment and diarrheal diseases, discussed in Chapter 8—are usually caused by poor diets and poverty. Some have worried about the impact of climate change on national security because of potential conflicts caused by droughts and food shortages and the resulting international mass migrations.

It turns out that the linkage between climate change and agriculture is more subtle than just a simple effect of temperature changes on crop yields, however. One important factor is that agriculture is a heavily managed activity, particularly in technologically advanced, information-rich economies. I discussed examples of management in Chapter 6—how irrigation systems can offset the variability of rainfall, or how sheds can protect cows from the desert sun. The potential for human management of agriculture systems raises important questions: How will different societies manage the changing climate? Will they take adaptive steps that could even enhance productivity? And what will farm technologies look like a century hence, with all the developments in genetically modified seeds and new information systems?

Yet another set of questions involves the interaction of climate change and economic growth. In the next section, we will see that the extent of impacts depends critically on the pace of economic growth, which in turn will determine how dependent societies are on farming

ECONOMIC GROWTH, CLIMATE CHANGE, AND DAMAGE FROM CLIMATE CHANGE

Before discussing the impacts of climate change on farming, it is important to understand two central points about the relationship between climate change and economic growth. <u>The extent of climate change, and the size and severity of damages on sectors like farming, will depend primarily on the pace of economic growth over the next century and beyond.</u> But the flip side of this is that societies are likely to be much wealthier in the future when they confront the dangers of global warming.

The best way to see these connections is to compare two futures: one with and one without economic growth. Let's examine the outlook for each scenario of climate change and climate damages using a standard integrated assessment model.

The *baseline scenario* is the one used to project economic growth, emissions, and climate change without emissions reductions or other climate-change policies. This scenario serves as the standard no-policy baseline throughout this book. For this discussion, I rely on the Yale DICE model discussed in Chapter 3. In the baseline run, per capita consumption continues to rise rapidly over the coming decades. The projected growth in global per capita output is a little under 2 percent per year for the twenty-first century, and just below 1 percent per year for the twenty-second century. After two centuries of growth, the world would be an affluent place by today's standards: Global per capita consumption would be almost three times the current level for the United States. The rapid growth in the baseline case also leads to rapid changes in global temperatures. These growth projections are standard to the integrated economic-climate models described in Part I (see particularly Figure 9).[1]

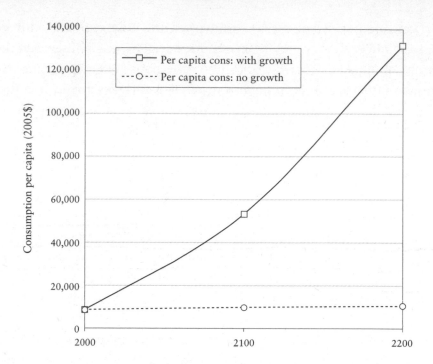

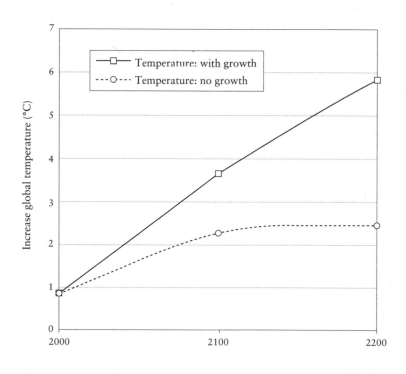

Now contrast the standard path with a situation with no economic growth. I use the term "no growth" to mean no new or improved products or processes—no growth in total factor productivity, to use the economist's technical language. In this stagnationist vision (unrealistic but useful to consider) societies would no longer benefit from continuing improvements in computers, health care, electronics, or other areas that have experienced rapid growth in recent decades. The era of technological miracles would end with the iPhone 5.

Figure 13 shows the two scenarios graphically.[2] These are stylized scenarios but will usefully make the point about incomes and climate change. The top part of the figure shows the two economic scenarios of growth and no growth. They are obviously dramatically different. In the no-growth scenario, global per capita consumption after two centuries is around $10,000 per person, well under that of today's rich countries. In the growth scenario, world per capita consumption grows to over $130,000 per capita. This sounds like a fantasy, but it is the result of exponential growth of living standards.[3]

Now look at the bottom half of Figure 13, which shows the difference in warming between the growth and no-growth scenarios. With growth, global temperatures increase by around $3\frac{1}{2}°C$ by 2100 and by 6°C by the end of the second century. This is the nightmare scenario of scientists.

Under the no-growth scenario, climate change is much smaller. The global mean temperature in the no-growth future rises by about $2\frac{1}{2}°C$ by 2200, even without any emissions controls. Some environmental advocates might like the impacts of the no-growth scenario—until they

Figure 13 opposite. Living standards and climate change with and without economic growth. This figure shows two possible futures. One is "no growth," which turns off productivity growth immediately. The other shows the projection of productivity growth built into most integrated assessment models. The top half compares the paths of per capita consumption. ("Per capita cons" represents average consumption of food, shelter, education, and other items.) The bottom half shows the difference in climate paths of growth and no growth without any climate policies. Rapid climate change is the unintentional by-product of rapid economic growth with no abatement policies.

contemplate the implications for the billions of people who will be stuck in poverty and disease for the indefinite future.

The central finding here is that the climate-change problem is largely a by-product of rapid economic growth without emissions reductions. But the scenario of continued productivity growth also implies that people will on average be richer in the future—which in turn implies that nations will be better able to afford steps to slow climate change or adapt to its adverse effects.

So we have a paradox. Rapid economic growth without abatement policies will produce rapid climate change and substantial damages. Slow growth will leave us poor but with fewer damages. However, even with substantial climate-change damages, consumption will still be much larger in the growth world than in the no-growth world. People will have substantially higher living standards in the growth world even after subtracting the damages from the changing climate.

The likelihood that people will be richer in the future is no excuse for ignoring climate change today. But it is also a reminder that we will leave our grandchildren a more productive economy alongside a degraded climate. If you compare the projected living standards in 2100 or 2200 in the two economic scenarios shown in Figure 13, you can see that it would take an enormous amount of climate damage to offset the fruits of future productivity growth on our living standards.

Should we conclude from this example that our problem is too much economic growth? That we should aim for zero economic growth? Few people today draw this conclusion.[4] It would be like throwing out all the groceries because the milk is sour. The appropriate response is to fix the market failure by repairing the flawed economic externality involved in climate change. Throw out the sour milk and fix the faulty refrigerator. Understanding how to do this will be our task in Parts III and IV.

IMPACT OF CLIMATE CHANGE ON AGRICULTURE

Almost daily we read about global famine, decadal droughts, and major areas at risk. For example, *The New York Times* published a long article, "A Warming Planet Struggles to Feed Itself." After recounting many anecdotes, the article concludes, "Many of the failed harvests of the past decade were a consequence of weather disasters, like floods in the United States, drought in Australia and blistering heat waves in Europe and Russia. Scientists believe some, though not all, of those events were caused or worsened by human-induced global warming."[5]

An even more somber projection was made by the prominent *Stern Review:* "Declining crop yields are likely to leave hundreds of millions without the ability to produce or purchase sufficient food, particularly in the poorest parts of the world. . . . Once temperatures increase by 3°C, 250–550 million additional people may be at risk—over half in Africa and Western Asia."[6]

The impact of climate change on agriculture is the most carefully studied area of impacts analysis. Do these pictures accurately reflect current assessments? It is worth looking at the summaries of the IPCC Fourth Assessment Report, which provided a careful review by experts in the field.

> Globally, the potential for food production is projected to increase with increases in local average temperature over a range of 1–3°C, but above this it is projected to decrease. Increases in the frequency of droughts and floods are projected to affect local crop production negatively, especially in subsistence sectors at low latitudes. Adaptations such as altered cultivars and planting times allow low- and mid- to high-latitude cereal yields to be maintained at or above baseline yields for modest warming.[7]

It is striking how this summary of the scientific evidence contrasts with the popular rhetoric. Crop productivity or yields are the output per acre of land under cultivation. The findings here are that productivity will increase in many regions for "modest warming," which generally means up to 3°C of local warming. The temperature projections in Figure 9 indicate that temperature increase is expected to remain in the modest range until the last quarter of this century.

These projections need to be qualified by the uncertainties of both climate and agricultural models. Moreover, there will clearly be losers as well as winners. Even more worrisome is that current models do not include the potential impacts of tipping points, or major changes in global weather patterns. Even given these uncertainties, the pictures of the grain belt turning into the Sahara Desert are posters for persuasion rather than the results of careful scholarly studies.

Adverse assessments of the impacts of global warming on farming rely on two major factors. First, climate change is likely to lead to warmer climates with declining soil moisture in many regions of the world where climates are already close to the margin. Work of my Yale colleague Robert Mendelsohn suggests that current climates in many parts of Latin America, Africa, and Asia are already warmer than is optimal for food production, and further warming would reduce yields in those regions.[8]

A second factor is that climate change may lead to adverse impacts on the "hydrological cycle," that is, systems that provide water for agriculture. Examples of adverse impacts include declines in mountain snowpack and major changes in seasonal river runoff. These trends would reduce the availability of water for irrigation, again harming agricultural productivity. These two elements have been extensively investigated with climate projections incorporating water and crop models.

ADAPTATION AND MITIGATING FACTORS

The crystal ball is just as cloudy for agriculture as for other areas, but there are several factors that could reduce the harmful impacts of climate change, including carbon fertilization, adaptation, trade, and the declining share of agriculture in our economies. One important mitigating factor for agriculture is carbon fertilization. Carbon dioxide is a fertilizer for many plants. In the presence of increased CO_2, yields for wheat, cotton, and clover—particularly when other inputs were adjusted appropriately—have increased sharply in field experiments. One review of multiple field studies found that doubling atmospheric concentrations of CO_2 would increase yields of rice, wheat, and soybeans 10–15 percent. Certain plants such as corn, which fix atmospheric carbon via what is known as the C4 pathway, are expected to show smaller increases in CO_2-induced yields. There are many questions about how

CO$_2$ fertilization will interact with other stresses. However, experts like Paul Waggoner, former director of the Connecticut Agricultural Experiment Station and one of the pioneers on the effects of climate change on agriculture, concludes that CO$_2$ fertilization could offset many of the adverse effects of warmer and drier conditions.

A second important mitigating factor is adaptation, which is another term to describe what we call management. Adaptation refers to the adjustments that human or natural systems make in response to changes in environmental conditions. Many of the studies that project large declines in yields make limited allowance for adaptation. So understanding adaptation is important in this context, as elsewhere.

Adaptations occur on multiple levels. Some occur without human assistance, such as when a species migrates to a friendlier climatic zone in response to a changing climate. In agriculture we usually consider the most important adaptations to be those undertaken by farmers. Short-run adaptations include adjusting sowing and harvesting dates, changing seeds and crops, and modifying production techniques such as fertilizer application, tillage methods, grain drying, and other field operations.

In the longer run, farmers can move into new areas and abandon infertile ones, plant new varieties of seeds that are drought and heat resistant, and shift land to other uses. One of the most important adaptations is the use of more water-efficient irrigation systems.[9]

Studies of agriculture have looked extensively at impacts with and without adaptation, and it is useful to examine a specific example. Figure 14 shows the synthesis of studies of the effect of climate change on the yields of wheat in low-latitude regions (such as India and Brazil).[10] The horizontal axis shows the change in average temperature in low-latitude regions, while the vertical axis shows the change in the yield (production per acre) of wheat production. The dashed lower line shows the summary impact of warming without CO$_2$ fertilization or adaptation. The upper solid line shows the summary impact of warming with CO$_2$ fertilization and some other adaptations.

In the case without adaptation or CO$_2$ fertilization, yields begin to decline after local warming of around $1\frac{1}{2}$°C. However, the story is quite

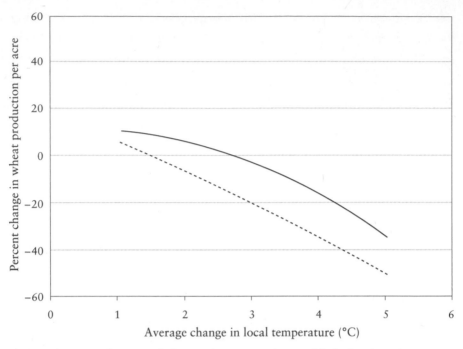

Figure 14. Estimated impact of climate change on wheat yields for low-latitude regions. The lines show the summary results drawn from about fifty published studies at multiple sites of yields per acre as a function of mean local temperature change. The lower line shows the response without adaptations, while the upper line shows yield changes with a limited set of adaptations, including CO_2 fertilization.

different with adaptation and CO_2 fertilization. Wheat yields in low-latitude regions with adaptation would be positive for temperature increases up to 3°C. This is the climate change that would be expected late in this century. Yields would begin to decline after the 3°C change and would decline as much as 30 percent at a 5°C temperature increase. The same survey found that the break-even temperature change for rice in low-latitude regions is estimated to be 4°C. For warming less than 4°C, rice yields with adaptation are predicted to increase. It should be added that most studies are very conservative in their assumptions about adaptations and probably underestimate the potential for upward shifts in the adaptation curve in Figure 14.[11]

One of the major factors affecting all aspects of climate change is technological change. It affects emissions through its impact on eco-

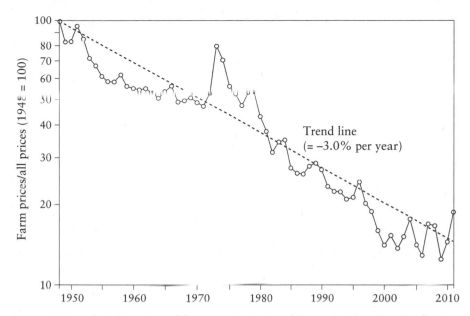

Figure 15. Trends in the prices of farm products, United States, 1948–2011. The figure shows the movement of farm prices relative to all prices.

nomic growth, as we saw earlier in this chapter. It will affect our ability to reduce emissions at low cost (see Part III). But here, we need to examine the interaction of new technologies and climate change in determining food prices. One would expect adverse climatic conditions that reduce yields to increase food prices. In economic terms, they would be an adverse shift in the supply curve.

What are the trends and prospects for farm prices? Figure 15 shows the trend in real farm prices over the last half century for the United States.[12] This index shows the ratio of the prices of all products produced on farms to economy-wide prices. Farm prices are the prices received by farmers, and this is the sector that is most sensitive to climate change. (Note that farm prices move differently than food prices: Food prices paid by consumers include other factors such as packaging, transportation, and retail margins that are largely unaffected by climate change, and these downstream costs move differently than farm prices.) Over the last several decades, farm prices have declined at an average rate of 3 percent per year. Real farm prices in 2011 were less than one-fifth of their level after World War II. The long-term decline in farm prices has been driven by large-scale technological improvements in that sector.

But what of the future? We have no crystal ball that tells us whether the downward trend of past food prices will continue or reverse. Perhaps the increased use of biofuels will increase the demand for crops and drive up food prices (see Chapter 22). But the issue here is the differential impact of global warming on farming. A climate-induced food shortage would tilt the price trend shown in Figure 15 upward.

What do studies suggest? A review of world food models in the IPCC Fourth Assessment Report showed a range of results.[13] Studies that allow for adaptation and international trade generally showed that warming would reduce world food prices relative to a no-warming baseline for increases up to 3°C. These results are consistent with studies that find increasing agricultural yields up to 3°C temperature increase, as shown in Figure 14. So one very important result of agriculture models is that global warming is estimated to reduce rather than increase food prices over the next few decades.

This leads to a third mitigating factor—the role of international trade in agriculture. Increasingly, farming is a market activity, not a subsistence activity. There is a world market for many agricultural products. This means that a shock to yields in one region will be cushioned by the world market. Assume, for example, that wheat yields in Kansas decline by 10 percent because of climate change. Calculations by scholars like MIT economist John Reilly indicate that there will be virtually no impact on food prices or on consumers because production of wheat and other crops elsewhere in the world will largely fill the gap.[14]

The final mitigating factor is the declining share over time of agriculture in the economy and in the workforce. Most people are surprised to learn how small the U.S. farm sector is. Farming declined from about 10 percent of GDP in 1929 to less than 1 percent by 2010. This trend is seen around the world. The downward trend is most striking in East Asia, where the share of agriculture fell from 40 percent in 1962 to 12 percent in 2008. Farming in sub-Saharan Africa is only 13 percent of the economy, and the share has fallen sharply there as well. The movement of jobs from rural farms to industrial and service-based cities is one of the most important and universal features of the process of economic development.[15]

If the trend continues, then shocks to agriculture from climate change are likely to have a small and declining impact on economies in many other regions—comparable to that of the United States today. The declining vulnerability to agriculture shocks is a critical point. The declining share indicates that the impacts of agricultural shocks on people's incomes and spending will be reduced as the share declines. The intuition is straightforward. Suppose you spend 20 percent of your income on housing and 4 percent on food. Now assume that the cost of each goes up by 25 percent (because of a shock to climate or other factors). To maintain the same housing consumption, you would have to reduce your nonhousing consumption by 5 (=0.25×20) percent, while it would require only a 1 (=0.25×4) percent change in nonfood consumption to maintain your food consumption. So as the share of a particular item in your budget goes down, the impact of price shocks on real incomes will decline roughly proportionally.

We can take the actual share of farming in the U.S. economy to illustrate this point. If we go back to the 1930s and 1940s, a 25 percent shock to farm prices would have reduced consumer real incomes by around 2 percent because farm products made up a large share of consumer budgets. However, with the declining importance of farming in economic activity, the same 25 percent shock to farm prices would produce only a 0.3 percent reduction in consumer incomes in the 1990s and 2000s. So while food is clearly critical to our health and well-being, the economy can absorb a large shock to the farm sector without a major loss of welfare.[16]

I have devoted an extensive discussion to agriculture not only because it is the most climate-sensitive industry but also because it illustrates the tug-of-war between climatic impacts and adaptive behavior. Experts are sharply divided on the impacts of climate change on farming because it is clear that powerful forces are acting in different directions. Yes, farming productivity is intrinsically highly localized and heterogeneous.

Yes, the impacts are highly dependent on local climatic conditions as well as soils, management practices, and market availability. Yes, some regions will experience warmer and drier conditions. So some regions will undoubtedly be severely affected, particularly if adaptation is limited.

But adaptive forces are also very powerful. Farm technologies have evolved greatly in most regions. Over the last century, the prices of farm products have been declining, and the share of most economies devoted to farming has been shrinking. The output of farms is increasingly sold in global markets, so the impact of localized climate change on consumption will be buffered by market forces and adaptation. Moreover, people can and do move away from regions that experience severe shocks to local industries, particularly over the longer run. Most important, societies have many adaptations they can make in the face of changing conditions.

However, while studies suggest that impacts on farming will be small for the next half century or so, we must also put in the balance concerns about the longer run. The odds in the Climate Casino become increasingly unfavorable with more extensive climate change, particularly when the global temperature increase exceeds 3°C. In the long run, with unchecked accumulations of CO_2 and the accompanying changes, the projections become much more uncertain and the risks rise of tipping points such as changes in monsoonal patterns or major changes in ocean currents.

What is the summary judgment here? The best evidence is that the economic impact of climate change on overall economic welfare through agriculture is likely to be small over the next few decades. The impact will be declining as countries develop and move their labor force out of the farm sector. Over the longer run, the outlook is cloudier, especially if climate change is unchecked. If global temperatures rise sharply, changes in precipitation patterns and abrupt changes are more likely to cause substantial impacts on food production.

8 THE IMPACT ON HUMAN HEALTH

Among the frightening impacts of global warming is the potential for major impacts on health. The concerns include malnutrition, heat stress, air pollution, and the spread of tropical diseases like malaria.[1] The *Stern Review* put forth the following somber warning: "Just a 1°C increase in global temperature above pre-industrial [levels] could double annual deaths from climate change to at least 300,000. . . . At higher temperatures, death rates will increase sharply, for example millions more people dying from malnutrition each year."[2]

This all sounds extremely grave. However, as with agriculture, we need to look carefully at the assumptions underlying these projections and to examine mitigating factors and adaptation. What are the assumptions about economic growth implicit in the estimates? How large are the health impacts compared to the background of improvements in health status around the world? Most important, how will the impacts be alleviated by the effects of economic growth and improving medical technologies?

POTENTIAL IMPACT OF WARMING ON HUMAN HEALTH

Estimating the impacts of climate change on health is yet another difficult task. It requires estimates of climate change by region and year. Then it requires estimates of the impacts of changing climate conditions on health for different diseases. This is challenging because the changes take place well into the future in a world where incomes, medical technologies, and health status are evolving rapidly. I sketch some estimates in this chapter, but it must be emphasized that these are at best educated guesses, and the potential health outcomes range from none to serious.

The most detailed assessment of the impacts on health was a study undertaken by a team of health and climate scientists for the World Health Organization (WHO).[3] Their report analyzed two mechanisms through which health impacts occur. The first is the direct effect of increasing environmental stress on people due to heat waves, pollution, and floods. The second is the indirect effect that occurs because global warming may lower living standards, increase the geographical range of some infectious diseases such as malaria, and worsen malnutrition and diarrheal disorders.

The study team began by examining evidence of the relationship between different diseases and climatic conditions. They then estimated the increased risk of contracting the diseases due to changing climate. By combining these estimates, they projected the total health risk from climate change.

More precisely, they began with estimates of the health status of different regions in a no-warming scenario; then they used one of the standard warming scenarios from climate models and produced a new estimate of health status; they then took the difference between the two scenarios to calculate the impacts of global warming in a particular year.[4] The team identified three major areas of concern: malnutrition (from inadequate incomes), diarrheal diseases (from poor sanitation and health systems), and malaria (from an expansion of malarial regions).

The report used an interesting innovation in public health research—the concept of the disability-adjusted life year (DALY).[5] The DALY measures the loss in healthy years of life from different diseases. It counts two factors: the number of years of life lost and the fraction of healthy years lost. For example, if an elderly 70-year-old person with a life expectancy of 10 years dies of heart failure, this would be 10 DALYs lost. If a young girl in Tanzania contracts malaria, her life expectancy would be reduced by about 33 years, so this would represent a loss of 33 DALYs.[6]

Additionally, if someone is not in perfect health, they are counted as having a disability and this enters into the DALY calculation. For example, if someone goes blind from river blindness (onchocerciasis to doctors), this syndrome would be equivalent to 62 percent of a death. Deafness is counted as one-third of a death. The methods are highly controversial even though the general idea of trying to avoid death and illness is sound.

The techniques used to estimate the impact of climate change on human health are challenging and not without criticism. Therefore I provide a detailed look at the estimates, particularly for diarrheal diseases. This section is more technical than most others and can be skipped by the reader who wishes to get the broad picture, but it will provide background on the analytical difficulties for those interested in the details.

There are currently no global studies of the impact of climate change on diarrheal diseases, so the team had to put together its own methods. The study assumed that there were no adverse impacts on countries with per capita incomes more than $6,000 per year. It then assumed that the incidence of diarrheal diseases in low-income countries would increase either 10 percent per °C increase for the high estimate or 0 percent response as the low estimate. These estimates were based on limited studies in Peru and Fiji, but more general studies were not available. Moreover, the studies assumed that, under this threshold, improvements in income and health technologies did not lower the vulnerability of people to these diseases.

Table 3 shows a simplified set of results for the health losses from climate change in the mid-twenty-first century using relative risk estimates of the WHO team. They estimated the loss in DALYs (disability-adjusted life years) from climate change, here shown for two different regions. Note that this estimate is the upper-bound of health impacts. For this table, we have shown only two regions, Africa and high-income countries. I show these two regions because these are at the extreme ends of the estimated impacts and allow an assessment of the overall impacts and trends.[7]

The top part of Table 3 shows the estimated DALYs lost due to each of the three most important diseases. The first row refers to Africa. For

Table 3. Estimated health impact of global warming, 2050.

Increased risk from climate change	Total	Diarrheal diseases	Malaria	Nutritional deficiencies
	Disability-adjusted life years lost per 1,000 persons			
Africa	14.91	6.99	7.13	0.80
High-income countries	0.02	0.02	0.00	0.00

Increased risk as percentage of baseline mortality	Total	Diarrheal diseases	Malaria	Nutritional deficiencies
	Losses from climate change as % of all losses			
Africa	2.92	1.37	1.40	0.16
High-income countries	0.01	0.01	0.00	0.00

the table, I have taken the WHO upper-bound estimate of health impact so as not to underestimate the impacts. The lower bound is zero impact. I take the WHO temperature estimate, which is labeled 2050. According to their estimates, climate change will lead to a total increase of about 15 DALYs lost per 1,000 persons in Africa. Put differently, on average a person's life will be shortened by 0.015 years, or about 5 days. Diarrheal diseases and malaria are each about half of the health risks for Africa. Now look at Africa in the bottom part of Table 3, again in the first row. This shows the effects of climate change as a percentage of baseline mortality, or projected deaths in that year. Again, this is shown both for the total and for the three specific important diseases. For Africa, the total estimated losses from climate change make up almost 3 percent of the total lost DALYs from all diseases. The estimate of the high-end impact of climate change is therefore a small increase in health risks (moreover, remember that the low-end estimate is zero).

Next look at the estimates for developing countries (which include primarily the United States, western Europe, and Japan). The estimated health risks here, even in the highest-risk case, are negligible, comprising about 0.01 percent of total lost DALYs. The reasons for the low impacts are primarily high incomes and good public health structures, and partially the temperate climates.

If we look at the world as a whole, we find increased health risks arise primarily for Africa and Southeast Asia. For the developed regions of North America and western Europe, the increased health risks are minimal. Other regions, such as Latin America, are in between.

Diarrheal diseases constitute about half the estimated global health risks from climate change, with malaria and malnutrition each responsible for about a quarter. Note that Table 3 excludes a number of other health risks, such as flooding, other tropical diseases, and heat stress, but the total for the other ailments as estimated by the WHO team was much smaller. A table with results for all regions and the world is in the endnotes.[8]

HEALTH RISKS IN THE CONTEXT OF ECONOMIC DEVELOPMENT

Having struggled in this field for many years, I have come to view impacts analysis as a kind of house-to-house combat. It pits dedicated analysts against fragmentary data and murky future trends. Nowhere is the terrain more treacherous than in mapping out future health impacts. Health is central to people's well-being and to economic performance. Health care is a large and growing part of the global economy, and it is changing rapidly as new knowledge, drugs, equipment, and information technology transform the sector.

The health status of poor countries has improved rapidly in recent years. Consider, for example, the sixty countries with per capita income less than $2,000 in 1980. In these countries, life expectancy rose by 14 years in the last three decades. Moreover, improvements in health status are clearly associated with higher incomes. Economic studies indicate that a rise of 10 percent in per capita income is associated with an increase in life expectancy of 0.3 years.

If one evaluates the major threats to health in poor countries, they have been primarily due not to climate change but to AIDS. In countries such as Zimbabwe, Botswana, Zambia, and South Africa, health improvements in other areas have been swamped by the effects of the

AIDS epidemic, which has lowered life expectancies by 20 years in the worst-hit areas.[9]

The health risks from climate change shown in Table 3 can be evaluated in the context of the overall health improvements in developing countries. Take sub-Saharan Africa as an example. For this region, life expectancy has increased about 10 years over the last four decades. The upper-bound health losses from climate change shown in Table 3 are about 1 year of life expectancy per person over the next four decades. This implies that the health risks from climate change are equivalent to a loss in health improvements of about four years at historical rates. In other regions, the losses are estimated to be much smaller.[10] Moreover, as I discuss in the next section, these health impacts reflect unrealistic assumptions and are likely to be exaggerated.

ADAPTATION AND MITIGATING FACTORS

The numbers in Table 3 are likely to overestimate the health impacts because they do not take into account technological improvements in health along with rising incomes. To begin with, they assume minimal adaptations to increasing temperatures and the associated health burdens. For example, we expect that people would adapt their structures and lifestyles to the higher temperatures through such means as air conditioning as their incomes rose. You might think this is a mixed blessing.

A story on the dramatic growth in the use of air conditioning in India pointed to the growth of electricity demand and CO_2 emissions resulting from powering the air conditioners. This growing demand for energy is indeed a central factor in the growth of CO_2 emissions and the rapid warming in the scenarios analyzed above. At the same time, we should not forget that air conditioning promotes human welfare—it cools the homes of people in the hot regions of rapidly growing countries like India and China, making them healthier and more productive.

However, the WHO analysis assumed no adaptation at all to heat stress. Similarly, no adaptations were made to combat the potential spread of malaria with warming, despite the wider array of adaptive options that would be available with higher incomes. Additionally, the projection of rising malnutrition is incompatible with the assessment of relatively stable yields and declining prices for agriculture, discussed in Chapter 7.

More generally, the WHO health analysis did not factor in the major improvements in health care and life expectancies that have already occurred and can be expected to continue given increasing incomes. As we saw in the last section, there is a strong historical relationship between incomes and life expectancy: Wealthier is healthier. With higher incomes, countries upgrade their public health services and other health-related infrastructure, and families have more resources to devote to health care. Higher incomes pay for more doctors and nurses, more clinics, and higher levels of education, and all of these are powerful contributors to better health. Moreover, the causality goes both ways because better health improves growth as well.

The point can be seen by looking at the difference in impacts for the two groups of countries in Table 3. The bottom half of the table shows that the health losses from climate change for Africa are about 3 percent of all losses measured in DALY terms. By contrast, the losses in high-income countries are negligible. The estimated impacts on middle-income countries (see the table in note 8) are much smaller than on African countries. To the extent that poor countries grow rapidly, they will have impacts that look more like those of middle-income and even rich countries.

But will poor countries actually grow fast enough to outrun the adverse health effects of climate change? We cannot be sure, but that assumption is buried in the climate projections. The average of the integrated assessment models projects that India's per capita GDP will grow by a factor of almost 40 over the 2000–2100 period. By the end of the next century, the low-income regions are expected to have incomes close to those of today's high-income regions. And it is critical to recall that this rapid economic growth is a central feature of scenarios that are producing warming in the first place (see Figure 9).

Since this point is so important, let's look in detail at the important case of diarrheal diseases, which comprise almost half of the health impact for Africa. Recall that the WHO study assumed that the impacts of diarrheal diseases fell only on countries with per capita incomes less than $6,000 per year. I went back to examine the projections underlying the DICE model, which include a set of regional estimates for sub-Saharan Africa. Combining these with detailed regional data, the model estimates the fraction of the African population with income below the $6,000 threshold for the recent past and in the future. Whereas more than 90 percent of the population fell below this threshold in 2000, the model projections indicate that only about half will fall below this threshold by the mid-twenty-first century. By this century's end, less than 10 percent of the African population is projected to be below the $6,000 threshold.[11]

Although these are just estimates, they have the advantage of being consistent with the assumptions of the integrated-assessment model used to predict the temperature increases. So the estimates of growing malnutrition and related diseases in the climate-health scenarios are incompatible with the estimates of growing incomes that produce the very emissions that lead to the rapid warming.

The projected incidence of malaria provides another example of a pessimistic bias in the WHO study. The IPCC Fourth Assessment Report states that by 2100, there will be a 16–28 percent increase in exposure to malaria in Africa.[12] These proportions are slightly higher than those used in the estimates in Table 3. However, these estimates assume that there are no socioeconomic adaptations in the coming years. This assumption is contrary to the view among public health researchers that poverty is a substantial contributor to the incidence of malaria. With higher incomes, people tend to move from mosquito-infested rural areas to cities. Higher incomes also enable people to pay for insecticide-treated bed nets, kidney treatment, and antimalarial drugs.[13] Moreover, the projections would be completely wrong if medical research over the next century were to produce an economical malaria vaccine or treatment. We might be skeptical about Bill Gates's patent to reduce hurricane intensity (see Chapter 6), but surely the Gates Foundation's program to eradicate malaria should be taken seriously.

These examples suggest that many of the serious health impacts of climate change are likely to be manageable and managed in a world of rapidly growing incomes. The limitations of projections like those of the WHO and IPCC reports highlight the importance of evaluating impacts in the context of the future economy—the economy that actually produces the climate-change scenarios—rather than making projections based solely on current economic conditions.

In addition, this discussion illustrates the more general point about the role of managed systems when considering the impacts of climate change. Health care is one of the most intensively managed of all human systems. In the case of malaria and other diseases that might be aggravated by climate change, we would expect governments to take steps to reduce vulnerabilities through research, preventive measures, and treatment programs. This analysis is consistent with trends in malaria incidence over the last decade. According to WHO, the deaths per person at risk fell by 33 percent over the decade from 2000 to 2010.[14]

The summary on health effects is similar to that for agriculture in the last chapter. In looking forward, we must remember that human societies increasingly devote resources to insulate their lives and property from environmental conditions as their incomes rise. This is true in all areas of human activity—in adaptive housing, storm warning systems, more and better trained doctors and nurses, and improved public health infrastructure. There is never a guarantee that this trend will continue, or that it will always be successful, or that surprises will not occasionally overwhelm the defenses. So while it would be imprudent to rule out adverse impacts of climate change on human health, the degree of vulnerability for the market economies seems very different from that of the unmanaged systems that are discussed starting in Chapter 9.

9 PERILS FOR THE OCEANS

The last two chapters, on agriculture and health, involved intensively managed systems. While the impacts in those areas may be unfavorable, particularly if they are badly managed, the risks are within the range of economic shocks experienced in normal times. A complete analysis, which is beyond the scope of this book, would add other managed or manageable sectors to that list, such as national security, forests, fisheries, construction, and energy production. However, the real concerns about global warming lie elsewhere—outside economic sectors that are increasingly managed and insulated from adverse environmental conditions.

I turn to four of these most serious and unmanageable threats in the next chapters: sea-level rise (SLR), ocean acidification, hurricane intensification, and ecosystem losses. Along with the tipping points discussed earlier, these issues are properly the areas of greatest concern over the coming decades. They are areas where the forces at work are most unmanageable, where the impacts may prove particularly damaging, and where the obstacles to adaptations may be most formidable.

THE RISING SEAS

I begin our analysis of unmanageable impacts of climate change by looking at the impacts on the oceans, starting with SLR. One of the challenges for policy is that SLR is so delayed. While the impacts on farming and health may arrive relatively quickly, the sea level will rise slowly for many centuries because of the thermal inertia in oceans and the long delays in melting the giant ice sheets. The long delays pose special challenges because they require envisioning the shape of our landscape and societies deep into the future and taking steps today that will produce most of their benefits well beyond the present century.

THE FUZZY TELESCOPE: ENVISIONING FUTURE SOCIETIES

As a boy, I loved high-powered telescopes. I once bought a cheap one that was advertised as twenty power. When it arrived, I was crestfallen. While I could see Sandia Peak off in the distance, it was fuzzy and distorted.

I call this the fuzzy telescope problem. In the current context, the further we look into the future for economic, social, and political calculations, the more things look fuzzy and uncertain. So before beginning my substantive discussion of SLR, I pause to consider the fuzzy telescope problem. This causes severe difficulties for analyses of climate-change impacts because it requires us to consider the impact of climate change on human societies that have already evolved for decades or even centuries.

To grasp the difficulty of this task, imagine your hometown around 1910 and think of all the changes since then. My hometown of Albuquerque had just seen its first railroad. The United States had no central bank, no income tax, and no airplanes. The most advanced computational device was the Monroe Calculator, which could perform about three operations per second, compared to the computer I am now using, which works 1 trillion times faster. Wages in the United States were about 19 cents an hour. Social networks were built over your back fence.

Look at a map for 1910. Europe was under the thumb of three now-defunct regimes: the Ottoman, Czarist, and Austro-Hungarian empires. Virtually the entire African continent was divided into colonies under the control of Belgium, France, Britain, and Germany. The nuclear model of the atom had not yet been discovered. Scientists did not know how traits were transmitted from parents to children.

You can see how daunting is the task of trying to project the impact of global warming on the world of 2110. In areas where models rely primarily on fundamental physical laws, we can be reasonably certain about our estimates. For example, if we are confident about our temperature projections, then the SLR due to thermal expansion of the oceans is straightforward. And in fact we see good agreement among physical models about this impact.[1]

At the other end of the spectrum are potential impacts that are highly contingent on future economic and social structures. What will our cities look like? How will we transport people and goods? What bio-engineered foods will we eat? What devilish weapons will be invented? Will computers be in charge of everything from surveillance to financial markets?

THE CASE OF ENVIRONMENTAL MIGRATION

The challenge of projecting impacts in a vastly different world can be illustrated with "environmental migration," which features prominently in many discussions of climate change. One report states that "unless strong preventative action is taken, between now and 2050, climate change will push the number of displaced people globally to at least 1 billion."[2] Another report declaims: "More poverty, more forced migrations, higher unemployment. Those conditions are ripe for extremists and terrorists."[3]

In reality, we know virtually nothing about the impact of global warming on future human migrations. Consider some of the issues we would need to understand to project migration over the next century. We would need to know the national boundaries, populations, and per capita incomes of major countries. What would be the boundary of the European Union and the Eurozone? Would there even be a Eurozone? (I doubt that there will be a recognizable Eurozone in a century, but I leave it to future readers to provide the updated answer.) What will be the economic and political structure of Africa? Would transportation costs be much lower, perhaps with personal aircraft that could zip across borders in a flash? What would be the impact on migration of the hypothetical virtual social networking device "Mindbook," which produces a synthetic reality so vivid that people do not care where they live?

In addition, we would need to guess at future immigration policies along with the technologies for enforcing these policies. Would borders be more or less porous than today? What kind of personal identification systems would be available? Would electronic detection and monitoring be so advanced that advanced hybrid road-air-water drones would be patrolling the borders and ready to zap transgressors with some as-yet-undiscovered device so frightening that even a coyote would hesi-tate to cross?

Perhaps we could take a stab at answering these questions. But even then our job would be only half done. Recall that people migrate primar-ily to improve their economic fortunes. We would then need to mea-sure the impact of global warming on the future incomes of countries and infer the impact of these income changes on migration trends. To be realistic, we could probably make an estimate of the impact of global warming on today's world, incomes, borders, and technologies. But these elements are likely to change dramatically over the coming century, so we need to be very cautious in any assessment of the impacts of global warming on migration more than a few years into the future.

Environmental migration exemplifies the difficulties of projecting climatic impacts. Human societies and economies are extensively man-aged systems. If climate change increases exposure to heat waves or vulnerability to the rising seas, we would expect that societies would take steps to reduce vulnerabilities through air conditioning and coastal policies. Moreover, if most countries continue to improve technologies and living standards, we would expect that most poor countries (who today can barely afford such investments) will increasingly be able to protect themselves against climatic extremes just as Miami and Rotter-dam do today. While no law of economics ensures that historical trends will continue, it seems likely that the poorer countries will follow the path of richer countries and will protect their peoples and societies from environmental stresses.

The lesson here is that we are likely to overestimate the economic impacts if we simply impose estimated climate changes on current soci-eties. In considering the impact of climate change in the late twenty-first century, two major trends can be seen—even through the fuzzy telescope. The first is that, under the scenarios that produce dangerous climatic change, most countries will be much richer than they are today. Clearly we should not assume that African countries will have incomes comparable to those of North America today and also assume that large numbers will still be nomads herding cattle across the desert.

Second, one of the regularities of economic development is that societies increasingly insulate their populations from all kinds of adverse shocks. We see this in the area of public and private health, agricultural shocks, environmental disasters and degradation, and violence. We would expect that adaptation to the dangers of future climate change would be added to this list of tasks of the modern state.

SEA-LEVEL RISE AND COASTAL SYSTEMS

One of the major concerns over coming decades and centuries is the impact of SLR on coastal systems and human settlements near the coast. I begin with the scientific background and projections and then discuss the potential impacts.

The long-term movement in sea level since the last ice age is remarkable. About 20,000 years ago, the earth reached a glacial maximum. At that point, global temperature was 4–5°C colder than today. The level of the ocean was about 120 meters (400 feet) lower. If you stood on today's east coast of Florida, the ocean would have been below the horizon 100 miles away.

Sea-level rise has two major components: thermal expansion and melting of terrestrial ice. Thermal expansion occurs because water density changes with different levels of temperature, salinity, and pressure. On average, as the oceans warm, they will expand, thereby raising sea level. This part of SLR is well understood and can be accurately modeled.

The oceans have been rising slowly since the last ice age. Current estimates are that the rate of SLR is approximately 3 millimeters (0.1 inch) per year. Under standard climate-change projections, thermal expansion will raise the oceans by about 0.2 meters (8 inches) by 2100. This is only slightly more rapid than the rate of SLR over the twentieth century.[4]

The other major component of SLR is melting ice from glaciers and ice caps, but the estimates here are highly uncertain. What most worries scientists is the vast quantity of water locked up in the three major ice sheets. The first is the Greenland Ice Sheet, which has about 7 meters (23 feet) of SLR equivalent of ice. This means that if the Greenland Ice Sheet were to melt completely, sea level would rise about 7 meters. A second concern is the West Antarctic Ice Sheet, which has an SLR equivalent of about 5 meters (16 feet). The balance of the Antarctic ice sheet has a much larger volume of ice, but the ice there is so cold and firmly grounded that there seems little risk of melting for several centuries.

Chapter 5 discussed the processes and possible tipping points associated with the melting of the Greenland Ice Sheet. Modeling ice caps is extremely difficult, according to specialists in this area. Recent estimates are that melting glaciers and ice caps will contribute 0.2 meters (8 inches) of SLR by 2100. Other projections using statistical techniques have produced larger estimates, but these have not been validated by ice sheet modeling.[5] This number indicates that land ice might contribute as much to SLR as thermal expansion. It must be emphasized, however, that this is an active area of scientific research, and we must be prepared for "inevitable surprises" in the future.[6]

As I have emphasized above, a major goal of climate research is to integrate economic and environment projections. This applies to SLR as well. The standard scenarios for SLR are decoupled from the economy, and vice versa.

How do integrated economy-SLR models behave? To illustrate this question, I have used the DICE model to make projections of climate-change impacts for different scenarios over the coming centuries. The model includes all sources of SLR, although the dynamics of the ice caps are very uncertain. The projections are consistent with standard ocean-climate models but additionally are linked to the economic and emissions models.[7]

For this exercise, we can look at two different emissions trajectories. One scenario uses baseline (unconstrained) emissions. I discussed the baseline concept in earlier chapters. The second model run assumes that global temperature increase is limited to a 2°C increase over the 1900 level. This target was endorsed in the Copenhagen Accord and is further analyzed in later chapters.

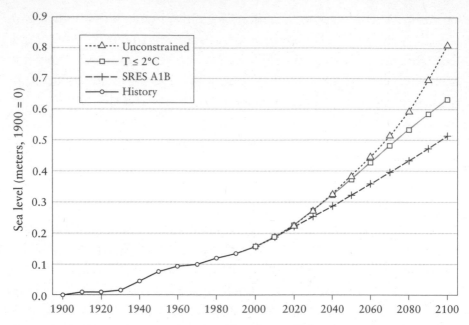

Figure 16. History and projected sea level for uncontrolled and temperature-limited scenarios, 1900–2100. The figure shows the history and a comparison of two DICE model SLR projections (unconstrained emissions and a limit of 2°C increase in global temperature) with that of the average of IPCC models for unconstrained emissions (SRES A1B) over the next century. Note that, even with an ambitious policy to limit warming, there will be substantial SLR.

Figures 16 and 17 show the DICE model SLR projections for the two policies along with the related IPCC run closest to this projection (IPCC SRES scenario A1B). Figure 16 shows the history of the global sea level over the last century plus three scenarios for the twenty-first century.[8] The DICE model for unconstrained emissions has higher estimates of SLR than comparable IPCC climate scenarios. This result occurs because the DICE model includes all ice sheets and uses parameters that show greater sensitivity to temperature increases than most models.

Note that there are only small differences among the alternative models and scenarios over the next few decades. The similarity among the paths during the early decades of this century illustrates the tremendous inertia of many earth systems, which is one of the recurring themes of climate change.

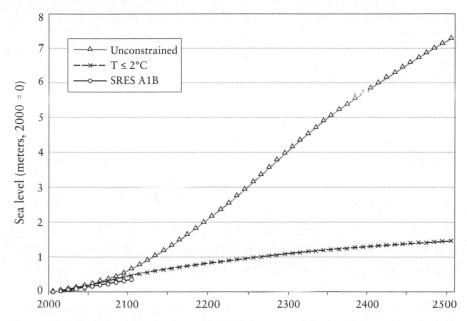

Figure 17. Projected sea level relative to 2000 for uncontrolled and temperature-limited scenarios. The figure shows illustrative sea-level projections over the coming half millennium from the DICE model. Note that even in the case of strong climate-change policies, substantial SLR is projected because of the inertia in ocean response.

Figure 17 shows illustrative projections for the next 500 years. These are even more uncertain than those in Figure 16 because of difficulties in modeling the response of the ice caps, but they are consistent with current climate estimates.[9] These sobering projections indicate that, even with extremely ambitious climate policies, there will be substantial SLR over the coming centuries. The model suggests that limiting climate change to 2°C will still lead to around 1.5 meters (5 feet) of eventual SLR over the next five centuries, with more in the pipeline after that.

The really worrisome projection, however, is the impact of an uncontrolled emissions scenario. This is projected to produce SLR of more than 7 meters (23 feet) over the next half millennium—with a further rise beyond the period covered by this projection. This upper-end result is produced by a combination of thermal expansion, substantial melting of the Greenland Ice Sheet, and discharge from the West Antarctic Ice Sheet. While these projections come from a highly stylized integrated assessment model, they are consistent with the projections of more detailed modeling studies.[10]

IMPACTS

What are the potential impacts of SLR over the coming century and beyond? We know that the oceans have risen and fallen over geological history. When humans first came to America, the oceans were at least 90 meters (300 feet) lower than today. (Ice age discovery of the New World is an example of how environmental changes can lead to innovative behavior.) In the last warm period, when global temperatures were 1–2°C warmer than today, the oceans were about 3 meters (10 feet) higher. In still earlier periods, sea level was perhaps 180 meters (600 feet) higher in the age of the dinosaurs, when glaciers were largely absent.

However, the pace of SLR over the coming century and beyond is unprecedented for the period of human civilizations. Reconstructions suggest that the level of the ocean has changed by less than 1 meter (3 feet) over the last 4,000 years. Ecologists are particularly concerned about the impact of the rising ocean as it interacts with coastal ecosystems. Here I concentrate on the social dimensions.

I discussed earlier the problem of the fuzzy telescope—that projecting impacts becomes increasingly difficult the further we go into the future. This can be seen dramatically for SLR. In many places, cities are built, grow, and decline over the course of a century. So while we can easily measure the impact of SLR on current settlements, the impact on those in a century or more looks fuzzy indeed.

We can, however, examine the extent of current vulnerability to SLR by looking at where people live and work today. About 4 percent of the world's population and output are in regions at elevations at or below 10 meters (33 feet). I call this the "red zone" at risk of SLR, although it probably exaggerates the extent of endangered people or output. Because people and economic activity tend to cluster near coastlines, there are more people and output than land in the red zone.

The vulnerability of regions is determined not just by their elevation, however. In areas subject to hurricanes or intense storms, flooding can pose major risks even for higher locations. But, for the most part, areas more than 10 meters above sea level are relatively invulnerable to SLR for the next century or two.

The global total might be of less concern if people, output, and eco-systems could migrate freely around the world. In that unrealistic case, people threatened by floods in Bangladesh would simply move to India or Thailand or some other high ground, and continue their lives in a new spot. Or take the case of Pudong, which is part of Shanghai, China. It lies in a river delta, and geologists might worry whether this is a good place for the tallest building in China. Yet the population of Pudong has grown from 300,000 in 1950 to over 5 million today. Will they simply let the building sink, or build a seawall, or move away when the oceans rise?

I emphasized above the difficulties of projecting migration patterns over long time horizons. Over short time horizons of less than a decade, there is relatively little international migration for most countries. We can take the extreme case—which is probably unrealistic over the time frame of SLR—where people cannot move outside their country, or where the cost of moving is large. For this question, we can examine the distribution of human settlements in the red zone by country. Table 4 shows countries at risk.[11] This measure considers the fraction of the 2005 population of each country living at or below 10 meters of elevation. The top part of Table 4 shows the ten countries that are most at risk from SLR. More than half of the population and output of these countries is in the 10-meter red zone. Most of these at-risk countries are relatively small, but two are populous: the Netherlands and Bangladesh.

The bottom part of Table 4 lists the eleven most populous countries and shows the fraction of their populations, output, and area at risk. Aside from Bangladesh, less than 10 percent of the populations and output of the large countries are at risk. However, between 5 and 10 percent of the populations of the three most populous countries live in the red zone.

Table 4 also illustrates the large differences in climate-change impacts among different regions. Some countries will be greatly affected by SLR (Bangladesh, the Netherlands, and the Bahamas), while others will be completely untouched (land-locked Austria, Kazakhstan, and Bo-

Table 4. Countries at risk from sea-level rise.

Country	Fraction at risk Population, 2005	Fraction at risk Output, 2005	Area	Total population, 2005 (000)	Population at risks, 2005 (000)
Most at-risk countries:					
Bahamas	100.0	100.0	100.0	323	323
Maldives	100.0	100.0	100.0	295	295
Bahrain	91.9	60.3	65.9	725	666
Kiribati	91.8	91.2	9.0	99	91
Netherlands	74.9	76.9	76.3	16,300	12,200
Tonga	69.0	58.1	17.5	99	69
Gambia	63.2	62.9	30.5	1,620	1,020
Bangladesh	60.1	58.0	50.6	153,000	92,100
Kuwait	48.8	9.5	7.8	2,540	1,240
Guinea Bissau	48.2	48.2	29.2	1,600	770
Most populous countries:					
China	9.0	14.4	1.8	1,300,000	117,000
India	7.3	7.2	2.8	1,100,000	80,100
United States	6.1	5.9	2.9	297,000	18,100
Indonesia	2.8	3.6	7.5	221,000	6,270
Brazil	2.9	1.7	1.4	187,000	5,410
Pakistan	6.8	3.5	2.4	156,000	10,500
Bangladesh	60.1	58.0	50.6	153,000	92,100
Russia	1.8	1.0	2.4	143,000	2,520
Nigeria	3.7	12.9	2.3	141,000	5,170
Japan	0.0	0.0	0.0	128,000	0
Mexico	3.2	2.9	3.3	103,000	3,260

Note: Table shows the 2005 population, area, and output that are located at or below 10 meters of elevation.

livia). This weak correlation of impacts and incomes is true for other impacts, such as those affecting agriculture, human health, national security, and storm intensification. While people tend to believe that poor countries are most likely to be affected, that is not accurate for SLR. The United States is highly vulnerable, while Canada is not. Bangladesh is vulnerable, while Chad is not. A careful look at the data shows that low-elevation regions tend to have higher per capita income than high-elevation regions.[12]

WORLD HERITAGE SITES

The people of Pudong may relocate, but buildings and ski areas cannot. This raises the issue of whether global warming threatens a significant number of the world's cultural and natural treasures. Many places are precious to people: Venice to artists, Yellowstone National Park to Americans, and New Mexico's Hermit's Peak to me. How vulnerable are such spots?

We can assess this question because the UNESCO World Heritage Convention has a systematic process for listing major treasures. These sites are according to UNESCO "among the priceless and irreplaceable assets, not only of each nation, but of humanity as a whole." The list currently includes 936 sites in 153 countries including religious, ecological, and architectural monuments.

The convention places sites on its danger list if they are "threatened by serious and specific dangers" as defined by the Convention Concerning the Protection of the World Cultural and Natural Heritage.[13] When this was written, thirty-five sites were on the endangered list. A review indicates that the major threats are armed conflict and war, earthquakes and other natural disasters, pollution, poaching, uncontrolled urbanization, and unchecked tourist development. Global warming was not mentioned as a problem for any of the endangered heritage sites, but this probably reflects inertia in setting priorities and determining threats.

The deliberations of the World Heritage Convention are catching up with today's concerns, and they have recently examined the impact of climate change on different groups of monuments. A report concluded that there are major dangers to four classes of sites: large glaciers, marine and terrestrial biodiversity, archaeological sites, and historical cities and settlements. With respect to SLR, major threatened sites listed by the report are the cities of London and Venice and several low-lying coastal ecosystems.[14]

From an economic point of view, the challenge here is to place values on these unique systems. I return to the thorny problem of valuation in Chapter 11, which discusses species preservation. The conclusion from the later discussion is that putting reliable values on the economic losses from unique natural and cultural heritage sites is extremely challenging. Nevertheless, we need to put them on the balance when weighing costs and benefits, which is on the agenda for economists in this field.

Sea-level rise is one of the most worrisome impacts of climate change because it has global effects and is difficult to stop once under way. The economic costs found in most studies are modest relative to overall output or to some of the other losses.[15] However, while the economic and land losses may be small on a global scale, the threatened areas rank among the most precious parts of our natural and human heritage. So losses from SLR cannot simply be written off the way a bank writes off a bad mortgage.

Although it is hard to stop SLR, societies can take steps to reduce the damages. A good example is choosing whether to "retreat or defend" against the rising seas. Defending often takes the form of building dikes and seawalls to protect existing structures and towns. The Netherlands has taken this strategy for centuries. For densely populated or highly valued sites, like the Netherlands or Manhattan Island, this is a sensible approach.

In other cases, a strategy of retreat is more sensible for the long run. The best economic strategy for dealing with sea-level rise has been addressed in a serious of pioneering studies by Wesleyan economist Gary Yohe. It is prudent and not defeatist, because it ultimately may protect social values by accommodating natural forces rather than going to war with them.[16] Natural systems have adapted over geological time to even larger changes in sea level than are projected over the coming decades and centuries. Waterfront properties do not disappear with SLR—instead, the waterfront relocates. Alas, this is little comfort for coastal property owners who find their houses washed away and their property values destroyed while their inland neighbors get a windfall. But over a period of decades and more, allowing natural processes to shift the beaches, ponds, and dunes will protect the overall value of land and ecosystems better than a Maginot Line mentality of protecting every parcel. This is yet another example of the value of migration—of people, of capital, and in this case of sand and ecosystems—in reducing the long-run costs of climate change.

OCEAN ACIDIFICATION

One of the themes of our survey of climate-change impacts is that the most troubling issues involve unmanaged or unmanageable systems. From an ecological perspective, humans are increasingly managing their environment. Over the last millennia, we have cleared fields and forests, moved from caves to houses, centralized exchange of goods in markets, and introduced technologies to control our personal and industrial climates.

But some areas are difficult or impossible to control. According to legend, King Canute found that when he commanded the tides to halt, they did not obey his order. In the modern era, we can build dikes and seawalls, but the ocean continues to rise around them. We will see similar issues in this chapter's review of acidification as well as in the next two chapters' analyses of hurricanes and species loss.

In each of these unintended consequences of human activity, we can echo King Canute's lament, "Let all men know how empty and worthless is the power of kings, for there is none worthy of the name but God, whose eternal laws heaven, earth, and sea obey." This will be the cry of future generations if we do not take forceful steps to reverse the rising tide of CO_2 and other greenhouse gases.

CARBONIZATION AND ACIDIFICATION

Another particularly unmanageable consequence of rising CO_2 concentrations is the carbonization and acidification of the oceans. Here, the issue is quite distinct from global warming because the problem does not result primarily from warming but from the carbon itself. Rising CO_2 concentrations in the atmosphere are quickly mixed into the upper layer of the oceans. While the transport of the carbon into the ocean reduces atmospheric concentrations, it also causes changes in ocean chemistry.

The chemistry is relatively straightforward. When CO_2 dissolves in the oceans, it makes the oceans more acidic and lowers the concentrations of calcium carbonate.[17] Many marine organisms form shells from calcium carbonate, including corals, mollusks, crustaceans, and some plankton. Because climate change and ocean acidification are both caused by increasing atmospheric CO_2, acidification is sometimes referred to as "the other CO_2 problem."

Ocean acidification has several important features. First, it depends primarily on the carbon cycle and does not have the uncertainties associated with climate modeling. Either because the chemistry is hard to challenge, or because the trend is clear, there is little controversy about ocean acidification. I have not yet read that ocean acidification is a hoax.

Second, the entire phenomenon was only recently recognized. The first major publications appeared over the past decade.[18] Indeed, the biological problems of acidification were not even recognized in the IPCC Third Assessment Report of 2001. This is a sobering example of what we call "inevitable surprises."

Third, the major predictions of the ocean acidification hypothesis have been confirmed by measurements in the world's oceans. There is a tight link between atmospheric and oceanic CO_2 concentrations and the falling pH (rising acidity) of the oceans.[19]

Marine scientists are just beginning to reckon with the consequences of acidification on ocean organisms and ecosystems. I discussed in Chapter 5 the warning from marine biologists about the catastrophic decline in corals that is already beginning and is likely to become irreversible if CO_2 concentrations continue their trend for two or three decades.

Field experiments indicate a complex set of responses to ocean acidification. In many of the organisms studied (particularly corals and mollusks), the rate of calcification and reproduction slows with higher CO_2 concentrations, and this is especially pronounced at high latitudes. These changes will lead to a major redistribution of species, with those depending upon calcification declining and the noncalcifiers increasing. There is evidence of a sharp increase in ocean CO_2 during an episode known as the Paleocene-Eocene thermal maximum (PETM), 55 million years ago. Based on data from earlier episodes of spiking CO_2 like the PETM, it appears that most species survived, but we should expect the current increase in CO_2 to result in the extinction of some species.

The impacts upon humans and the economy are most easily seen for fisheries. Those species most likely to be harmed are oysters, corals, plankton, and shellfish. The magnitude of losses, and the extent to which the losses in human consumption can be replaced by fish farms or other foods, is unclear at this point. Some studies have found that the mortality rate of fish increases dramatically as CO_2 concentrations rise above three times current levels.[20]

Ocean acidification is one of the most troubling features of CO_2 accumulation. It is an extreme example of an unmanageable system. Humans are likely to add at least 3 to 4 trillion tons of CO_2 to the upper layer of the oceans by 2100. There are no easy technological solutions here. We will see later that geoengineering solutions to the climate-change problem may slow warming, but they will do almost nothing to address ocean acidification.

Moreover, while it is reassuring that the earth has previously experienced spikes in CO_2 concentrations similar to that which humans are causing, the distribution of species in earlier periods was different, and we do not have reliable records of how different species fared in those periods. Because the oceans are so complex, even with the most talented and diligent scientists trying to understand its consequences, we are unlikely to have a full understanding of the impacts of ocean acidification until they are upon us.

10 INTENSIFICATION OF HURRICANES

Nothing illustrates the Climate Casino better than the impact of warming on tropical storms. When they begin to form, we don't know how intense they will become, where they will hit, and how much damage they will cause. A major question is how much global warming will intensify and redistribute hurricanes over the coming decades—and how much damage these changes will cause.

You are unlikely to see a video on the rising sea because the rise is imperceptible. In most places, tidal changes over a few hours are larger than sea-level rise over the next century. By contrast, hurricanes are swift, localized, dramatic events, tearing through cities and burying houses under a wall of water. There are TV shows about "hurricane trackers," and perhaps there may soon be a "Hurricane Channel," but you are unlikely ever to see the "Sea-Level Rise Channel," even with 10,000 stations.

I have witnessed hurricane after hurricane near my home. A few people remember the Great New England Hurricane of 1938. An entire community on Napatree Point in southwest Rhode Island was wiped off the face of the earth as the storm washed over the low-lying spit of land. Superstorm Sandy in 2012 struck the New York area and caused at least $75 billion of damages. Hurricanes are a particularly thorny problem because they are an unmanageable system that is clearly affected by global warming. Hurricanes differ from sea-level rise and ocean acidification in being extremely local and highly differentiated in impact.

THE EFFECT OF GLOBAL WARMING ON HURRICANES

A hurricane is the name given to the North Atlantic version of a spectacular natural phenomenon known as a tropical cyclone. If sustained winds from a North Atlantic tropical storm reach 74 miles per hour, the storm is classified as a hurricane.[1] Hurricanes are huge engines that use the heat from warm waters to power churning winds. They are fed by a reinforcing feedback loop in which stronger winds lead to lower pressures, which increases evaporation and condensation, which in turn causes stronger winds. The main factor generating hurricanes is warm surface water in the oceans. To get one started requires a sea surface temperature of at least $26\frac{1}{2}°C$ (80°F). The areal extent of warm water will increase as the earth warms, which will probably increase the areal extent of the spawning ground for hurricanes and will make them more intense.

We can use basic physics and historical data to estimate the impacts of global warming on hurricanes. The U.S. data are the most complete, and I have gathered information about the characteristics and economic damages for 234 hurricanes that made landfall in the United States between 1900 and 2012. The data cover thirty storms before 1933 and all storms since then. Figure 18 shows the trend in annual normalized hurricane damages (dollar damages divided by GDP) since 1900.[2] Hurricanes caused damages that averaged 0.05 percent of GDP per year over this period, with the maximum being 1.3 percent of GDP in 2005 (the spike there is produced primarily by Hurricane Katrina).

One interesting feature is that—unlike many other environmental impacts—the damages from hurricanes appear to have an upward trend relative to the total economy. Statistical analysis indicates that, after correcting for the number of storms and their intensity, damages have risen around 2 percent per year faster than GDP. The reason for this increased vulnerability has not been fully explained. It is clearly not primarily due to global warming and is probably the result of people's fondness for living near the coast. (I plead guilty to that syndrome.)

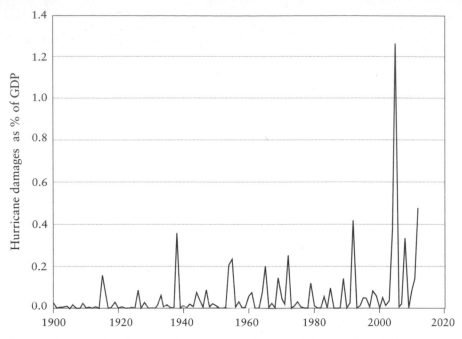

Figure 18. Normalized costs of hurricanes for the United States, 1900–2012. This figure shows the ratio of damages to GDP for all hurricanes for the given year. Damages are highly skewed, with high damages in a few years, but little or no damages in most years.

The effect of global warming on tropical cyclones has been studied carefully, and the basic physics is clear. Global warming may affect several dimensions of hurricanes, including frequency, size, intensity, duration, and geographic distribution. Of the five, the only clear link from basic physics is between global warming and intensity. As sea surface temperature rises, the "potential intensity" or upper limit of wind speed increases, holding other factors constant. Recent calculations suggest that a warming of 4°C would increase the average intensity by about one category (say, from a category 2 to a category 3 hurricane, or about 16 miles per hour).

A further question is whether other extreme storm events, such as tornadoes or thunderstorms, are likely to increase in frequency or intensity. The answers here are less clear than for hurricanes because the underlying causes (unlike the effects of warmer water on hurricanes) do not point to a straightforward answer. Some climate scientists believe that the intensity of thunderstorms will increase, but this is still an open question.

IMPACTS OF WARMING

There have been several assessments of the impact of global warming on hurricanes. As with rising sea levels, the physical effects can be estimated using models, but the socioeconomic impacts will depend upon how humans adapt to increased storm intensity and rising sea levels. I have estimated that the impact of warming over the twenty-first century will lead to slightly more than a doubling of hurricane damages in the United States if no measures are taken to reduce vulnerability. This would amount to around 0.08 percent of GDP, or about $12 billion per year at current levels of output. This is not a substantial fraction of total national output over the next century. However, the impacts are highly localized and devastating to individual communities, as was seen when Hurricane Sandy hit the New Jersey and New York region in 2012.

A careful study of the effects of global warming on hurricanes by climate scientists and economists estimated the range of hurricane impacts by country and region. Figure 19 shows the impacts by major region.[3] Central America (including the Caribbean) is projected to be the most vulnerable region, followed by North America (primarily the United States). Some regions are negligibly affected (western Europe and South America).

If we look at the country data (provided by the authors of the study), this study projects less hurricane damage from global warming than some other studies do. But the interesting finding is that some important countries may experience reduced damages from hurricanes in a warmer world. For example, Bangladesh is estimated to experience reduced hurricane damages. This paradoxical result occurs because warming causes hurricane redistribution as well as intensification.

Another interesting finding, which is parallel to the finding on sea-level rise in Chapter 9, is that hurricane damages are only weakly correlated with affluence. The United States is heavily affected, while the

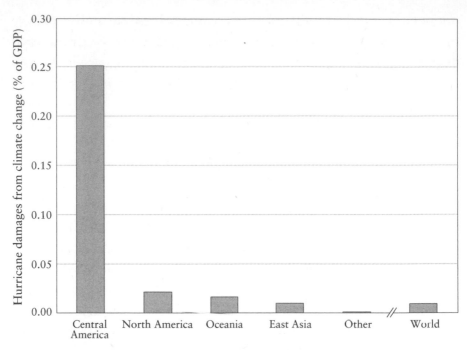

Figure 19. Impacts of climate-change hurricane intensification and redistribution on different regions. Which regions are likely to be most adversely affected by the hurricane intensification induced by global warming? A study finds that Central America is the most vulnerable by far of any region, followed by North America (primarily the U.S.).

impact of hurricane intensification on Africa is essentially zero. These results show again how the impacts of climate change are distributed widely and unpredictably.

ADAPTATION

Societies can take many steps to reduce vulnerability to more intense hurricanes. For example, better forecasting has dramatically reduced the fatalities from hurricanes over the past half century. While better forecasting protects people, who can evacuate, it cannot protect houses and other immobile structures. In the longer run, vulnerable immobile structures depreciate, and incentives should be in place so that people will rebuild their structures on higher and safer ground.

A small rate of capital migration can offset the impacts of greater hurricane intensity. About 3 percent of the U.S. capital stock is located below 10 meters of altitude and is in the hurricane zones of the Atlantic coast. Assuming that the major vulnerable items are structures, this amounts to about $600 billion of capital today. The average lifetime of structures is around 50 years. Assume for simplicity that all vulnerable capital assets (such as houses, roads, and hospitals) are moved to safer locations as they depreciate. The only costs would be relocation. If these relocation costs were one-fifth of the replacement capital costs, securing the nation's capital from hurricanes would cost about 0.01 percent of GDP annually over the next half century. This is much smaller than the costs if no such adaptations are made.[4]

This example illustrates how strategic planning for the impacts of climate change can significantly reduce the damages. But this point must be qualified by the reality that the distribution of winners and losers makes orderly planning difficult. Inlanders may feel little sympathy for rich people in fancy beach mansions whose vulnerable coastal properties are threatened; highlanders may not wish to contribute their tax dollars to build dikes and levees for those threatened by flooding; thriving towns will be disinclined to transfer precious resources to towns whose tax bases are declining. Moving all the facilities in a coastal town to a more secure location may reduce vulnerability, but that will provide little solace to those who are attached to their homes and communities.

The need for far-sighted strategies to deal with coastal settlements, for both hurricanes and sea-level rise, is one of the major challenges in dealing with climate change. Orderly planning can reduce the most dangerous impacts significantly, but the process of adaptation is likely to be politically contentious and messy.

11 WILDLIFE AND SPECIES LOSS

Finally, climate change has dangerous impacts on wildlife and, more generally, species and ecosystems around the world. Ecosystems have two interesting features. To begin with, they are largely unmanaged or unmanageable systems, and, second, they are economically far removed from the marketplace.

The nonmarket aspect raises new questions for impacts analysis: How can we measure the "value" of ecosystems or of endangered species? How can we put losses in this area in a metric that can be compared to those in market sectors such as agriculture and the costs of abatement? This chapter begins with a review of the potential impact of climate change on species extinctions and ecosystems and then turns to the thorny issues of valuing those impacts.

THE SIXTH MASS EXTINCTION?

According to biologists, there have been five mass extinctions on earth in the last half-billion years. Conservation biologists warn us that the combination of climate change and other human influences will cause a sixth mass extinction over the next century.[1]

The history of life has witnessed several distinct surges and extinctions of life on earth. Figure 20 shows an estimate of the extinction rate for marine organisms, for which records are more complete than is terrestrial history.[2] Major extinctions have occurred at periods shown by the spikes, and scientists attribute them to events such as asteroid collisions, volcanic eruptions, glaciations, and sea-level rise. The Permian-

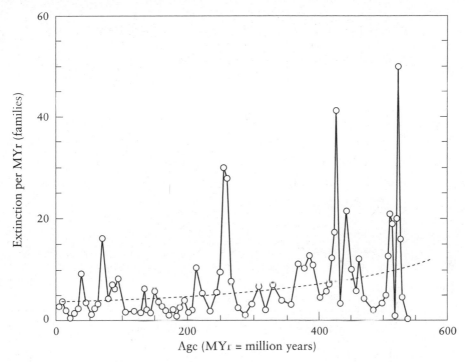

Figure 20. Estimate of extinction rate for marine life for the last 600 million years. The extinction rate is the number of families of known marine organisms that became extinct per unit of time. Spikes represent major extinction events. The dotted line is the time trend.

Triassic extinction about 250 million years ago wiped out about 90 percent of all species.

The extinction rate of the last 15,000 years has been relatively low in the chronology for marine life shown in Figure 20. Indeed, many of the dramatic extinctions in the most recent period were due to human interventions. For example, more than half of the large mammal species of the Americas disappeared in a short period around when humans first arrived about 13,000 years ago, and they were probably annihilated by our spear-carrying ancestors. There is evidence that humans have had a similarly disastrous effect on species on other continents and islands. In earlier periods, preservation of species was of no interest, and when a species disappeared, as in the case of the dodo bird, that event was unmourned and sometimes even unremarked.

CLIMATE CHANGE AND THE POTENTIAL FOR EXTINCTIONS

We know that past rapid climate changes have sometimes been accompanied by mass extinctions. Will that happen again in the coming decades and beyond? The estimates here are particularly difficult to pin down. To begin with, estimates of the current rate of extinction vary greatly. The observed number of extinctions is relatively small, while theoretical calculations give much larger numbers.[3]

Scientists who have studied potential extinctions project dire consequences in the case of rapid warming. A review suggests that the threat

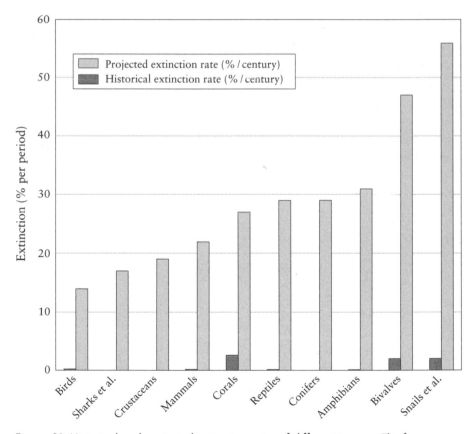

Figure 21. Historical and projected extinction rates of different groups. The figure shows a recent compilation of estimates of historical and projected extinction rates for major groups. Historical estimates are for species that became extinct in the wild. The projections are for threatened groups.

of extinction for many groups will rise from the current rate of extinction or 0 to 0.2 percent per century to 10–50 percent of species in the next century or so, as shown in Figure 21.[4] The most recent summary by the IPCC concluded that about 25 percent of species on a global scale will be at high risk of extinction with unchecked climate change. To this outlook we should add the dangers to marine organisms from ocean acidification, which are generally not included in these calculations.[5]

While these numbers are frightening, I must emphasize that the estimates are also subject to many qualifications, as we will see below.

THE CHALLENGE OF VALUING NONMARKET SERVICES

Oscar Wilde once remarked that a cynic is a man who knows the price of everything and the value of nothing. This saying has sometimes been incorrectly applied to economists because they study primarily market processes—stock prices and interest rates, food and housing— those areas that can be measured in hard cash.

Before discussing why this stereotype is dead wrong, we must acknowledge that food and housing are not inconsequential. Just ask the 10 million American families who lost their homes during the recent recession, or the 46 million people on food stamps in 2012. Perhaps money can't buy happiness, but it can buy food.

Economists have long recognized that people do not live by bread alone—there is a definite value of nonmarket activity. Many things that people care about are not produced and sold in markets. Some of these are close to the market, such as home-cooked meals or do-it-yourself carpentry. Others are intrinsically nonmarket, such as caring for our families or visiting the Grand Canyon.

To illustrate this point, do the following exercise: Take out a piece of paper. Write down ten activities that are most precious to you. Then ask how many of them you can buy at a local store or on the Internet. Typically, many things of value are not available in markets, and this is exactly the challenge we confront here because they do not carry monetary price tags.

Understanding the economics of nonmarket activities is important because many of the impacts of climate change fall outside the marketplace. Consider the four areas that have been highlighted as major concerns—the rising seas, the acidification of the oceans, hurricanes, and species loss. These are primarily natural systems rather than market processes. None of these is in any real sense produced by firms or measured in the marketplace the way food and housing are.

It is no accident that many of the most significant impacts of climate change occur outside the market. Markets are mechanisms for social control and management of natural resources and other systems. Architects design houses to protect their occupants from heat and cold, flood and earthquake, bugs and wild animals. Agricultural specialists design irrigation systems, pesticides, and seeds to protect crops against natural hazards that ruined farmers in earlier times. Dikes and seawalls are designed to prevent water damage from storms. All these systems sometimes fail spectacularly, as did the seawalls in Japan during the 2011 tsunami, because human designs are intelligent but not perfect.

Of all the areas we have examined, the impacts of climate change on species and ecosystems are the furthest from the market. They consequently raise the deepest issues of both analysis and valuation.

VALUING ECOSYSTEMS AND SPECIES

Most people agree that we should prevent the loss of species and valuable ecosystems. However, major difficulties arise when we try to measure the value of these systems. How much will people pay or sacrifice to prevent the loss of wildlife and species? How much for iconic creatures like polar bears? How about coral reefs? How do we think about protecting the estimated 700,000 as-yet-undiscovered species of spiders?

Some may object that even asking these questions displays a crude materialism—that trying to weigh life against money is an immoral act. But this is surely wrong. The real immoral act involves omitting the values of these species when we count up the losses from climate change. Some people believe that ecosystem impacts are indeed the most significant damages to put on the scales when we weigh costs and benefits.

Moreover, preventing loss of ecosystems and species, particularly those associated with rising CO_2 concentrations and global warming, is not a simple matter. It involves, as we will see in coming chapters, taking steps to change energy systems. And those involve very large costs. So there is an inevitable trade-off between the costs of our emissions reductions and the risks of ecosystem and species losses.

How do economists and ecologists go about measuring this trade-off? This turns out to be the most difficult area of all for estimating the economic damages from climate change. The natural and social sciences have great difficulty in making reliable estimates of the value of preserving ecosystems and species. There are two difficulties—getting reliable estimates of the losses, and then valuing the losses.

Start with problem one: the difficulty in making reliable projections of species losses over time. I illustrate the difficulties by examining an influential study on species losses and global warming by Thomas et al. This study concluded that between 18 and 35 percent of species are "committed to extinction" given current trends in climate change.[6]

How did they reach this conclusion? The study began by estimating the climatic range of existing species (including mammals, birds, and amphibians) in a particular region. Then the team estimated how the size of the climatic range would change under a particular scenario. For example, they examined the impact of a 3°C warming on the Proteaceae species in South Africa (Proteaceae are a family of beautiful flowering plants).

Next they applied a technique known as the species-area relationship. This is an empirical law holding that the number of species increases as the area of the habitat increases. For the regions considered by the team, the climatic range for most species was estimated to shrink with global warming, implying that the number of species will also shrink. For example, under the assumed 3°C increase for South Africa, the researchers concluded that 38 percent of the Proteaceae species will become extinct because the climatic range supporting the plants will decline. Perhaps the most carefully studied area of potential extinctions is the reef-building corals.[7]

While these studies are widely cited, the methods have severe limitations. To begin with, most studies consider "vulnerable" species as well as those that are on the brink of extinction. Additionally, some of the species can be preserved through human intervention, so the extinctions generally refer to species in the wild. Moreover, the techniques used in these studies are quite controversial and may not apply to situations where species have adapted to human habitations. In other cases, the damage is being done by habitat destruction, overuse, overfishing, over-hunting, and pollution that would occur even in the absence of climate change. Finally, the estimates of the climatic ranges are often statis-tically biased by assuming that the ranges shrink but cannot expand, which leads to a declining number of species by assumption. In reality, some climatic ranges will shift, and some areas might grow, so the number of species for growing ranges would be predicted to increase rather than decline.

Perhaps we can solve problem one. Perhaps we can devise reliable estimates of the risk of extinction for different species. We must now confront problem two: Ecologists and economists have not developed reliable techniques for valuing ecosystem and species losses. There is no price tag on the value of a species or a rare ecosystem.

Let's take some specific examples of species that are threatened by climate change: the Arctic fox, the leatherback turtle, and the koala bear. Consider specific endangered ecosystems such as Australia's Great Barrier Reef or South Africa's Cape Floral Kingdom. How can we place a value on these species and ecosystems so that we can weigh the costs and benefits of different climate-change policies?

The difficulty can be described by comparing this issue with the eco-nomic impacts of damage to wheat production, discussed earlier. When the production of wheat declines, economists typically value that loss at the market price of wheat. If climate change leads wheat production to decline by 100 million bushels and the price of wheat is unchanged at $5 per bushel, then the social cost is calculated as $500 million. (There are still lots of further refinements, such as whether this decline will raise the price of wheat, and whether the impact is particularly severe on low-income families, but we ignore those for now.)

How can we value these natural systems? Specialists have looked at the market or near-market values, and at the "externality" values. Begin with the market or near-market value of these losses, often called the "use value" in the technical literature. A market value is the price that a good commands in the store or on the Internet. A near-market value is the market price of something that is obtained outside the market, as in the price of the home repair job. It has been tempting for scientists concerned about ecosystem and species losses to point to the use, market, or near-market damages that might occur with species loss. One argument is that the potential losses are large because a substantial fraction of Western pharmaceuticals are derived from rain forest ingredients.[8] A caricature of such assertions would be the claim that, when a fern species disappears, we are foregoing the miracle cure to AIDS that lurks hidden in the Brazilian forest.

The reality is more complicated. A recent review of new drug entities found that natural products are indeed important for developing new drugs. For example, almost half of the new cancer drugs developed over the last six decades were either natural products or directly derived from natural products. The natural source varies greatly, however, from ones discovered in laboratories to ancient Chinese herbal remedies. Only one new drug in the last three decades came from the rain forest (Taxol), and it was from a temperate rather than a tropical rain forest. Many drugs have natural products as ancestors if we follow their family tree back far enough, but they have since been optimized in the laboratory, and they have often been synthesized once their natural product structures were analyzed.[9]

On the whole, having worked with a team of students for a summer studying this question, I found it impossible to evaluate the hypothesis that significant medicinal riches will be lost in the disappearing rain forests of the world. There is simply no compelling evidence on either side. However, we can make one point with confidence: Most of the economic value of threatened species and ecosystems will not be found in the marketplace. Perhaps preserving species is important, but the value of the preservation will not be found on the stock market. Ecosystems and species simply do not have much cash-and-carry value in today's market economies.

Where then does their value come from? It comes from the externality or "nonuse" values. While we usually think of externalities as negative (such as pollution), this is an example of a positive externality value. The classic example of a positive externality is lighthouses. They save lives and cargoes by warning ships of lurking dangers. But lighthouse keepers cannot reach out to collect fees from ships. Even if they could, it would serve no social purpose for them to exact an economic penalty on ships that use their services. The light can be provided most efficiently free of charge, for it costs no more to warn 100 ships than to warn a single ship of the nearby rocks.[10]

Species and ecosystems are biological analogies to lighthouses. The value of the Arctic fox or the Great Barrier Reef cannot be captured by charging people to visit and observe them. The gain from preserving these endangered systems is primarily the nonuse pleasure of having such a beautiful animal or place on earth. Polar bears might have some monetary touristic value to Arctic communities, but that is likely to be miniscule relative to their externality values.

The difficulty comes in attempting to estimate the externality value of endangered species and ecosystems. Perhaps in some fantastic world, there would be a market for the ability to see an Arctic fox or visit the Great Barrier Reef. I have done neither, but I might pay $100 to be assured that they would be available in the future. Because nothing remotely like such a market exists, however, we have no reliable scale to measure the gain from protecting these things for the future.

In the absence of markets, environmental economists have devised methods to simulate missing markets. The most important technique is known as contingent valuation methodology (CVM), which estimates the value of nonmarket activities and resources. CVM uses surveys of a representative sample of the relevant population to ask what people would be willing to pay for a given good or service. These are essentially highly structured surveys in which people are asked, in effect, "What would you pay to protect or preserve the Arctic fox?" or "What is it worth to you to be able to visit the Great Barrier Reef in the future?"

We have seen that climate change may affect the health of ecosystems. Here is a specific example of how a CVM might be used to determine values.[11] The U.S. government is required to determine the impact on fish populations when deciding whether to build or replace dams. In considering dam projects in the state of Washington, one question was the value of salmon, steelhead, and other migratory fish populations. We could estimate the market value of the fish catch in the supermarkets, but that would leave out the nonuse values.

A study by Layton, Brown, and Plummer can illustrate how the CVM can be used to estimate the value to local households of changes in fish populations under different scenarios. Specifically, the authors conducted a contingent value survey to estimate the value of returning the fish populations to current levels in 20 years rather than continuing to allow the fish populations to decline. The authors estimated that on average, Washington households were willing to pay $736 per year for this increase in migratory fish populations.[12] If 5 million people are affected, this comes to a total of $3.7 billion a year.

While CVM techniques have been applied in many areas, to date they have not been used on the scale and scope necessary for estimating the impacts of global warming. There are formidable, even insuperable, obstacles to undertaking a complete appraisal of the impact of climate change on the value of lost species and damaged ecosystems. One difficulty is that scientists have great difficulty in specifying the changes that need valuation. We saw above how disparate are the estimates of the number of species that would be lost, and the timing of losses would add another complication. A second difficulty is the sheer scale of the task. It involves undertaking evaluations not just for migratory fish in the state of Washington but for species and ecosystems around the world, in remote corners where there are very scant measurements to begin with.

Additionally, the use of CVM has been highly controversial in economics and is not universally accepted. Some argue that "some number is better than no number." Others argue that in the absence of reliable methods, "no number is better than a flaky number." Many years of debate and further research have not produced a consensus on this approach.[13]

Some experts argue that the responses are unreliable given the inherent difficulty in thinking about the relevant questions. People are asked about a counterfactual situation that they may not understand.

The answers are hypothetical and do not correspond to actual behavior. Additionally, people may exaggerate the values of saving threatened species or ecosystems if they feel a "warm glow effect" about the subject— for example, they may think of beautiful pictures of jumping salmon that have no relationship with the actual fish involved. There are many subjective biases that must be overcome.

Skeptics further point out that the numbers from CVM studies are sometimes implausibly large. We can look at the results for the migratory fish survey described above as an example. Median household income in Washington at the time of the survey was $46,400, so the value of the fish population was estimated to be 1.6 percent of income, which seems a large sum. We might wonder what people would say about other environmental issues. Suppose we did surveys on the value of migratory birds in Washington, of other threatened species, of water quality or air pollution in Washington, and of removing the dangers from nuclear waste sites across the state. These might well elicit similar-sized answers. We might further inquire into the value of remote sites like Yellowstone National Park and the Himalayan glaciers, and about Arctic foxes and polar bears. A good bet is that some creativity would produce a total value from all these potential losses that was more than household income.

If we go back and ask people what they would pay for all the environmental issues combined, it seems unlikely they would pay anything nearly as large as the sum of the individual answers. Or if they were asked to vote in a tax referendum, they might well vote to pay nothing at all.

My personal appraisal here is that CVM and similar survey-type techniques are illustrative but too unreliable at present to be used for assessing the costs of ecosystem effects triggered by the rising CO_2 concentrations and climate change. The two shortcomings discussed above—incomplete scientific assessment of the risks and controversial economic tools for valuation—indicate that we are a long way from having reliable estimates of the economic impact for losses to wildlife, species, and ecosystems to use in our estimates of the impacts of global warming.

This does not mean we should simply throw up our hands and walk away from the problem. At the least, we need a better way to sort out ecosystems and species in urgent need of preservation from those of lower priority. Some biologists suggest that simply estimating the number of species at risk is an inappropriate measure of biological importance.

Other metrics would emphasize such characteristics as functional or behavioral diversity and the ability to rebound after an environmental shock. These aspects were analyzed by biologists Sean Nee and Robert May. They studied how much of the genetic diversity or information coded in DNA—the tree of life, in Charles Darwin's phrase—was lost in past extinctions. The idea is that all species are not equally important. For example, the extinction of the dodo bird, with no genetically close relatives, would lead to a greater loss in diversity than the loss of one of the 3,000 mosquito species. Their surprising finding was that approximately 80 percent of the underlying tree of life survived even when 95 percent of species were lost.[14]

Other scholars such as Harvard economist Martin Weitzman have developed measures of the "importance" of different species.[15] This is an important task. Modern biology will need to develop better metrics of importance for species and ecosystems to guide our conservation decisions in the context of global climate change.

And we should encourage ecologists and economists to work together to develop more comprehensive estimates of the value of lost species and ecosystems even though this is a daunting task.

The short summary on the valuation of impacts on species and ecosystems is that estimating these impacts is one of the most difficult tasks of all. We have insufficient understanding of the risks, and indeed we do not even know how many species exist in the world today. We cannot today value ecosystems in a reliable way, nor can we rank them in terms of their importance.

Moreover, many people feel that strong ethical issues are involved in extinguishing life. Many feel that humans have a fundamental responsibility as stewards of planet earth. To allow the sixth mass extinction on our watch would be immoral. We have been given fair warning about the risks, and we cannot plead ignorance and inadvertence. The evolution of polar bears, monarch butterflies, cutthroat trout, South African protea—and, yes, even those ingenious but irritating mosquitoes—is the greatest wonder of the natural world. To undo a substantial part of that heritage in a century is a terrible step. As the philosopher Arthur Schopenhauer wrote, "The assumption that animals are without rights and the illusion that our treatment of them has no moral significance is a positively outrageous example of Western crudity and barbarity."[16]

This ends the discussion of particularly intractable impacts of climate change. They are not necessarily catastrophic for humans, although they are likely to have grave consequences for other species and precious natural systems. The main obstacle is that humans are unable to effectively control the impacts in these areas. Perhaps, someday, societies will be able to do what King Canute could not and hold back the seas. Perhaps future biologists can regenerate the dodo bird from an earlier era and revive the Arctic fox should it go extinct. But until that day, the large-scale impacts of climate change and elevated CO_2 levels on natural systems are likely to be pervasive, changing the natural world in ways that will be unwelcome and even perilous.

12 ADDING UP THE DAMAGES FROM CLIMATE CHANGE

The last few chapters have taken an extensive look at the major impacts of climate change. I described this as scientific house-to-house combat because each sector has its own special dynamics and relation to climate change. Soil moisture is critical to agriculture, sea surface temperature to hurricanes, atmospheric concentrations of CO_2 for ocean acidification, and so on.

But having gone house to house, we can now stand back and look at the overall picture. What are the overall impacts as best we can judge? Five overarching themes emerged from our review of impacts, and it is worth emphasizing them.

- We found that climate damages are closely linked to economics. They are unintended by-products or externalities resulting from rapid economic growth. Zero economic growth would greatly reduce the threats from warming.
- Additionally, we saw the important distinction between managed systems (such as the industrial economy) and unmanageable systems (such as ocean acidification). We emphasized that the major focus of our concerns should be on those impacts that are unmanaged or unmanageable.
- We have seen that market economies of high-income countries are increasingly insulated from the vicissitudes of climate and other disturbances of nature. This is partly because the nature-based sectors such as agriculture are shrinking relative to services, and

partly because nature-based sectors are becoming less dependent on unmitigated natural influences.

- This point then raises a fourth and deeper issue regarding impacts. If our societies do indeed evolve and grow rapidly over the coming decades, as is projected by all economic and climate models, how can we forecast the impacts on those different structures a century or more from now? Assessment is difficult because technological change is rapid in areas such as agriculture, human health, and migration. Assessing the shape of our economies and making reliable impacts analysis in the distant future is like viewing a landscape through a fuzzy telescope.

- As a final point, we found that the most troubling impacts are in areas that are far removed from the market and thus from human management. This point applies particularly to areas such as human and natural treasures, ecosystems, ocean acidification, and species. Valuing the impacts in these areas is doubly challenging because of the difficulty of estimating impacts and the lack of reliable techniques for measuring impacts. Economics can contribute least in areas where we need it most.

VULNERABILITY BY ECONOMIC SECTOR

With these observations about individual sectors behind us, let's look at the overall picture. We do this first for the market economy of the United States for the period 1948–2011. The industrial composition of the United States is representative of high-income countries today, and it is likely that middle-income countries will have a similar structure by the middle of this century.

For this purpose, I have classified U.S. industries into three groups: heavily impacted sectors, moderately impacted sectors, and lightly or negligibly impacted sectors (Table 5).[1] Detailed studies on impacts indicate that the heavily affected or vulnerable sectors are likely to be agriculture and forestry. In these sectors, productivity might decline substantially under extreme scenarios (recall the discussion about agriculture in Chapter 7 as well as the yield diagram in Figure 14).

Table 5. Vulnerability of the U.S. economy to climate change by sector, 1948–2011.

Sector by impact	Share of total national income in sector		
	1948	1973	2011
Heavily impacted sectors	9.1	3.9	1.2
Farming	8.2	3.4	1.0
Forestry, fishing	0.8	0.5	0.2
Moderately impacted sectors	11.6	11.4	9.0
Real estate (coastal)	0.3	0.4	0.5
Transportation	5.8	3.9	3.0
Construction	4.1	4.9	3.5
Utilities	1.4	2.1	2.0
Lightly or negligibly impacted sectors	79.3	84.7	89.8
Real estate (noncoastal)	7.2	9.3	10.8
Mining	2.9	1.4	1.9
Manufacturing			
Durable goods	13.5	13.5	6.0
Nondurable goods	12.7	8.5	5.4
Wholesale trade	6.4	6.6	5.6
Retail trade	9.1	7.8	6.0
Warehousing and storage	0.2	0.2	0.3
Information	2.8	3.6	4.3
Finance and insurance	2.5	4.1	7.7
Rental and leasing services	0.5	0.9	1.3
Services and residual	10.5	14.0	27.2
Government	11.1	14.6	13.2
Total	**100.0**	**100.0**	**100.0**

A second group of industries includes those that are affected by weather and climate but can adapt at modest costs. One example is the transportation industry. Extreme weather such as snow or floods can cause delays and impose costs, but the impacts of climate change on road and air travel is likely to be relatively small, with impacts of at most a few percentage points of output over the next century.

Industries in the third group are likely to experience little or no direct effects from climate change. They include primarily services such as health care, finance, education, and the arts. For example, take neurosurgery, which is a major specialty of health care. Office visits and operations take place in highly controlled environments, and climatic variations are unlikely to have a measurable effect on this activity. Services have grown from 25 percent of the economy in 1929 to 52 percent today, which indicates the trend of increasing insulation of the market economy from weather and climate.

The numbers shown in Table 5 provide a striking picture of the changing vulnerability of the U.S. economy over the last six decades. The first point is that the share of the heavily impacted sectors is currently only 1 percent of the U.S. economy. The moderately impacted sectors—coastal real estate, transportation, construction, and utilities—constitute less than one-tenth of the economy. As of 2011, the sectors least susceptible to the impacts of climate change constituted 90 percent of the total market economy.

The second important historical feature is the sharp decline in the sectors most vulnerable to climate change. The share of the heavily impacted sectors has declined from 9 percent of the economy in 1948 to 1 percent today. This trend is largely due to the declining share of agriculture in the U.S. economy. As of 2012, only 1 percent of the workforce was in farming.

The trends shown in Table 5 are found in most other regions around the world. As economies mature, people move from rural farming to urban industry and services. Farming is about 1 percent of output and 3 percent of employment for all high-income countries. For low-income and middle-income countries, the share of agriculture in their economies declined from 25 percent in 1970 to 10 percent in 2010. Here is a dramatic historical fact: Of the 166 countries for which the World Bank provides data on the share of agriculture in GDP, only four show a rising trend over the last four decades—the Democratic Republic of Congo, Sierra Leone, Central African Republic, and Zambia. All other countries show a stable or more frequently a declining trend.[2]

These trends are assumed to continue in the long-term economic projections of climate-economy models. If countries do in fact show the rapid growth in output and emissions assumed in the standard projections, then market economies will become increasingly less vulnerable to climate change as activity shifts from farming and land-based activities to industry and services. This pattern is not inevitable. But it is pervasive across time and space, and we should consider it to be one of the central findings of the economics of climate change.

ESTIMATES OF AGGREGATE DAMAGES

Economists have labored for many years to estimate the aggregate damages from climate change. They gather all the available findings from studies for different sectors and different countries. There are studies for market or near market areas like agriculture, forestry, fisheries, energy, sea-level rise, and health. Inevitably, analyses primarily examine regions with plentiful data, such as the United States and western Europe. Estimates for developing countries and nonmarket sectors cover only a few sectors in a few countries.

Figure 22 shows the results of a comprehensive survey of the aggregate damages from climate change for different levels of warming. The dots indicate the results of different studies as compiled by a leading scholar in this area, Richard Tol.[3]

Several interesting findings emerge from these results. The first surprise is that, for the range of changes that have been calculated, the estimated impacts of climate change are relatively small. The largest damage estimate is around 5 percent of output. The most carefully studied scenario shows 2½°C of warming (which we estimate to occur around 2070). For this warming, the central damage estimate is around 1.5 percent of global output.

Additionally, Figure 22 shows estimates from the DICE model as a solid line. These aggregate estimates are drawn from a number of different areas (agriculture, sea-level rise, hurricanes, and the like) and take the global damages as a percentage of global output for different temperature increases. They are subject to large uncertainties, as I have emphasized in

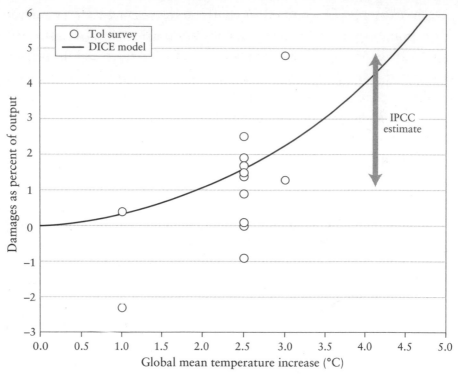

Figure 22. Estimates of the impact of global warming on the global economy. The figure shows a compilation of estimates of the aggregate damages from global warming for each temperature increase. Dots are individual studies. The solid line is the global damage function used in the DICE model. The arrow is the estimate from the most recent IPCC survey of impacts. The estimates generally include only partial estimates of damages to nonmarket sectors.

earlier chapters, because of the difficulty of estimating impacts in areas such as the value of lost species and damage to ecosystems.

The final estimate is shown by the vertical arrow at 4°C. This estimate is a range that was provided by the IPCC in its Third Assessment Report. It is drawn largely from the same studies that Tol surveyed and is therefore an expert appraisal rather than an independent estimate.[4]

Finally, note that the impacts are estimated to be nonlinear and convex (with increasing slope). Some studies find that the first degree or so of warming may have economic benefits (see the example of agriculture in Chapter 7). But after some point, the damages begin to rise, and they rise ever more sharply. In other words, each additional degree of warming is estimated to be increasingly costly. Tol's estimates suggest that the impact of the first 1°C of warming might be beneficial rather than harmful, primarily because of the fertilization effect of CO_2 for agriculture. Above that, however, the impact turns negative. Moreover, the incremental cost of warming at 3°C is approximately twice as large as that at 2°C. These studies have not incorporated potential tipping points in a reliable manner, which might make the damage curve turn up even more steeply.[5]

A RISK PREMIUM FOR THE HAZARDS IN THE CLIMATE CASINO

The leitmotif that runs through this book is the unknown dangers that lie in wait for us as CO_2 and other gases accumulate and the climate changes. Some of these hazards are well identified, such as the uncertainty about the sensitivity of climate to greenhouse-gas accumulations. But others appear unexpectedly as scientists study the subject more deeply. There are continuing open questions about the future of the huge ice sheets of Greenland and West Antarctica; the impact of aerosols on global and regional climates; the risks in thawing of vast deposits of frozen methane and permafrost; changes in the circulation patterns of the North Atlantic; the potential for runaway warming; and the impacts of ocean carbonization and acidification.

Our economic models have great difficulties incorporating these major geophysical changes and their impacts in a reliable manner. It might be useful to consider how we might insure our planet against the risks we are encountering in the Climate Casino.

To illustrate the risks inside the Climate Casino, we might think of the large-scale risks as a kind of planetary roulette. Every year that we inject more CO_2 into the atmosphere, we spin the planetary roulette wheel. When the wheel stops, we find out whether we have a favorable outcome or a particularly damaging one. On the first spin, a ball in a black pocket produces a slow growth in emissions, while a ball in a red one produces a rapid growth in emissions. On the next spin, we find out what will happen when CO_2 concentrations double. Perhaps doubling will increase equilibrium global temperatures by 3°C. But there is a wide range of estimates on this number. A further spin might find that farmers can adapt well and global food production is unaffected, while a ball in a red pocket might lead to particularly adverse climate impacts in the current grain belts of the world and therefore much greater damages than we had anticipated.

But in the Climate Casino, the ball also might land on zero or double zero. If it lands on zero, we find significant loss of species, ecosystems, and cultural landmarks like Venice. If it lands on double zero, we see those impacts and even more serious ones. We might begin to see a rapid collapse of the West Antarctic Ice Sheet, or melting of vast portions of permafrost, or changes in the ocean currents that currently warm the North Atlantic community, or mass extinction in the oceans because of the cascading impacts of ocean acidification.

We might also worry that the climatic roulette wheel has a weird construction. We might not even know what the numbers are, and perhaps there are many more red pockets than we thought because we underestimated the number of tipping points. Also, the numbers might change depending upon the outcome of the earlier wheel spins. We also find that when there are multiple unfavorable spins, the outcomes are even more costly because of nonlinearities in the physical system. Three reds in a row plus a double zero might lead to even more unfavorable outcomes as rapid growth in emissions adds up to a larger-than-expected climate impact plus a shift in monsoonal patterns that has a yet further impact on the Indian subcontinent. In the Climate Casino, the total climate impacts are more than the sum of the individual parts.

A sensible strategy would suggest an insurance premium to avoid the roulette wheel in the Climate Casino. We should add a premium in our damage estimates to reflect the casino risks on top of the identified damages shown in Figure 22. We need to incorporate a risk premium not only to cover the known uncertainties such as those involving climate sensitivity and health risks but also the zero and double zero uncertainties such as tipping points, including ones that are not yet discovered.

How large a risk premium should we add? This is the subject of intensive research and discussion among specialists today, and experts have different answers from very small to perhaps doubling or tripling the damage estimates. All that can be said with confidence is that we should not ignore the risks in the Climate Casino.

CAUTIONARY RESERVATIONS ABOUT THE ESTIMATES

The estimates of the impacts of climate change presented here represent the state of the art, and they are a necessary ingredient for calculating economically efficient climate-change policies. However, they should be used with great caution.

Some of my reservations are related to the discussion of individual sectors in earlier chapters. To begin with, these estimates include only the quantifiable impacts and largely concentrate on market or near-market sectors such as agriculture, real estate, land, forestry, and human health. Since we have found that much of the economy is relatively invulnerable to climate change, it is not surprising that the market damages are relatively modest, particularly in high-income countries.

It is also important to understand what these studies omit. They exclude several small negative and positive items: the impact on energy expenditures (less space heating, more space cooling), lower expenditures on winter coats, the costs of cooling plants for electricity generation, increased accessibility of Arctic harbors, greater cost of snowmaking for skiing, decreased amenities from winter recreation and greater amenities from warm-weather recreation, loss of income from fisheries, and so on. It is possible that many small impacts could add up to a large total—in effect, economic death by 1,000 climatic cuts. While this seems to me unlikely, it must be emphasized that, with all the sectors in all the regions for all the possible scenarios, the aggregate impact of these numerous minor injuries is hard to assess reliably.

A more important reservation concerns impacts that are either too uncertain or too difficult to estimate reliably. For instance, I discussed the difficulties of calculating the economic impacts of species losses and ecosystem damages. Estimating impacts here is doubly difficult because the physical impacts are generally too complex to determine and because economists have not yet produced reliable estimates of the costs of biodiversity losses.

The major qualification centers on the difficulty of assessing the impacts of tipping points—the potentially discontinuous, abrupt, and catastrophic climate changes and consequences. The economic impacts of the potential singularities are difficult to estimate for the same reasons as those of species and ecosystem losses. They are hard to forecast; the physical impacts are unknown; and the consequences generally lie far outside the marketplace. The challenges are compounded here because the effects may threaten the biological and physical foundations of human and natural societies. In this respect, they are similar to existential debates about national security, where it is difficult to measure the costs and benefits of different strategies. At this stage, the physical sciences still have far to go in understanding the threats from these large-scale tipping points. Once those are better known, we can attempt to understand the dangers they pose to social and natural systems as well as the steps required to prevent these geophysical bank runs.

What should we conclude at the end of this review of the impacts of future climate change? The first point to emphasize is the difficulty of estimating impacts. They combine the uncertainties of emissions projections and climate models. Even if we overlook the uncertainties about future climate change, the reactions of human and other living systems to these changes are very poorly understood. In part, reactions of social systems are hard to forecast because they are so complex. In addition, humans increasingly manage their own environment, so that a small investment in adaptation may offset the impact of climate change on human societies. Moreover, climate changes are almost certain to occur in the context of technologies and economic structures that will differ vastly from those of today.

However, we must look through the fuzzy telescope as best we can. A second conclusion involves the estimated economic impacts of climate change from sectors that we can reliably measure, particularly for high-income countries of today or the future. The estimates here are that the economic impacts from climate change will be small relative to the likely overall changes in economic activity over the next half century to century. Our estimated impacts are in the range of 1–5 percent of output for a 3°C warming. This compares to projected improvements in per capita GDP in the range of 500 to 1,000 percent over the same period for poor and middle-income countries. The loss in income would represent approximately one year's growth for most countries spread over several decades.

This projection will surprise many people. However, it is based on the finding that managed systems are surprisingly resilient to climate changes if they have the time and resources to adapt. This finding applies especially to high-income market economies with small agricultural sectors. While some might worry that this dooms poor countries to be laid low by climatic shocks, this concern overlooks the economic growth that underlies the projections of major climate change. China and India, with more than 2.5 billion people, have seen their per capita incomes rise by a factor of almost ten over the past half century.[6] Another half century of similar growth will raise the per capita incomes in India and China to around $50,000, with most people working in services and few left in rural farming. The vulnerability of today's poor countries to climate-change impacts is likely to decline significantly by the end of the twenty-first century.

A third major conclusion is that the most damaging impacts of climate change—in unmanaged and unmanageable human and natural systems—lie well outside the conventional marketplace. I identified four specific areas of special concern: sea-level rise, hurricane intensification, ocean acidification, and loss of biodiversity. For each of these, the scale of the changes is at present beyond the capability of human efforts to stop. To this list we must add concerns about earth system singularities and tipping points, such as those involved in unstable ice sheets and reversing ocean currents. These impacts are not only hard to measure and quantify in economic terms; they are also hard to manage from an economic and engineering perspective. But to say that they are hard to quantify and control does not mean they should be ignored. Quite the contrary, these unmanaged or unmanageable systems are the ones that should be studied most carefully because they are likely to be the most dangerous over the longer run.

To put this in perspective, the total volume of ice in the endangered ice caps is equivalent to approximately 1,600,000,000,000,000,000 gallons of water. This is far beyond what humans can easily pack up to store in some convenient location. The implications of sea-level rise and more intense hurricanes are easily comprehended, and in reality human societies can adapt to them without catastrophic losses. But the implications of ocean acidification and the potential loss of large numbers of species are difficult to comprehend and value reliably. We cannot rule out the possibility that future technologies—the analogs of Bill Gates's patent on hurricane modification—will change the outlook for these worrisome areas. But the hurdles here are much higher than for managed systems such as health and agriculture—and the prudent course is to assume these will not be manageable over the next century or so.

Finally, given what is known about impacts, is there a natural limit for which we can say, "Go up to this point but no further"? It would simplify policy if we could find some focal point, some precise numerical target for climate policy. Scientists and policymakers at Copenhagen in 2009 determined that a temperature increase of 2°C compared to preindustrial levels was the maximum that was within the safety margin for earth systems. What does our study of impacts suggest about the Copenhagen target?

A balanced approach suggests that the 2°C target is both too low and too high. It is too low given the identified damages analyzed above and the high costs of attaining such an objective discussed in Part III. But it is too high a target if we believe, along with many earth scientists, that the earth has already crossed the thresholds of some of the dangerous tipping points.

How can we resolve this dilemma of whether policies are aiming too high or too low? The answer lies in the realm of costs. Faced with the dilemma of deciding between too high and too low, we need to consider the costs of slowing climate change and of attaining different targets, to which I turn next. When that is completed, we can compare costs and benefits and propose a solution going forward—one that balances the twin objectives of preserving our environment for the future while economizing on losses in living standards along the way.

PART III

SLOWING CLIMATE CHANGE: STRATEGIES AND COSTS

> Gambling: The sure way of getting nothing for something.
> —*Wilson Mizner*

13 DEALING WITH CLIMATE CHANGE: ADAPTATION AND GEOENGINEERING

Earlier chapters explained how uncontrolled growth in carbon dioxide emissions and other gases is leading to vast changes in our climate systems along with human and natural systems. Most changes are likely to happen gradually, like a long freight train gathering speed and momentum. We cannot predict the impacts with precision, but they are unwelcome at best and dangerous at worst. And like the accelerating freight train, they will be hard to stop once they get under way.

The chapters in this part consider steps to deal with the threat of climate change. There are three major approaches. A first approach is adaptation, which involves learning to cope with a warmer world rather than trying to prevent it. Relying only on adaptation is favored by those who oppose taking costly steps to slow climate change as well as those who believe that the effects of warming are likely to be small, but adaptation will be part of any portfolio of strategies.

A second approach is geoengineering, which would offset the CO_2-induced warming by introducing cooling elements. Geoengineering is likely to be at least partially effective but is unproven and may have dangerous side effects.

The third approach, often called mitigation, consists of actions to reduce emissions and atmospheric concentrations of CO_2 and other greenhouse gases. Mitigation has been the focus of international negotiations and is the safest solution from an environmental standpoint. It is also the most expensive in the short run and therefore the most difficult to achieve.

Before entering a discussion of alternative strategies, I will provide a succinct summary of the results. Economic evidence suggests that it would be relatively inexpensive to slow climate change if nations adopted efficient control strategies in a timely and near-universal fashion. The necessary steps—which involve rapidly developing new technologies and raising the price of carbon emissions as an incentive to reduce emissions—rely on economic mechanisms that have worked effectively around the world for many years. But tried and true are not necessarily popular and achievable. Indeed, these policies have met fierce resistance, as we will see in Part V.

Most of Part III discusses mitigation strategies. It explores the techniques, the necessity of high participation, estimates of cost of mitigation, and the role of new technologies. But before turning to mitigation proper, I devote this chapter to the siren song of relying solely on adaptation or geoengineering. These two polar approaches look very attractive from a distance; they are alluring because they appear to be the low-cost way of attaining our environmental goals. In reality, they may soften the blows, but they cannot completely offset the damaging impacts of carbon accumulation and climate change. They may be part of a strategy of risk management, but even the best geoengineering and adaptation will still leave significant and unacceptable risks to the planet.

ADAPTATION: LEARNING TO LIVE WITH CLIMATE CHANGE

If climate models are correct in their projections, the world will change dramatically over the coming century and beyond. We have seen many of the important impacts in earlier chapters: rising seas, ocean acidification, melting ice sheets, more intense storms, changing agricultural zones, and ecological distress. Some people think we should learn to live with these changes rather than take expensive steps to prevent them. In other words, they propose that we primarily adapt to rather than prevent global climate change.

The term "adaptation" refers to adjustments that can avert or reduce the damaging impacts of climate change on human and other living systems. For example, farmers can change their crops and planting dates, and build irrigation systems. If heat waves become more frequent, then people can install air conditioning. In some situations, adaptation might reduce the impacts to virtually nothing. In other cases adaptation may accomplish very little.

Adaptation is seldom costless, however. Farmers have to invest real money when they install and operate irrigation systems to adapt to a drier climate. You and I will have to put out cash to install and run air conditioners. But, for the United States, at least, estimates suggest that adaptation to modest climate change (say, an increase of 2–3°C) will offset most of the potential damage to humans and their enterprises.[1]

In still other areas, including unmanaged or unmanageable systems such as ocean acidification, sea-level rise, and threatened species and ecosystems, the necessary adaptations are extremely costly or impossible. Let's take a flight of fancy for sea-level rise. Someone might propose that we adapt by pumping the excess seawater on top of Antarctica to prevent sea-level rise. Some calculations indicate that this would require pumping 800,000,000,000,000,000 gallons per year and would be astronomically expensive.[2] Similarly, we might try to store the DNA of threatened species until new biotechnologies could regenerate them, but there is no guarantee that we will actually be able to perform this task. So if one takes unmanaged or unmanageable systems into consideration, adaptation is at best an incomplete solution to the vast changes that are likely to occur in the coming centuries.

Specialists here make two fundamental points about adaptation. First, adaptation is local while prevention is global. We prevent climate change by reducing global emissions and concentrations. It does no good if you or I reduce our emissions while the rest of the world continues its energy business as usual. On the other hand, adaptation is local because the costs and benefits accrue to the people who undertake the adaptation. If a farmer changes crops or installs an irrigation system, the farmer pays for the adaptation and the farmer also benefits from it. If I move my sea-front cottage to higher ground to reduce the threat from hurricanes, I pay and I benefit. These examples are oversimplified because of realistic complications such as government subsidies, impacts on neighbors, and market distortions, but these are complicating wrinkles within the basic cost-benefit pattern. The local nature of adaptation implies that most of the necessary decisions can be taken locally, or perhaps by nations, rather than globally.

Second, adaptation is completely different from mitigation, geoengineering, or carbon removal. Adaptation puts the emphasis on living with climate change, while the other options emphasize prevention. We can use an analogy of house fires. Suppose I live in a remote mountain house in New Mexico that has a high fire risk. It is near a forest just waiting for a wildfire. I can consider prevention or adaptation. Prevention would involve such things as clearing the trees near my house, putting on a metal roof, and keeping my yard free of combustible materials. The point of these steps is to prevent my house from burning down.

Another approach might be to prepare for a fire. This would involve an evacuation plan, keeping my valuables in a remote location or fireproof safe, and staying tuned to local fire reports. This strategy is to adapt if a fire occurs. While both are sensible strategies in certain situations, and most people would actually do both, they are fundamentally different approaches.

So adaptation is likely to be a necessary and useful part of the portfolio of actions to reduce the dangers from global warming. It is a complement, not a substitute, for mitigation. Particularly in areas that are heavily managed by humans, such as health care and farming, adaptation can remove many of the damaging impacts. A careful look reveals, however, that some of the most important dangers are unmanageable and cannot realistically be removed by adaptation; these include effects such as ocean carbonization and ecosystem losses. The only sure way to avoid such long-run dangers is to reduce CO_2 and other greenhouse-gas concentrations.

GEOENGINEERING: COUNTERACTING GLOBAL WARMING WITH ARTIFICIAL VOLCANOES

Relying solely on adaptation to cope with climate change is not a recommended option. However, is it possible that modern technologies can slow or stop global warming through interventions in the earth's physics or chemistry? Such approaches are called geoengineering. Geoengineering is generally divided into two categories: First are techniques that remove CO_2 from the atmosphere; second are solar radiation management techniques that reflect sunlight and heat back into space.[3] In this section, I consider the second option of solar radiation management, while the option of CO_2 removal, which is genuinely attractive, is postponed to later chapters.

The principle underlying solar radiation management is to slow or reverse warming by changing the energy balance of the earth. You can think of the process as making the earth "whiter" or more reflective, so that less sunlight reaches the surface. This cooling effect will offset the warming that comes from the accumulation of CO_2 in the atmosphere.

The whitening process is similar to changes that occur after large volcanic eruptions. After Mount Pinatubo blasted 20 million tons of particles into the stratosphere in 1991, global temperatures fell by about 0.4°C. Geoengineering can be viewed as creating artificial volcanic eruptions, and five or ten artificial Pinatubo eruptions might need to be created every year to offset the warming effects of CO_2 accumulation.

In recent years there have been many proposals for geoengineering through solar radiation management. Some involve literally making the earth whiter (say, by using white roofs and roads). Perhaps the easiest to visualize is putting millions of little mirror-like particles 20 miles above the earth. For example, we might artificially increase sulfate aerosols in the stratosphere above background levels. This would increase the planetary albedo or whiteness and reduce incoming solar radiation. Climate scientists have calculated that reflecting about 2 percent of solar output could offset the warming effect of a doubling of CO_2. The right number of particles in the right place could reduce solar radiation and cool the earth by the desired amount.

Cost estimates indicate that, if successful, geoengineering is likely to be much less expensive than reducing CO_2 emissions. Current estimates are that geoengineering would cost between one-tenth and one-hundredth as much as reducing CO_2 emissions for an equivalent amount of cooling. In economic terms, it is useful to view geoengineering as essentially costless. The major issues connected with this approach revolve around its effectiveness and its side effects.

At present, there have been no large-scale geoengineering experiments on our globe (other than volcanoes themselves), so the estimates of its impacts and side effects are based on computer modeling. The major concern is that geoengineering is not really a perfect offset to the greenhouse effect. The little particles or mirrors would reduce incoming radiation while the greenhouse effect decreases outgoing radiation. The two effects might lead to zero net warming, but they are very different physically.

A useful analogy is turning on your home air conditioner during a heat wave. Perhaps your house will be, on average, the same temperature as on a normal day, but some of the rooms might be colder and others warmer, and you definitely will be spending a small fortune on electricity.

So what are the net effects of combined CO_2 warming and "little mirror" cooling? Here is a summary of current findings: It will definitely not solve the problem of ocean acidification because altering the earth's energy balance has little impact on atmospheric CO_2 concentrations. The results of climate modeling to date suggest that at the right dosage, the planet could be cooled to present levels by injection of reflective particles into the atmosphere. However, modeling suggests some important side effects. One effect that is predicted by fundamental physics and confirmed by modeling is a general decrease in precipitation. In other words, it does not seem possible to return to the current temperature and precipitation patterns with CO_2 elevation and geoengineering. One study found that using enhanced stratospheric aerosols would modify the Asian and African summer monsoons.[4]

Additionally, active climate management may create a whole new set of political problems. In today's world, where everyone is guilty of causing global warming, no one can be held responsible. However, if certain countries engage in active climate management, then affected parties can point the finger at them if some undesirable weather pattern emerges. This means that any responsible geoengineering program will need to be negotiated among countries, and it might require some kind of compensation scheme if some regions are damaged.

This leads to a cautionary note about the strategic aspects of geoengineering. It has potentially destructive as well as constructive uses. If it can be used benignly to cool the earth, it can be used maliciously to wreck another country's harvest. This prospect of climatic warfare was emphasized by the founder of game theory, John von Neumann:

> The most constructive schemes of climate control would have to be based on insights and techniques that would also lend themselves to forms of climatic warfare as yet unimagined. . . . Useful and harmful techniques lie everywhere so close together that it is never possible to separate the lions from the lambs. This is known to all who have so laboriously tried to separate secret, classified science or technology (military) from the open kind; success is never more nor intended to be more than transient, lasting perhaps half a decade. Similarly, a separation into useful and harmful subjects in any technological sphere would probably diffuse into nothing in a decade.[5]

To me, geoengineering resembles what the doctors call "salvage therapy"—a potentially dangerous treatment to be used when all else fails. Doctors prescribe salvage therapy for people who are very ill and when less dangerous treatments are not available. No responsible doctor would prescribe salvage therapy for a patient who has just been diagnosed with the early stage of a treatable illness. Similarly, no responsible country should undertake geoengineering as the first line of defense against global warming.

Geoengineering is particularly valuable exactly because it is salvage therapy—it can be used in situations where it is most needed. In this respect, it is like a fire truck rather than fire insurance. The fire truck of geoengineering can come to the rescue to slow or reverse rapid and potentially dangerous warming. But this is no panacea. When a fire truck puts out a fire, many of our prized possessions are wrecked by water damage, and much cleanup is necessary. So fire trucks and geoengineering are useful for the worst emergencies but not as the first line of defense.

Putting this differently, it is prudent to have a portfolio of measures available for the geophysical equivalent of a terminal illness. Unfortunately, many people shy away from serious research on geoengineering. They fear that considering geoengineering would lead to "moral hazard." By this they mean that reliance on geoengineering would take the pressure off the need to reduce CO_2 and other greenhouse-gas emissions.

Moral hazard is present in many government policies, but its force here is probably exaggerated. Societies take many steps to reduce vulnerability that may also increase risk taking. Firefighters, central banks, and ski rescue services all reduce vulnerability to risks and by so doing may encourage risk taking. But on balance, I would definitely prefer to live in a society that has a central bank and ski rescue services even if they lead bankers and skiers to increase their risk taking.

So the balance sheet on geoengineering is mixed. A careful weighing of costs and benefits suggests that preparing for geoengineering would reduce the risks of the most dangerous climatic outcomes. But it leaves many of the problems unsolved and may produce dangerous side effects, so I would definitely prefer to reduce CO_2 emissions and concentrations as the first line of defense. However, we need to understand the salvage therapy of geoengineering better. A cautious plan of research and experimentation should be drawn up. Just as important is that nations should consider a treaty that places geoengineering under international regulation and control to prevent it being used strategically by individual countries for their own narrow benefits.[6]

14 SLOWING CLIMATE CHANGE BY REDUCING EMISSIONS: MITIGATION

The discussion up to now suggests that neither adaptation nor geoengineering is a satisfactory solution to the threats of global warming. The only genuine solution for the long run is to reverse the accumulation of greenhouse gases (GHGs). This is typically called mitigation or, more accurately, prevention.

Mitigation involves reducing the concentrations of GHG emissions. The most important GHG is CO_2, produced primarily by the burning of fossil fuels. There are other long-lived GHGs, such as methane (the natural gas that heats our homes). Other GHGs are short-lived, including particulate matter (also called aerosols). Some of these tend to cool the globe, which complicates the picture.

It will be helpful to spell out the magnitudes here. Scientists estimate that a doubling of atmospheric CO_2 would lead to an increase in radiative forcing (roughly, heating) of 3.8 watts per square meter (W/m^2) of the earth's surface. This is approximately one one-hundredth of the radiation that the earth receives from the sun. As of 2011, the total human-caused forcings since 1750 totaled 2.4 W/m^2.

This total is the sum of many positive and some negative numbers. The largest single contributor in 2011 was CO_2, which contributed 1.7 W/m^2 of heating. Other long-lived GHGs, like methane, contributed another 1.1 W/m^2. The contributions of CO_2 and other long-lived gases are well measured, and we can have confidence in these calculations.

The other contributions to warming are much more poorly measured. The most difficult factor to measure is aerosols. Human-caused aerosols come largely from power plants and from burning biomass. The best estimates suggest that these contributed a negative forcing of about 0.7 W/m² in 2011. In other words, aerosols tend to cool the earth and mask the warming forces.

Most projections indicate that by 2100, CO_2 will be the major contributor to global warming. The contribution of other factors, particularly aerosols, is highly speculative. One of the difficulties of projecting aerosols is that we do not know how much power will be generated by coal, nor how much of the emissions of coal-burning plants will be cleaned up in the future.

In the present analysis, I generally simplify the story by concentrating on CO_2 emissions, which captures the essential issues. I discuss other factors when they enter the picture.[1]

WHERE DO CO_2 EMISSIONS COME FROM?

The task of reducing CO_2 emissions is simple in principle but difficult in practice. It "simply" requires the world either to use less fossil fuel, or to find a way to remove the CO_2 emissions if fossil fuels are burned. Figure 23 shows the major contributors to CO_2 emissions.[2] Coal and oil are each 35–40 percent of global energy CO_2 emissions; natural gas contributes about one-fifth of the total. Percentages for the United States differ little from those of the world as a whole. There are other sectors that emit CO_2, such as cement production, but it is most useful to focus on fossil fuels, where the economic stakes are largest and the contribution to warming the greatest.

Figure 23 shows the physical volumes of CO_2 emissions. We can also examine the relative economic value of the CO_2 emissions. By this is meant the dollar value the market places on the fuel to which the CO_2 is attached. Some fuels are more expensive than others. For example, when you use gasoline in your car, the amount of CO_2 released is low per dollar of spending. By contrast, when an electric utility burns coal, the amount of CO_2 released is high per dollar.

Here are the estimates of the tons of CO_2 emissions per $1,000 of expenditures on fuel:

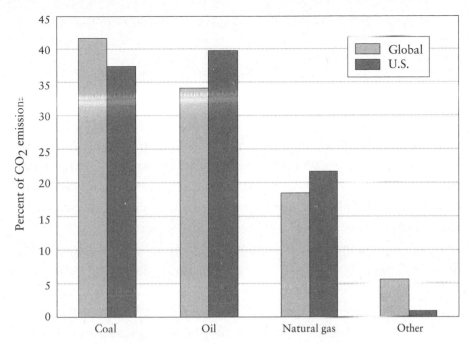

Figure 23. Sources of CO_2 emissions, 2010. This figure shows the percentage break-down of CO_2 emissions in 2010 for all countries (left bars) and for the United States (right bars).

- Petroleum emits 0.9 tons of CO_2 per $1,000 of fuel.
- Natural gas emits 2 tons of CO_2 per $1,000 of fuel.
- Coal emits 11 tons of CO_2 per $1,000 of fuel.

The results are striking: Coal has about six times more CO_2 emissions per dollar of cost than natural gas and about twelve times more than petroleum. Coal is a very inexpensive fuel per unit of energy but it has the disadvantage that much CO_2 is released per dollar of expenditure.[3]

The economics of emissions shown in the list above has important implications. It suggests that the most economical way to reduce energy emissions is to reduce coal use. This implication is not proven by the bulleted numbers because it requires further economic analysis of the capital and labor costs involved in using different fuels. However, this preliminary result survives the most careful scrutiny, as we see in the next section. This point deserves repetition because it is so critical: The most cost-effective way to reduce CO_2 emissions is to reduce the use of coal first and most sharply.

CO_2 EMISSIONS FROM THE HOUSEHOLD PERSPECTIVE

This is all very abstract. So let us move to the statistically average American household. We can calculate household emissions by dividing the national totals by the 115 million households in the United States. Table 6 shows the CO_2 emissions per household from different activities.[4] Driving is the largest single source of emissions, at about 8 tons per year. Heating and cooling are also large items. If we add all the listed sources, they total 20 tons per household per year.

But this still leaves about 32 tons per year for everything else. You might well wonder what that "everything else" in Table 6 is. In fact, CO_2 releases are involved in every aspect of household life because fossil fuels are used directly or indirectly in the production of all goods and services used by households. CO_2 is emitted from the coal used to produce the steel used to produce the kitchen table; from the natural gas used to heat the hospital to provide emergency services; from the diesel fuel used to power the tractor used to grow the wheat used in the baker's bread.

However, all activities are not equally CO_2 intensive. Coal-fired electricity generation is the biggest single source of CO_2 emissions in the United States, so activities that rely heavily on this input are CO_2 intensive. Other CO_2-intensive activities include cement, iron, and steel production. There are yet further non-CO_2 GHGs that affect the climate. One example is the methane released through "enteric fermentation," which refers to the methane released from the digestive tracts of cattle. Even an innocuous-looking glass of milk has an effect on future climate.

What sectors are relatively CO_2 free, or have only the tiniest climatic impact per unit of expenditure? The emissions per dollar of output are smallest in services. For example, health, architectural, accounting, insurance, finance, and legal services have emissions per unit of output about one-fifth of the economy as a whole. So while you may dislike your bank, it has the virtue of having a tiny carbon footprint.[5]

Table 6. Emissions for different activities by U.S. households, 2008. What household activities produce the most CO_2 emissions? Driving is the single biggest source. Most of emissions ("everything else") are not from direct fuel use but rather from indirect uses or "embodied" CO_2 where the carbon dioxide has been emitted to make the goods and services used by households.

End use	CO_2 emissions per household (tons, 2008)	Percentage of emissions
Automotive travel	7.9	15.2
Space heating	3.2	6.2
Air travel	1.6	3.0
Air conditioning	1.3	2.5
Water heating	1.3	2.5
Lighting	1.1	2.2
Refrigeration	0.8	1.5
Electronics	0.8	1.5
Cleaning	0.5	1.0
Computers	0.1	0.2
Everything else (including nonhousehold)	33.4	64.3
Total	51.9	100.0

TECHNOLOGIES FOR REDUCING CO_2

Suppose we decide to reduce CO_2 emissions and concentrations. How would we do this? Here are the main approaches:

- We can slow the overall growth of the economy. For example, during the 2009 recession U.S. emissions declined by 7 percent. Causing recessions is a painful way to accomplish the task and is definitely not recommended.
- We can reduce our energy consumption. Energy services are the useful activities listed in Table 6, such as driving or heating our homes. This route is a possible approach. We can surely trim some fat here. But most people resist major lifestyle changes, and we

definitely cannot reduce our carbon emissions to zero by reducing our consumption by fifty or ninety percent.

- Reduce the carbon intensity of production of goods and services. This would involve changing the *how* rather than the *what* of production processes. For example, we might substitute natural gas for coal in electricity generation, which would reduce CO_2 emissions by about half. Or we might go even further and use zero-carbon wind generation. Studies indicate that the real gold is likely to be found here—in changing production technologies and processes, particularly when we develop low-carbon technologies. And maybe some miraculous, unheard-of technology will be discovered that will produce our energy not only without carbon but also less expensively than current fuels.
- Remove carbon from the atmosphere. A final approach is postcombustion CO_2 removal. There are several strategies here, but most look expensive and massive in scale, as will be discussed later.

I do not discuss the details of these approaches. They have been analyzed by experts on many occasions, and readers can look to those for careful descriptions.[6] Instead, I provide some illustrative examples in the balance of this chapter: a short-run example of fuel switching; a second example of postcombustion removal; and then some futuristic examples. The final section discusses the way that potential technological breakthroughs enter the analysis in the context of the Climate Casino.

Natural gas is the cleanest of the fossil fuels, emitting about half as much CO_2 per kilowatt hour (kWh) as coal when burned for electricity generation. Shifting a greater fraction of electricity to natural gas is an important way of reducing CO_2 emissions. According to expert reports (see Table 14), new natural gas combined-cycle power plants produce electricity less expensively than new coal plants. For example, the total cost of electricity from a new conventional coal plant is estimated to be about 9.5 cents per kWh, while the total cost from a natural gas station is estimated to be 6.6 cents per kWh. At the same time, the CO_2 emissions per kilowatt hour from a coal plant are approximately double those from a natural gas plant.[7]

You might naturally ask why the United States generates any electricity from coal if it is so expensive. The answer is that the short-run costs of coal are much lower than those for gas. For efficient existing plants, the costs of generation from natural gas are about twice as high as those from coal. The difference between the long run and the short run is the high capital cost of a new coal plant as compared to a new natural gas plant. You will not be surprised that most new facilities being built or planned in the United States are gas fired rather than coal fired. But the existing plants still have significant emissions and will operate for many years without environmental regulations or taxes.

What about removing CO_2 from the atmosphere? Natural processes will eventually remove most of the CO_2 that human activities are adding to the atmosphere. But these processes operate very slowly—on a time scale of tens of thousands of years, which is too long to prevent rapid climate change and its impacts. For example, suppose that countries continue on a path of rapid emissions growth through 2100 and then completely stop all emissions. CO_2 concentrations would remain well above preindustrial levels for a millennium, and global temperature would peak at around 4°C above 1900 levels. This striking result shows the tremendous inertia in the carbon cycle and the climate system.[8]

Perhaps we should consider a completely different approach to mitigation. Is it possible to remove the CO_2 after the fossil fuels have been burned? This could take place either as an integrated process or after the gases have entered the atmosphere. The advantage of postcombustion processes is that we can continue to use the abundant fossil fuels to power our economies and still reduce their climatic impacts.

The most promising of the postcombustion technologies today is called carbon capture and sequestration (CCS). This technology would burn fossil fuels (such as natural gas or coal) and then capture the CO_2. Burning is easy, while economical capture is difficult.

How would CCS work? The following description is based on a careful study by a team of engineers and economists from MIT.[9] The basic idea is simple. CCS would capture CO_2 at the time of combustion and then ship it off and store it in some location where it would remain for hundreds of years and thus not enter the atmosphere.

I use the example of coal because that is the most plentiful fossil fuel and a leading candidate for a large-scale CCS deployment. Engineers think that CCS with natural gas will be less expensive at today's natural gas prices in the United States, but the basic principles outlined for coal are similar for natural gas. We can simplify by assuming coal is pure carbon. Then the basic process is:

$$\text{Carbon} + \text{oxygen} \rightarrow \text{energy as heat} + CO_2$$

So combustion produces a desired output (heat that can be used for electricity generation) plus an undesirable externality, CO_2.

The trick is to capture the CO_2 molecules before they enter the atmosphere. CO_2 separation is currently in operation today in oil and natural gas fields. However, existing techniques operate at a small scale and are not appropriate for deployment in large coal-fired electrical generation. One promising technology is integrated gasification combined cycle with CO_2 capture. This process would start with pulverized coal; gasify it to produce hydrogen and carbon monoxide; further react the carbon monoxide to produce highly concentrated CO_2 and hydrogen; separate out the CO_2 with a solvent; then compress the CO_2; and finally ship the CO_2 and store it. All this sounds complicated, and it is, but it is not much more complicated than the technologies that are currently used in generating electricity from coal.

The major issues with CCS are cost and storage. The cost of electricity rises when CCS is added because energy is necessary to separate the CO_2 from the emission stream. According to the MIT study, the cost of electricity generation rises by 3 to 4 cents per kWh with CO_2 capture. This adds about 60 percent to the generation cost for current technologies, but the MIT team projected that it would add only 30 percent to the cost of generation for advanced technologies.[10]

While the CO_2 capture is the expensive part of the process, transportation and storage are likely to be the more controversial parts. One problem is simply the scale of the materials that would be stored. The most likely storage sites are porous underground rock formations such as depleted oil and natural gas fields. Another issue is the risk of leakage. This would not only reduce the value of the project (because the

CO_2 would enter the atmosphere) but could pose problems for health and safety. My favorite option would use gravitational storage in the deep oceans. If CO_2 is deposited in the deep ocean, the CO_2 would be heavier than water and would remain there for many centuries [11]

At present, CCS faces many hurdles. It is expensive, untested, and would need to be scaled up to handle tens of billions of tons of CO_2 each year. We have inadequate data on the performance of underground storage, and extensive experience is necessary to ensure scientific and public acceptability. People are frightened of the prospect of a huge burp of CO_2 causing unforeseen damage.

Like many other large-scale and capital-intensive technologies, CCS is caught in a vicious cycle. Firms will not invest in CCS on a large scale because it is financially risky; it is financially risky because public acceptance is low and there are big hurdles to large-scale deployment; and public acceptance is low because there is so little experience with CCS at a large scale. Breaking out of this vicious cycle is a major dilemma for public policy in this as in other new, large-scale energy systems.

SOME FUTURISTIC TECHNOLOGIES

Other proposals for removal of CO_2 from the atmosphere sound more like science fiction than hard-headed engineering. One cute example is to grow billions of trees, cut them down, and store them along with their carbon in some remote location to prevent decomposition. One variant of this was suggested by the distinguished physicist Freeman Dyson:

> After we have mastered biotechnology, the rules of the climate game will be radically changed. In a world economy based on biotechnology, some low-cost and environmentally benign backstop to carbon emissions is likely to become a reality. . . . [For example,] it is likely that we shall have "genetically engineered carbon-eating trees" within twenty years, and almost certainly within fifty years. Carbon-eating trees could convert most of the carbon that they absorb from the atmosphere into some chemically stable form and bury it underground.[12]

Scientists are working on other technologies that could speed up natural CO_2-storing processes. A "synthetic tree" that would remove CO_2 from the atmosphere has been proposed by Columbia University's Klaus Lackner.[13] Some scientists have proposed methods for using the oceans to absorb excessive carbon.

All of these ideas face two major obstacles. They are likely to be expensive, and the required scale of removal is vast. These points can be illustrated with an example that is definitely feasible today. The Canadian province of British Columbia has vast tracts of forest that are largely untouched. Suppose that British Columbia were to devote half of its forest land, or about 300,000 square kilometers, to carbon removal. This would involve growing trees, cutting them after they mature, and storing them in a way that prevents leakage of the CO_2 into the atmosphere. British Columbia would soon have a huge mountain of trees, but devoting half the province to the project would offset less than 0.5 percent of the world's CO_2 emissions in coming years.

Perhaps a large number of carbon-eating trees, BC-type tree projects, and Lackner-style synthetic trees could tilt the CO_2 trajectory downward, but it is a gigantic undertaking. Such efforts are more likely to supplement rather than substitute for emissions reductions, unless some completely different and more efficient carbon-removal process is discovered.

Most of the options for sharp reductions in CO_2 emissions look costly, as calculations in Chapter 15 will show. Are we unduly pessimistic because today's technologies were developed in a world that was unconcerned about climate change? Is it possible that, with the appropriate incentives and by devoting sufficient scientific talent to the task, global warming might be solved by a revolution in energy technologies that simply makes the problem disappear?

Look back for a moment at Figure 3. This figure shows that the carbon intensity of the U.S. economy has declined around 2 percent per year over the last eight decades, with only small variations on that trend. Is it possible that a major revolution in energy technologies might increase the rate of decarbonization to 10 or 20 percent per year and thereby bend down the emissions trajectory sharply? I consider how such a scenario might unfold and then discuss its implications for global warming policy.

Forecasting future technological developments is inherently difficult. If I knew what future technologies would succeed, then, as with forecasting future stock market movements, I could be fabulously famous and wealthy. But let's consider some technological science fiction. Scientists and technologists who speculate about future trends generally anticipate that breakthroughs might come from some combination of advanced computation, robotics, and new materials.

Inventor-futurist Ray Kurzweil has proposed a vision for a low-carbon but energy-rich future. He suggests that molecular nanotechnology can reduce the fabrication costs of solar power to a tiny fraction of the current level, enabling placement of inexpensive solar cells on buildings, vehicles, and even clothing. He also envisions using solar power in space to beam vast quantities of energy to earth via microwaves, with the materials lifted to space using a space elevator.[14]

As with other forecasts of revolutionary breakthroughs, it is hard to know how seriously to take them. Is the likelihood of such a breakthrough in the next half century 20 percent? Or 2 percent? Or 0.002 percent?

To begin with, we definitely should not rule out these kinds of radical technological breakthroughs. A century ago, no one would have dreamed of today's Internet, artificial intelligence, or DNA sequencing. Moreover, if we look at Figure 39, we see that solar photovoltaic costs have declined sharply in the past five decades.

But a little reflection suggests that potential radical technological breakthroughs will not solve the global warming dilemma. The reason is that we need insurance against bad outcomes, not to cover good outcomes. Fire insurance is a useful analogy. We buy fire insurance in case our house burns down, not for the surviving house, or for a house whose value rises sharply. Our premiums insure against the worst-case scenario, not the best-case scenario.

Here is a fable that will make the point. Suppose someone invents an ingenious bug that eats carbon in the atmosphere and then flies into space when it is full. Should we relax all our efforts to slow climate change? A little reflection suggests not. The bug might in reality eat nothing and fly nowhere, and we will then be faced with unchecked climate change. We need policies for when the bug does not eat, not for when it does eat. So to the extent that global warming policies are largely insurance against uncertain but very damaging outcomes in the Climate Casino, the possibility of favorable outcomes from potential revolutionary breakthroughs does not substantially reduce the insurance premium to cover the adverse impacts of global warming.

So what is the conclusion on mitigation? There are many options for reducing CO_2 and other greenhouse gases. Some are available today, such as shifting electricity generation from coal to natural gas and other low-carbon sources. Others are more speculative, such as carbon capture and sequestration. Still others are dreams, such as carbon-eating trees and bugs. Economists who have studied this problem are generally in agreement: We can slow global warming through mitigation if the task is taken seriously and managed efficiently. It need not be ruinously expensive, and the use of market-friendly tools will reduce the expense and the intrusiveness of policies on our everyday lives. The impact on living standards over the next half century would be very modest if mitigation is efficiently managed. All these are big assumptions, to which I turn in the next few chapters.

15 THE COSTS OF SLOWING CLIMATE CHANGE

The previous chapter concluded that limiting climate change requires focusing primarily on reducing concentrations of CO_2 and other greenhouse gases (GHGs). We saw that there are four basic ways to accomplish this. The first, which is really not in contention, would reduce our living standards by slowing economic growth.

The other three are worth serious consideration. We might change our lifestyle by curbing our carbon-intensive activities, such as deciding not to fly around the world. Additionally, we might produce our goods and services with low-carbon or no-carbon technologies or fuels, such as substituting natural gas or wind for coal in our electricity generation. And finally, we might burn fossil fuels but remove the CO_2 after combustion.

The purpose of climate-change policies is to encourage all three of these actions. Effective and efficient policies must affect the decisions of billions of people, firms, and governments around the world to induce them to use low-carbon consumption and technologies. Some technologies are obvious, such as reducing the net CO_2 emissions from coal-fired electricity. Others are subtle, such as operating factories more efficiently. Yet others, which will be the most promising for the long run, involve encouraging the development of new and improved technologies.

However, for the most part, each of these involves costs. New electricity from wind is more expensive than power from efficient coal plants. A hybrid car costs more than a standard car. And, from the point of view of happiness, it is costly to stay home because we were really looking forward to our trip to New Mexico. Some of these substitutions may be inexpensive, while others will be costly. But the central lesson from economics is that attaining the goals of climate-change policy— particularly the ambitious ones—will require substantial investments.

THE METRIC FOR MEASURING COSTS

The usual way to measure the costs in this area is "dollars per ton of CO_2 reduced." At first, this seems strange, but it is just a price. We are used to paying "dollars per pound of potatoes." The difference here is that we are paying not to produce something rather than to produce something. It is like paying someone to cart off the trash. The logic is simple. Suppose that you can reduce your CO_2 emissions 10 tons by spending $1,000; then the cost is $100 per ton (=$1,000/10).

Let's take two specific examples.

Example 1: New refrigerator. I have an old refrigerator and am thinking of buying a new energy-efficient model that costs $1,000. Each refrigerator will last 10 years and has identical size and cooling. The new one uses less electricity, and I calculate the cost savings to be $50 per year, so (ignoring discounting) the new refrigerator will have a net cost of $500. A little research shows that the new fridge emits about 0.3 tons of CO_2 per year less than the old one. So over the 10 years I can reduce my CO_2 emissions by 3 tons for a cost of $500. This comes to $167 per ton of CO_2 reduced [=$500/(0.3×10)]. This cost is a little higher if we discount the costs, as we should for investments.[1]

Example 2: Natural gas electricity generation. The cost of reducing emissions by replacing my old refrigerator turns out to be high. Let's turn to another example, which is motivated by my discussion in Chapter 14 of the advantage of substituting natural gas for coal in electricity generation. Suppose the old coal plant is inefficient and has variable cost about 1 cent per kWh more than the new gas plant. The difference in CO_2 emissions is about half a ton of CO_2 per 1,000 kWh. Dividing these, we get a cost of $20 per ton of CO_2 removed. The arithmetic is ($10/1,000 kWh)/(0.5 tons of CO_2/1,000 kWh) = $20/ton of CO_2. So this is much less costly than replacing the refrigerator.[2]

ESTIMATING THE COSTS OF REDUCING CO_2 EMISSIONS

The cost of reducing CO_2 emissions is one of the most important topics in climate-change economics. The basic idea is simple. You need energy for services such as lighting, heating, or driving. You can get these services in different ways. You can get your lighting with cheap, inefficient bulbs or expensive, efficient ones. You can get your vehicle miles with gas guzzlers or with hybrids.

If you use less energy, you will use less fuel and therefore emit less CO_2. However, in each case you will need to spend a little more up front for the energy-efficient equipment. The question is, when you take everything into account, what is the net cost of reducing a given amount of CO_2?

Energy experts have made many studies of the costs of reducing CO_2 and other GHG emissions. Here are some of the important findings.

- The economy contains many inexpensive opportunities. Some may even have "negative costs" in the sense that the discounted savings in energy costs more than offset the up-front investments.
- The costs begin to rise steeply as we restrict emissions ever more tightly. Studies indicate that countries can achieve 10 or 20 percent reductions with relatively modest and possibly even zero costs. But reducing emissions by 80 or 90 percent in a few years would be extremely expensive.
- There is today no "silver bullet" technology that will solve the climate problem in one shot. Rather, there are countless opportunities around the world, in virtually every sector of every country.
- Finally, even though we focus here on CO_2 from fossil fuels, a complete portfolio of policies should not neglect sources outside the burning of fossil fuels. There are many sources of GHGs that can be reduced economically. For example, replacing the chlorofluorocarbons that depleted the ozone layer led to reductions in GHGs that would have had large warming effects. Similar steps are available in other areas, some discussed in note 3, but I put those aside to simplify this discussion.[3]

Many scientific studies of global warming present future technological scenarios in great detail. I do not take that approach here. One reason is that we really don't know the answer. Economists and policymakers do not have the information to micromanage the energy system for 315 million Americans or 7 billion earthlings. The economy is too complicated and evolves too rapidly. Rather, as discussed in Part IV, economists emphasize that policy should be designed to provide strong incentives to reduce CO_2 emissions and to develop new low-carbon technologies.

Even though we may not know the technological details of a global warming strategy, we do have some educated hunches on where the major areas for reduction should come. I illustrate this with an analysis of a specific policy proposal. For this example, I examine a proposal that targeted a 40 percent reduction in U.S. GHGs in 2030 relative to a no-control baseline. The details of the proposal are not important for my purpose; rather, the emphasis is on the efficient manner of reaching an ambitious target.

The policy was analyzed using a very detailed energy model developed by the U.S. Energy Information Administration. Figure 24 shows that most of the emissions reductions would come from reducing coal use.[4] Coal consumption would be reduced 90 percent, while petroleum and natural gas use would be reduced about 5 percent each. The reason for this result is that coal has much higher CO_2 emissions per dollar of energy content. Additionally, natural gas can be economically substituted for coal in electricity generation, as we saw in example 2 earlier in this chapter. Finally, the price of natural gas has fallen sharply in recent years, reducing the cost penalty of reducing coal use even further.

The results of detailed energy models suggest an important and troubling conclusion. The favorite policies of most countries today are energy efficiency regulations such as those for automobiles and appliances like refrigerators. However, such regulations will not touch the area where reductions are most economical—electricity generation from coal. While energy-efficiency regulation may be popular, reducing coal use meets with ferocious opposition from coal regions and their hired guns. But careful analyses show that coal is king when it comes to reducing CO_2 emissions.

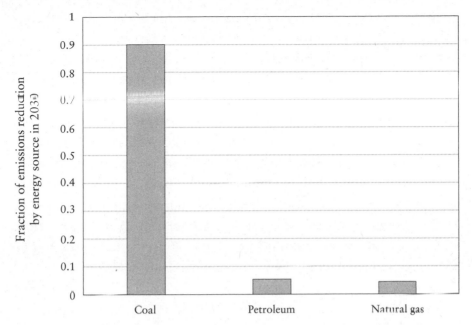

Figure 24. A projection of the most economical way for the United States to reduce CO_2 emissions by fuel type. According to a study by the U.S. Energy Information Administration, we should reduce coal use most sharply. These results are similar to those of other economic models.

This leads to one further point. The costs involved in reducing CO_2 emissions are potentially very large. Significant reductions in emissions cannot be done easily, quickly, or cheaply with today's technologies or those that are ready for large-scale deployment. It will require considerable ingenuity to craft inexpensive ways to reduce emissions. Yet we need to ensure that societies rely on the least expensive approaches. Returning to our examples of refrigerators versus electricity generation, we saw a cost difference of a factor of almost ten. When we are talking about reducing emissions by billions of tons, the economic stakes are enormous.

THE AGGREGATE COST-REDUCTION CURVE

The discussion above illustrated CO_2 cost reductions using typical decisions such as the choice of refrigerators for households and power plants for electric utilities. But ultimately we are interested in the cost for the entire economy. Experts have studied the CO_2 cost reduction

question for many years. I summarize the results but must also emphasize the difficulties and dynamic nature of the analysis.

There are many estimates, and they vary widely. Figure 25 shows
the results from two different methodologies—the engineering or
bottom-up approach and economic modeling or top-down approach.[5]
Start with the bottom-up models. A bottom-up approach estimates the
costs by looking at a suite of different technologies, such as those used
in cars, blast furnaces, power plants, and the like. It then asks how we
can reduce emissions for each sector, and at what cost. Our examples of
refrigerators and power plants were rudimentary bottom-up estimates.
These are typical of how an engineer would approach the question,
looking at different products or processes and asking how they can be
redesigned to reduce carbon emissions in an efficient manner.

Now look at Figure 25. The vertical axis shows the average cost of
emissions reductions as a percentage of income, while the horizontal axis

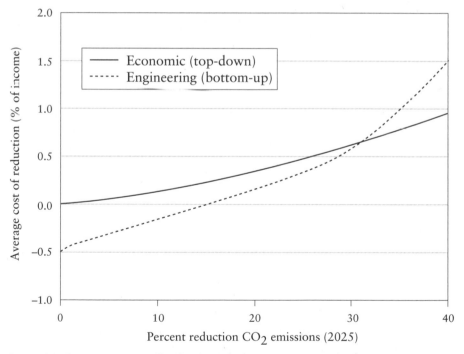

Figure 25. The average cost of reducing GHG emissions, 2025. This figure shows an
estimate of the average cost of reducing emissions in the most efficient manner for the
world as a whole. Estimates for the United States differ slightly but have the same shape.

shows the percentage of CO_2 reduction for a given year, here 2025. Take, for example, the cost estimates for a 30 percent reduction in CO_2 emissions. The two methods are consistent in estimating that the average cost of reductions at that level is a little more than 0.5 percent of national income. If we put this in terms of cost for the U.S. economy in 2012, it would average about $15 per ton of CO_2 reduced and an aggregate cost around $100 billion per year. Aiming for sharper rates of emissions reductions will raise the costs.

One interesting finding from the bottom-up studies is the claim that there exist many negative-cost measures, that is, ones that save money. They involve such things as using natural gas power plants and improving automotive fuel efficiency. According to most bottom-up studies, we can reduce emissions by around 15 percent and actually save money at the same time. Another 15 percent or so of emissions reductions can be achieved with relatively low cost, but it still adds up to $100 billion for the United States.

The other curve shows the cost estimates from top-down or economic models. These typically use statistical estimates that relate energy use and emissions to prices and incomes. This approach is described as "top-down" to reflect the fact that it works with totals or aggregates rather than looking at individual technologies. Economic models typically assume that there are no negative-cost options. The economic approach assumes that if there were negative-cost technologies, they would already have been adopted and would not need climate-change policies to encourage them.

Note that the two curves have different slopes. The engineering or bottom-up estimates start lower with negative costs but rise more rapidly than the economic or top-down approach. I explained the lower starting point for the bottom-up approach as reflecting the engineering finding of negative-cost technologies. The higher slope results because the bottom-up models typically analyze only a limited number of technologies. They are likely to overlook some emissions-reducing options because they simply cannot include everything, whereas the economic models in principle allow for all the possible approaches. Most bottom-up estimates focus on a few dozen technologies in their calculations (automobiles, refrigerators, electricity generation, and so forth). But there are many ways to reduce emissions other than changing technologies. One way is through changing our consumption patterns. For example, perhaps I can satisfy my vacation needs by not flying long distances; this kind of emissions-reducing process would not be accounted for in the engineering or bottom-up approaches but would be included in the economic or top-down models.

Which approach is the correct one? In my own work, I tend to use the economic top-down approaches because they are consistent with observed behavior in many countries and at different times. Moreover, the bottom-up models often include unrealistic assumptions.[6] I acknowledge that there are many negative-cost items. But knowing that negative-cost options exist does not imply we have the knowledge to find them and the wisdom to exploit them efficiently. So when I cast my vote, I choose the economic approach in my modeling.

But I also recognize that this area has been the subject of heated and well-informed debates among economists and engineers. The jury is still out on which is the correct approach, and indeed the jury has been languishing for decades. For nonspecialists, it is surely unnerving to find that the experts are so divided on the costs of emissions reductions. But these differences reflect genuine uncertainties about what will be required to make radical changes in such a complex part of the economy.

Notwithstanding these debates, the basic contour of efficient cost reduction is similar in all the models. The cost of modest reductions is relatively small, but as we increase the depth of the cuts and shorten the time horizon, the costs rise sharply.

THE COST OF MEETING GLOBAL TEMPERATURE TARGETS

Having examined the costs of slowing climate change, we can now put this apparatus to work. This section examines the costs of meeting a specific climate-change objective. This calculation is more demanding than estimating cost curves because it requires integrating costs into a climate model.

For this purpose, I present estimates of the costs of meeting different temperature targets. One is the Copenhagen target, which proposed limiting the global temperature rise to 2°C. We can do similar calculations for other temperature targets. The estimates that follow use the Yale DICE model, but they are representative of other models.

Figure 26 shows the results.[7] Begin with estimates of abatement costs using the most efficient set of policies. The lines show the cost of meeting different temperature targets shown on the horizontal axis. The solid left-hand cost curve in Figure 26 shows the utopian ideal of

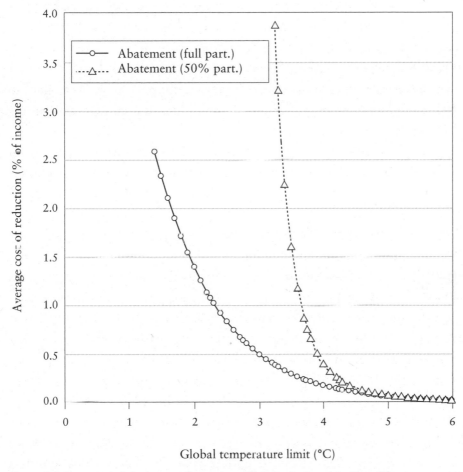

Global temperature limit (°C)

Figure 26. Estimated global costs of meeting different climate objectives. The two curves show the fraction of global income needed to attain given temperature objectives. The left-hand curve assumes 100 percent participation and efficient policy design, while the right-hand curve assumes 50 percent participation. Low participation makes it virtually impossible to achieve the 2°C Copenhagen target.

100 percent efficient policies with 100 percent participation of countries. In addition to universal country participation, the minimum-cost curve further assumes that interventions are efficiently timed and universally applied—no exemptions for farmers, exporters, or the politically connected are allowed. Note that the costs are calculated as a percentage of world income. (These results also use discounted costs, a concept explained in Chapter 16.)

The utopian policy indicates that meeting the Copenhagen objective of 2°C would be modest if it is undertaken efficiently. It would require spending about 1.5 percent of world income, or about one year's growth in average income. However, to aim for a lower target (say 1°C) would become much more expensive. So the important point is that the world can meet ambitious temperature targets at low cost if it is done efficiently and with universal participation.

Next, move to limited participation. One of the first insights from the economic models is the importance of near-universal participation in emissions reduction programs. Put differently, the cost of meeting a climate objective depends greatly on how many countries participate. The reason is that efficiency requires that all regions exploit their negative-cost and low-cost reduction options. If, for example, India makes no reductions, then other countries would have to adopt more expensive reductions to meet a given global climate policy target.

We must be realistic about country behavior. Some countries will refuse to join the effort. Moreover, only one-fifth of global emissions were covered by the Kyoto Protocol in 2012. So assume that countries with only half of emissions participate, although they do so very soon. These might be all the rich countries and some of the middle-income countries but not the poor countries. The other countries would join the plan in the next century. The right-hand curve in Figure 26 shows the costs for this limited-participation case. This second case still has an idealistic flavor because it assumes that policies are implemented in an efficient manner—again, no exemptions for farmers, exporters, or other groups.

The limited participation curve is sobering. It shows that meeting any temperature target will be much more costly if only half the countries join the effort. The costs rise very quickly for temperature targets below 4°C. The reason is simple: If half the countries make no efforts to reduce emissions, substantial warming will be inevitable even if the other half of countries make maximum efforts. This calculation also indicates that delayed participation of a substantial part of the world will make it virtually impossible—not just costly—to meet the Copenhagen objective of 2°C.

Finally, consider inefficient policies. I discuss the efficient design of policies in later chapters, but the basic idea is that the marginal costs of emissions reductions should be equal in all sectors and countries. If this is a bit mysterious, I will explain it carefully in short order.

This further case is relevant because no country comes close to passing the efficiency test. Policies are generally a hodgepodge of regulations, energy taxes, and green subsidies. For example, the United States regulates the fuel efficiency of automobiles, but the regulations apply only to new cars. The U.S. government has proposed regulating CO_2 emissions from new power plants, but the CO_2 emissions of existing power plants are not regulated. Many European countries tax carbon emissions, but they also exempt or give special breaks to export industries and small businesses.

As a result of the inconsistent treatment of different industries, the costs of meeting temperature objectives are higher than the efficient level shown in Figure 26. I do not provide a graphic here, but readers can easily draw one for themselves. A typical finding is that using inefficient regulations or approaches will double the costs of meeting environment objectives. Put this finding together with the assumption of a 50 percent participation rate. Then the cost curve in Figure 26 would shift upward by a factor of 2. You can pencil in this new curve and label it "Mitigation cost: 50 percent participation and inefficient regulations." The cost of meeting the 3½°C target would rise from 1.5 percent of income to 3 percent of income; the cost of meeting a 3¼°C target would rise from 4 percent of income to 8 percent of income; and so forth.

This simplified example emphasizes the importance of designing policies efficiently. Poor design and limited participation can raise the cost sharply and can even make our objectives infeasible.

For those interested in other modeling results, we can look to the EMF-22 modeling comparison discussed in Part I. The eleven models ran scenarios very similar to the two shown in Figure 26. The results were roughly parallel. In the case of universal participation, about half the models found that it was possible to attain the 2°C target. For partial participation, twenty of twenty-two model runs found the 2°C target infeasible. In reality, "infeasible" means that it would require causing a horrible economic depression. These results have been confirmed by other modelers as well.

The models also estimated the costs of different scenarios. The costs from the EMF models were generally higher than the DICE model calculations shown in Figure 26. There were also large differences among the models. If we take a scenario that was feasible for all the models, the largest-cost model estimate for meeting the objective was twelve times the minimum-cost model estimate.[8]

Why are the cost uncertainties so large? One reason is that models use different cost structures: Some are top-down while others are bottom-up. Additionally, they have different growth rates of output and emissions. A model with a high growth rate has to spend much more to get temperature down to the desired level. A third difference is the vision of energy technologies. For example, one model might see a constrained nuclear power industry, which would raise costs.

However, we should view these model differences as genuine and not imaginary ones. They cannot be resolved by getting the modelers together to insist that they find the "right" answer. The cost estimates reflect carefully considered judgments about future economic and energy systems, and we should take them as reflecting uncertainties about the future as seen by the world's leading modeling teams.

So the bottom line on costs is this. Suppose we live in an ideal world—one where countries work together cooperatively to introduce emissions reductions, take care to ensure that all countries and sectors participate, and time their actions efficiently. For this world, slowing climate change to meet the Copenhagen objective of a 2°C limit or something close to it would be a feasible objective. Estimates from economic models suggest that attaining this goal would take between 1 and 2 percent of total world income on an annual basis.

But we need to be realistic about country behavior and the efficiency of our policies. To the extent that countries do not participate, or that inefficient measures are used, or that the timing of actions is inefficient, then we cannot realistically attain an ambitious temperature target such as that adopted at Copenhagen. Under such circumstances, we might be able to achieve a less ambitious goal, perhaps limiting global warming to an increase of 3°C.

So unless virtually all countries participate very soon, and do so in an efficient manner, achieving the Copenhagen target of limiting the increase in global temperature to 2°C is not possible with current or readily available technologies. This does not mean that we should give up. We need to strive to develop more efficient technologies; we need to design social mechanisms that will encourage economic efficiency and high participation; we should provide help to poor countries that have limited resources; and we will need to recalibrate our objectives toward achievable goals rather than fail in the ambitious but impossible ones.

16 DISCOUNTING AND THE VALUE OF TIME

Any consideration of the costs of meeting climate objectives requires confronting one of the thorniest issues in all of climate-change economics: How should we compare present and future costs and benefits? This is a moderately complex issue and extends to the frontier of current economic theory. However, it is also of central importance for understanding the temporal trade-offs involved. These are trade-offs between the costs of emissions reductions today and the societal value of reduced damages in the future. So a full appreciation of the economics of climate change cannot proceed without dealing with discounting.

Here is the issue in a nutshell: When we make investments to reduce emissions, these costs are paid largely in the near term. The benefits in the form of reduced damages from climate change come far in the future. As an example, suppose that we replace a coal-fired power plant with a wind farm. If we follow the chain of effects from building the wind farm to reduced CO_2 emissions and concentrations to temperature change to reduced damages, there is a delay of many decades from building the wind farm emissions to the reduction in damages.

OUR FIRST MORTGAGE

Economists generally advocate that we discount benefits in the future relative to costs incurred today. Others hold that it is unethical to give lower priority to future generations than to people living today. How can we sort this out?

All of us confront this question in our everyday lives. Suppose you want to buy your first house, which costs $200,000, but you have only $50,000 in cash. You need to get an additional $150,000. You go to the bank and find that it is willing to lend you the $150,000, but it requires you to pay a 6 percent interest rate on the loan. A quick calculation shows that if you were to borrow $150,000 for 30 years at 6 percent interest, you would need to pay the bank $323,759.

Your first instinct might be to say, "Now I know why bankers are so rich." But on further reflection, you realize that the extra $173,759 is interest and reflects the fact that you get $150,000 of buying power today instead of having to wait for years to become a homeowner. Money is more valuable today than tomorrow, and that is why people and businesses are willing to pay interest on borrowed money.

REAL VERSUS NOMINAL INTEREST RATES

We need to pause for one financial detail. In my discussion of mortgages, the interest rate was 6 percent per year. But suppose that prices go up by 2 percent per year. So we will be paying back in dollars that are worth less in the future because of inflation. How should we deal with this fact?

When we think of interest, we usually have the "nominal" or dollar interest rate in mind. Interest is quoted in dollar terms, meaning we pay back dollars in the future for dollars borrowed today. But suppose prices are going up at 2 percent per year. Then while you pay $6 for every $100 borrowed, the $6 is worth less next year. Because prices changed over the year, you would not sacrifice $6 of future goods.

The concept financial economists use to deal with inflation is the "real interest rate." It measures the quantity of goods we get tomorrow for goods foregone today and is obtained by correcting nominal or dollar interest rates for the rate of inflation. In our example, with a nominal interest rate of 6 percent per year and an inflation rate of 2 percent per year, the real interest rate is $6 - 2 = 4$ percent per year. When we borrow, we are really only paying back 4 cents of goods next year for each dollar's worth of goods borrowed this year. From now on we will talk about real interest rates because inflation just confuses the measurements.

A DISCOUNTING EXAMPLE

The following example illustrates the issues posed by discounting. Suppose a sterling character is selling a special bond that pays $1,000 in real terms (in dollars corrected for inflation) in 50 years. What is the maximum amount that you would be willing to pay today for such a bond?

You turn to a trusted financial consultant. She advises you to calculate the appropriate current contribution by taking the future $1,000 and "discounting" its value back to the present using an appropriate discount rate. That discount rate should reflect the amount you could earn on equivalent investments over the same period. The $1,000 is inflation corrected, so we want to use a real discount rate. In addition, we need to recognize that investments always carry some kind of risk. So in the case of the special bond, we might need to add a risk premium. We would need to recognize that our sterling character might turn out to be the bankrupt Lehman Brothers or a Cyprus bank rather than Uncle Sam.

So how much is the $1,000 bond worth today? I will use 4 percent for our hypothetical investment scenario. Applying this discount rate to the $1,000 bond would yield a present value of $141. This is the right value because if you take $141 and invest it for 50 years at a compound interest rate of 4 percent per year, the end value would be $1,000.

DETERMINANTS OF INTEREST

What is the underlying economic reason for interest? Interest reflects the fact that investments are productive. In other words, if the economy puts resources into investment projects, the projects yield more resources in the future. This applies to building a factory, sending children to school, investing in energy-saving appliances, or writing better software. Typically, an investment of $100 in new capital would yield between 4 and 20 percent per year in more goods in the future. If the return is 4 percent, this means that to get $1 next year requires only $1/$1.04 = $0.96 today.

Figure 27. Discounting reduces the value of distant goods. Discounting is like visual perspective, reducing the value of goods and services in the future.

Because dollars are less valuable in the future than today, they are reduced or "discounted" in the future. We can use the analogy of visual perspective to show the impact of the future on values. If you look down a railroad track, distant objects look smaller (see Figure 27). This is the way distant economic dollars should look as well because goods received in the future have lower economic value than goods received today.[1]

CONSUMPTION TODAY VERSUS CONSUMPTION TOMORROW

Discounting compares goods today with goods tomorrow. People ultimately care about their living standards, or what economists call "consumption of goods and services." Consumption is the ultimate goal of economic life, and it is the focus of my discussion.

Consumption refers to the vast array of goods and services that people enjoy. You should think of it as a comprehensive concept. It includes market goods like cars, nonmarket items like home-cooked meals, and environmental services such as a swim in the ocean. It would properly correct for deficiencies in standard measures by subtracting the costs of pollution and adding the value of public parks.

The major trade-off in climate-change policy involves trading off consumption today for consumption in the future. When we reduce CO_2 emissions today, that requires sacrificing current consumption. The return for our investment is reduced climate-change damages and therefore higher consumption in the future. If we reduce consumption by taking fewer airline trips today, thereby reducing CO_2 emissions, this will help preserve national parks and wildlife for vacations in the future.

Now we see why discounting becomes so important. Suppose that a climate investment sacrificing 100 units of consumption today increases consumption by 200 units in the future. How can we put these into comparable units to determine whether that is a good investment? We do this by discounting.

PRESCRIPTIVE AND OPPORTUNITY-COST VIEWS OF DISCOUNTING

The discounting controversy has centered primarily on the question of whether the discount rate should be derived from a prescriptive (normative) approach, or whether it should rely upon a descriptive (opportunity-cost) basis.[2]

Begin with the prescriptive approach. This approach was forcefully advocated by the distinguished British economist Nicholas Stern, in a major study he led on climate-change policy, the *Stern Review*. Along with others, Stern argued that it is unethical to discount the welfare of future generations. They believe that we should therefore apply a very low discount rate on goods to calculate the present value of future climate damages. Advocates of the normative view often advocate discount rates on goods around 1 percent per year.[3] An alternative approach based on sustainability has been developed by Yale political scientist John Roemer.

While this is an appealing argument, there are important qualifications. In analyzing the issues, we need to distinguish the *discount rate on goods*, which applies to things like houses or energy spending, from the *discount rate on welfare*, which applies to the treatment of people in different times or generations. We might treat all generations equally but still discount future goods. If people in the future are richer than people today, we might count their consumption as less valuable than the consumption of the present generation (i.e., discount it). So putting different values on goods is not the same as putting different values on people.

Here is a different way of seeing this point. Most philosophers and economists hold that rich generations have a lower ethical claim on resources than poor generations. This would imply that we would discount the value of future consumption relative to today's consumption because we think that future generations will be richer than present generations. Exactly how high the discount rate on goods should be would depend upon how much richer future generations are expected to be as well as the relative valuations of the consumption of rich and poor generations.[4]

Those who advocate the alternative descriptive approach might agree with the philosophy underlying the prescriptive approach. However, the descriptive school holds that these philosophical reflections are largely irrelevant to decisions about climate-change investments. Instead, the descriptive analysis holds that the discount rate should depend primarily on the actual returns that societies can get on alternative investments. Countries have a range of possible investments: homes, education, preventive health care, carbon reduction, and investing abroad. Particularly in a period of tight government budgets and financial constraints, the yields on such investments might be very high. In such a context, the prescriptive approach of a very low ethical discount rate just does not make any economic sense. A country would be poorly served to put its scarce funds into wind farms yielding 1 percent per year when it is borrowing money in international financial markets at 5 or 10 percent. According to the descriptive view, the discount rate should be primarily determined by the opportunity cost of capital, which is determined by the rate of return on alternative investments.

ESTIMATES OF DISCOUNT RATES

In estimating the opportunity cost for the descriptive approach, economists have looked at the rate of return on alternative investments. Here are some examples. The posttax real returns on corporate capital are estimated to be 6 percent per year for the United States over the past four decades. Real rates of return on investments in human capital (education) range from 4 to 20 percent per year depending upon the place, time, and kind of education. Investments in real estate have typically enjoyed real returns in the range of 6 to 10 percent per year, although they have done poorly since the bursting of the housing price bubble after 2006. Investments in energy savings (say through higher fuel efficiency of cars or improvements in buildings) are often calculated to have real returns of more than 10 and sometimes as high as 20 percent per year.[5]

My own studies usually rely on the descriptive or opportunity cost approach. Using a variety of estimates, I generally use a real rate of return on capital of around 4 percent per year for the United States, along with a slightly higher rate of return on capital in the rest of the world. I adopt the descriptive approach because it reflects the reality that capital is scarce, that societies have valuable alternative investments, and that climate investments should compete with investments in other areas.

Governments need to use discount rates in making their investment decisions—on roads, dams, levees, and environmental regulations. In its current regulations (OMB Circular A-94), the U.S. federal government instructs agencies to use a real discount rate of 7 percent per year in their base-case analysis. The rationale is basically the same as that for the descriptive approach given above: "This rate approximates the marginal pretax rate of return on an average investment in the private sector in recent years." In addition, the federal government uses an alternative approach that appears motivated by the prescriptive one. This is described as follows: "When regulation primarily and directly affects private consumption . . . , a lower discount rate is appropriate. The alternative most often used is sometimes called the 'social rate of time preference.' This simply means the rate at which 'society' discounts future consumption flows to their present value. If we take the rate that the average saver uses to discount future consumption as our measure of the social rate of time preference, then the real rate of return on long-term government debt may provide a fair approximation. Over the last thirty years, this rate has averaged around 3 percent in real terms on a pre-tax basis."[6]

Unfortunately, the OMB discussion is completely confused. The 7 percent rate is a risky rate of profit on leveraged corporate capital, while the 3 percent rate is a risk-free borrowing rate by the U.S. federal government. The difference is not the difference between investment and consumption, or pretax versus posttax. The difference is the risk premium on leveraged corporate capital (sometimes called the equity premium). Luckily, even though the analysis is wrong, the numbers are generally reasonable ones to apply.

DISCOUNTING AND GROWTH

The opportunity-cost approach assumes that the United States and other economies will continue to grow over the next century in a manner roughly similar to that of the last century. As a result, living standards are assumed to rise rapidly in the coming decades. Is this really a good assumption? Or will technological change dry up?

Of course, there is no way to answer these questions definitively. However, most research on long-term economic growth suggests that continued growth is a good bet. After all, the information and bio-technology revolutions have just begun. Moreover, other countries can grow significantly just by catching up with best practices around the world. The forces of globalization are bringing major productivity gains to low-income regions.

But remember that, if this projection is wrong, then the economic projections underlying the climate models' projections are also wrong. The models projecting rapid warming over the next century also assume rapid growth in living standards and therefore in CO_2 emissions.

A look back at Figure 13 indicates that slow economic growth would lead to a very different future compared to standard projections—both economically and climatically.

People look at the slow growth in the United States and other countries since 2007 and worry about economic stagnation. However, the slow growth was caused by inadequate demand, not by declining productivity. Moreover, poor countries have performed much better than rich countries. Per capita GDP in the developing countries of East Asia grew at 8.5 percent per year over the last decade, and the developing countries of sub-Saharan Africa grew at 2.5 percent per year during this period.[7]

This is not necessarily a picture of future wine and roses for the world. But it reminds us that the climate-change problem results from strong economic growth without adequate climate-change policies—it is not consistent with a pattern of economic stagnation and slow growth in living standards.[8]

APPLICATION TO CLIMATE-CHANGE INVESTMENTS

I now apply the discounting concepts to climate-change policy. In this area, I generally compare the cost of emissions reductions today with the value of reduced damages in the future. So suppose a $10 million investment in wind energy today would reduce CO_2 climate-change damages by $100 million in 50 years. Is this a worthwhile investment given the available alternatives?

To answer this question, I reduce the $100 million benefit by the factor $(1+r)^{-50}$ where r is the discount rate. In the specific case of the discount rate of 4 percent per year, this discount factor is $(1.04)^{-50} = 0.141$. The calculation indicates that with a 4 percent discount rate, a future benefit of $100 million in 50 years has a present value or benefit of $14.1 million. Since the present value of the benefit exceeds the $10 million cost for wind energy, it is economically justifiable.

Table 7 shows the present value at different discount rates. Note how much a high discount rate reduces the present value. At the government discount rate of 7 percent, the $100 million investment would not pass a cost-benefit test because the net value is minus $6.6 million

Table 7. Illustration of how discounting changes the present value of $100 million received 50 years from now.

Discount rate (% per year, real)	Present value of $100 million reduction in damages in 50 years
1	60,803,882
4	14,071,262
7	3,394,776
10	851,855

(present value of $3,394,776 minus $10,000,000 cost). But low discount rates such as 1 percent per year hardly reduce future values at all.

Table 7 suggests that the discount rate may be the single most important factor in determining the value of a long-term investment. Yet our intuition usually takes flight for calculations over very long time horizons. To test your intuition, ask how much Columbus would be worth had he invested $100 at a 6 percent return in 1492 and came back to collect it today. I tried to do the calculation in my head, but I greatly underestimated the number. When I used a calculator, I was surprised to learn that he would collect a sum that is greater than the entire wealth of the world.

ETHICS AND DISCOUNTING

Many people are worried about placing a small value on future climate damages. How can we care so little about the future? Are we not shortchanging future generations?

Discounting future benefits does not mean indifference to the future. Rather, it reflects two important interacting forces. We must first remember that capital is productive. Societies have a vast array of productive investments from which to choose. One investment is to slow climate change. But others will also be valuable. We need to invest in research and development on new low-carbon energy technologies; in technologies that enable low-income countries to prosper in a warmer world; in health care research to combat tropical diseases; and in education to prepare a workforce to cope with the inevitable surprises that will arise in the future. These are all productive investments whose benefits accrue to future generations.

The second factor is compound interest, which so successfully eludes our intuition. The power of compound growth turns tiny investment acorns into giant financial oaks. Here is one further example: At a 6 percent money interest rate, the $26 paid for Manhattan in 1626 would yield $152 billion today. This is approximately equal to the land value of the world's most valuable island.

As a final point, note the difference between the very low discount rate and the other discount rates in Table 7. Note that the lowest discount rate in Table 7 calculates that the value of 50-year climate investments is more than four times larger than the value calculated at the 4 percent discount rate. The difference would be even greater with 100- or 200-year payoff periods. This single point helps us understand the logic behind the favorable cost-benefit analysis of the *Stern Review* and many other activist arguments. With low discount rates, early action is so favorable primarily because future damages count for so much.

THE HEAVY BURDEN OF VERY LOW DISCOUNTING

How might we think about our obligations to our children, grandchildren, and so on further down the generational line? I will use the example of parental concerns to illustrate the point. As parents, we naturally feel intense concern for our children, worrying about their safety, well-being, health, and happiness. We also care deeply for our grandchildren, but our anxieties are mediated by the knowledge that their parents—our children—are also caring for them. Similarly, our great-grandchildren and great-great-grandchildren are more remote from our anxieties. In a sense, they have an "anxiety discount" because we cannot judge the circumstances in which they will live, and because our children and grandchildren will be there to care for them after we are gone.

Just to make this point numerically, suppose our generational anxiety discount is one-half. So anxieties have a weight of 1 for our children, $1/2$ for our grandchildren, $(1/2)^2 = 1/4$ for the next generation, and so on. The sum of the cares is $1 + 1/2 + (1/2)^2 + (1/2)^3 + \cdots = 2$. In this world, we weigh our children and all their descendants about equally in our concerns. We might use different generational discount weights, but we can deal with the problems as long as there is some discounting of the future.

Now take the example of zero discounting, which is sometimes advocated by philosophers. In this family example, suppose that we have no anxiety discounting for future generations, so we are just as anxious about our grandchildren as about our children, and about our great-great-great-grandchildren as our grandchildren. To use our numerical example, the sum of undiscounted anxieties would be infinite (i.e., equal to $1 + 1 + 1 + \cdots = \infty$). In this situation, most of us would dissolve in a sea of anxiety about all the things that could go wrong for distant generations from asteroids, wars, out-of-control robots, fat tails, smart dust, and other disasters. We would simply be unable to decide what to do. Zero discounting is like an infinitely heavy load on our shoulders. This argument sounds like a bit of flaky pseudo-mathematics, but it is exactly the nub of the deep mathematical analysis of zero discounting made by Nobel Prize–winning economist Tjalling Koopmans.[9]

So here is the short summary. We need to use a discount rate that reflects the actual market opportunities that societies face, not an abstract definition of equity taken out of the context of market realities. The logic of market discounting is not just a selfish view that the future should take care of itself. It does not hold that we should consume all our income and make no investments to protect our world or future generations. Nor does it hold that we should ignore impacts a few decades in the future. Rather, it reflects the fact that there are many high-yield investments that would improve the quality of life for future generations. The discount rate should be set so that our investable funds are devoted to the most productive uses. A portfolio of efficient investments would definitely include ones to slow global warming. But it also includes investments in other priority areas—health systems at home, cures for tropical diseases, education around the world, and basic research on all kinds of new technologies.

Investments to slow global warming should compete with other investments, and the discount rate is the measuring rod for comparing competing investments.

SUMMARY ON APPROACHES TO SLOWING CLIMATE CHANGE

Here are the important points to emphasize on the costs of slowing climate change that I have reviewed in Part III.

First, economic and engineering analyses indicate that it is feasible to keep climate change within safe limits. If the world takes strenuous and efficient efforts with full participation, it can stay with the Copenhagen target of limiting change to 2°C. Even if efforts are delayed and some countries do not participate, the world can remain within a limit of 3°C change. Economic studies suggest that the cost of limiting climate change to 2½ or 3°C would be 1 percent or less of discounted world income if policies are reasonably efficient.

Second, this optimistic outlook must be qualified by the strong warning that it requires cooperative and efficient measures. Cooperation requires that most countries participate in the efforts relatively quickly—say, within a couple of decades. If the poor and middle-income countries decline to join the effort, and particularly if the United States continues to stay on the sidelines, then the costs of meeting an ambitious temperature target will rise very sharply, and the Copenhagen targets become infeasible.

Third, efficiency requires not only near-universal participation but cost effectiveness. It requires that all sectors and countries have roughly equal marginal costs of emissions reductions. An efficient program cannot have wildly different marginal abatement costs in different sectors and countries.

This summary leaves many open questions. What targets should governments set for climate change? How do all these relate to the targets that were established at Copenhagen? What mechanisms should be used to induce people and businesses to make the decisions that are necessary to bend down the curve of CO_2 emissions? These are the questions we turn to in Part IV.

PART IV
POLICIES AND INSTITUTIONS FOR SLOWING CLIMATE CHANGE

The best throw of the dice is to throw
them away.
—*English proverb*

17 HISTORICAL PERSPECTIVES ON CLIMATE POLICY

Earlier parts have examined different aspects of the climate-change puzzle: climate science, climate-change impacts, and the costs of abatement. We concluded that the only reliable way to avoid dangerous climate change is to reduce the concentrations of CO_2 and other greenhouse gases. However, doing so is potentially costly, particularly if nations do not act in concert and use efficient control mechanisms. It is now time to put all the pieces together.

- How can governments set a sensible temperature target for climate-change policy? This involves the question of how much emissions should be reduced.
- How will policies relate to the declarations that have been signed at Kyoto, Copenhagen, Cancun, and other environmental summit meetings?
- Does effective action on climate change require that all countries coordinate their policies? What enforcement mechanism will bring in the reluctant free riders?
- How can governments ensure that people and firms take the necessary steps?
- What policies will produce the inventions, innovations, and deployment of the low-carbon technologies essential for making a transition to a stabilized climate?

Scientists and policymakers have been struggling for many years to understand the dangers of unchecked climate change. A U.S. National

Academy of Sciences report endorsed a 2°C temperature limit for the world as well as sharply declining emissions limits for the United States.[1] Similar statements have come from other scientific bodies around the world. World leaders in recent years have also agreed on the approach of limiting temperature increases.

Our task in this chapter is to look inside the covers of such reports to examine how these objectives have been derived. It might seem straightforward to set objectives for climate-change policy. We could, for example, pick a temperature target to keep the world a safe distance away from dangerous tipping points. Or we might attempt to prevent the loss of a significant number of species. Perhaps we could select a target to prevent the melting of the Greenland Ice Sheet. In fact, none of these choices provides a simple and unambiguous guide for determining climate targets.

I will discuss how temperature objectives became so central. This discussion will show that the policy of a specific numerical target rests on weak scientific support. There is no bright line for targets at $1^1/_2$°C or 2°C or 3°C or any specific temperature increase. The best target will depend upon the costs of achieving it. We should aim for a lower temperature target if it is inexpensive, but we might have to live with a higher target if costs are high or policies are ineffective.

The final conclusion of this chapter is that we cannot sensibly set climate policy targets without economics. We need to consider both costs and benefits—both where we are going and what it costs to get there.

INTERNATIONAL AGREEMENTS ON CLIMATE CHANGE

Begin with the first statement on climate-change objectives. The foundation for international climate-change deliberations is the "United Nations Framework Convention on Climate Change," ratified in 1994. This treaty states that "the ultimate objective . . . is to achieve . . . stabilization of greenhouse-gas concentrations in the atmosphere at a level that would prevent dangerous anthropogenic [i.e., human] interference with the climate system."[2] This lofty goal is too vague to be useful for policy because there is no definition or obvious way to determine what would amount to "dangerous" anthropogenic interference. But it is a good starting point.

The first and to date only binding international agreement on climate change was the Kyoto Protocol, signed in 1997. The protocol cited the objective from the Framework Convention to prevent dangerous anthropogenic interference with the climate system.[3] When it came to mandates, the protocol required Annex I countries to reduce emissions but exempted other countries. (Annex I consists of the high-income countries and those in "transition to a market economy.") As a whole, the participants agreed to reduce their CO_2 and other greenhouse-gas emissions to a level 7 percent below the 1990 total, with the agreement to take force during the period 2008–2012. There was, however, no direct link between the emissions reductions and an environmental target, and there was no mechanism to encourage participation or prevent free riding.

I discuss the difficulties of the Kyoto Protocol in later chapters. The short verdict is that it failed to reduce emissions substantially or attract countries, and it expired at the end of 2012.

Now move to the meeting in Copenhagen in December 2009. This meeting was called to establish a replacement for the Kyoto Protocol, whose agreed-upon limits expired at the end of 2012. The meeting failed its key goal of establishing binding emissions limits after 2012. However, it did adopt a target temperature limit to be used for climate policy-making. In the Copenhagen Accord, countries recognized "the scientific view that the increase in global temperature should be below 2 degrees Celsius."[4] This was the first time that any climate target had been established at a global conference.

The target of limiting climate change to 2°C above preindustrial levels has been widely accepted among governments, scientists, and environmentalists. In 2007 the European Commission considered proposals "to prevent global climate change from irrevocable consequences. This means limiting global warming to no more than 2°C above the temperature in pre-industrial times." The Group of 8 richest countries declared at the L'Aquila Summit in July 2009, "We recognize the scientific view that the increase in global average temperature above pre-industrial levels ought not to exceed 2 degrees C." These statements are representative of the aspirational targets set by many governments.[5]

THE SCIENTIFIC BASIS OF THE 2°C TARGET

The declarations quoted above refer to "the scientific view" on the appropriate target. Where does this scientific view come from? Was the 2°C target based on a strong body of evidence that suggests there is a threshold at 2°C? Would there be "dangerous" or at least serious consequences if the earth's climate system passes this threshold?

The surprising answer is that the scientific rationale for the 2°C target is not really very scientific.[6] For example, in explaining the 2°C target, the most recent report of the U.S. National Academy of Science did little more than connect the circularity of the argument: "Subsequent scientific research has sought to better understand and quantify the links among GHG emissions, atmospheric GHG concentrations, changes in global climate, and the impacts of those changes on human and environmental systems. Based on this research, many policy makers in the international community recognize limiting the increase in global mean surface temperature to 2°C above preindustrial levels as an important benchmark; this goal was embodied in the Copenhagen Accords, at a 2009 meeting of the G-8, and in other policy forums."[7] So the politicians refer to the science, and the scientists refer to the politics.

If we sift through the arguments, we find three justifications for the temperature target. The first is that the maximum experienced global temperature for the last half-million years is about 2°C more than today, and to exceed that would be potentially dangerous. A second rationale is that ecological adjustments may be difficult beyond this temperature increase. A final reason is that many dangerous thresholds will be crossed once the temperature surpasses 2°C.

We begin with the first reason, which is based on historical climate data. Figure 28 shows a reconstruction of global temperature change over the last half-million years. These estimates are derived from Antarctic ice cores.[8] The numbers have a large potential error because they measure trends over Antarctica; additionally, they are based on a regional temperature proxy rather than on actual temperature measure-

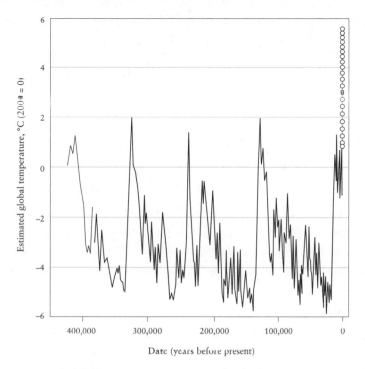

Figure 28. Estimated global temperature variations for the last 400,000 years along with model projections for the next two centuries. This figure shows a reconstruction of global temperatures using Antarctic ice core data for the last half-million years. The present temperature is normalized at 0°C. The line with dots shooting up at the far right shows a projection of future temperature increases from the DICE model in a no-controls baseline scenario. If global warming continues unchecked, future temperatures will soon surpass the historical maximum of the last half-million years.

ments.[9] The year 2000 is assigned the value of 0°C to make the present a baseline for comparison. Where the line dips below zero, it reflects cooling trends and ice ages (low global temperatures), and where it rises above zero, it indicates warm or interglacial periods (high global temperatures).

According to this reconstruction, global temperatures may have been as much as 2°C higher than today, but these warm periods lasted for relatively short intervals. As best we can tell, global temperatures have not exceeded today's temperatures by more than 2°C for the last half-million years.

We also show a sharply rising line of dots at the upper right in Figure 28; these are the temperature projections for the next two centuries from the Yale DICE model with uncontrolled climate change (these estimates are representative of other models). Our temperature projections with unchecked CO_2 emissions would push global temperature far beyond the upper end of the ice core record.

It would be necessary to go back much further in geological time and biological history to find temperatures as high as those projected for the coming centuries. While the proxy record is necessarily approximate, it appears that the earth reached maximum temperatures of 4–8°C above today if we go back 500 million years. CO_2 concentrations were as much as eight times current levels in the Jurassic period, and even higher in earlier periods. These higher levels are not surprising because today's fossil fuels are the result of decaying vegetation from these earlier periods of much higher CO_2 concentrations.

Many years ago, I suggested the paleoclimatic temperature extremes could serve as an appropriate target. The reasoning was as follows: "As a first approximation, it seems reasonable to argue that the climatic effects of carbon dioxide should be kept within the normal range of long-term climatic variation. According to most sources the range of variation between distinct climatic regimes is in the order of ±5°C, and at the present time the global climate is at the high end of this range. If there were global temperatures more than 2 or 3° above the current average temperature, this would take the climate outside of the range of observations which have been made over the last several hundred thousand years."[10]

Setting targets with reference to historical trends was adopted by the influential German Advisory Council on Global Change back in 1995. The council suggested that climate policy should be set with reference to a "tolerable temperature window." This window would look at the range of fluctuation for the earth's mean temperature in the last few hundred thousand years. It estimated that the planet today is near the upper end of the range and proposed somewhat arbitrarily extending the historical range by $1/2$°C at either end. With this window, the council calculated that the tolerable maximum increase above the 1900 temperature would be about 2°C.[11]

The second rationale for the 2°C target is based on ecological arguments. According to an advisory group to the World Meteorological Organization in 1990, a global warming of 2°C would be "an upper limit beyond which the risks of grave damage to ecosystems, and of nonlinear responses, are expected to increase rapidly." There was relatively little support for this statement at that time. Several of these ecological problems are discussed earlier in this book (see the impact analysis in Part II). They do appear to worsen with more rapid climate change, but there is no clear threshold at any specific level of warming.

The IPCC Fourth Assessment Report looked at dangerous results that are likely to occur at different temperature thresholds.[12] Here is a summary of the impacts at different thresholds:

- At 1°C: increased water shortages; increased coral bleaching; increased coastal flooding; increasing amphibian extinctions.
- At 2°C, in addition to the above: about 20–30 percent of species at increasingly high risk of extinctions; increasing burden of diseases.
- At 3°C, in addition to the above: decrease in productivity of food crops; long-term commitment to several meters of sea-level rise due to melting ice sheets; substantial burden on health systems.
- At 5°C, in addition to the above: major extinctions around the globe; major decreases in food productivity; 30 percent loss in coastal wetlands; major coastal flooding and inundation; reconfiguration of the world's coastlines; major change in ocean circulation.

These projections definitely paint a disturbing picture. But they enter in an increasingly severe manner and do not suddenly occur at a single threshold temperature.

The third rationale for limiting the temperature increase to 2°C is based on the notion that higher temperatures might trigger major instabilities and tipping points (see Chapter 5). I concluded that research on tipping points in climate change is in its infancy. But we know in many areas from biology to economics that large and potentially dangerous discontinuities can occur suddenly and unexpectedly in complex systems. Current research indicates that a number of particularly dangerous risks may be incurred over the next century or so once the earth has warmed by 3°C or more. So on this basis, the target threshold might be set at 3°C rather than 2°C. At the same time, there is a large margin of error in these estimates. Since we don't have a clear idea of where the different thresholds are crossed, it might be prudent to target a lower limit for temperature increase.

From this evidence, I conclude the following. If the costs are small, then we would surely want to keep climate change and increases in CO_2 concentrations to the bare minimum. Why risk any damages to coastlines, ecosystems, and small islands if we can avoid them at a small cost? On the other hand, if aiming for a very low temperature increase involves cutting back drastically on central human priorities such as food, shelter, education, health, and safety, then we would need to take a careful look at the trade-offs. We might be willing to run some risks on wheat yields or sea-level rise rather than spend a fortune limiting warming to the lowest feasible level. After all, we might be able to spend that money more fruitfully on improving seeds, water management, and infrastructure. Moreover, we might find inexpensive technologies for carbon removal—the carbon capture and carbon-eating trees that technologists are designing—so that we can drive down CO_2 concentrations quickly in a few decades. So short of catastrophic impacts, we should look at the price tag before committing to any specific target.

The implication is that we cannot realistically set climate-change targets without considering both the costs of slowing climate change and benefits of avoiding the damages. This is where economics comes back into the picture.

18 CLIMATE POLICY BY BALANCING COSTS AND BENEFITS

Chapter 17 concluded that a sensible target for climate-change policy would require balancing abatement costs and climate damages. This approach is often used by economists in analyzing different options and is called cost-benefit analysis. The basic idea is quite intuitive. In a world of limited resources, we should make investments that produce the greatest net social benefits—that is, ones that have the greatest margin of social benefits over social costs.[1]

People perform cost-benefit analysis all the time in their daily lives. Sometimes, the calculations are straightforward. A neighborhood gasoline station is convenient, but it charges 10 cents per gallon more than the station near the mall. Is the $2 saving from going to the mall worth the extra time and gas to get there?

A more challenging choice involves selecting a college. Suppose you have been accepted at three colleges and need to choose among them. Not only do the economic costs differ, but the schools provide different benefits. Some of the benefits are market returns, such as tuition and postgraduate salary prospects. Others are nonmarket, such as the quality of student life, the climate, and the music. For some very rich students, the costs are largely irrelevant, and they can focus solely on the benefits. Most people, however, must take into account both costs and benefits. Some of these benefits might be hard to monetize, or put in dollar terms. But, at least implicitly, we put all costs and benefits onto the scale when we choose among available options.

COST-BENEFIT ANALYSIS APPLIED TO CLIMATE CHANGE

I now apply the cost-benefit approach to evaluate different targets for slowing climate change. I do this in a simplified way that asks which temperature objective minimizes the sum of abatement investments and damages from climate change. This is the same as choosing a policy that maximizes net benefits.

I do this by putting abatement costs and climate damages together in a single graph, as shown in Figure 29 (as well as Figures 30 through 32). This important figure requires some explanation because it combines several elements.

The idea is to examine the costs, damages, and net impact for different climate objectives. I take targets of 2°C, 3°C, 4°C, and so forth. For each objective, I calculate the abatement costs required to keep the global temperature increase below the selected target; this cost curve is the downward-sloping line. I calculate the damages from climate change at that temperature target; this is the upward-sloping line. The costs and damages are added together to arrive at the total costs, shown as the U-shaped curve. Each curve is plotted as a ratio of the costs divided by total global income on an annualized basis.

Each of these curves has been discussed in earlier chapters (12 and 15), so here I am simply putting them together. For example, the costs of using emissions reductions to meet each of the temperature targets was shown in Figure 26. Similarly, the damage curve uses the estimates summarized in Figure 22. Note that these estimates do not include all the costs of tipping points or of the less easily quantified impacts, such as ocean acidification.[2] They also simplify by omitting the dynamics of adjustment. Figures 29 through 32 all use the same graph to show the damages and costs under four scenarios.

Begin with an economic analysis of efficient policies without discounting in Figure 29. This means that costs and benefits are calculated as if they occur in the same year. While this is a polar extreme of discount rates (and an approach that I definitely do not recommend for realistic analyses), it has the virtue of transparency. I further assume

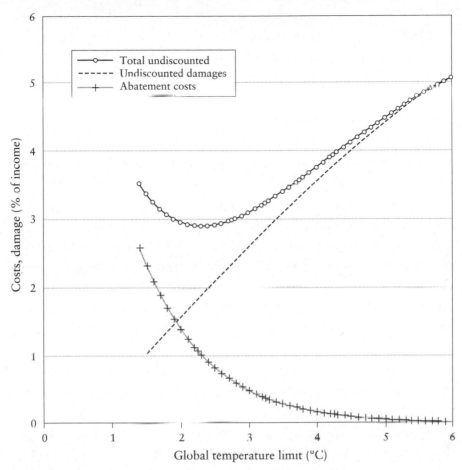

Figure 29. Total costs of different temperature targets assuming 100 percent efficiency and no discounting. This figure shows the undiscounted annual costs of emissions reductions (the downward-sloping line), damages (upward-sloping line), and total costs (U-shaped curve) for each temperature limit. All values are undiscounted. This takes the idealized case of efficient abatement and universal participation. The damage curve here assumes that there are no catastrophic damages or tipping points.

that implementation is perfectly efficient and that there is 100 percent participation, so the abatement costs are at the bare minimum.

The total undiscounted cost curve is U-shaped because it is costly at the two extremes of very low and very high temperature limits. At the upper temperature changes, the high costs are due to extreme damages with small abatement costs. At the lower temperature limits, the costs come primarily from high abatement costs, and little of the total cost is attributable to damages.

In this first optimistic scenario, the minimum cost comes at 2.3°C (in all our calculations, the temperatures are relative to 1900, which was about 0.8°C lower than today's mean global temperature). At the minimum, the total costs are 2.9 percent of total income, with damages being about twice the abatement costs. As we move outside this temperature range in either direction, the total costs increase sharply.

Here is a first and centrally important conclusion: If climate-change policies are well designed and perfectly efficient, and if current and future costs count equally, then a target of 2¼°C is justified from an economic perspective. In this optimistic case, the cost of investments to slow climate change is modest, about 1 percent of global income. So this first approach suggests that the 2°C target that has been the consensus of many governmental and scientific reports is very close to the optimal target under certain conditions.

Let's now move in the direction of greater realism by recognizing that nations are unlikely to attain perfect efficiency in their abatement actions. Some countries will not participate in the near term.

A simple case assumes that the unenthusiastic countries do not participate in an emissions reduction program. Recall that the Kyoto Protocol covered barely one-fifth of global emissions by 2012. So for our second scenario we assume that a program covers only 50 percent of global emissions over the next century. (Recall that we examined the effects of limited participation in Figure 26.) We continue to assume a zero discount rate so as to isolate the effect of low participation.

Figure 30 shows the outcome. The only difference here is that the abatement-cost curve shifts up and to the right relative to Figure 29 because of the higher costs of reaching each temperature target. Indeed, with a 50 percent participation rate, it is not possible to attain the 2°C target—the emissions of the uncontrolled regions necessarily push the globe beyond that limit. The cost-minimizing temperature target in this second case rises to 3.8°C. Note as well that the total costs rise sub-

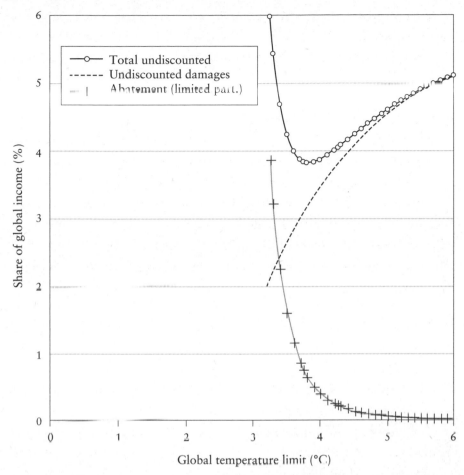

Figure 30. The temperature target rises with inefficient abatement without discounting. The second case assumes inefficient abatement because of limited participation. Again, curves are the annual costs of emissions reductions (the downward-sloping line), the undiscounted damages (upward-sloping line), and total costs (the U-shaped curve). This version assumes no catastrophic damages or tipping points and that future values are not discounted.

stantially from the idealized case in Figure 29—from 2.9 percent of income in the first case to 3.8 percent of income in the second case. Most of the costs in the limited-participation case are damages, paradoxically. Because abatement has become so expensive, it is economically beneficial to abate relatively little and live with the damages.

Economists generally recommend discounting when comparing investments today with payoffs in the future, as we saw in Chapter 16. Therefore, the third case introduces discounting into the limited participation scenario. Recall that discounting plays an important role in climate-change policies because the costs of emissions reductions occur in the near future while the damages occur in the distant future.

Economic modelers generally solve for the best temperature by calculating the entire path of discounted costs and damages, which can be accomplished with a computerized integrated assessment model. However, we can simplify by putting everything in a single year. This is done by assuming that the damages occur 50 years after the abatement. This lag reflects the inertial physics of the global climate system that causes temperature increases to occur well after CO_2 emissions.[3] In addition, I apply a discount rate of 4 percent per year to reflect the productivity of investments.[4]

Figure 31 shows the results of the calculations with discounting and with limited participation. It is thus Figure 30 plus discounting. The cost curve for emissions reduction is identical to that of Figure 30, but the damage curve has shifted downward to reflect that discounting reduces the present value of distant damages.

The discounted total cost curve indicates that the cost-minimizing temperature is 4.0°C, which is only marginally above the target with limited participation and no discounting. Therefore, the realistic case of discounting and limited participation results in a higher target temperature than the idealized case in Figure 29. But the primary reason for the higher optimal temperature target is limited participation, which raises the cost of meeting the target. If we look at the participation effect alone, it raises the target temperature from 2.3°C (see Figure 29) to 3.8°C (Figure 30). Discounting raises the target by only another 0.2°C.

The result on discounting shown in Figure 31 is surprising (indeed, it surprised me). Why does discounting change the outcome so much less than limited participation? The reason is subtle, found in the shapes of the damage and cost curves. The abatement cost curve is highly nonlinear with limited participation. For temperature limits above 4°C, the additional abatement cost of changing the limit is small, while for costs

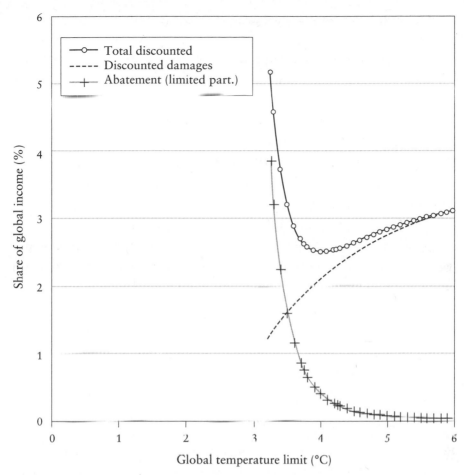

Figure 31. Total costs of different targets assuming limited participation and discounting of future incomes. This calculation shows the annualized costs when damages are discounted at 4 percent per year but still assuming inefficient abatement because of limited participation. Here, the economic calculus indicates an optimal temperature limit of 4°C.

below 4°C the additional abatement cost is high. By contrast, the damage curve around 4°C has a near-constant slope; changes in the slope of the damage curve contribute relatively little to the minimum cost calculation. Therefore, as I lowered the damage curve through discounting, the minimum point moved relatively little. We should not take the exact numbers here as the last word on the choice of an optimal target. Rather, they point to the role of nonlinearities in costs and damages as key factors in selecting targets, a point which is reinforced in the next section.

The next scenario, which is not shown graphically, is full participation and discounting. This case would be the ideal for "discount-prone optimists," who believe that we should discount future benefits but are optimistic about achieving near-universal participation of different countries. The optimal temperature target in this last case is 2.8°C. This is about ½°C higher than the no-discounting case shown in Figure 29, but lower than the zero-discounting case with low participation. This again shows how important participation is in reaching the ideal of limited climate change and low abatement costs.

What should we conclude from these analyses of costs and benefits? These diagrams are simplified but not overly so. They capture the major forces at work:

- The higher damages with higher temperatures
- The higher costs of abatement with lower temperature targets
- The increase in costs with low participation and inefficient abatement
- The lower damage costs with discounting

The full integrated assessment models contain more detail and examine the dynamics of moving from today's starting point to different targets. But the basic points of integrated assessment analysis are retained in these stylized examples.

COST-BENEFIT ANALYSIS WITH TIPPING POINTS

Most economic analyses of climate change do not include estimates of the impacts of major earth system tipping points and discontinuities. Look at the damage curves in Figures 29 to 31. Damages rise gradually as global temperatures increase on the horizontal scale. This shape derives from the economic damage studies reviewed in Chapter 17 and is the standard approach used in economic integrated assessment models. They generally exclude the tipping points because we have no reliable assessment of their likelihood, the thresholds at which they might occur, and their economic impacts.

With some scientific and economic imagination, we can include tipping points. Suppose that a careful analysis concluded that damages rise sharply when global temperature exceeds a certain threshold. Perhaps disintegration of the giant ice sheets of Greenland and West Antarctica will lead to rapid sea-level rise. Perhaps agricultural yields will drop off catastrophically. Perhaps some instability in monsoonal patterns will disrupt commerce around the world. The impacts are at present speculative, but we can show how to deal with them in our analysis.

Thresholds can be introduced as a cliff or ⌐-shaped damage function.[5] I use a stylized tipping-point damage function that turns up very sharply at 3½°C, reflecting the earlier discussion. For this example, I assume the damages from the tipping elements add up to 0.5 percent of world income at 3½°C. Above 3½°C, tipping-point damages rise rapidly. Damages are 9 percent of world income at 4°C; they shoot up to 29 percent of world income at 4¼°C; and on upward from there. These assumptions are at the outer limit of what seems plausible and have no solid basis in empirical estimates of damages, so they should be interpreted as illustrating how tipping points might affect the analysis.

Now repeat the cost-benefit analysis of Figure 31 (discounting and limited participation) but add the threshold damages. Figure 32 is thus Figure 31 plus the sharp threshold damages. The damage curve is now very steep above 3½°C. As a result, the total cost curve is now a very sharply defined V-shaped curve with a minimum cost at 3½°C. In other words, the optimal policy is to take very strenuous actions to make sure that temperature does not exceed the 3½°C threshold. Additionally, note that total costs are much larger than in earlier cases. We need to incur much higher abatement costs to avoid the high tipping-point damages, but there are still high damages even after the strenuous abatement efforts of participants.

One important lesson here is that cost-benefit analysis (or economic analysis, more generally) can definitely incorporate strange and singular

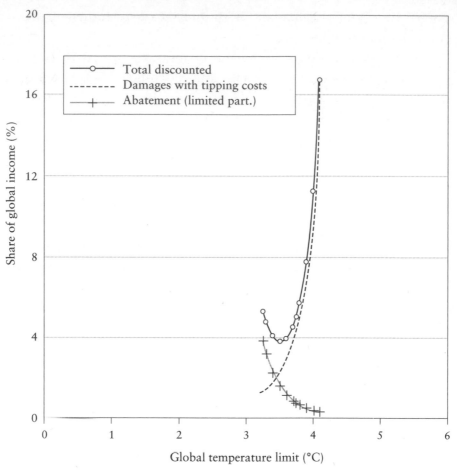

Figure 32. Climate policy with a sharp tipping point at 3½°C. The final example has a threshold or tipping point at a temperature increase of 3½°C in a situation with discounting and limited participation. This shows that the optimal temperature increase is very close to the threshold. It is constrained on the low side by abatement costs and on the high side by the sharp increase in damages.

elements such as tipping points, abrupt climate change, sharp discontinuities, and catastrophes.

The difficulty of including tipping points is not the analytical one of adding these strange elements to our models. Rather, it is an empirical problem that comes from our inability to predict the impacts of the threshold damages reliably. Take the threshold damage function shown in Figure 32 as an example. This curve makes assumptions about three parameters: the threshold temperature, the damages at that temperature, and the convexity of the curve.

However, we do not know any of these parameters even to a first approximation. The first parameter is the tipping point, here assumed to be 3½°C. We saw in the earlier chapters that the exact point at which the tipping elements enter is poorly understood. Second, we need estimates of damages at the threshold. I assume that the total damages are about 0.5 percent of income at the threshold, but that is just an assumption and has no empirical basis. A final uncertainty involves the curvature of the damage function. I assumed that it is extremely convex as represented by a function of temperature to the twentieth power, but this is just an illustration. There is no empirical evidence on the curvature and that the function should be raised to the twentieth rather than the fourth or the fiftieth power.

So at this point, the focal temperature target shown in Figure 32 is just an illustration. Different assumptions would lead to very different results—some to higher targets, some to lower targets.

COST-BENEFIT ANALYSIS IN THE CASINO

We can use the cost-benefit approach of the previous section to illustrate how uncertainties of the Climate Casino can affect climate policy. There are many possibilities, but we can easily illustrate two polar cases.

In the first example, policy follows an *expected value* principle. For this case, we take the nontipping scenarios shown in Figures 29 through 31 but assume that we do not know the magnitude of the damages. More precisely, assume that there is uncertainty about the size of the damages at each temperature increase. Suppose that at a 2°C increase, the damage is either 1 percent of income or 3 percent of income with even odds, which gives an expected value damage of 2 percent of income. (Expected value here means the statistical average; for example, the expected value of a roll of a die is 3.5 dots.) A similar uncertainty arises at each temperature level, and it might hold for costs as well. For this case, a little analysis will show that we only need to consider the average damage and cost, and the uncertainty does not affect the best decision.[6]

A second polar case involves uncertainties about where the tipping points occur, which leads to a quite different outcome of acting in a highly risk-averse manner. In the polar case, we would adopt a more risk-avoiding path in the spirit of the *precautionary principle*. This principle is used in many different areas. In 1992, the United Nations' Rio Declaration on Environment and Development stated, "Where there are threats of serious or irreversible damage, lack of full scientific certainty shall not be used as a reason for postponing cost-effective measures to prevent environmental degradation."[7] A more radical statement is that in the absence of scientific certainty, society should make policies that would prevent the worst outcome (a "minimax" strategy in game theory).

Without adopting a particular doctrine here, we can use our cost-benefit approach to determine what the optimal policy would be with uncertain tipping points. Begin with limited participation and discounting. Then assume that scientists have discovered a sharp tipping point. It might be some runaway greenhouse effect or a rapid disintegration of the giant ice sheets. If we ignore uncertainty, the cost-benefit analysis would look like Figure 32.

But suppose that further analysis reveals uncertainty about the temperature at which the tipping point enters. Perhaps there are two equally likely outcomes in which the tipping point might be either 3°C or 4°C. So we should really draw two different damage curves, one turning up sharply at 3°C and the other turning up at 4°C. We would then give each of these a weight of one-half (because that is the probability of each) and make this the new damage curve. We now have a super-strange W-shaped damage curve.

If we go through this exercise, we find that the lower temperature threshold dominates and drives our policies. We should aim for policies that are around 3°C even though the expected value of the tipping point is 3½ °C. The reason is intuitive. If there are multiple catastrophic outcomes, we want to avoid all of them if we can afford to. So we take policies to avoid the first catastrophic threshold we are likely to encounter, which in this case is the 3°C threshold.

While this example supports the minimax version of the precautionary principle, it rests on extreme assumptions. Using a minimax strategy assumes that there are only a limited number of potential cliffs in the damage function, and further that it is not ruinously expensive to avoid all of them. However, in other situations, we would not go to the minimax solution if the cliffs are just bumps, or if there are too many cliffs, or if the cost of avoiding the first cliff is so high that we must choose among the least bad alternatives.

Under these alternative conditions, the precautionary principle would not hold. Instead, the analysis would lead to an extra insurance premium to avoid the tipping element, but not paying all costs to avoid it. For example, scientists might think that there is a small probability that the Gulf Stream will reverse course when temperatures rise above 2°C, but that the costs of stopping the reversal are extremely high and the damages are not catastrophic. In this case, we might add an additional step to the damage function at 2°C, but this would not necessarily lead to an optimal temperature limit at that level.[8]

The general point here is that if the damages are uncertain, highly nonlinear, and clifflike in the Climate Casino, then our cost-benefit analysis will generally lower the optimal target to provide insurance against the worst-case outcomes.

CRITIQUES OF APPLYING COST-BENEFIT ANALYSIS TO CLIMATE CHANGE

Cost-benefit analysis is often criticized. Skeptics argue that it is inappropriate for weighing decisions on climate change. Some of its drawbacks in this context are technical: there are great uncertainties, and sometimes the probabilities of different events cannot even be determined; the costs and benefits may accrue to different people or generations; and there are difficulties in comparing costs today with benefits in the distant future.

However, climate change also raises important philosophical issues. For example, in making choices about health impacts, are we ethically justified in putting a price on human health and life? Perhaps the greatest difficulty is that climate-change impacts involve natural systems such as ecosystems and biodiversity, and our tools are currently inadequate for valuing these changes.

How do economists respond to these questions? Most would agree that doing a sound cost-benefit analysis for climate-change policy is a daunting task. But it is necessary if people are to make reasoned choices about policies. We might not be able to make definitive estimates about the impacts of higher temperatures on different sectors, but by a process of careful study and analysis, we can get order-of-magnitude estimates and use them in our analyses. Care must be taken to include all impacts—market, nonmarket, environmental, and ecosystem impacts. Moreover, in those areas where the estimates are particularly sparse, such as ecosystem valuation, economists and natural scientists need to cooperate to produce better estimates. However, if we are to act responsibly with people's money and not make foolish investments, we need to compare the price tag with the things we are buying.

Consider the following thought experiment. Suppose that you have a trusted team of experts who provide you cost estimates for attaining different climate objectives. Suppose the estimates look like those in Figures 29 to 32. What target would you pick?

You would need to study the impact analysis and think about tipping points. Perhaps you would modify the damage functions to add an insurance premium for damages to ecosystems and species, which are often omitted from damages.

You would also need to make a realistic estimate of country participation. If you really thought that only half of all countries would participate, then aiming for 2°C is like hoping you can take Amtrak to the moon. On the other hand, if you thought you could induce all countries to get on board very quickly, with no free riding, and that the policy tools you could realistically deploy are efficient ones, then you might well aim for the Copenhagen target.

Based on the analysis in the last two chapters, what should we conclude about setting objectives for climate policy? To begin with, it is important to have coherent and valuable objectives. Some scientists are convinced that a temperature target is the right goal. While that argument is not beyond debate, limiting climate change is definitely a worthy goal. By contrast, emissions limits or concentration objectives are instrumental objectives, not ultimate goals.

Yet, while simple temperature targets make an attractive approach, they are insufficient in a world of competing goals. People want to be assured that these targets are not simply the result of overly concerned environmentalists who are intent on saving their ecosystems at the expense of humans. Nations will want to make sure that they are not subsidizing undeserving countries or feeding corrupt dictators whose green policies are really an excuse for skimming greenbacks.

If large sums are involved, people want to get their money's worth. And this means that people want to compare costs and benefits. The benefits need not be completely monetized, but it will not be sufficient to say "Ecosystems are priceless" or "We must pay any cost to save the polar bears." That is why costs and benefits must be put on the balance when weighing the options on global warming. Depending upon how optimistic you are about participation and your view on discounting, you can probably use the four figures in this chapter as a guide for picking a target for climate-change policy.

19 THE CENTRAL ROLE OF CARBON PRICES

Climate-change policy is a tale of two sciences. The natural sciences have done an admirable job of describing the geophysical aspects of climate change. The science behind global warming is well established. While the timing and regional effects of the changes are not known with certainty, natural scientists have persuasively shown that un-checked CO_2 emissions will have dangerous consequences.

But understanding the natural science of climate change is only the first step. Designing an effective strategy to control climate change will require the social sciences—the disciplines that study how nations can harness their economic and political systems to achieve their climate goals effectively. These questions are distinct from those addressed by the natural sciences. They involve not only estimating the economic impacts of climate change along with the costs of slowing climate change, as we have seen, but also designing policy tools that society can deploy to attain the desired emissions reductions.

I discuss these questions in the chapters that follow. The present chapter discusses the central role of pricing the CO_2 externality, or the design of "carbon prices." Chapter 20 discusses how governments actually go about setting carbon prices. And Chapter 21 examines how the goals of climate policy can be effectively and efficiently implemented among the community of nations. We confront here the politically charged issues of institutional design for a low-carbon world.

WHAT ARE CARBON PRICES?

Something crucial is missing from our survey. We have concluded that reducing concentrations of CO_2 and other greenhouse gases is the only reliable way to slow the freight train of global warming. We saw how much it costs to reduce emissions, and why all countries must participate if we are to keep the costs down and why it is important to shift power generation from coal to natural gas or low-carbon sources, to develop energy-efficient equipment, and to invent new low-carbon technologies. People who are serious about slowing climate change would probably agree with all these steps.

But this leaves individual choices out of the equation. What will persuade you and me and everyone else to undertake the necessary actions? How can we be induced to buy fuel-efficient cars? To vacation close to home rather than flying around the world? What incentives will lead firms to redesign their operations in ways that reduce carbon emissions while keeping their stockholders happy by maximizing profits? What will convince scientists and engineers and venture capitalists that a promising area for their talents is investing in new low-carbon processes and products?

These questions are likely to make your head spin. Fortunately, there is a simple answer. The history of economic interventions in the energy sector and elsewhere shows that the best approach is to use market mechanisms. And the single most important market mechanism that is missing today is a high price on CO_2 emissions, or what is called "carbon prices."

Carbon prices? On first hearing the idea of placing a price on carbon, and a high price at that, many people wonder whether this is some hare-brained fantasy. Actually, the idea is firmly based in economic theory and history. The main insight is that people must have economic incentives to change their activities in ways that lower emissions of CO_2 and other greenhouse gases. The best way to accomplish this is by putting a price on CO_2 emissions. This will in turn raise the relative prices of carbon-intensive goods and lower the relative prices of carbon-free goods, thereby bending down the trend of CO_2 emissions.

Let's begin with the economic analysis. Recall that carbon emissions are economic externalities—activities in which people consume things but do not pay the full social costs. When I turn on my air conditioner, I pay for the electricity. But I do not pay for the damage done by the CO_2 emissions because the price of CO_2 emissions in the United States is zero. If you look back at the list of carbon-producing household activities in Table 6, you will see that none of these includes a CO_2 price that reflects the social costs.

How can we fix this omission? This is one of the few areas where the economic answer is very simple. Governments must ensure that people do pay the full costs of their emissions. Everyone, everywhere, and for the indefinite future must face prices that reflect the social costs of their activities.

Putting this differently, putting a price on carbon represents a societal decision about the priority of reducing CO_2 emissions. The signal is similar to the one given by a high price of land. When land in central Manhattan sells for an astronomical price, that high price indicates that this is not an economical place for a golf course. A price tag on carbon emissions will provide a signal that emissions are harmful and should be reduced.

So much for the economic theory. What is a carbon price in practice? It is the price attached to the burning of fossil fuels (and similar activities). In other words, whenever a firm or person burns fossil fuels, and the CO_2 enters the atmosphere, the firm or person must pay an additional price that is proportional to the quantity of CO_2 emitted. In the examples that follow, I generally use a carbon price of $25 per metric ton of CO_2 so that readers can become familiar with this price. I suggest later that this is a reasonable target to aim for in near-term policies.

Electricity generation provides an example for understanding the role of carbon pricing. Consider a household that consumes 10,000 kilowatt hours (kWh) of electricity each year at the current price of 10 cents per kWh, or $1,000 per year. If half the electricity is generated from coal and half from natural gas, the generation would produce 8 tons of CO_2 emissions. If the carbon price were $25 per ton of CO_2, this would increase the annual cost of electricity generation by $200 and raise household electricity expenditures by 20 percent.

RAISING PRICES THROUGH TRADABLE PERMITS OR TAXES

How do governments actually put a price on CO_2 emissions? I discuss this at length in Chapter 20, but it should be introduced very early to highlight the idea. There are two ways to raise the price of carbon.

- The easiest way is simply to tax CO_2 emissions: a "carbon tax." It would require firms and people to pay a tax on their emissions much the same way as they do when buying gasoline.
- A second and more indirect method requires firms to have permits to emit CO_2, and to allow them to be bought and sold. This is called "cap and trade" because the quantity of emissions is capped, but the rights to emit can be traded for a price among firms.

While these two mechanisms sound different, they both accomplish the same economic goal of raising carbon prices. I discuss their similarities and differences in Chapter 20, but it is central to understand that these are the two ways, and in reality the only two ways, to put a market price on the externality of greenhouse-gas emissions.

There is one technical but important detail: Who actually pays the price? You might naturally say, "Look, I didn't burn the coal. In fact, I don't even know how or where my electricity is made. How can anyone calculate the right price?"

This is an astute observation. An important administrative issue in designing a carbon pricing system is deciding who writes the check. Consider the oil flowing out of the well, into the pipeline, to the refinery, then perhaps on a truck to the gas station, into the storage tank, through the gas pump, and then into your car. Who would pay for the CO_2 emissions? In principle, anyone along the chain of production might pay. However, the most economical system would probably have refineries pay the price rather than gas stations or consumers. For coal, since there are a few large users, perhaps power plants would write the check. Imports and exports would need to be included in the system as well.

Political scientists point out that the public acceptability of a price-raising regulation or tax may be affected by the point in the production chain at which it is levied. "The only good tax is an invisible tax," as the adage goes. For example, by law one-half of Social Security taxes are "paid" by firms, and most people don't count them as part of their own tax burden. Labor economists firmly believe that both parts of the Social Security taxes come out of wages (or, in technical language, are shifted to wages). Given these behavioral perceptions, or misperceptions, it might be advisable to place regulations or carbon taxes upstream from consumers so that they are less prominent and meet less public opposition.

From an economic point of view, however, it does not make any difference whether the producer, the refiner, or the gas station pays. The carbon price will be passed on to the consumer in the form of higher prices, and the impact on the price of gasoline or other goods does not depend upon who writes the check.

THE ECONOMIC FUNCTIONS OF PUTTING A PRICE ON CARBON EMISSIONS

Putting a price on the use of carbon serves the primary purpose of providing strong incentives to reduce carbon emissions. It does this through three mechanisms: by affecting consumers, producers, and innovators.

First, a carbon price will provide signals to consumers about what goods and services have high carbon content and should therefore be used more sparingly. Consumers will find that air travel becomes relatively more expensive than visiting local sights or taking the train, which will reduce air travel and therefore the emissions from air travel.

Second, it will provide signals to producers about which inputs use more carbon and which use less or none. It thereby induces firms to move to low-carbon technologies so as to lower their costs and increase their profits. One of the most important signals will come in electric power generation. The costs of generating electricity from coal will rise sharply; costs from natural gas will rise somewhat less; and those from nuclear power and renewable sources like wind will rise not at all. Of all the adjustments, reducing CO_2 emissions from coal is probably the most important step for the United States.

A high carbon price will get the attention of electricity generators. Indeed, many companies already build the possibility of high carbon prices into their long-term plans, even though the current price in the United States is zero. For example, a survey of twenty-one electric utilities in 2012 in the United States found that sixteen had built a positive CO_2 price into their planning, with the average price for 2020 being slightly below $25 per ton of CO_2.[1]

A third and more subtle effect is that carbon prices will give market incentives for inventors and innovators to develop and introduce low-carbon products and processes to replace current technologies. Suppose you are the executive in charge of research and development (R&D) at a large company like GE, which had an R&D budget of $5 billion in 2012. You make equipment for generating electricity from different sources—coal, nuclear energy, and wind. Most generating facilities will last for decades. If carbon prices are going to be zero or very low, then coal-burning plants will continue to be an important source of profits, and you will continue to do substantial R&D for coal technologies.

On the other hand, if you expect carbon prices to rise sharply, few conventional coal stations will be built, and zero-carbon technologies like wind and nuclear power will be the areas on which to place your bets. In other areas where consumer or producer demand is sensitive to carbon prices—air travel, consumer appliances, and automobiles being good examples—companies with big R&D budgets will be sensitive to the signals given by carbon prices and redirect their investments accordingly. I discuss the economics of innovation at length in Chapter 23.

CARBON PRICING AND ENVIRONMENTAL ETHICS

People often wonder why economists recommend such a complicated approach as carbon pricing. Why not just tell people to stop using so much CO_2, or shut down coal production? Perhaps we should all have bumper stickers: "Just say no to carbon."

I return to regulatory and other alternatives below. But the interesting point is that carbon pricing actually simplifies life. Decisions about emissions reductions are complicated, diverse, and pervasive. One of the beautiful aspects of using carbon prices rather than other mechanisms is that it simplifies the complex carbon-related decisions. It does this by reducing the amount of information that is required to undertake the different tasks.

Suppose you take environmental ethics seriously. You desire to reduce your carbon footprint—the amount of carbon emissions your activities produce. How might you go about adapting your daily life to include carbon-related decisions?

Here is a story that describes the way carbon prices simplify decisions. Perhaps you and your brother live in Denver and want to visit your father in Albuquerque. Should you drive or fly? You consult an online carbon calculator and find that flying produces 350 kilograms of CO_2 while driving your Toyota produces 400 kilograms. So flying is better from a pure carbon footprint viewpoint.

But then you remember that you have to get to and from the airport, so you need to calculate the carbon emissions for those activities. You also wonder whether the calculator takes into account whether the flight is full or not. You further consider whether these calculators include only the carbon in the gasoline and jet fuel but have excluded the CO_2 released in the production of the tires, aluminum, steel, cushions, and everything else that goes into making the air travel possible, not to mention the carbon costs of flying the crew in from Los Angeles.

Maybe you should just forget the trip and stay home. You would save carbon, but you would then have an unhappy father to deal with. You might well decide that all these carbon calculations are too complicated and try to find some other way to be a responsible citizen of the world.[2]

This is where the advantages of a carbon price as an aid to decision making become so clear. If a price were charged on all carbon emissions, the costs would already be included in the price of the gasoline for the car trip, in the ticket and taxi fares for the air travel, and in the costs of all the alternative activities. Once the carbon price is universally applied, the market price of all activities using carbon would rise by the carbon price times the carbon content of fuels they used. We would not know how much of the price is due to the carbon content, but we would not need to care. We could make our decisions confident that we are paying for the social cost of the carbon we use.

To summarize: You can see why economists emphasize the many advantages of using carbon prices to reduce carbon emissions. They provide strong incentives to reduce emissions; they do so in an even-handed way; they affect all aspects of the economy from production to innovation; and they economize on the information that people need to make efficient decisions.

SETTING THE RIGHT CARBON PRICE

Economics teaches us that unregulated markets will not put the correct price on externalities like CO_2—because they are external to the marketplace. So how should the price be determined? Economists have used two approaches to estimating the appropriate carbon price. The first is to estimate the damages from climate change with a concept called the "social cost of carbon." The second is to estimate the required price of carbon that would attain different environmental objectives using integrated assessment models.

Begin with the social cost of carbon. This concept represents the economic damage caused by an additional ton of CO_2 emissions (or, more succinctly, carbon) or its equivalent.[3] Estimates of the social cost of carbon are a critical ingredient in climate-change policy. They provide policymakers a target to aim for in setting a carbon tax, or in setting the level of emissions reductions in a cap-and-trade system, or in international negotiations on minimum carbon prices.

Another application is in rule making where countries do not have comprehensive policies covering all greenhouse gases. In this context, regulators might use the social cost of carbon in a calculation of social costs and benefits of policies involving energy or climate-affecting decisions. For example, the U.S. government has used the social cost of carbon in setting regulations or subsidies for installation of low-carbon energy sources, for efficiency standards in buildings, for fuel efficiency standards for motor vehicles (discussed shortly), and for setting emissions standards for new power plants.

There are currently many estimates of the social cost of carbon. A U.S. government report provided a best estimate of about $25 per ton of CO_2 for 2015.[4] This is consistent with numbers that come from models, as I show next, so I use this as the target price in the discussion that follows.

A second approach used to determine an appropriate carbon price is to employ integrated assessment models. For example, we might estimate what trajectory of CO_2 prices would be required to attain a given temperature objective. Figure 33 shows an example, where for these calculations I have chosen a temperature limit of 2½°C.[5] This target is consistent with Chapter 18's discussion of cost-benefit analysis.

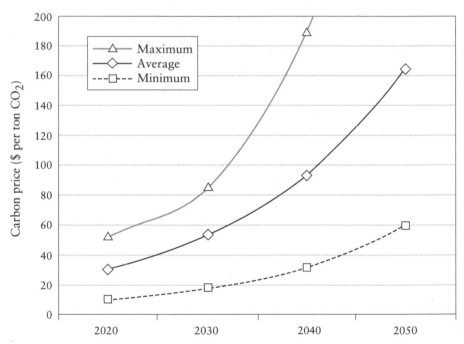

Figure 33. Illustrative carbon prices needed for a 2½°C temperature limit. This figure shows target price paths for CO_2 that would lead to a maximum temperature rise of around 2½°C. These results are from a group of thirteen models and show the central tendency as well as maximum and minimum required carbon prices across models. The path assumes full participation and efficient policies.

Figure 33 shows the trajectory of carbon prices over the next half century under the idealized situation of universal participation and efficient implementation.[6] It would start at about $25 per ton in 2015. The required carbon price rises rapidly over time, at around 5 percent per year in real or inflation-corrected terms, reaching $53 per ton of CO_2 in 2030 and $93 per ton of CO_2 in 2040. The sharp price rise is needed to choke off the rapid projected growth in CO_2 emissions that is assumed in most economic models.

The figure also shows the range of estimates of different models. You can see the substantial uncertainty across different models about just what carbon price would be required to contain global warming at the 2½°C limit. The large range reflects intrinsic uncertainties about future economic growth, energy technologies, and climate models.

IMPACT OF CARBON PRICES ON ENERGY PRICES

To understand how a carbon tax would affect daily life, Table 8 shows the impact of a $25 per ton carbon price on representative energy products at the wholesale level.[7] The increases are determined by the CO_2 content per dollar of cost. Coal is the most heavily affected, while petroleum shows the smallest impact because it has high value per unit of CO_2 emissions.

Table 8. Impact of a $25 per ton carbon tax on wholesale energy prices. This table shows the impact on the wholesale prices of major energy products. The effect on coal will be substantial because it is so carbon intensive. Petroleum has the smallest increase because it has high value per unit of CO_2 emissions.

Item	Unit	Without carbon price	With carbon price	Change (%)
Prices (2005 $):				
Petroleum	$ per million btu	17.2	19.1	11
Coal	$ per million btu	1.8	4.1	134
Natural gas	$ per million btu	4.5	5.8	30
Electricity (industrial)	cents per kWh	6.9	9.0	31

What is the impact of carbon prices on overall expenditures of the statistically average American family? Table 9 shows some examples for a carbon price of $25 per ton.[8] The prices of carbon-intensive goods rise sharply, while those of carbon-light goods rise much less. The largest increase would come in electricity prices, because so much electricity generation in the United States comes from CO_2-intensive coal. A typical year's motor fuels would cost 8 percent more. The percentage increase for an airline ticket would be slightly less. The prices of phone or banking services would rise hardly at all because they use so little CO_2. The cost of all consumption for the average U.S. household, from abacuses to zwieback, would rise slightly less than 1 percent.

Table 9 shows one of the important ways that putting a price on emissions can slow global warming. The prices of carbon-intensive goods go up relative to those of low-carbon goods. This will lead to behavioral responses in which consumers will buy more of the low-carbon and less of the high-carbon items. The higher the carbon price, the more CO_2 emissions will be reduced. This "law of downward-sloping demand"—meaning that quantity demanded goes down as price goes up—is one of the universally confirmed findings in all of economics.

Table 9. Impacts of a $25 per ton CO_2 price.

Example	Tons of CO_2	Increase in spending due to $25 CO_2 price	Increase in spending (%)
Year's electricity use	9.34	$233.40	19.45
Year's driving	4.68	$116.90	7.79
Economy class transcontinental flight	0.67	$16.80	5.61
One year's household communication services	0.01	$0.36	0.04
One year's household financial services	0.02	$0.41	0.04
One year's household consumption	29.48	$737.00	0.92

CARBON TAXES AND THE FISCAL PICTURE

Table 10 shows the aggregates for the U.S. economy based on the prices used in Figure 33. For these calculations, I assume that CO_2 prices are raised by carbon taxes (but it could also be done by auctioning emissions allowances). The carbon tax analyzed here would start at $25 per ton of CO_2 in 2015, assuming that the economy has attained full employment at that time. It would raise substantial revenues, on the order of 1 percent of GDP. Over the period to 2030, the tax would cause U.S. emissions to stabilize at about the 2000 level. Models indicate that this path of carbon prices, if met with parallel policies in all other countries, would limit the global temperature increase to around 2½°C.

We generally think of energy and climate policy in isolation from overall economic policy, but there is an important fiscal interaction. Most major countries need to curb growing government debts, and a carbon tax can make a major contribution to that effort.

I will illustrate this point for the United States. The Congressional Budget Office in 2012 estimated that the federal debt–GDP ratio will rise from 36 percent in 2007 to 76 percent of GDP in 2013.[9] The debt ratio is increasing rapidly as a result of the collapse of revenues in the current extended downturn, as well as the economic stimulus programs. The long-term outlook is for a rapidly rising debt ratio unless major fiscal corrections are taken.

Table 10. Economic impacts of proposed carbon tax, United States, 2010–2030.

Year	Tax rate (2005 $/ton CO_2)	Emissions (billion tons CO_2)	Revenues (2005 billion $)	Revenues (% of GDP)
2010	0	6.3	0	0.00
2015	25	5.9	147	0.96
2020	30	5.5	168	0.97
2025	42	5.4	225	1.14
2030	53	5.2	277	1.25

A carbon tax is the closest thing to an ideal tax that can be imagined. It is the only tax under consideration that will increase economic efficiency because it reduces the output of an undesirable activity (emitting CO_2). It goes a long way toward implementing the U.S. goals for climate-change policy and meeting international obligations that the United States has undertaken. It will have substantial public health benefits because it will reduce harmful emissions, particularly those associated with burning coal. A carbon tax can buttress or replace many inefficient regulatory initiatives and will thereby provide yet further improvements in economic efficiency.

As Table 10 shows, the recommended carbon tax would yield $168 billion of revenues in 2020, equal to about 1 percent of GDP. Because the tax rate would rise sharply, the revenues would also increase substantially over time. Implementing a carbon tax can be a compromise for fiscal conservatives and environmental activists as a way to reduce growing fiscal deficits, slow global warming, and do both of these in a market-friendly manner.

20 CLIMATE-CHANGE POLICIES AT THE NATIONAL LEVEL

Economics brings two central lessons to policies on global warming. The first, discussed in Chapter 19, is that people and firms must face economic incentives to tilt their behavior toward low-carbon activities. Activities that lead to emissions of CO_2 and other greenhouse gases (GHGs) must become more expensive, which primarily requires raising the prices of carbon-based fuels. This is an inconvenient economic truth because people resist paying more for energy.

The second economic truth is that markets alone will not solve this problem. There is no genuine "free-market solution" to global warming. We need new national and international institutions to coordinate and guide decisions about global warming policies. These mechanisms can use the market, but they must be legislated and enforced by governments. This second truth is the focus of this and the following chapter.

THE TWO MECHANISMS FOR CARBON PRICING

Governments can limit emissions and raise the price of CO_2 and other GHGs through two mechanisms: cap-and-trade systems and carbon taxes. The present chapter discusses these systems and their relative merits.

The first approach raises the price of CO_2 emissions by making them scarce and is called "cap and trade." It begins with legislation in which a country caps or limits its CO_2 and other GHG emissions. The country then issues a limited number of allowances that convey the right to

CERTIFICATE 1031144AH23.
EMISSIONS ALLOWANCE FOR THE UNITED STATES OF PACIFICA

1000 tons of carbon dioxide equivalent

This certificate provides that the registered owner is allowed to emit a designated quantity of emissions of carbon dioxide into the atmosphere. The rules governing the measurement of emissions are governed by USP Reg. 120.12.12 in the USP Register of August 18, 2013. Use and transfer of the allowances will be governed by the prevailing regulations.

The registered owner is Hypo Utility Co. incorporated in the State of Marylondia USP.

These allowances are fully transferable for emissions within the territory of the USP upon registration with the Allowance Management System of the Pacifica Environmental Protection Agency.

Emissions under this certificate are available beginning on January 15, 2015, and may be used until December 31, 2019.

Dr. E. N. Viron — *January 20, 2014*
Signature — ***Date***

Figure 34. Whimsical certificate for emissions allowance for the United States of Pacifica.

emit a given quantity of CO_2 or other GHG. This kind of regulation has been used by governments around the world to reduce pollution.

Just for fun, Figure 34 shows a hypothetical allowance certificate. In the modern era, certificates are electronic and contain complex regulatory requirements, but this gives the basic idea that emissions allowances are ownership rights that can be bought and sold like cars and houses.

The next stage is a brilliant innovation by environmental economists: the "trade" in cap and trade. In addition to having emissions allowances, firms can buy and sell the allowances. Perhaps firm A owns 1,000 tons of allowances and decides to shut down an obsolete power plant; perhaps firm B desires to open a profitable new computer server farm that will emit 1,000 tons of CO_2. Firm A can sell its valuable allowances to firm B.

How would they set the emissions price? There might be an exchange where allowances are bought and sold; or dealers might link up buyers and sellers. Firm A would look for the highest bids, and firm B would seek the lowest offers. They might settle on a price of $25 per ton.

The advantage of establishing a market in allowances is to ensure that emissions are used in the most productive manner. In our example, firm A might have stayed in business if it couldn't sell the allowance, but the value might be only $2 per ton. Similarly, purchasing firm B might find that the allowances are actually contributing $202 of net value in the new product. Hence, by allowing the trade, economic welfare is improved by $200 per ton.

These ideas are not just some wild theoretical scheme. They have been used in a wide variety of contexts over the last half century. Permits are auctioned for the rights to drill for oil, to harvest trees, and to use the electromagnetic spectrum. In the environmental area, the most successful example is the use of allowances to limit the emissions of sulfur dioxide (SO_2) since 1990. This program proved very successful in reducing overall emissions and did so much less expensively than many analysts had predicted. The U.S. SO_2 program was so successful that it was used as the basis for the Kyoto Protocol's GHG emissions plan and then for the European Union's CO_2 Emissions Trading Scheme.

In the context of CO_2 emissions, the cap-and-trade plan squeezes the most economic value out of the limited emissions. It accomplishes this through the mechanism of prices and markets, not through governmental micromanaging of businesses. Because emissions are capped below the unregulated or free-market level, they are a scarce resource, like land or oil. The market price of CO_2 allowances rises high enough to reduce emissions to the quantitative limit. Just as a high corn price squeezes corn demand to fit into the available supply, the carbon price induces producers and consumers to reduce their use of carbon-emitting goods to fit within the capped quantity. A binding cap-and-trade regime would indirectly lead to a positive rather than zero price for carbon.

The cap-and-trade idea for CO_2 was implemented by the European Union through its Emissions Trading Scheme. Figure 35 shows the price of CO_2 emissions in the scheme over the period 2006–2012.[1] The

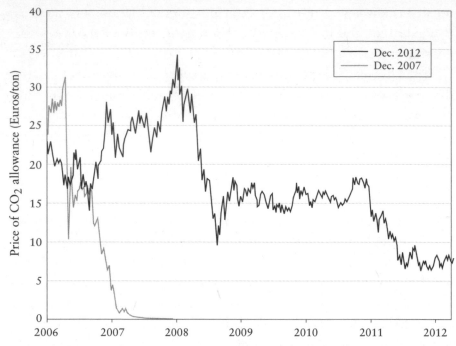

Figure 35. The market price of CO_2 under the European Trading Scheme. This figure shows the history of CO_2 prices under the EU Emissions Trading Scheme from 2006 to 2012. The price declined sharply during the financial crisis and at the end of 2012, when the future of global climate-change agreements was in doubt. Note: The vertical scale uses metric tons rather than American tons (2,205 versus 2,000 pounds). The euro averaged \$1.36/€ during this period.

number of allowances from the first phase was greater than actual emissions, and the price fell to zero in 2007. For the second phase, prices started around 20 euros (\$27) per ton, but fell by 2012 to around 8 euros (\$11) per ton.

In the second approach to raising the carbon price, known as carbon taxation, governments directly tax CO_2 emissions. The basic idea is simple. When a firm burns fossil fuels, the combustion leads to a certain quantity of CO_2 entering the atmosphere. The tax would be levied on the CO_2 content of each fuel. The definitional issues are the same for carbon taxes and emissions caps. The only difference is that one taxes a quantity while the other limits the quantity. The definitions of the quantities are the same.[2]

Let's take an example. Suppose a company generates electricity using coal. A large plant might burn around 5 million tons of coal each year. At a tax of $25 per ton of CO_2, the plant would pay almost $400 million per year in carbon taxes. This would be the single most important component of costs and would definitely get the attention of management.

A universal carbon tax would be similar to this example but would apply to all sources of CO_2 (and other GHGs as well). Coal, oil, and petroleum are the major sources of CO_2, but other areas such as cement production and deforestation would also come under a universal tax. As in any tax system, there are many lawyerly details.

Carbon taxes (or more frequently their relatives such as energy taxes) featured in the early discussions of climate-change policy. They were shunted aside in the late 1990s because the political negotiators at international meetings believed that quantitative restrictions were more familiar and more likely to be acceptable to the public and national governments. Since 1997, as a consequence, quantitative restrictions such as cap and trade along with regulations have been the norm in international negotiations.

However, carbon taxes have been used by a few countries to raise revenues. Some western European countries have carbon taxes or mixed energy-carbon taxes on the books. India levied a $1 per ton carbon tax on coal, and China is considering such a tax. Similar proposals have been considered in Korea, Australia, New Zealand, Canada, and the European Union. Up to 2012, no country has introduced a high carbon tax that is applied to the entire economy.

CARBON TAXES AND CAP AND TRADE: THE CENTRAL EQUIVALENCY

How do the two regimes—cap and trade and carbon taxation—compare? Most people will be surprised to learn that they are fundamentally the same. That is, in an idealized situation, they have the same effects on emissions reductions, on carbon prices, on consumers, and on economic efficiency. People may argue strenuously about which is better, but each of them has the effect of reducing CO_2 emissions by giving strong incentives to consumers and firms to reduce emissions by raising the price of carbon emissions.

The similarity can be seen with the following example. Assume that uncontrolled emissions for the United States are 5 billion tons of CO_2 per year. Then the United States passes cap-and-trade legislation that limits emissions to 4 billion tons. This is done by auctioning off emissions allowances for 4 billion tons. (These are the real-world equivalent of the little cartoon in Figure 34.) Allowances are then traded so that the reductions are undertaken in the most economical manner. Because it is costly to reduce emissions, the price of an allowance would rise to the cost of reducing the last ton. Assume that the cost of the last ton removed is $25 per ton of CO_2. The price of allowances would then rise to $25 per ton because that is the price at which emitters are indifferent between incurring the cost of abatement and buying an allowance. From the point of view of a firm doing business, it would cost $25 to buy the right to emit a ton of CO_2.

Now assume instead that the United States imposed a tax of $25 per ton of CO_2. At that tax rate, firms would find it economical to reduce emissions by 1 billion tons. From the ground view of individual firms, in both cases the price of adding a ton of CO_2 to the atmosphere is $25 per ton, so firms will behave identically in both situations. In one case, they pay a tax of $25 to emit a ton; in the other case, they buy a permit for $25 a ton. The quantity of emissions and the price of CO_2 are exactly the same for the cap-and-trade regime as for the carbon tax. The only difference is that in the one case government employs a market-based "quantity" regulation, while in the other case government uses a "price" regulation in the form of taxes.

In the end, firms pay $100 billion (4 billion tons × $25 per ton) to emit the 4 billion tons of CO_2. In one case it is $100 billion of taxes; in the other case, it is $100 billion for allowances. The government gets $100 billion of revenues in either case. Cap and trade operates just like a tax on pollution.

CARBON TAXES AND CAP AND TRADE: THE IMPORTANT DIFFERENCES

Once we move from an idealized analysis to a realistic situation, significant differences emerge. Generally, economists lean toward carbon taxation as preferable, while negotiators and environmental specialists lean toward the cap-and-trade approach. The following are some of the major considerations.[3]

Carbon tax advocates point out that tax systems are mature and universal institutions of policy. Every country uses taxes. Countries have administrative tax systems, tax collectors, tax lawyers, and tax courts. Countries need revenues, and indeed many countries face large fiscal deficits today. By contrast, there is limited experience with cap-and-trade systems in most countries and virtually no international experience.

A related point is that quantitative limits produce severe volatility in the market price of carbon under an emissions-targeting approach, which can be seen in Figure 35 for the European system. Note how wildly prices fluctuated in 2008, declining by almost 75 percent in a few months. The volatility arises because both supply and demand for permits are insensitive to the permit price. The high level of volatility is economically costly and sends inconsistent signals to private sector decision makers. Clearly, a carbon tax would provide consistent price signals and would not vary so widely from year to year, or even day to day.

One important difference between standard cap-and-trade systems and taxes concerns who pays and who gets the revenues. Historically, the permits or allowances under cap-and-trade plans were allocated free of charge to firms who were regulated. For example, under the U.S. SO_2 program of 1990, virtually all the emissions permits were allocated for free to electric utilities and firms who were historically large emitters and were to be regulated. Allowances were valuable assets, and the free allocation helped reduce the political opposition to the plan by the regulated firms. Similarly, in the early stages of the European CO_2 trading plan, permits were allocated to firms. Economists find the free allocation of emissions allowances objectionable because it wastes fiscal resources and is not necessary to offset the impacts of the emissions cap on the profits of firms.

Under a carbon tax, the valuable revenues go to the government to be used for recycling to consumers or to buy important collective goods. Some current cap-and-trade proposals require the government to auction the allowances. With auctions, the two systems have equivalent fiscal impacts.

Carbon taxes have two major disadvantages relative to cap-and-trade systems. The first is that the quantity of emissions is uncertain under a carbon tax. If we set a universal carbon tax of $25 per ton, we would not know the actual quantity of emissions. If we have a definite idea of a dangerous level of emissions, this would be a major disadvantage of carbon taxes. So here is a genuine difference. The price of carbon would fluctuate under a cap-and-trade regime while the quantity of CO_2 emitted would remain constant. Under a carbon tax, the quantity emitted would fluctuate while the price would be stable. This suggests that, unless it can be periodically changed, a carbon tax cannot automatically ensure that the globe remains on the safe side of "dangerous anthropogenic interferences" with the climate system.

A further point, emphasized by its advocates, is that cap-and-trade systems have greater political appeal and greater durability. One reason is that political opposition from industry groups who would be disadvantaged by tighter regulation are bought off by allocation of free allowances. Indeed, the value of the free allowances appears to be much greater than the lost profits from the tighter regulations. This source of political glue from cap and trade would disappear if governments moved to auctioning allowances.

A final political argument is that taxes are hard to introduce but easy to cut. Perhaps scientists would persuade the government to introduce a high carbon tax, which would give a strong signal to firms to begin making low-carbon investments. But if the political winds shifted, the next government might reverse that policy and repeal the tax. In a sense, the price volatility in Figure 35 might be replaced by political volatility with a carbon tax if the tax gets caught in partisan political struggles.

The history of regulation suggests that environmental rules tend to have greater durability and have generally been irreversible. Congress introduced a tightening of the rules with respect to SO_2 emissions in 1990. Even with the major political changes in the United States since that time, emissions standards have not changed appreciably. For this reason, many analysts believe that the regulatory route of a cap-and-trade policy would be more durable and have a larger chance of being a credible long-term policy.

How do I come out after weighing the arguments? My first choice is . . . either one! The most important goal is to raise the price of CO_2 and other GHG emissions. If countries find it easier to raise prices with cap and trade, particularly with auctions, that will accomplish the goal. Other countries might find they need a stable and reliable revenue source and lean toward carbon taxes, and I would applaud them. As I will emphasize in Chapter 21's discussion of alternatives, either one is so far superior to other approaches that we must focus on the major goal—raising GHG prices—and not let the differences be obstacles to effective policies.

If I were put on the rack and forced to choose, I would admit that the economic arguments for carbon taxation are compelling, particularly those relating to revenues, volatility, transparency, and predictability. So if a country is genuinely unsure, I would recommend it use the carbon tax approach. However, if a country like the United States has a powerful aversion to new taxes but can swallow a cap-and-trade system, particularly one with the allowances auctioned, then that is definitely better than allowing unchecked climate change or relying on ineffective substitute approaches.

HYBRIDS

There are many competing considerations in weighing carbon taxes versus cap and trade. Is there a compromise, crossing the strengths of the carbon tax regime with cap and trade to produce a hardy hybrid? Perhaps the most promising approach would be to fashion a hybrid mechanism that has quantitative limits with a price floor and a safety valve price at the higher end. For example, a system might have quantitative targets with a minimum CO_2 price as a carbon tax floor. Some countries might organize their climate-change policies around a cap-and-trade model, as Europe does. They could also incorporate an upper-end safety valve into the system wherein nations could sell carbon emissions permits at a multiple of the tax, perhaps at a 50 percent premium of the base level, to reduce volatility and ensure that the economic costs of the program are contained.

A hybrid system would share the strengths and weaknesses of the two options. It would not have firm quantitative limits of a pure cap-and-trade system. But the soft quantitative limits would guide firms and countries and would generate confidence that the climatic targets were being achieved. The hybrid would have some but not all of the advantages of a carbon tax system. It would have more favorable public finance characteristics, reduce price volatility, mitigate the incentives for corruption, and help alleviate uncertainties. The narrower the difference between the price floor and the safety valve price, the more the program would have the advantages of a carbon tax; the wider the difference, the more it would have the advantages of a cap-and-trade system.

As with systems as complex as the economy and the climate, many design details are just sketches in a brief treatment. The reader can refer to specialized legal or economic analyses for a more detailed analysis.[4] One particularly thorny issue is the treatment of carbon sequestered in forests and soils. In principle, a system would give carbon credits when carbon is accumulated in trees, and the owners would be debited when trees are cut and burned. In practice, keeping an accurate record of these flows is beyond current capabilities, so including forests in an international GHG control system presents real problems.

Another complication is the measurement of flows of GHGs across national borders when the national emissions control systems are not harmonized. Suppose that the United States has a tax of $50 per ton of CO_2 while Canada has a tax of $20 per ton. In an ideal world, imports of CO_2 from Canada to the United States might receive an additional tax of the difference of $30 per ton. The difficulty comes in how to treat indirect or "embodied" CO_2 and other GHGs. Should we include only fossil fuels in the border tax? Or goods that are highly CO_2 intensive, like steel? Or should we include an estimate for all imports? Border tax treatment will be manageable if the carbon prices are low. But if prices are in the range of $500 or $1,000 per ton of CO_2, as is found in some proposals, then a few percentage points in the CO_2 price can make a substantial difference for the prices and competitiveness of goods in international trade.

These are just two examples of the many realistic details that will need to be ironed out in any global climate policy. They sound tedious for nonspecialists and will make work for lawyers. But working through the details and establishing a price for CO_2 and other GHGs is a critical step on the road to slowing global warming.

21 FROM NATIONAL TO HARMONIZED INTERNATIONAL POLICIES

The last two chapters discussed how governments can harness the market to slow the pace of global warming. We saw that a key element is putting a price on CO_2 and other greenhouse gases (GHGs). We next explained the two potential systems that would accomplish this: cap and trade and carbon taxes. These would work at the level of individual nations and indeed have been implemented for almost a decade by the EU in its Emissions Trading Scheme.

One final facet of an effective global warming policy is . . . that it be global. The present chapter discusses alternative approaches, including the failed Kyoto Protocol, and considers ways to introduce more effective international policies. A key innovation in a new international agreement will be to introduce incentives to prevent free riding.

APPROACHES TO GLOBAL EXTERNALITIES

Global warming is an unusual economic phenomenon known as a global externality. Global externalities are not new, but they are becoming increasingly important because of rapid technological change and declining transportation and communication costs—what people sometimes call "globalization." Global externalities are different from other economic activities because the economic and political mechanisms for dealing with them efficiently and effectively are weak or absent.

Global externalities have long challenged national governments. In earlier centuries, countries faced religious conflicts, marauding armies, and the spread of infectious diseases like the plague. In the modern world, the older global challenges have not disappeared, while new ones have arisen—including not only global warming but others like the threat of nuclear proliferation, drug trafficking, international financial crises, and the growing threat of cyber warfare.

Further reflection will reveal that nations have had limited success with agreements to deal with global economic externalities. Two successful cases include handling international trade disputes (today primarily through the World Trade Organization) and the protocols to limit the use of ozone-killing chlorofluorocarbons. The study of economic aspects of environmental treaties has been pioneered by Columbia University economist Scott Barrett. He and other scholars believe these two treaties were successful because the benefits far outweighed the costs and because effective institutions were created to foster cooperation among nations.[1]

Governance is a central issue in dealing with global externalities because effective management requires the concerted action of major countries. But, under current international law, there is no legal mechanism by which disinterested majorities or even supermajorities of countries can require other nations to share in the responsibility for managing global externalities. Moreover, extralegal methods such as armed force are hardly recommended when the point is to persuade countries to behave cooperatively rather than free riding.

Earlier chapters demonstrated that effective actions to slow global warming require both near-universal participation and harmonized policies. Most countries need to join an agreement. By doing so, policies can be harmonized so that the marginal costs of emissions reductions are equalized across nations and sectors. The strict conditions for effective policies are the reason why international agreements and institutions are necessary.

What are the proposals and the actual institutions for dealing with the global externality of climate change? Here are the four main approaches.[2]

1. Inaction, in which no measures are taken to override market supply and demand, and the climate-change externality is not corrected.

This has been the approach of most nations up to now, but it will not solve the problem.

2. Unilateral actions, in which countries set their own objectives and policies but do not coordinate them with other countries. This has been the route increasingly followed by most countries. For example, the United States has included climate-change objectives in regulatory policies since 2008. The U.S. climate-change policy proposed by the Obama administration in 2009 had a cap-and-trade mechanism that applied only to the United States but did not coordinate policies with other countries. Similarly, China has pledged to lower its CO_2 emissions per unit of GDP by 40 to 45 percent by 2020 compared to 2005, but China also stated that it is not obliged to subject its programs to international monitoring and accountability.

3. Regional approaches, an important example of which is the EU's Emissions Trading Scheme. It sets limits for all members of the EU, covering approximately half of EU CO_2 emissions. It is a cap-and-trade plan in which countries are allocated emissions allowances, which can be traded on carbon exchange markets. Regional agreements have the potential to decrease the number of bargaining units and might lead to an effective international agreement. However, at present the EU is unique among regional federations, and other groups of countries (such as the Arab League or the African Union) have not forged emission control arrangements.

4. Binding international agreements among most nations to limit GHG emissions using a combination of regulatory and tax measures. The history of this approach is discussed in the next section.

A SHORT HISTORY OF INTERNATIONAL CLIMATE AGREEMENTS

The risks of climate change were recognized in the United Nations Framework Convention on Climate Change, ratified in 1994. That document stated, "The ultimate objective . . . is to achieve . . . stabilization of greenhouse-gas concentrations in the atmosphere at a level that would prevent dangerous anthropogenic interference with the climate system."[3]

The first step to implement the Framework Convention was taken in the Kyoto Protocol in 1997. High-income countries agreed to limit their emissions to 5 percent below 1990 levels for the 2008–2012 budget period. Under the protocol, important institutional features were established, such as reporting requirements. The protocol also introduced a method for calculating the relative importance of different GHGs. Its most important innovation was an international cap-and-trade system of emissions trading as a means of coordinating policies among countries.

The Kyoto Protocol was an ambitious attempt to construct an international architecture that would effectively harmonize the policies of different countries. But countries did not find it economically attractive. The United States withdrew very early. It did not attract any new participants from middle-income and developing countries. As a result, there was significant attrition in the coverage of emissions under the Kyoto Protocol. Also, emissions grew more rapidly in noncovered countries, particularly developing countries like China. The protocol as first designed would have covered two-thirds of global emissions in 1990, but the actual scope in 2012 was barely one-fifth of world emissions. Analyses showed that, even if indefinitely extended, the Kyoto reductions would have a very limited impact on future climate change. It died a quiet death, mourned by few, on December 31, 2012 (see Figure 36).[4]

The 2009 Copenhagen meeting was designed to negotiate a successor agreement for the post-Kyoto period. It produced an agreement known as the Copenhagen Accord. The accord adopted a global temperature target, "recognizing the scientific view that the increase . . . should be below 2 degrees Celsius." However, because countries were unwilling to make binding commitments and were concerned about the division of costs, the meeting concluded without a substantive agreement to limit emissions.

What is the implication of the demise of the Kyoto Protocol and the failure of the Copenhagen Accord? For the near term, it seems likely that climate policy will at best take the route of parallel but uncoordinated national policies—the second of the four approaches listed above. Some countries (such as those of the EU) will continue to use cap and trade. Others (perhaps India and China) may introduce cap-and-trade limits or carbon taxes. Still others (such as the U.S.) will rely largely on

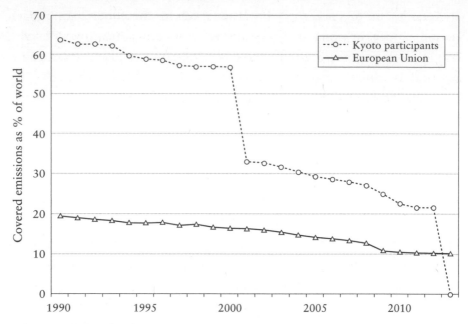

Figure 36. Share of global emissions. The Kyoto Protocol (the dashed line) covered almost two-thirds of emissions when it began. However, the growth of developing countries and the departure of the United States and Canada reduced that share to about one-fifth by the time it expired in 2012. The EU was the major stalwart throughout this period (its share of global emissions is shown as the solid line).

regulatory measures that limit emissions on specific technologies. These policies may bend down the trajectory of emissions slightly in the coming years. But they are unlikely to do so efficiently, and, given the high costs of inefficient measures (discussed in Chapter 22), countries acting unilaterally are unlikely to take sufficiently energetic measures to ensure that climate change stays short of the dangerous thresholds.

It is painful to conclude that an important and well-meaning approach—in which so many invested so much time and hope—has failed. But it is hard to reach any other conclusion about the Kyoto model. At present, global actions lag far behind the steps that would be necessary to limit global warming to the 3°C increase indicated by economic cost-benefit analysis, while the ambitious 2°C target announced at Copenhagen is probably infeasible.

Nations are in a stalemate in negotiations on climate change. Every year sees further rounds of international meetings and negotiations in conferences of the parties: Nairobi in 2006, Bali in 2007, Poznan in 2008, Copenhagen in 2009, Cancun in 2010, Durban in 2011, Doha in 2012. Every meeting ends with several reports and decisions, along with complaints that nothing is being achieved.[5] The Kyoto model is a dead end.

STRUCTURE OF INTERNATIONAL AGREEMENTS

An efficient policy to slow global warming requires that national policies be harmonized among countries. Strictly speaking, policy harmonization means that the marginal costs of emissions reductions in each country are the same. The idea here is exactly parallel to my discussion of the rationale of national emissions trading. Suppose an optimal emissions target is 30 billion tons of CO_2 per year. To minimize the costs of meeting this objective, the cost of the last unit reduced (which is the marginal cost in economists' language) would need to be equal in every sector of every country. Go back and read the text around Figure 34. Just replace "firm" with "country," and the reasoning is exactly the same.

The easiest way to achieve harmonization of marginal costs is by ensuring that the prices of CO_2 emissions are equalized in every country. This means that every firm will set its marginal costs of abatement equal to the CO_2 price, and that will mean that every firm in every country will have the same marginal cost. This will imply that the cost of meeting the global emissions objectives is minimized. While this objective will strike many as utopian to the nth degree, it is important to keep that ideal in mind when considering different approaches to national and global policies.

As with approaches inside countries, there are two approaches that can harmonize policies across countries. One way to do this is through an international cap-and-trade policy, such as the one run by the EU or that envisioned in the Kyoto Protocol. Under such plans, country emissions would be limited (cap), and the emissions allowances could be bought and sold among countries (trade). The market mechanism would ensure that the prices were equalized across different countries, and this would lead to equalizing marginal costs of abatement across countries and to a global minimum cost.

A second approach would be a regime in which countries agree upon a harmonized minimum carbon price; countries then undertake to penalize carbon emissions at this minimum price. I describe the system in the next section and then compare the two approaches.

A CARBON PRICE REGIME

While the structure of a cap-and-trade system is relatively familiar to those who have followed climate-change negotiations, the structure of a carbon price regime is a novel idea and requires some explanation. The basic idea is that countries would agree on a carbon price rather than an emissions limitation. The actual implementation would be under the control of individual countries subject to agreed-upon norms of monitoring, verification, and enforcement.

The first step is to agree upon a target carbon price. There is a substantial literature on carbon prices that countries could draw upon. For this discussion, I have chosen a price path that would be consistent with a temperature limit of 2½°C. While other targets might be chosen, this range is suggested by the cost-benefit analysis in Chapter 18 as well as more complete integrated assessment models. Look back to Figure 33 to see the path of carbon prices that were generated from several economic models under the idealized situation of universal participation and efficient implementation. For this discussion, I use as an example the midpoint of the estimates in Figure 33, which is $25 per ton of CO_2 in 2015 and rises sharply after that. Note however that there is a wide range of estimates of the carbon prices necessary to attain that target, that changing the target would also change the carbon price, and finally that the target path would change with changing economic and scientific information.

The next question is the obligation that countries would undertake in a carbon price treaty. At a minimum, all countries should agree to penalize carbon and other GHG emissions by the agreed-upon minimum price. Countries could set their price at a higher level if they desired. Verifying the actual carbon prices would require transparent reporting by countries.

The process of setting the international norm price would require a framework treaty. Decisions might take the form of weighted voting, but they would clearly be a major and contentious set of international negotiations. A key point to recognize is that negotiating the minimum price would be much simpler compared to negotiating a complete set of individual national emissions caps. The simplicity of a single carbon price compared to country-specific emissions caps is an important but elusive point. It can be illustrated with the example of negotiations over dues to a club. Suppose that several people want to set up a club—for golf, cricket, or duck hunting. People differ in their enthusiasm, proximity, family size, and income. One approach is to negotiate dues on a member-by-member basis, where each member would have a certain share of the total. This procedure would require a long and painful negotiation over shares. There may be clubs that negotiate dues on a member-by-member basis, but I have never seen one in operation. This is the approach of the Kyoto model, and you can see why it is has proven so difficult and eventually fruitless.

Negotiating a single minimum price would be much easier than negotiating emissions quotas. Germans might argue for a high price, while Canadians argue for a low price, and Saudi Arabia for a penny price. But once the price is set, there is no need for any further negotiations about the differentiated prices for each country. You can see from the example of club dues why negotiating an international carbon price is simpler and more likely to produce a constructive outcome than negotiating emissions reductions country by country.

The administration of the harmonized price would be different from the cap-and-trade system. Countries could determine the price using whatever mechanism they choose. Even though countries would agree to meet the minimum international price, the agreement would not dictate the mechanism by which countries meet their obligations. Some countries might simply use carbon taxes. Others might implement their commitment using a cap-and-trade mechanism such as was envisioned by the Kyoto Protocol and embedded in U.S. legislation. Yet another approach would be a hybrid cap and trade with a minimum price floor (perhaps by using an auction with a reservation price).

From an economic and environmental point of view, the comparison between an international cap-and-trade system and a harmonized carbon tax system parallels the discussion above about domestic variants. Many of the advantages and disadvantages are the same. However, the real issues are not technical ones of design but fundamental political ones. Any treaty will need to tread softly on country sovereignty and domestic prerogatives. Countries will need to believe that they have wide latitude to shape their climate policies under an international agreement. The minimum-price regime is a friendly approach, more like agreements on tariffs or tax treaties that countries already engage in. It is less likely to trigger nationalistic jealousies and taboos than the highly intrusive cap-and-trade approach of the Kyoto Protocol.

OBLIGATIONS FOR RICH AND POOR

International agreements often differentiate the responsibilities of poor and rich nations. Under the Kyoto Protocol, for example, rich countries had binding emissions limitations, while middle-income and poor countries had no binding emissions limits and were required only to report their emissions. In a future and more comprehensive arrangement, rich countries would take immediate steps to curb emissions; middle-income countries would need to join the agreement and reduce emissions in the near term; and, as is discussed shortly, poorer countries could postpone participation or would receive assistance for their emissions reductions.

What is the distribution of emissions among countries by different income groups? Table 11 shows CO_2 emissions by country groups. I have taken 167 countries for which the World Bank provides data and divided them into five groups ranked by per capita income.[6] Today's high-income countries (per capita income of $20,000 or more) are responsible for

Table 11. Distribution of emissions by country income level.

Country group	Lower limit of per capita income (2005 U.S. $)	Cumulative share of global CO_2 emissions (%)	Number of countries
High income	20,000	46.3	35
Middle income	10,000	60.8	30
Low-middle income	5,000	89.9	30
Low income	2,000	99.1	35
Lowest income	280	100.0	37

slightly less than half of all CO_2 emissions. The top three groups, representing 90 percent of current emissions, include not only rich countries but also China, South Africa, Ukraine, Thailand, Kazakhstan, Egypt, Algeria, Colombia, Turkmenistan, Peru, and Azerbaijan.

High-income countries had commitments under the Kyoto Protocol (although not all of them met these commitments, and the United States and Canada withdrew). They will serve as the critical mass for an effective agreement.

However, as I have emphasized repeatedly, this problem cannot be solved if rich countries act alone. Meeting an ambitious temperature target will require that countries representing virtually all emissions participate. As Table 11 shows, an effective agreement will require including most middle-income and low-middle-income countries, particularly China and India. For these countries, joining in the carbon price regime would seem a reasonable goal for an international climate-change treaty. On the other hand, the prospects of India or China joining a Kyoto-like agreement in the near future seem remote. The range of institutional structures and integration in the global economy and in international institutions differs greatly among these countries, but they need to be persuaded to join a global agreement if it is to be effective, and the agreement needs to be designed in a way that is not overly burdensome for middle-income countries. A minimum carbon price regime does that.

What about the poorest countries? On the one hand, we have seen the importance of universal participation. On the other hand, it is unfair and unrealistic to expect countries struggling to provide clean drinking water and primary schooling to make sacrifices for people in richer countries many decades in the future. Fortunately, this is not a major loss. Aside from Nigeria, the current emissions of the lowest-income countries are negligible. As we see in Table 11, the bottom 72 countries produce only 10 percent of global emissions. If the top 100 countries plus India and China are included, this would account for 90 percent of global emissions.

The best mechanisms for encouraging the participation of low-income countries would be a combination of financial and technological assistance in adopting low-carbon technologies as well as a campaign to persuade these countries to substitute carbon taxes for other taxes. The advantage of carbon taxes relative to binding emissions reductions is particularly applicable to countries with weak governance structures. It seems unlikely that these countries could run a cap-and-trade system without pervasive problems of corruption and evasion.[7] By contrast, a carbon tax could meet the revenue needs of governments while reducing other burdensome taxes and would pose no especially difficult governance problems.

COMBATING FREE RIDING WITH ENFORCEMENT MECHANISMS

Whatever the international regime to slow climate change—whether it be a revived Kyoto approach or a carbon price regime—it must confront the tendency of countries to free ride on the efforts of others. A critical component of a new regime will be to design a mechanism to overcome the free-rider problem. Countries have strong incentives to proclaim lofty and ambitious goals—and then to ignore these goals and go about business as usual. When national economic interests collide with international agreements, there will be a temptation to shirk, dissemble, and withdraw.

Canada is an interesting case. Canada was an early enthusiast for the Kyoto Protocol. It signed up for a 6 percent reduction in emissions and ratified the treaty. However, the Canadian energy market changed dramatically in the following years, with rapid growth in production from the Alberta oil sands. By 2009, Canadian emissions were 17 percent above 1990 levels, far above its target. Finally, in December 2011, Canada withdrew from the protocol. There were no adverse consequences except for some scolding from environmentalists. The Canadian experience shows that the Kyoto Protocol had yet a further disadvantage of being a toothless treaty, without sanctions or any mechanism for enforcement. In a deep sense, participation was voluntary.[8]

How might international climate-change treaties introduce enforcement mechanisms? The only serious candidate would be to link participation and compliance with international trade. For example, countries that do not participate or live up to their obligations would be subject to trade sanctions. The standard way to employ sanctions under current international law is to put tariffs on the imports from countries that are not complying with a treaty's provisions. This approach is commonly used when countries violate their trade agreements, and is also included in several international environmental agreements.[9]

Two specific approaches might be considered. The simplest one is to impose a straight percentage tariff (perhaps 5 percent) on all imports from the noncomplying country. This has the advantage of simplicity and transparency, although it does not relate the tariff specifically to the carbon content of the import.

A second proposal—more commonly promoted by scholars who have advocated this enforcement mechanism—would put tariffs on goods in relation to their carbon content. This mechanism is known as "border tax adjustment." Under this plan, imports into a country would be taxed at the border by an amount that would be equal to the agreed-upon international carbon price times the carbon content of the import.

Let's work through an example of the border tax adjustment approach. Suppose that the internationally negotiated minimum carbon price was \$25 per ton of CO_2. Assume that noncomplying Canada exports a ton of steel to Europe. If calculations show that the ton of steel has used 1.2 tons of CO_2 in its production, then Europe would levy a border tax of \$30 per ton of steel on this import.[10] On the other hand, if

Korea complied with the treaty and had a domestic CO_2 price of at least $25 per ton of CO_2, its trade would be treated as normal international commerce with no border tax adjustments.

This all sounds simple, but in reality, the border tax adjustment regime would become terribly complicated for noncomplying countries. How exactly would we calculate the carbon content for imports? Should we apply the tax to all products? Imports of oil or natural gas would be easy to tax at the border, but different kinds of coal have differing carbon contents, and countries would need to deal with that. Conventional goods would be even more difficult. If we included cars, would we count the CO_2 that comes from the coal that goes into the steel that goes into the cars? Trade specialists warn that relying on trade sanctions would open the door to protectionism, which is always lurking in the shadows looking for excuses to keep out foreign goods and services.

In analyzing the impact of the border tax adjustment enforcement mechanism, we need to consider that trade sanctions affect only goods in international trade, while much of a country's CO_2 emissions come only from domestic production. For example, virtually none of the energy used by U.S. residences, in transportation, or in electricity generation enters directly into international trade. Yet it forms 95 percent of U.S. CO_2 emissions. To look at this from another angle, consider the question of reducing U.S. CO_2 emissions from coal-fired electricity generation. Studies indicate that this would be the single most efficient way to reduce emissions. But the United States exports less than 1 percent of its electricity generation, so the effect of tariffs here would be tiny.

Given the complexity of the border tax adjustment approach, the alternative of a uniform percentage tariff on imports might be preferable. The rationale is that nonparticipants are damaging other countries because of their total emissions of GHGs, not only from those embodied in traded goods. While the trade is the instrument, it is not the target of the sanctions. The size of the tariff should relate to the damages in a fashion that gives countries incentives to be part of the solution, not just the problem.

This discussion suggests that the major motivation for countries to join the carbon treaty would come from the stigma and messiness of being outside the carbon-compliant region. But would it work? The main cost of noncompliance would be an array of proceedings that would be visible, costly, contentious, and undesirable for noncomplying countries. In effect, there would be a free-trade zone of complying countries and a tangle of regulations and penalties for noncomplying countries.

While harnessing the world trading system to a climate agreement is the most promising route to overcoming the tendency of countries to ride free on the efforts of others, it must be used with great caution. The current free and open trading system is the result of hard-fought efforts to combat protectionism. It has produced large gains to living standards around the world. It should be tied to a climate-change agreement only if the benefits to the climate regime are clear and the dangers to the trading system are worth the benefits.

Let's summarize the lessons on devising incentives to participate. To begin with, past approaches such as the Kyoto Protocol contained completely inadequate enforcement mechanisms, with the result that countries could stay out without any adverse consequences. Trade measures that impose duties on imports from nonparticipating countries are likely to be the most useful instrument for overcoming free riding and inducing participation. However, trade measures are only indirectly related to emissions, and the need to calibrate and apply them effectively is uncharted territory in environmental and trade policy.

Establishing effective policies to slow global warming will require four important steps. First, it will require focusing on raising the price of CO_2 and other GHG emissions in the marketplace. Second, because free markets will not do the job, it will require nations to use either a cap-and-trade or carbon tax system to raise CO_2 prices. Third, it will require most nations to agree to the first two steps and to coordinate their policies at a global level. And finally, an international climate-change agreement must contain an effective mechanism to combat free riding.

The hurdles facing global coordination are extremely high. Countries guard their sovereignty like the family jewels. They are loath to cede power to any international organization or group of other countries. Given the urgency of reaching an agreement and the realities of national reluctance, the most fruitful approach is a harmonized carbon price with trade sanctions as a way to prevent countries from free riding on the investments of others.

22 SECOND BEST AND BEYOND

Many people who think global warming is a grave concern may agree with the proposals of the three previous chapters. They see the important role of carbon pricing; they may like cap and trade or carbon taxes or both; they recognize that a global effort is necessary for effective and efficient management of our global commons. At the same time, they might say, "Alas, these are utopian ideas. Scientists and economists may agree with such plans. But the people have other priorities. They are worried about their jobs, their declining incomes, and their health care. Americans are not ready for such radical surgery."

A sober assessment of current attitudes and policies would have to agree with a pessimistic assessment of trends in public attitudes and national policies. Europe is the only major region where countries have actually raised the price of carbon, through its Emissions Trading Scheme. The U.S. Congress has repeatedly failed to enact strong climate-change policies. Part of the difficulty is that people resist raising the price of energy goods and services, particularly if it takes the form of taxes. This sentiment is widely shared around the world, although the United States exhibits an extreme allergy to taxes in its rhetoric and politics.

In response to the resistance to price-raising measures, countries have often turned to other approaches. We can take the United States as an example. The Clinton administration advocated the binding emissions caps negotiated in the Kyoto Protocol in 1997. However, because of

Congressional resistance, the treaty was never submitted for ratification. Later, the Obama administration proposed cap-and-trade legislation in 2009. It passed the House of Representatives but failed in the Senate.

After his reelection to a second term, President Obama continued to argue strongly for policies to slow global warming. Because his economy-wide measures were making no progress, he warned that he would push forward with regulatory proposals:

> But if Congress won't act soon to protect future generations, I will. I will direct my Cabinet to come up with executive actions we can take, now and in the future, to reduce pollution, prepare our communities for the consequences of climate change, and speed the transition to more sustainable sources of energy.[1]

The actions to "reduce pollution," by which is meant CO_2 and other GHG emissions, would involve regulations on fuel efficiency in new cars, CO_2 emissions in new power plants, and possible regulations of GHGs in existing power plants.

Given the importance of alternatives to price-raising policies, we need to assess other approaches to climate-change policy. What are the major alternatives to raising the prices of CO_2 emissions, through either cap-and-trade plans or carbon taxes?

- Virtually all countries rely on regulations. These require improved energy efficiency for major energy-using capital such as automobiles, appliances, and buildings.
- Many countries have subsidies on "green" technologies. These include fiscal incentives to lower the cost and increase the use of renewable power such as wind or solar electricity generation, hybrid vehicles, and biofuels such as ethanol.
- Virtually all countries have some taxes on energy. Except for oil producers, countries generally have high taxes on motor fuels.
- Virtually all countries have voluntary approaches. These are generally commitments by industry to reduce emissions. For example, large oil companies have made commitments to reduce their emissions by 10–20 percent.

I will put aside for the moment one special category of program, research and development. These policies attempt to foster new low-carbon technologies or basic energy sciences. New technologies play a central role in a transition to a low-carbon world. As discussed in Chapter 23, the need to encourage fundamental science and technology in energy efficiency is a central part of any strategy to reduce CO_2 emissions over the long run, with or without carbon-pricing policies.

Most of the policies in the list above have been carefully analyzed and have been shown to be inefficient and ineffective ways to slow global warming. These alternative approaches can supplement and buttress more comprehensive greenhouse-gas emissions limits or carbon taxes. However, they are inefficient because they require spending substantial sums for minimal impacts. Some are small and modestly effective; others are just expensive; while some are counterproductive and actually increase emissions.

I cannot review the alternatives in a comprehensive manner. Rather, I focus primarily on regulatory alternatives, which have been most widely used. I illustrate the major difficulties raised by alternatives, which is that they tend to be expensive and ineffective relative to more direct approaches to limiting greenhouse-gas emissions. The first part of this chapter looks at some alternative approaches, while the second part examines a special kind of myopia that looms over different policy proposals.

MAJOR ALTERNATIVE APPROACHES TO CLIMATE POLICY

A central issue examined in this chapter is the relative efficiency of different approaches. Public finance economists have developed the idea of "deadweight loss" to measure the inefficiency of different policies. Measuring deadweight loss sounds complicated, but the idea is simple. The deadweight loss is the net loss to society in terms of foregone goods and services. For example, in the estimates of the cost of slowing climate change discussed in Chapter 15, I estimated that the costs (really deadweight losses) were generally on the order of 1 percent of world income. This is equivalent to a reduction in potential consumption by that amount.

A specific example would be a government appliance regulation. Suppose that the government mandates that furnaces reduce their fuel use per unit of heating. A low-fuel furnace costs $500 more in capital and fuel costs over its lifetime. It also reduces lifetime CO_2 emissions by 10 tons. We would therefore say that the cost of the CO_2 reduction is $50 per ton.

Note that we do not count taxes as efficiency losses. Suppose that there is a $25 per ton carbon tax. If my total direct and indirect CO_2 use is 10 tons per year, I would pay $250 in carbon taxes (not only directly, but also indirectly as higher costs embedded in my purchases of goods and services). However, this cost is not a deadweight loss but a transfer. The government gets $250 of revenue and can spend that on governmental services or serve up $250 in tax cuts. If I pay $250 of carbon taxes and my income taxes are reduced by $250, then my real income is essentially back where it started. This shows why to a first approximation we should not count the tax revenues as a deadweight loss.[2]

A REGULATORY EXAMPLE: AUTOMOBILE FUEL EFFICIENCY STANDARDS

It will be useful to begin with an example of the regulatory approach: automobile fuel efficiency standards. They are used in virtually every major country; they are popular; and they are costly.

The most recent standard issued by the Obama administration in 2012 was a good example of the pros and cons of a regulatory approach. It set standards that would decrease automotive CO_2 emissions in new cars over the 2012–2025 period by as much as 40 percent. The estimated technology costs were $120 billion in higher costs of cars and light trucks over the 2011–2015 model years.

The implementation is complicated. The standards differ by vehicle category: Small cars will be required to get 52 miles per gallon (mpg), while large light trucks (big SUVs and pickups) will only be required to get 38 mpg. Such an arrangement creates a perverse incentive for people to buy large SUVs rather than small cars compared to a standard where all cars and SUVs have the same fuel efficiency standard. Thus different standards undermine the effectiveness of the fuel efficiency mandate.

This would be similar to a gasoline tax that is lower on large cars than small cars.

Moreover, an economic analysis of the regulation shows that most of the "benefits" come from fuel savings, not from reduced CO_2 emissions or reduced pollution.³ The rule is primarily justified by what I call "energy-cost myopia," discussed in the second half of this chapter.

The cost of different approaches is illustrated in a careful study by a team at Resources for the Future (RfF), a nonpartisan research institute that focuses on environmental and resource economics. The RfF team evaluated the effectiveness of CAFE (Corporate Average Fuel Economy) standards along with other approaches to reducing CO_2 emissions. It estimated the emissions reductions and the cost (deadweight loss) per unit of CO_2 emission reduction.⁴

Begin with their findings for the standard economic approach, called "no market failures." This approach assumes that markets work efficiently and that consumers understand the fuel costs and savings. The team calculated that the gold standard for emissions reduction is a carbon-pricing system like cap and trade or carbon taxes. They then examined the costs and CO_2 savings from different fuel efficiency standards under the assumption of no market failures. (An alternative assumption is discussed shortly.) The team found that with no market failures, the CAFE standards were much more expensive than a first-best, efficient carbon tax or cap and trade. The cost was $85 per ton of CO_2 removed for CAFE standards compared to $12 per ton for the economically efficient policies.

The regulatory policy is so expensive for two reasons. First, in the case of no market failures, automobile manufacturers are assumed to incorporate the price of gasoline into car designs. Designs would be optimized so that the cost of an additional gallon of gasoline is just balanced by the cost of the gallon saved by improved fuel economy. Additionally, because the 2012 rule required very large miles-per-gallon changes, the costs of the last fuel efficiency improvements are extremely expensive. The basic point is that, without market failures, the cost of reducing CO_2 emissions through CAFE standards will exceed the cost of reducing emissions through the first-best approaches of carbon taxation or cap and trade.

Automotive fuel efficiency is just one of many regulatory interventions that are used to reduce energy or CO_2 emissions. Can we generalize from that case to ask about the effectiveness of programs that use targeted regulations?

This topic has been studied intensively by energy economists. Table 12 provides a partial list of the cost effectiveness of different regulatory and tax measures, drawn from the RfF study.[5] The table shows two metrics. The first is the effect, which is defined as how much a given regulation would contribute to achieving the U.S. benchmark climate-change policy.[6] The second column shows the cost per ton of CO_2 reduction, which is the deadweight loss efficiency measure discussed above.

Start with the bottom row, showing the gold standard for minimum cost—a program of universal cap and trade or carbon tax. Calculations show that they would both have an average cost of $12 per ton of CO_2 reduction of attaining the benchmark U.S. emissions-reduction goal. The remaining policies are ranked from least costly to most costly. As Table 12 shows, and as is consistent with the economic theory discussed above, the other policies are all more expensive and less effective than the ideal policies, assuming no other market failures. As we noted

Table 12. Effects and costs of alternative regulatory and tax policies. A study by a team at Resources for the Future examined the cost-effectiveness of different policies in reducing CO_2 emissions. Note how much more the indirect approaches cost compared to the direct and efficient approaches.

Policy	Effect (as % of 2010–2030 emissions)	Cost ($ per ton of CO_2)
Gasoline tax	1.8	40
Building codes	0.1	51
Tighter auto standards	0.6	85
Liquid natural gas trucks	1.5	85
Weatherization tax credits	0.3	255
Federal interest subsidy	0.0	71,075
Cap and trade/Carbon tax	10.2	12

above, automobile standards are expensive to implement because requiring such large miles-per-gallon improvements is uneconomical. Other policies range from modestly to horribly ineffective.

It should be noted that Table 12 has biases in both a negative and positive direction. It is likely to understate the costs of CO_2 reduction because it assumes that the policies are optimally designed. If there are exemptions or loopholes, then the costs will be higher. At the same time, it overstates costs to the extent that consumers make poor decisions (as discussed later in this chapter).

Other policies, not shown in Table 12, actually have a perverse effect. The best example is a subsidy to ethanol production for automotive fuels. The ethanol provisions (in place for many years but expired at the end of 2011) provided a subsidy of 45 cents a gallon to ethanol when blended with gasoline. You might think that this is a good idea because ethanol replaces fossil fuels. Not so. Careful studies indicate that corn-based ethanol emits about as much CO_2-equivalent as gasoline when all fossil fuels and greenhouse gas–producing fertilizers are included. Ethanol is truly a medicine that causes rather than cures diseases.

NONREGULATORY APPROACHES

There are many other ideas about how to tackle global warming, which cannot be systematically analyzed within the scope of this book. However, it will be useful to sketch them here.

Some policies are complementary to putting a market price on emissions. For example, strong support for public and private research and development on low-carbon energy technologies would lower the costs of these technologies and is definitely recommended. They would lead to greater emissions reductions and lower costs for attaining the targets. These policies are analyzed in Chapter 23.

Some alternatives are in the dubious category. One example is the "clean development mechanism" included in the Kyoto Protocol and the European Emissions Trading Scheme, which allows poor countries to sell emissions reductions to rich countries, which then get credit for the reductions in a cap-and-trade regime. For example, China built a hydroelectric power station, which (it claimed) would replace a coal-fired station. It obtained 31,261 tons of CO_2 credits, which it sold to the Netherlands. The dubious element here is that we have no way of knowing whether China would have built this hydroelectric power station even without the incentive of selling credits. Without effective caps on country CO_2 emissions, we can never know whether schemes to buy emissions reduction in poor countries, or to offset our carbon footprint, are having any net impact on emissions.

Another set of questionable proposals is to subsidize "green energy" or "green jobs." The spirit of these proposals is that certain activities are low carbon and should be encouraged. However, we always need to look behind the "green" label to determine whether that is really a cover for politically favored but inefficient subsidies such as the one for ethanol described earlier.

Subsidies pose a more general problem in this context. They attempt to discourage carbon-intensive activities by making other activities more attractive. One difficulty with subsidies is identifying the eligible low-carbon activities. Why subsidize hybrid cars (which we do) and not biking (which we do not)? Is the answer to subsidize all low-carbon activities? Of course, that is impossible because there are just too many low-carbon activities, and it would prove astronomically expensive. Another problem is that subsidies are so uneven in their impact. A recent study by the National Academy of Sciences looked at the impact of several subsidies on GHG emissions. It found a vast difference in their effectiveness in terms of CO_2 removed per dollar of subsidy. None of the subsidies were efficient; some were horribly inefficient; and others such as the ethanol subsidy were perverse and actually increased GHG emissions. The net effect of all the subsidies taken together was effectively zero![7]

So in the end, it is much more effective to penalize carbon emissions than to subsidize everything else.

Three tentative points emerge from the analysis of alternatives to carbon pricing. First, alternatives such as regulation are generally more expensive per unit of emissions reduction than a price-based policy.

The reason is that they cannot fine-tune the response of different producers and sectors. Second, even a robust set of regulations is unlikely to achieve ambitious targets such as those set at the Copenhagen climate convention. They might contribute in some sectors, but they are insufficient to make a substantial contribution. Third, the selection of the portfolio of regulations is a difficult problem because some options are extremely expensive or even counterproductive, such as the use of corn-based ethanol. Therefore, the regulatory approach alone is unlikely to effectively address the climate-change problem, and definitely will not solve the problem efficiently.

This analysis indicates that the best approach to preventing "dangerous interferences" with the climate is actually straightforward from an economic perspective. The countries of the world need to move quickly to a high and rising price on CO_2 emissions and other greenhouse gases, and these prices should be harmonized so that they are roughly equivalent in all countries. Such policies can be undertaken with either taxes or tradable emissions limits. While the two mechanisms are not identical, either could, if well designed, reduce emissions to attain environmental objectives; would provide governments with precious revenues to pay for public services or reduce other taxes; and would do so in a manner that improves rather than impedes economic efficiency. This is one of those rare cases where the right solution is a simple solution.

THE COMPLICATION OF ENERGY-COST MYOPIA

The previous section concluded that regulatory approaches to reduce CO_2 emissions are inefficient and sometimes even counterproductive. If that were the whole story, we could write off regulations as a political convenience with little to recommend them.

But the regulatory story is more complex than this simple picture. Analyses of energy markets have found many market failures and impediments on the road to energy efficiency. Some involve institutional factors, such as the fact that people who rent houses have little incentive to make energy-saving investments that may pay off in the long run. A similar problem is seen in energy use in college dormitories.

Since rooms are not individually metered, students have weak incentives to turn the lights off or the heat down.

On top of these, one of the most important and puzzling phenomena is "energy-cost myopia." This refers to the syndrome in which people invest too little in energy efficiency because they underweigh (or over-discount) future fuel savings. If we could resolve this puzzle, the role of regulation would be much clearer.[8]

Here is a little fable. Suppose I go to the Volkswagen dealer looking for a new car. The salesperson shows me two models, one with a gasoline engine and one with a diesel engine. The gasoline gets 31 miles per gallon, while the diesel gets 42 miles per gallon. But the diesel version costs $2,000 more.

If I am like most people, I will choose the gasoline model. After all, if I am having trouble keeping on top of my credit card debt or am facing steep college tuitions for the children or had to postpone our family vacation, then $2,000 is not a welcome extra expense. And so I choose the gasoline car.

But suppose the salesperson explains the life cycle costs of the car. I tell him we drive 12,000 miles a year. He gets out his little life cycle calculator and finds that the gasoline version will use 100 more gallons of fuel per year than the diesel version. At $4 a gallon, this totals $400 per year of higher running costs for a gasoline engine. Over a 10-year lifetime and without discounting, we will spend $4,000 more in fuel costs to save $2,000 of up-front costs. Even with proper discounting, the fuel savings are more than the up-front costs.[9]

So enlightened by the facts, what do we do? Evidence from studies in many areas indicates that most of us will still buy the car with the lower up-front cost. For comparable models, gasoline engines outsell diesel ones by more than two to one in the United States.[10] More generally, evidence suggests that when people make purchases—from cars to appliances to home insulation—they systematically underinvest in energy efficiency. Some studies indicate that we could save a substantial fraction of energy use (between 10 and 40 percent depending upon the study) with zero net costs. The savings are lost in part because we suffer from a condition where we count mainly the near-term costs and ignore the distant savings. This is energy-cost myopia.

I have read academic studies about energy-cost myopia and have taught about it in classes. Still, I have succumbed to this syndrome myself on several occasions. For example, an energy audit of my house three years ago produced a list of suggestions that would save hundreds of dollars in heating and cooling costs with a modest up-front investment. Yet the audit is still sitting in my "To Do" box.

What are the reasons for energy-cost myopia? Some say that people have poor information: They do not know how poorly their homes are insulated or what the excess energy is costing them. Also, they may have trouble with the complicated calculations to determine the present value of energy savings. Yet another reason is that many people are cash starved—after all, if you are paying 29.99 percent annual interest on your credit card debt, long-term fuel savings are not a good investment. Perhaps people just systematically undervalue the future—their personal discount rate is much higher than the money discount rate. My excuse is simply that I am busy doing other things and tend to procrastinate on boring but noncritical tasks.

I should emphasize that decision failures of this kind are not limited to purchases of cars and home insulation. People often make questionable decisions about health care (they don't take their medications), about finance (they don't read the mortgage document and lose their houses), about business (half of small businesses fail in the first year), and in many other areas. Failures to make the most economical decisions are common features of human behavior that are increasingly studied in the fields of psychology and behavioral economics.[11]

Whatever the reason, the syndrome of energy-cost myopia is a realistic feature of human behavior that must be incorporated into our analysis.

Energy-cost myopia provides an important justification for regulatory approaches to global warming policy. Suppose that people do indeed systematically undervalue future energy costs. By requiring manufacturers to improve energy efficiency, we save energy, reduce carbon emissions, and simultaneously provide a good investment for consumers. It is similar to requiring automobile companies to install airbags, which consumers might not buy without a mandate. Since people do not always behave in their long-run self-interest, careful use of regulatory mandates can save lives (in the case of airbags) or money and CO_2 emissions (in the case of effective energy regulations).

How would we evaluate energy regulations when energy-cost myopia is factored in? This turns out to be a deep question because we do not know exactly why people exhibit energy-cost myopia. One interesting approach is to assume that people "overdiscount" future energy savings. That is, people implicitly apply a very high discount rate to future fuel savings. In the case discussed above, overdiscounting would reduce the long-term $4,000 savings. Suppose I apply a 20 percent annual discount rate to future fuel savings. A spreadsheet analysis will calculate a discounted gasoline savings of only $1,837, versus the extra $2,000 of up-front cost. Applying the super-high discount rate, I would indeed buy the gasoline-fueled car.

A finance specialist might tell me that I am behaving myopically. I would be better off putting my money in the diesel car rather than in my savings account. I respond, "Hold on before you call me myopic, dude!" I have a long list of reasons for my behavior. I need my savings for a rainy day; gasoline prices might go up; the bank deposit is guaranteed by the federal government; maybe I will wreck the car; perhaps I won't like the car and will sell it for a steep discount in a couple of years. So $2,000 in the bank—as opposed to in the diesel car—might seem completely sensible. These may not be sound reasons, but they might be sufficient to tilt people toward investments with low up-front costs and higher deferred costs.

In this context, let us revisit the efficiency of different regulations under the assumption that purchasers are myopic and overdiscount future energy savings. This would in reality apply mainly to consumer purchases, since businesses are more consistent in their economic decisions. The team that produced the estimates in Table 12 also investigated the cost of regulations when consumers use a high discount rate. They label this scenario "complete market failures" to represent the case where consumers base their investment decisions on a very high discount rate of 20 percent per year.

Table 13 compares the costs of CO_2 emissions reductions under assumptions of no market failures and full market failures.[12] In the case of automobile efficiency standards, if consumers discount future fuel savings at 20 percent per year, then the number changes sign, and there is actually a negative cost of $22 per ton of CO_2 removed. In other words, if we assume that consumers overdiscount future savings, this regulation can reduce CO_2 emissions and save money. This was the rationale for the most recent CAFE standards. The finding was similar for building codes, where the cost of the regulation in the context of overdiscounting was negative $15 per ton rather than a positive $51 per ton when discounting at the normal 5 percent per year. The two other cases in Table 13 show lower but positive costs even with energy-cost myopia.

The question of consumer rationality is indeed an important aspect of regulatory policy. If decisions are contaminated by energy-cost myopia, then there may be many negative cost options for reducing energy use and greenhouse-gas emissions.

Table 13. Costs and effects of alternative regulatory policies with energy-cost myopia. The table shows the cost of reducing CO_2 emissions under alternative discounting assumptions: no distortions (5 percent per year) and overdiscounting (20 percent per year).

	Cost ($ per ton of CO_2 reduced)	
Policy	No distortions in energy decisions (5% discount rate)	Overdiscounting in energy decisions (20% discount rate)
Gasoline tax	38	6
Building codes	51	−15
Tighter auto standards	85	−22
Liquid natural gas trucks	85	69

BALANCE SHEET ON ALTERNATIVE APPROACHES

This chapter has examined alternative approaches to raising carbon prices as tools for reducing CO_2 and other greenhouse gases. To begin with the positive side, it is clear that the economy is full of inefficient decisions on energy use. The syndrome of energy-cost myopia seems pervasive among consumers. Carefully designed regulations in a few areas can probably reduce CO_2 emissions at low or possibly zero cost.

Moreover, efficient regulations can supplement and buttress carbon price policies. Even if countries implement policies that raise carbon prices using cap and trade or tax approaches, there will always remain political uncertainties about whether the winds will shift and the regulations or taxes will be reduced. In this environment, regulatory emissions limits will ensure that businesses continue to move toward a low-carbon economy through the changing political weather.

But the shortcomings of relying primarily on regulations are severe. One problem is that undertaking most of the emissions reductions by regulation would involve literally thousands of technologies and millions of decisions. Governments would be saying, "Do this, but don't do that" about the entire economy. Realistically, governments do not have sufficient information to write regulations for the entire economy. Additionally, people in market democracies will not tolerate so much intrusion into their lives.

This leads to the second point: Regulatory policies alone cannot come close to solving the global warming problem by themselves. It is impossible to design regulations for every sector, energy good, and service. So while governments can write regulations for automobile fuel efficiency, they cannot realistically order people not to drive or order airlines not to use jet fuel.

Third, regulations can be very costly or even counterproductive if they are not carefully designed. The example of ethanol subsidies in the United States is a reminder that seemingly sensible policies can end up worthless or even counterproductive.

Given the unfavorable record of the regulatory approach, you might wonder why governments universally employ regulatory tools when they have been shown to be so inefficient. Studies have shown again and again that gasoline taxes are more efficient than regulations in reducing gasoline consumption or reducing the CO_2 emissions from transportation. Yet most countries prefer to impose fuel efficiency standards rather than taxes. The United States has tightened its standards while leaving the gasoline tax to decline in inflation-corrected terms.

There are many reasons for the regulatory tilt. One is that the costs of regulations are hidden from consumers. In the gasoline example, fuel efficiency standards raise the price of automobiles without leaving any governmental fingerprint; by contrast, raising gasoline taxes has generally been highly contentious, and high fuel prices even provoke riots in some countries. An additional factor promoting the regulatory approach is that businesses usually find that they can manipulate regulations to their advantage and can even "capture" regulatory agencies (in the sense that the regulatory agency advances the interests of the regulated industry rather than the public interest), while taxes have proven harder to manipulate. A good example of why businesses prefer regulation is the cap-and-trade approach, in which existing polluters have generally been granted valuable pollution allowances for free. Giving preferences to businesses under a pollution tax is harder to engineer because it is so visible.

Pessimists might throw their hands up in despair. Regulations cannot do the job efficiently, yet governments continue to use them as the primary approach. Advocates of carbon pricing will not deny that there is opposition to their proposals. But humanity is faced with a new and profound peril in global warming. We will need new tools to deal effectively with this danger.

The truth is that unless we implement an effective policy of carbon pricing, we will get virtually nowhere in slowing climate change. It may take time for people to become comfortable with new approaches. Moreover, people tend to overestimate the net cost of regulatory taxes because they overlook the fact that the revenues can be recycled by lowering other taxes. Therefore, explaining the importance of the use of market-based approaches such as carbon pricing is just as important a part of the educational process as explaining the science behind climate change.

23 NEW TECHNOLOGIES FOR A LOW-CARBON ECONOMY

Earlier chapters have described economic policies that provide incentives for firms and individuals to make the transition to a low-carbon economy. The discussion has described only in a general fashion the exact technologies that will power that transition. But we don't drive or heat our homes on generalizations. We use actual energy in the form of jet fuel for our airplanes, electricity for our computers, and gasoline for our cars. How big a challenge is it to "decarbonize" our economy?

A second question is the technological one. Today's economy is driven largely by fossil fuels like oil and coal. What will replace these workhorses of the modern economy? What will fuel our cars and heat our schools in the low-carbon world? What are the roles of nuclear, solar, wind, and other fuels for electricity generation? These are exciting questions that engage engineers and scientists around the world.

A third question from economics is subtle but equally important. How will we get firms to invent and produce, and consumers to buy and use, these new technologies? It is not enough to have an idea about a solar-powered water heater or a carbon-eating tree. Someone must have the incentive to develop an efficient prototype. If firms are to invest millions or even billions of dollars to develop such technologies, they must find them profitable to produce and sell. Consumers must find them advantageous to buy. What are the mechanisms that will set in motion this chain of invention, investment, production, and purchase of new low-carbon technologies? This is the central question addressed by this chapter.

THE LAST REFUGE

As the Kyoto Protocol expired at the end of 2012, many observers turned pessimistic. The leading British scientific magazine, *Nature*, had a special issue with a cover headline, "The Heat Is On: A Survival Guide to the Post-Kyoto World." Its introduction opined, "the world can go back to emitting greenhouse gases with abandon."[1] Some have given up on emissions restraints and believe that energy efficiency and new technologies are the answer. The Obama administration is pushing ahead on regulatory approaches. Others believe we have no alternative but to adapt to rapid warming, droughts, and rising seas.

We should avoid these mood swings from excessive optimism about the signing of the Kyoto Protocol to grim pessimism about its demise. Most of this book is devoted to thinking through different successor regimes. But suppose that the pessimists are correct about emissions reduction plans; perhaps an effective international regime to raise carbon prices is beyond reach. The alternative siren song of regulatory constraints is inefficient and unlikely to achieve the appropriate limits on climate change. What hope is there for our world?

In reality, when active policies fail, the only remaining hope for a happy ending would be a revolutionary change in energy technologies—changes that made low-carbon or even negative-carbon activities so inexpensive that they would replace fossil fuels even without any nudge from policymakers. This would require very steep declines in the costs of current renewable fuels (wind, solar, and geothermal) or discoveries of new technologies that are currently not in widespread application.

At present, the odds for such a favorable technological outcome are low in the Climate Casino. But technological history is full of surprises. Particularly if we are pessimistic about other roads to a stabilized climate, we should use all means to make the positive—in the sense of low-carbon—technological surprises more likely. This chapter discusses the challenges and the options.

THE CHALLENGE OF A LOW-CARBON ECONOMY

The chances are slim that technology can do the job without government policies mainly because the required changes are so large. Take as an example the U.S. policy set by the Obama administration. Using 2005 levels as a baseline, the proposal was to reduce CO_2 and other greenhouse-gas emissions 17 percent by 2020 and by 83 percent by 2050. The general outline of this policy was endorsed by several advisory groups.

Meeting these targets with domestic reductions alone would require major changes in the behavior of the U.S. economy. We can show this using the past and projected "carbon intensity" of economic activity. This concept measures the ratio of CO_2 emissions to output.

Figure 37 shows on the left the historical trend of decarbonization in the United States.[2] In recent years, U.S. carbon intensity has declined about 2 percent per year. Beyond 2010 there is a line labeled "U.S. policy proposal." This shows the required rate of decarbonization over the coming four decades under the policy proposed by the Obama administration and several scientific advisory groups. Over the entire 2010–2050 period, the United States would need to decarbonize at 6 percent per year on average.[3] This is a giant change in the pattern of energy use. Outside of electronics, no sector has achieved long-term rates of productivity growth at that pace for extended periods of time.

We can perform the same calculation for the world as a whole. To achieve the 2°C target at a global level, the global rate of decarbonization would need to be 4 percent per year over the 2010–2050 period.[4] This is less ambitious than the U.S. objective because the United States is proposing steeper reductions for rich countries than for developing countries. However, at the global level, it is still an enormous challenge.

To summarize: Achieving the emissions reductions contemplated by U.S. policy and consistent with the Copenhagen 2°C temperature target would require more rapid technological shifts than have been seen in almost any industry. This technological fact underlines the daunting challenge posed by climate change.

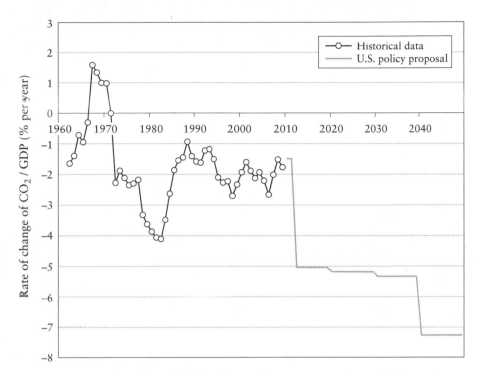

Figure 37. Historical and projected decarbonization in U.S. economy. The figure shows the rate of change in the CO_2-GDP ratio, or the rate of decarbonization. The left side shows the actual rate of decarbonization for the past half century. The right side shows the rate needed to achieve the ambitious goals for reducing CO_2 emissions by 83 percent by midcentury.

PROMISING TECHNOLOGIES

We can set the stage by viewing existing sources of energy. Figure 38 shows where the United States gets its energy today: almost 80 percent is from fossil fuels.[5] This implies right off the mark that about 80 percent of our energy will have to be produced either in different ways or from different sources if we are to move to a zero-carbon world. That in a nutshell is the problem.

THE TECHNOLOGICAL ROAD TO A LOW-CARBON WORLD

Given the enormity of the transition needed to achieve a low-carbon economy, what are the promising low-carbon energy sources?

Researchers such as Nebojsa Nakicenovic of IIASA and the Technical University in Vienna have made important contributions to our understanding of the underlying processes of innovation in energy systems. This is a major area of research today, and I can only scratch the surface of the topic. However, a few remarks will illustrate the nature of the transition.[6]

A good place to start is with the current and prospective costs of different kinds of electricity generation for the United States, shown in Table 14.[7] This shows the costs, the estimated dates of full-scale availability, and the level of maturity of the technology. The generation costs of existing plants include only the variable costs (since the capital and

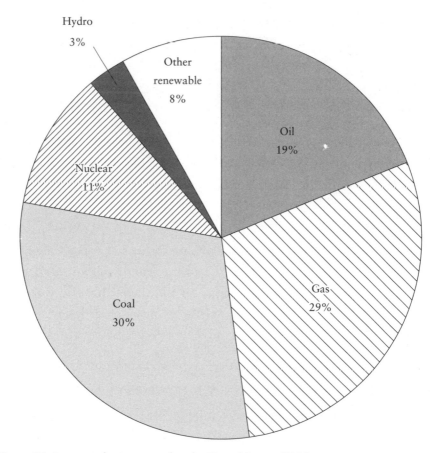

Figure 38. Sources of energy used in the United States, 2009.

Table 14. Estimates of the cost of near-term electricity generation. This table shows estimates by the U.S. Energy Information Administration of the costs of different kinds of power generation. Note that the renewable sources or low-carbon-emissions CCS are much more costly.

Plant type	Capital and other fixed	Variable	Total	Date of availability	Status of technology	Emissions rate (tCO$_2$/MWH)
Conventional combined-cycle natural gas	2.05	4.56	6.61	Today	Mature	0.60
Conventional coal	7.05	2.43	9.48	Today	Mature	1.06
Wind	9.70	0.00	9.70	Today	Mature	0.00
Geothermal	9.22	0.95	10.17	Today	Developing	0.00
Advanced coal	8.41	2.57	10.98	2020	Developing	0.76
Biomass	7.02	4.23	11.25	2020	Developing	0.00
Solar photovoltaic	21.07	0.00	21.07	Today	Developing	0.00
Solar thermal	31.18	0.00	31.18	Today	Developing	0.00
Advanced natural gas with CCS	3.97	4.96	8.93	2030	Early-stage	0.06
Advanced nuclear	10.22	1.17	11.39	2025	Early-stage	0.00
Advanced coal with CCS	10.31	3.31	13.62	2030	Early-stage	0.11

other fixed costs are already spent). Variable costs are low, generally less than 5 cents per kWh. As long as these plants are operational, and without any CO_2 emissions charges, they will continue to be profitable for many years. For new plants, natural gas is currently the most economical of mature technologies. Conventional coal and wind power are about 50 percent more expensive than new natural gas plants.

The central question going forward is the prospect for economical low-carbon electricity. Wind is the only mature low-carbon technology. It is 50 percent more expensive than the best existing technology. Moreover, its capacity is limited in the United States. The other promising technologies with the possibility of large-scale deployments are, from least to most expensive, advanced natural gas with carbon capture and storage (CCS), advanced nuclear power, and advanced coal with CCS. These are 50 to 100 percent more expensive than the most economical existing technology. Moreover, they are still a long way from being ready for large-scale deployment. Table 14 is worth careful study as it shows the gaps that must be reduced—either by technological improvements or by carbon pricing—to bring low-carbon technologies to the market.

It is sobering to recognize the hurdles on the road to a low-carbon economy. Chapter 14 analyzed the difficulties involved in deploying CCS on a large scale. The other major large-scale and proven nonfossil energy resource today is nuclear power. Nuclear power can be used for electricity, but there is currently no economical way to use it in many applications, such as air travel. In addition, nuclear power faces two hurdles. To begin with, it is more expensive than fossil fuels (see Table 14). An even greater obstacle is the huge number of plants that would be required to replace fossil fuel power generation. Moreover, because of widespread public concerns about safety, the expansion would have to occur in an environment where some countries (Germany, for example) plan to phase out nuclear power.

Given the constraints on using nuclear power, the transition to a low-carbon future will require new and unproven—or existing and expensive—technologies. The most attractive options in most people's minds are renewable energy sources such as solar, wind, and geothermal power. In most countries, these sources are currently much more expensive than fossil fuels and have grown primarily because of large subsidies. Without major improvements in cost, replacing fossil fuels with renewable energy would impose a huge expense—on the order of hundreds of billions of dollars annually—on the United States.

It will be useful to look closely at the nature of the transition to a low-carbon economy by examining projections from energy models. Take as an example an analysis of the technological requirements of stabilizing emissions over the next four decades. Two modeling teams (the Joint Global Change Research Institute and the National Renewable Energy Laboratories) examined the technological changes in the U.S. electricity sector that would be consistent with a temperature stabilization target. The two models are both state of the art. One (GCAM) is a global model with a detailed energy sector for major regions, while the other (ReEDS) is a model of the U.S. electricity sector with a detailed regional resolution.[8]

The models were calibrated to produce the same electricity generation over the 2010–2050 period. Then each model calculated the mix of technologies that would meet the electricity path at the lowest costs. Even though the models have completely different architectures, focus, economic structures, and scientific teams, they showed remarkably consistent results.

- The most prevalent technologies currently used to generate electricity—conventional coal and natural gas—are phased out by 2050.
- Nuclear power grows modestly, keeping approximately its current share of generation.
- A wholly undeveloped technology—coal and gas with CCS—has about half of the electricity market by 2050.
- Wind power has about one-quarter of the market by 2050.
- Advanced renewable generation of various kinds (solar photovoltaic, solar thermal, biopower, geothermal) captures another quarter of the market.

- The major difference between the two models is in the prospects for coal CCS and wind, which involve questions of cost and future availability.

I would highlight two major features of the study. First, the models require very high CO_2 prices to induce electricity suppliers to restructure their capital to meet the sharp emissions reductions. The prices in 2050 range from $150 to $500 per ton of CO_2 to meet the objectives. The lower end is approximately the price shown in Figure 33 and is consistent with many of the global integrated assessment models, while the higher number is at the high end of estimates and would impose serious economic stresses on energy markets.

The most important point to emphasize is the size of the technological transition that will be necessary to meet the objectives. Technologies that comprise 70 percent of current electricity generation (coal and natural gas) will need to be completely replaced. Fully half of the projected generation will be provided with technologies that are not currently operated at anywhere near the required scale. Another quarter (nuclear) will be provided by a technology that is generally unacceptable to the American public; indeed, not a single U.S. nuclear power plant was licensed between 1978 and 2012. The balance of the electricity will be generated by sources that are presently much more expensive than current technologies (wind) or are really just a gleam in the eyes of engineers (large-scale solar photovoltaic and geothermal power).

In reality, a technological transition of this magnitude requires years to go through the many stages of technological, political, regulatory, and economic approvals—and must pass the test of public acceptability and private profitability along the way. A technology like CCS might require a decade of research and development (R&D), another decade of pilot plant testing, continuous public and environmental and boardroom scrutiny, perhaps another decade of roll-out of large-scale plants in many countries, and only then—if it passes all the tests along the way—would it be ready for deployment on the scale needed to capture and store billions or tens of billions of tons of CO_2 every year.

This survey just touches on possible technological solutions to the climate problem. I conclude tentatively that for the foreseeable future there are no mature technologies that can meet ambitious emissions reduction targets economically. But we cannot reliably see far into the future, and technologies are developing rapidly in many areas. So we need to be attuned to new possibilities. Even more important, we need to encourage fundamental and applied science, and to ensure that markets provide the appropriate incentives for inventors and investors to discover and introduce new low-carbon technologies. That issue leads to the final section of this chapter, which explores innovation policies.

THE NATURE OF INNOVATION

Most energy decisions are made by private businesses and consumers on the basis of prices, profits, incomes, and habits. Governments influence energy use through regulations, subsidies, and taxes. But the central decisions are taken in the context of market supply and demand.

It is clear that a rapid decarbonization will require substantial changes in our energy technologies. How do technological changes arise? The answer is, usually through a complex interaction of individual brilliance, persistence, economic incentives, and market demand. The meandering history of the photoelectric cell used for solar power is a typical example.

The story begins in 1839, when the young French physicist Edmond Becquerel hit upon the photovoltaic effect while experimenting with an electrolytic cell. The physics underlying the photoelectric effect were explained by Albert Einstein in 1905, for which he won the Nobel Prize.

The first important practical applications for the photovoltaic cell were not created until more than a century after Becquerel's discovery. Scientists at Bell Telephone Labs developed solar cells in the mid-1950s, and governments got involved as they realized the potential of solar power for use in space satellites and remote locations. At that point, solar technology blossomed, with applications in space satellites, small arrays on houses, and large solar plants. Efficiency rose from 4 percent in the first solar cells to more than 40 percent in the best current applications. Costs have fallen dramatically since the first cells were produced, and some observers project that solar electricity will be competitive with fossil fuels within two or three decades. In recent years, as costs have dropped and climate-change policy has become more prominent, there has been steep growth in patenting of photovoltaic solar cells. Figure 39 shows the trend in the price of photovoltaic modules.[9]

If you look at the history of inventions, you will find that virtually every one entailed a similar interplay between basic science, applications, commercial interests, false starts, improvements, and profits in the marketplace when they succeeded. A study of technological history also shows the perils of forecasting technological advances—as difficult as predicting the stock market. As an example, in the 1958 first edition of the study by John Jewkes, David Sawers, and Richard Stillerman, that is wise in other respects, the authors did not include computers among their great inventions. Revisiting this a decade later, they wrote, "the Electronic Digital Computer seemed to have so uncertain a commercial future that we decided to exclude it from our case studies."[10] This prediction by three of the most prominent historians of technology is a sober reminder of the difficulties of forecasting future trends.

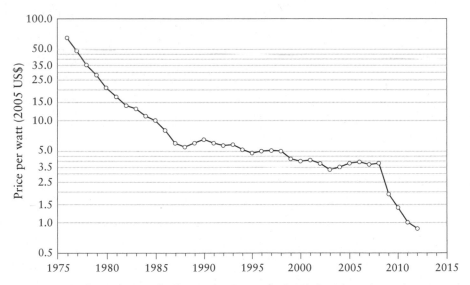

Figure 39. Decline in price of solar power. Prices declined sharply in the early era, reached a plateau, and then dropped again when China entered the market with large governmental subsidies.

Economists who study innovation and technological change emphasize one central feature that distinguishes them from normal goods: They have large externalities. Recall that an externality is an activity for which the person undertaking the activity does not pay or is not compensated fully for the full social cost or benefit of the action.[11]

All new technologies have this property. When you discover a new device or process, I can use it without making you less productive. Moreover, once a technology has been developed and revealed, it is not possible (without special laws such as those relating to patents and copyrights) to exclude others from using it. You might be surprised to learn that many of the great inventors in history died in poverty because they could not capture the fruits of their ideas.

From an economic point of view, fundamental inventions have the same basic characteristics as global warming. Their value spreads around to all corners of the world. Cell phone innovators probably did not dream that one of the major beneficiaries would be people in remote villages of tropical Africa. If you have mastered the externalities of global warming, you have also understood the basic economics of innovation. The only difference is that the externalities of innovations are largely beneficial while those of global warming are largely harmful.

This brings us to the main economic implication of innovational externalities. Because the creators of new knowledge cannot appropriate for themselves the full gains from new knowledge, the private returns on innovation are below the social returns. As a result, less innovation is undertaken than is optimal for society as a whole.

The history of inventions shows that they result from the purposive activities—often formal R&D—in the public and private sector. Who actually does the R&D today? The basic facts are clear. Governments and the nonprofit sector fund much of the nation's basic research, while industry funds most product development and investment in capital goods. This pattern suggests that support for low-carbon innovation will require two kinds of funding. First, government support for basic research is essential for fundamental science and engineering on energy and related fields. The United States has agencies such as the

National Science Foundation and the Department of Energy to support these activities.

For low-carbon technologies to move beyond the laboratories and into the marketplace requires funding from the profit-oriented firms that develop new products and processes to increase their profits.

One of the most difficult challenges is how to motivate the private sector to invest in low-carbon technologies. The main problem is that business investments in low-carbon innovation are inhibited by a double externality. The first externality is the fact, discussed above, that innovators capture but a small fraction of the social returns on innovation. The second hurdle is the environmental externality of global warming in the absence of a price on carbon emissions. In other words, investments in low-carbon technologies are depressed because the private returns on innovation are below the social returns, and private returns are further depressed because the market price of carbon is below its true social cost. The net effect is to doubly discourage profit-oriented R&D in low-carbon technologies.

A specific example will clarify the problem. One technology that definitely would not be profitable in a world without CO_2-limiting policies is CCS. Recall from the earlier description that this technology uses costly processes to capture CO_2 emissions and store them in a safe place where they can be sealed off for a century or more. Current estimates, based on data from several large demonstration projects, suggest that a large CCS plant could capture and sequester CO_2 at about $50 per ton.[12] If the price of CO_2 is zero, then the plant would lose money. No profit-oriented company would invest in this process if it knew the price of CO_2 would be zero forever.

Now suppose that a firm thought that countries were going to implement a tough global warming policy—one in which the price of carbon would rise to $100 per ton in a few years. At that price, businesses estimate that a CCS plant would be profitable because in effect it would be producing CO_2 at $50 per ton of CO_2 and selling it at $100 a ton. Firms would proceed cautiously, looking at different approaches, but they would have economic reasons to invest in this technology. This same logic would apply to investments in solar, wind, geothermal, and nuclear power.

This leads to an essential conclusion: A high price of carbon is necessary to induce profit-oriented business to undertake research, development, and investments in new low-carbon technologies.

The country may have the best climate scientists developing the best projections of climate change; it might have the best materials scientists working on high-efficiency CO_2 pipelines; it may have the best financial wizards developing new financial derivatives to fund all these investments. But if the carbon price is zero, then projects to develop promising low-carbon technologies like CCS will not get to the boardroom of a profit-oriented company.

CROSSING THE VALLEY OF DEATH

The U.S. economy has superb fundamental science and engineering in its universities and research labs. American firms are highly attuned to the marketplace and produce thousands of new and improved products every year. But in between the ivory tower and the jungle of the marketplace, the terrain dips into what Stanford economist John Weyant has called "the Valley of Death."[13] This is the no-man's-land where bright ideas from the laboratory do not survive the transition to the marketplace because they are starved of funds (see Figure 40).

This problem has been thoughtfully analyzed by a leading scholar in this area, F. M. Scherer:

Somewhere between the extremes of basic research and specific new product or process development lie investments in technological advances that have not matured enough to permit commercial embodiment, but that blaze the trail for concrete developments. Investments in such "precompetitive generic enabling" technologies are believed to be susceptible to private-sector market failures nearly as severe as those afflicting basic research. The investment outlays required to bring a technology forward to the point of commercial applicability may be substantial, but once decisive advances

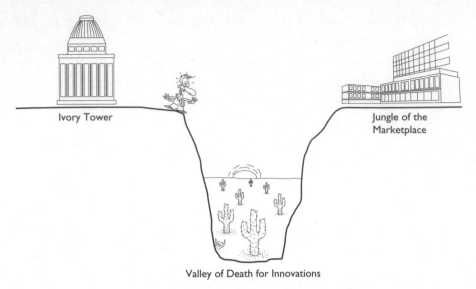

Ivory Tower

Jungle of the
Marketplace

Valley of Death for Innovations

Figure 40. Few innovations survive the transition from scientific laboratories to the marketplace.

have been made, their features are likely to be widely known and appropriable by others, and patent protection may be too weak to deter their use in others' R&D projects.[14]

How can we increase the survival rate of sound innovations across the Valley of Death? First, the global warming externality must be eliminated by having an appropriate price for carbon. As an additional incentive, governments might provide extra tax credits for precompetitive technologies.

An interesting governmental innovation is a program called Advanced Research Projects Agency-Energy or ARPA-E.[15] Its purpose is to fund early-stage energy research that profit-oriented firms are unlikely to support due to technical and financial uncertainties. These projects in the first years included new battery technologies, CO_2 capture, and improved turbines. To be realistic, the program is tiny by the standards of overall R&D, with a budget of $275 million for 2012, versus $5 billion spent on all energy R&D for the same year. But if the Valley of Death theory is correct, funds applied at this stage may generate extremely high returns. People will be watching this initiative closely to see if it helps bring innovative ideas to market.

This chapter leads to three major conclusions. First, it is essential that governments continue to support basic science and technology in energy and related fields. We don't know which scientific developments will pay off, so we need to fund research widely as well as wisely. Support for basic science should include support for early-stage projects in the perilous Valley of Death.

Second, we must recognize the importance of the private sector in developing new technologies—both not-for-profit researchers and for-profit entrepreneurs. Particularly critical is to ensure that profit-oriented firms have the proper incentives to promote a rapid and economical transition to a low-carbon economy. The major requirement is that carbon prices be sufficiently high so that investments in low-carbon technologies can expect tangible and secure financial payoffs. Without high carbon prices, innovators and firms will not be motivated to invest in low-carbon technologies. So once again, the carbon price becomes a central part of a strategy to tame the dangers of global warming.

Finally, I again emphasize the central role that rapid technological change must play in the transition to a low-carbon economy. Current low-carbon technologies cannot substitute for fossil fuels without a substantial economic penalty. Developing low-carbon technologies will lower the cost of achieving our climate goals. Moreover, if other policies fail, development of low-carbon technologies is the last refuge for achieving our climate goals.

PART V
CLIMATE POLITICS

There is no gambling like politics.
—*Benjamin Disraeli*

24 CLIMATE SCIENCE AND ITS CRITICS

If this were an academic treatise on the best economic strategy to deal with climate change, we would now be finished. We have reviewed the science, economics, and policies. We have concluded that climate change is serious and have laid out some of the options for governments to deal with it. End of story.

In reality, the story continues. This book takes climate science seriously. But there are skeptics. Many people misunderstand the issues. Doubts about the validity of mainstream climate science as well as policies to slow warming are central issues in American politics today. Here are some examples of the contentious dialogue:

> *A U.S. presidential candidate:* The greatest hoax I think that has been around for many, many years if not hundreds of years has been this hoax . . . global warming.
> *The title of a book by a U.S. senator: The Greatest Hoax: How the Global Warming Conspiracy Threatens Your Future*
> *An advocacy group:* "Cap and Trade—Taxing Our Way to Bankruptcy"[1]

Such views are not limited to the United States. Here are two from abroad:

> *A key adviser to Russian president Vladimir Putin:* No link has been established between carbon dioxide emissions and climate change.
> *The former president of the Czech Republic:* Global warming is a false myth and every serious person and scientist says so.[2]

The list could go on and on. While these debates may seem like amusing distractions, they pose serious challenges because of their impact on public opinion. So in this final part, I discuss the hurdles that confront climate-change policy today.

THE MEANING OF SCIENTIFIC CONSENSUS

Suppose you are a student assigned to write a paper on the role of humans in global climate change. In light of the dueling advocates on both sides, you want to determine what scientists believe. When you look at Wikipedia, you find the following: "Presently the scientific consensus on climate change is that human activity is very likely the cause for the rapid increase in global average temperatures over the past several decades. Consequently, the debate has largely shifted onto ways to reduce further human impact and to find ways to adapt to change that has already occurred."[3]

So at the very beginning, you are told that there is a scientific consensus. A little bell might go off in your head. What is a scientific consensus? How can we decide whether there is one? Who decides? Aren't there cases of past consensuses that turned out to be wrong?

A scientific consensus is the collective judgment of the community of informed and knowledgeable scientists in a particular field at a given time. But determining the "collective judgment" is very tricky. Science does not proceed by majority rule. There are no votes on scientific principles, and most scientists would scoff at the idea that science is decided by a plebiscite. Moreover, we know that even the most brilliant scientists have sometimes taken a wrong turn.

One way to identify a consensus is to examine authoritative textbooks and expert reports on the subject. Let's take an example of the concept of externalities, which is critical for understanding the economics of climate change. We might turn to the fine introductory textbook by distinguished Princeton economists William Baumol and Alan Blinder, now in its eleventh edition. They actually list externalities as one of the "10 Great Ideas" of economics. Here is what they write: "Some transactions affect third parties who were not involved in the decision. . . . Such social costs are called *externalities* because they affect parties external to the economic transactions that cause them. Externalities escape the control of the market mechanism because no financial incentive motivates polluters to minimize the damage they do."[4]

You would find a similar definition in other economics textbooks. So the use of the concept of externalities—and its utility in understanding the market failures of pollution—is an example of the scientific consensus in economics. Economists might and indeed do disagree about which externalities are important, about the best policies to correct externalities, and about how much to tighten the screws on externalities like toxic wastes or global warming. But mainstream economists do not claim that externalities are a hoax. Similarly, mainstream scientists do not claim that climate change is a hoax.

Suppose that we would like to find the collective judgment on a specific scientific question. How is that done in practice? In many areas of science, consensus is determined by the reports of expert groups. Take as a leading example the U.S. National Academies, which is the premier American scientific institution. That body has a carefully designed process for producing consensus reports. In writing reports, the National Academies insist on several ingredients: independence from external pressure, expertise, reliance on evidence, objectivity, approval by the Academies' leadership, and disclosure of conflicts of interest.[5]

For example, Congress was concerned about the use of evidence in criminal trials. In recent years, DNA evidence has shown that many people were sentenced to death based on faulty eyewitness testimony. The Congress asked the National Academies to prepare a report to "make recommendations for maximizing the use of forensic technologies and techniques to solve crimes, investigate deaths, and protect the public."

The Academies then convened a panel of experts to study and report on the subject. The panel reviewed the scientific literature, synthesized existing knowledge, and wrote a report. The output was a consensus of the panel members. It was peer reviewed by outside experts, and was then approved by the governing board of the Academies. In this case, you can read the report, *Strengthening Forensic Science in the United States: A Path Forward*, to see what the experts recommend.[6]

What have expert reports of the U.S. National Academies concluded on climate change? When President George W. Bush and his advisers arrived in 2001, they were skeptical about climate change, so they asked the National Academies for "assistance in identifying the areas in the science of climate change where there are the greatest certainties and uncertainties." The committee was chaired by a distinguished climate scientist, Ralph Cicerone (who later became president of the National Academy of Sciences), and produced a clear and forceful report. The report began with the following statement: "Greenhouse gases are accumulating in Earth's atmosphere as a result of human activities, causing surface air temperatures and subsurface ocean temperatures to rise."[7] The review hence concluded that the evidence for human-caused global warming was sound.

A decade later, the National Academies were asked similar questions by Congress, and it produced another consensus report. The first two sentences of the summary stated, "Emissions of carbon dioxide from the burning of fossil fuels have ushered in a new epoch where human activities will largely determine the evolution of Earth's climate. Because carbon dioxide in the atmosphere is long lived, it can effectively lock the Earth and future generations into a range of impacts, some of which could become very severe."[8] According to the report, there is no question about what is happening to the climate or about the primary cause.

Finally, we can turn to the latest published report of the IPCC, which is the authoritative international group reviewing climate-change science. This report reviewed the evidence and concluded, "Warming of the climate system is unequivocal, as is now evident from observations of increases in global average air and ocean temperatures, widespread melting of snow and ice, and rising global average sea level. . . . Most of the observed increase in globally averaged temperatures since the mid-20th century is very likely due to the observed increase in anthropogenic greenhouse gas concentrations."[9]

I could continue with further examples, but the basic findings of expert panels around the world are the same: The processes underlying projections of climate change are established science; the climate is changing unusually rapidly; and the earth is warming.

CONTRARIAN VIEWS ON GLOBAL WARMING

Previous chapters have presented mainstream scientific views on climate change—the established, the uncertain, and the unknown. Not every scientist or economist would agree with every finding, but most have a secure footing in the published and peer-reviewed literature.

Consensus does not imply unanimity. We find today a small and vocal group of contrarian scientists who argue that the consensus on climate change is poorly grounded and that policies to slow warming are not warranted. In 2012, an opinion piece by "sixteen scientists" was published in *The Wall Street Journal* titled, "No Need to Panic about Global Warming."[10] This was useful because it contained many of the standard criticisms in a succinct statement.[11]

The basic message of the article was that the globe is not warming, that models are wrong, and that delaying policies to slow climate change for 50 years will have no serious economic or environment consequences. I will analyze four of their claims as typical of the contrarian viewpoint.[12]

A first claim of contrarians is that the planet is not warming. The sixteen scientists wrote, "Perhaps the most inconvenient fact is the lack of global warming for well over 10 years now."

It is easy to get lost in the tiniest details here. Most people will benefit from stepping back and looking at the record of actual temperature measurements. I showed the global temperature history in Figure 8. I do not need any complicated statistical analysis to see that temperatures are rising, and furthermore that they are higher in the past decade than they were in earlier decades.[13]

Moreover, climate scientists have moved far beyond global mean surface temperature in looking for evidence of human-caused climate change. Scientists have found several indicators that point to a warming world with humans as the major cause, including melting of glaciers and ice sheets; changes in ocean heat content, rainfall patterns, atmospheric moisture, and river runoff; rising sea levels; stratospheric cooling; and the shrinking of Arctic sea ice. Those who look only at global temperature trends are like investigators using only eyewitness reports and ignoring fingerprints, video surveillance cameras, social media, and DNA-based evidence.[14] Yet the contrarians continue to repeat their claims using outmoded techniques and data.

A second argument is that the climate models are exaggerating the extent of warming. The sixteen scientists wrote, "The lack of warming for more than a decade—indeed, the smaller-than-predicted warming over the 22 years since the UN's Intergovernmental Panel on Climate Change (IPCC) began issuing projections—suggests that computer models have greatly exaggerated how much warming additional CO_2 can cause."

What is the evidence on the performance of climate models? Do they predict the historical trend accurately? Statisticians routinely address this kind of question. The standard approach is to perform an experiment in which modelers put the changes in CO_2 concentrations and other climate influences in a climate model and estimate the resulting temperature path ("with GHGs"); and then modelers calculate what would happen in the counterfactual situation where the only changes were due to natural sources, for example, the sun and volcanoes, with no human-induced changes ("without GHGs"). They then compare the actual temperature increases, the model predictions with all sources (with GHGs), and the model predictions with natural sources alone (without GHGs).

This experiment has been performed many times using climate models.[15] The experiments showed that the projections of climate models are consistent with recorded temperature trends over recent decades only if human impacts are included. The divergent trend is especially pronounced after 1980. By 2010, calculations using natural sources alone underpredict the actual temperature increases by about 1°C, while the calculations including human sources track the actual temperature trend closely.

In reviewing the results, the IPCC report concluded, "No climate model using natural forcings [i.e., natural warming factors] alone has reproduced the observed global warming trend in the second half of the twentieth century."[16]

One of the strangest claims of contrarians is the third argument: "The fact is that CO_2 is not a pollutant." What might this mean? Presumably, it means that CO_2 is not by itself toxic to humans or other organisms within the range of concentrations that we are likely to encounter, and indeed higher CO_2 concentrations may be beneficial.

However, this is not the meaning of pollution under U.S. law or in standard economics. The U.S. Clean Air Act defines an air pollutant as "any air pollution agent or combination of such agents, including any physical, chemical, biological, radioactive . . . substance or matter which is emitted into or otherwise enters the ambient air." In a 2007 decision on this question, the Supreme Court ruled on the question: "Carbon dioxide, methane, nitrous oxide, and hydrofluorocarbons are without a doubt 'physical [and] chemical . . . substance[s] which [are] emitted into . . . the ambient air.' . . . Greenhouse gases fit well within the Clean Air Act's capacious definition of 'air pollutant.'"[17]

In economics, a pollutant is a form of negative externality—that is, a by-product of economic activity that causes damages to innocent bystanders. The question here is whether emissions of CO_2 and other greenhouse gases will cause net damages, now and in the future. I reviewed this question in Chapter 20, and it may be useful to look back at the results shown in Figure 8. Eleven of the thirteen studies concluded that there are net damages, and the damages rise sharply for warming greater than 1°C.[18] CO_2 is indeed a pollutant because it is a damaging side effect of economic activity.

In their final point, the sixteen scientists argued that warming might be beneficial. In doing so, they cited my earlier work and claimed that my studies showed that policies to slow climate change would be unnecessary for the next half century: "A recent study of a wide variety of policy options by Yale economist William Nordhaus showed that nearly the highest benefit-to-cost ratio is achieved for a policy that allows 50 more years of economic growth unimpeded by greenhouse gas controls. . . . And it is likely that more CO_2 and the modest warming that may come with it will be an overall benefit to the planet."

The first problem with this claim is an elementary mistake in economic analysis. The authors use the concept of the "benefit-to-cost ratio" to support their argument. Cost-benefit and business economics teach that this is an incorrect criterion for selecting investments or policies. The appropriate criterion for decisions in this context is net benefits (that is, the difference between, and not the ratio of, benefits and costs).[19]

The major point, however, is that the sixteen scientists' summary of the economic analysis is incorrect. My research, along with that of virtually all other economic modelers, shows that acting now rather than waiting 50 years has substantial net benefits. I recalculated the economic impacts of waiting using the DICE-2012 model to determine the cost of delaying action for 50 years. The loss is calculated as $6.5 trillion. Waiting is not only economically costly but will also make the transition much more costly when it eventually takes place.

POLICIES IN THE CLIMATE CASINO

Contrarians often argue that we are uncertain about future climate change and impacts, and we should defer any costly abatement while gathering more information. The sixteen scientists were sufficiently relaxed about the risks that they recommended waiting 50 years before taking actions to slow climate change.

We can return to our parable of the Climate Casino to understand the dangers of waiting. Humans are in effect spinning the roulette wheel when we inject CO_2 and other gases into the atmosphere. The balls may land in the favorable black pockets or in the unfavorable red pockets, or possibly in the dangerous zero or double-zero pockets.

The contrarians suggest, in effect, that most of the balls will land in the favorable black pockets, and we should therefore postpone any abatement activities for 50 years. In fact, the contrarians have the impact of uncertainty exactly backward. A sensible policy would pay an insurance premium to avoid playing the roulette wheel of the Climate Casino. Economic model estimates of the costs of doing nothing for 50 years are understated because they cannot incorporate all the uncertainties—not just the obvious ones such as climate sensitivity but also the dangerous zero and double-zero uncertainties of tipping points, ecosystem risks, and ocean acidification.

The advice of climate science contrarians is to ignore the dangers in the Climate Casino. To heed that advice is a perilous gamble.

UNATTAINABLE CERTAINTY

I am often asked if, given all the uncertainties, we can be absolutely sure that humans are causing rising temperatures and that this trend will continue in the years ahead. The IPCC Fourth Assessment Report answered this question as follows: "Most of the observed increase in global average temperatures since the mid-20th century is *very likely* due to the observed increase in anthropogenic greenhouse gas concentrations."[20]

Critics continue to attack these and similar conclusions. One argument is that scientists are not really 100 percent sure about global warming. That is true. But a good scientist is never 100 percent sure of any empirical phenomenon. This was explained by Richard Feynman in a way that is humorous but very deep:

Some years ago I had a conversation with a layman about flying saucers. Because I am scientific, I know all about flying saucers! I said, "I don't think there are flying saucers." So my antagonist said, "Is it impossible that there are flying saucers? Can you prove that it's impossible?"

"No," I said, "I can't prove it's impossible. It's just very unlikely." At that he said, "You are very unscientific. If you can't prove it's impossible, then how can you say that it's unlikely?" But that is the way that is scientific. It is scientific only to say what is more likely and what is less likely, and not to be proving all the time the possible and impossible.

To define what I mean, I might have said to him, "Listen, I mean that from my knowledge of the world that I see around me, I think that it is much more likely that the reports of flying saucers are the results of the known irrational characteristics of terrestrial intelligence than of the unknown rational efforts of extra-terrestrial intelligence."[21]

Standing back from the shouting and debates, I would draw two lessons here. The first is a warning about the potential for a false scientific consensus. Many scientists are irritated by the nagging contrarians who are always pointing to some obscure piece of data or trend that points in a direction that seems to contradict the standard theory behind climate change. Perhaps contrarians point to the pause in warming such as occurred during the 2000–2010 period; or satellite observations that differ from ground-based observations; or studies that indicate that agriculture might benefit from CO_2 fertilization.

It is tempting to wish the critics would simply disappear. However, the history of science tells us that we need to be alert to the possibility of allowing a false consensus, of ignoring telltale inconsistencies, of holding too firmly to existing doctrines. So the correct response to critics is to look carefully at their arguments and determine whether they do indeed undermine standard theories. Scientists and economists need to confront contrary arguments with the same vigor with which they argue for the validity of their own approaches.

The second lesson in Feynman's story is a reminder about how good science proceeds—both in the natural sciences of space travel and in the social sciences like economics. There is a remote possibility that the world will not warm over the coming years. We can never say for sure that global warming theories are 100 percent correct.

Rather, it is better to say, "Given the fundamental science, the many climate models from around the world, the fiercely competitive scientific enterprise that tests assumptions and reasoning, and the accumulation of corroborating evidence, it is very likely that the theories are correct. Perhaps we are only 95 percent certain. But we cannot wait to be 100 percent certain because absolute certainty can never be achieved in an empirical science. And if we wait until we are completely certain, it will be too late to stop it."

25 PUBLIC OPINION ON CLIMATE CHANGE

In a democracy, effective and durable policies to slow global warming must ultimately rest on public support. While the scientific basis has become stronger over time, we observe a large and growing divide between climate scientists and popular opinion in the United States. What are popular views on climate change? What are the reasons for the growing gap in public understanding? These are the questions I examine in this chapter.

PUBLIC VIEWS ON SCIENCE AND GLOBAL WARMING

Before analyzing public opinion on global warming, let us step back to examine public opinion on science. Climate change is a scientific field. It will be instructive to look at what people believe about other scientific areas, some controversial, some not.

For several years, the U.S. National Science Foundation has sponsored surveys that measure public understanding of major scientific concepts, called indexes of scientific literacy. Figure 41 shows the percentage of respondents who answered "correctly" on six important scientific questions.[1] (I use the word "correct" with hesitancy. These statements are described as "basic constructs that are the intellectual foundation for reading and understanding contemporary issues." Without getting into deep discussions of epistemology, we might say that these propositions are almost surely "true," but as Feynman reminded us in Chapter 24, it is possible but very unlikely that these statements are incorrect.[2])

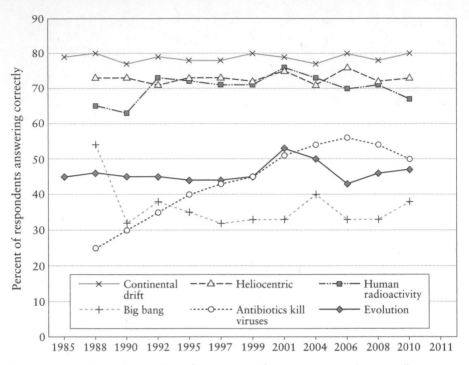

Figure 41. Popular understanding of major scientific concepts. People generally accept continental drift and the heliocentric view, while the big bang theory of the origin of the universe and evolutionary theories are correctly understood by less than half of Americans.

People are well informed on some concepts, such as the heliocentric view, the source of radioactivity, and the existence of continental drift. The concept of evolution does not fare well with many Americans. The big bang theory has actually lost ground among the public over the last quarter century. On the other hand, understanding of the effect of antibiotics on viruses has improved markedly. Perhaps people pay attention to scientists, as they do to their doctors, when it makes a difference to their personal welfare.

Now turn to views on global warming. Surveys on this topic have been conducted starting in 1997 in the United States. I gathered the major surveys conducted by different survey groups and selected the eight panels that had repeated the questions for several years; five by Gallup, two by Pew, and one from Harris. As an example, one of the Pew sur-

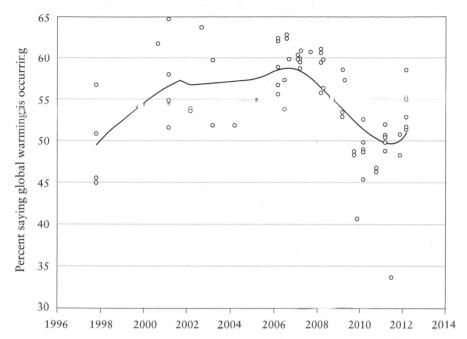

Figure 42. Fraction of population saying that global warming is real. This figure synthesizes data on public views in the United States on global warming. While the questions differ, they typically are "Do you think the earth is warming?" The dots are the individual surveys, while the solid line is a statistical fit.

veys asked, "From what you've read and heard, is there solid evidence that the average temperature on earth has been getting warmer over the past few decades, or not?" I linked the surveys together and created a composite survey. The results from the sixty-seven individual surveys and the composite are shown in Figure 42.[3]

The survey data indicate an interesting pattern, one not seen in the other results on scientific understanding. Public understanding and agreement with climate science in the United States rose markedly from the late 1990s to the mid-2000s. Then agreement with the science took a sharp nosedive after 2006. The composite series fell from a peak of about 58 percent agreement in 2007 to less than 50 percent in 2010.

Scientists may be glad to note that there appears to have been some upturn in public agreement with the basic science in the last two years.

Of ten questions that have been repeated since early 2011, the fraction of respondents holding that global warming is happening or of concern increased in every single survey.

Note the contrast between the trends on global warming and the background of little change in overall scientific literacy. For the eleven questions that have been asked since 1992 in the survey illustrated in Figure 41, the average ratio of correct answers has been virtually unchanged.[4]

UNDERSTANDING MISUNDERSTANDING

Teachers need to deal with misconceptions every day in the classroom. Most entering students do not know how unemployment is measured or what the Federal Reserve does. But they have open minds. They read their textbooks, go to class, and fire questions at me. After a semester of studying, they know the answers to these questions and much more.

When I grade exams and find that a student does not know what the Fed does, I want to understand why. Similarly, we need to know why people hold incorrect scientific views. The source of public views about evolution has been carefully studied. The International Social Survey Program asked respondents from thirty countries whether humans "evolved from older animal species." The United States had the highest percentage responding that humans did not evolve from older species (54 percent), followed by the Philippines, Poland, and Latvia, while Japan had the lowest rejection of evolution (10 percent).

Studies of the determinants of scientific views find different factors.[5] Education was an important determinant of correct views for most items that did not conflict with values. Religion was highly significant for evolution: 29 percent of those with strong religious views (holding that the Bible is the literal word of God) held evolution to be correct, while 79 percent of those who held that the Bible is an ancient book of fables held evolution to be correct.

Politics is sometimes associated with scientific views and sometimes not. It is definitely associated with beliefs about evolution. Among liberals, 68 percent believed that humans evolved from older animal species, as compared to 33 percent of conservatives. For many other scientific questions, however, politics appears to play no role. For example, conservatives tend to get a slightly higher proportion of correct answers on questions about astrology and antibiotics, whereas liberals do slightly better on radioactivity and chemistry.[6] The conclusion from these studies is that, when science collides with deep convictions (such as those on religion or politics), conviction often trumps science, even for those who are highly educated.

At present, there is limited evidence on the determinants of public views on global warming. We can look at existing surveys to get the basic results, however. In 1997, there was essentially no partisan difference in views about global warming, but a sharp partisan divide on global warming has emerged since then. The Pew survey in 2010 found that 89 percent of declared liberal Democrats think that the earth is warming, while only 33 percent of conservative Republicans do.

Another interesting feature is what people believe the scientists believe. Among Democrats, 59 percent say that most scientists agree that the earth is warming mostly due to human activity, while only 19 percent of tea party Republicans think that scientists agree the earth is warming.[7] People think scientists are divided and that the scientific disagreements are widening, but scientists are actually developing a greater consensus on the basic science of climate change.

We might hope that education would be the answer. However, there is no substantial difference by level of education: 61 percent with high school or less believe there is solid evidence for warming, while 60 percent with postcollege education hold that view. In this case, ideology trumps education.[8]

The increasing gap between public and scientific views on climate change shown in Figure 42 is a major concern for those who think vigorous steps should be taken soon. How can it be that highly educated Americans appear less informed about the science than those who never went to college? What accounts for the dramatic drop in public acceptance of mainstream climate science?

To understand this strange trend, we turn to studies of the formation of public opinion. To begin with, survey researchers have found that most people are poorly informed about public affairs. For example, one study found that less than 2 percent of Americans could name at least five members of the Supreme Court. Given all the things most people have to worry about, this might be rational but regrettable ignorance. People have a clear sense of their general stance on things ("I think the country needs to reduce spending," or "Things are going off track"). But they are usually vague on the details of many political, economic, or scientific questions, and the science of global warming seems to be one of the details.

A second finding, in part resulting from the first, is that people tend to form their opinions on specific issues by listening to and adopting the views of the elites of groups they adhere to. Today, most people get their news from the Internet and television, and relatively few from newspapers. They will get quite a different view of politically charged subjects depending upon the Web sites they visit or the talk shows they listen to.

The dependence of people on the views of elites is not surprising. After all, they cannot study every issue in depth. People have their experts on the role of government and social policy. Since they trust them, they are likely to adopt their views on the environment and foreign policy as well. This is particularly true if they spend only 10 minutes a month thinking about these issues and believe that fossil fuels are the fossilized remains of dinosaurs.[9]

Modern theories of public opinion, such as those in the writings of John Zaller, emphasize the points just made and then propose a mechanism by which people form opinions given these constraints.[10] Many people start out knowing little on most technical subjects. If a question is framed in a way that reminds them of something they know and care about, that will frame their answer.

One of the questions on global warming surveys is the following: "How worried are you about global warming?" Suppose the question was asked right after a snowstorm, when you had just spent an hour digging out your car. The answer might be "Not at all worried" because you remember the snowstorm and actually are dreaming of sitting on the beach.

On the other hand, suppose Hurricane Sandy has destroyed valuable parts of the northeast coast, and some scientists are discussing the linkage between hurricanes and global warming. Perhaps it is a record year for hurricanes. The next survey on attitudes about global warming takes place in this context, and people call up the memory of howling winds when they are asked whether they worry about global warming. Upon recalling the storms, their concerns about global warming increase.

Something is missing from the history, however. Why did public opinion become more skeptical about global warming in the past decade? What was the source of the sharp political divide? The most compelling explanation is the dynamics of modern American politics. Over the last three decades, the two major political parties have developed increasingly distinct ideologies in many areas—on tax policy, abortion, regulatory policy, and environmental policy.

As global warming took on greater importance, it attracted political entrepreneurs. The most important one in the United States was Albert Gore Jr., who was a Democratic senator, vice president, and candidate for president. He believed global warming was a defining issue of our time and talked about the dangers of the current trajectory. He proposed measures to reduce emissions by a tax on energy, a cap-and-trade system, and a carbon tax. He personally negotiated the Kyoto Protocol. So climate change as a scientific issue was joined by global warming on the political agenda.

Others in the U.S. Democratic Party moved solidly behind both the science of climate change and forceful policies to reduce CO_2 emissions. President Bill Clinton warned of global warming and approved the Kyoto Protocol in 1997, but he sent no legislation to Congress to implement the provisions or ratify the treaty. However, in 2009 President Barack Obama endorsed a strong cap-and-trade bill with the support of most congressional members of his party.

About the same time, conservatives turned in the opposite direction. Part of the reason for the anti-global warming policy focus of U.S. conservatism was an increasingly free-market philosophy, one skeptical of governmental regulations in all areas. The anti-global warming view was also buttressed by campaign support from major business groups and individuals with strong economic interests in reducing environmental costs and constraints.

The partisan divide became clear with the Obama administration's proposal for a cap-and-trade bill. It passed the House in 2009 with only eight Republican votes. If we look at the statements of major Republican political figures in 2010 and 2012, in virtually all cases they rejected climate-change science or economics. Hence, by 2011–2012, the two parties were clearly divided on global warming policies. Arguments against policies were usefully reinforced by arguments against the underlying science by a few contrarian scientists waiting in the wings (as we saw in Chapter 24).

The increasing political divide on environmental issues is shown in Figure 43, tracking the positions of the two parties using the environmental scorecard published by the League of Conservation Voters. They rank members of Congress between 0 and 100 based on votes on key environmental legislation. The sharpest increase in polarization came between 1988, when global warming emerged as a political issue, and 1997, when the Clinton administration negotiated the Kyoto Protocol. The difference in the "environmental score" between House Democrats and Republicans rose from 20 percentage points in the early 1970s to between 60 and 70 percentage points in the late 2000s.[11]

The messages from the political elites, therefore, became increasingly differentiated. Members of the public who were solidly conservative took the message that global warming was bad science and politics, while liberals took the opposite message from their leaders. You can see the effect in Figure 42, where public opinion moved sharply toward the skeptical viewpoint. This is a remarkable swing in public opinion in such a short time.

The standard theory of public opinion is clearly demonstrated here. The conservative elites moved toward opposition to global warming policies, and they welcomed contrarian scientists who helped undermine the scientific consensus. Conservatives among the public followed elite opinion with a lag. Those most intensely involved in politics, such as the tea party Republicans, swung further than less involved conservatives. The most educated conservatives shifted most sharply to the

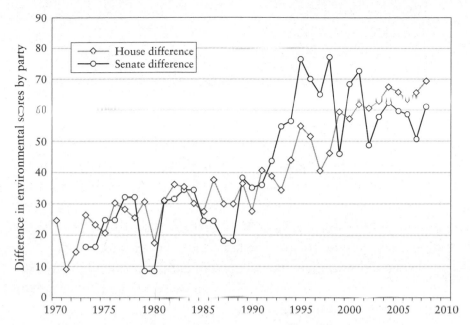

Figure 43. Widening partisan divide on environmental policies in the U.S. Congress. The figure shows the difference between the environmental scores of Democrats and Republicans in the House and Senate over the past four decades. In the early years, there was considerable overlap in views, but in recent years the two parties have become increasingly polarized.

skeptical view, as would be predicted, because they were paying more attention to the issue and could understand why global warming did not fit "the way things are."

Climate change is an area where the political leaders have led public opinion. As the parties have diverged over the last four decades, public opinion has followed with a lag. By 2013, public opinion on climate change largely reflected political ideology rather than what people learned in school or from environmental scientists.

This review is a sobering reminder how a large divide can arise between scientific views and public opinion. That divide opens up and becomes a chasm when powerful economic and political forces join to undermine mainstream science. The case of global warming is just one of many historical examples of the struggle to understand natural phenomena being hindered by the perversities of human nature.

CLOSING THE PARTISAN DIVIDE ON CLIMATE POLICY: A CONSERVATIVE PERSPECTIVE

We saw in the first part of this chapter that climate change has generated a sharp political divide in the United States. Some people think that slowing climate change is a liberal cause backed by those who are hostile to capitalism and want to bring the unfettered market to its knees. Others believe that global warming skeptics are oblivious to the dangers faced by many precious natural systems. While climate change has recently become a battleground issue between Republicans and Democrats in the United States, I believe that the partisan divide can be bridged if we consider the high stakes and potential solutions.

This section examines the issues from a different perspective. Suppose I am a conservative, libertarian, small-government advocate. But I am no defender of big oil, and I don't think that anyone should be allowed to despoil the earth at other people's expense. I desire a political and economic system that is efficient and equitable, and has maximum individual freedoms. Moreover, I desire to leave a better world for my children and grandchildren. These environmental values cross ideological boundaries, as can be seen in the following statement by the conservative U.S. president Ronald Reagan: "If we've learned any lessons during the past few decades, perhaps the most important is that preservation of our environment is not a partisan challenge; it's common sense. Our physical health, our social happiness, and our economic well-being will be sustained only by all of us working in partnership as thoughtful, effective stewards of our natural resources."[12]

So wearing my conservative hat, I consider the issues of global warming. What would I do? To begin with, I would read the scientific analyses very carefully. I would examine the arguments of the climate-change skeptics, such as those presented in Chapter 24. I would seek out someone who teaches earth sciences at my local university. After reading the science with an open mind, I would conclude that the evidence behind climate-change science is convincing, and the contrarian arguments are, to put it charitably, very thin. Clearly there are lots of ifs, ands, and qualifications. But the idea that an army of scientists around the world is perpetrating a giant hoax just seems silly.

I would then study the literature on impacts. The evidence here is much murkier because we are making uncertain climate projections on rapidly changing future societies. But I find the projections very unsettling. I might have a fine beach house and read that it is likely to wash into the sea. Or perhaps I am a ski fanatic and learn that the skiing season is getting shorter. I read about the forced migration of millions of people and wonder whether they will spill over to my town, state, and country. I worry about whether we are destroying many of the natural wonders of the world that I would hope to visit with my children and grandchildren. I conclude that we have enough problems without adding another huge mess to the pile.

Finally, I turn to the policymakers. I learn that many activists favor a cap-and-trade approach, which sets up an allocation of allowances to emit CO_2 and gives them away to "deserving" parties. They might give the allowances away to industries or to environmental groups, and some might go to poor countries with weak governance. I also see that activists are proposing regulations on automobiles, power plants, appliances, and lightbulbs. I heard one of my favorite conservative talk show hosts denounce this as "lightbulb socialism," and that sounded funny and right. As a conservative, I don't like the smell of extensive regulations and political allocation of valuable permits associated with cap and trade.

How about turning it over to the market? I quickly realize that we definitely cannot rely on the free-market solution, which involves a zero price of carbon emissions. A zero price is the wrong answer because it ignores the external costs of emissions to other people, to other countries, and to the future. So I recognize that some kind of governmental intervention in the market is necessary to slow global warming.

I turn to see what the economists say here. Many of them are advocates of something called a carbon tax, which would impose a tax on emissions of CO_2 and other greenhouse gases. It would be a "Pigovian tax," which is a tax on a negative externality. It would accomplish the goal of raising the price of CO_2 emissions to cover their social costs. This sounds like a good approach.

I wonder what conservative economists think. I look at the writings of Martin Feldstein (chief economist to Ronald Reagan), Michael Boskin (chief economist to George H. W. Bush), Greg Mankiw (chief economist to George W. Bush), Kevin Hassett (American Enterprise Institute), Arthur Laffer (of Laffer curve fame), George Schultz (economist and diplomat in the Reagan administration), and Gary Becker (Nobel Prize–winning Chicago-school economist). They all favor a carbon tax as the most efficient approach to slowing global warming.[13]

In discussing this question with some conservative friends, I find that they are unenthusiastic about carbon taxes. They contend that such policies are just another sad example of an antigrowth "tax and spend" economic philosophy. One argues in *The Wall Street Journal*, "Taxes create artificial incentives that misdirect capital formation from productive market applications."[14]

On reflection, I recognize that this argument fundamentally misunderstands the economic rationale of carbon taxes. Those who burn fossil fuels are enjoying an economic subsidy—in effect, they are grazing on the global commons and not paying for what they eat. Raising the carbon price would improve rather than reduce economic efficiency because it would correct for the implicit subsidy on the use of carbon fuels. European countries have found that they can levy energy taxes, reduce taxes on labor and other worthwhile activities, reduce CO_2 emissions, and improve overall economic performance. Moreover, carbon taxes can help reduce the government debt without harming the incentives to work and to save.

I also think about governmental policies in other areas. Do I like the government giving away the country's oil or land? Do I like banks running excessive risks with government guarantees and then having the taxpayers bail them out when the investments turn sour? As a conservative, the answer to these questions is "No!" I realize that allowing firms to put carbon in the atmosphere cost-free is a similar valuable subsidy—it is the right to harm others. Just as we auction oil and gas rights on public lands, just as we should end the privileges of banks that are called too big to fail, just so should we tax firms on the greenhouse gases they emit.

I know that many "conservative" business groups oppose any limits on their activities, particularly ones that are involved with the environment. But I also know that they are really looking out for their profits and not for the public welfare.

I conclude that carbon taxes are an ideal policy for true conservatives who care about preserving our beautiful planet but want to do so with well-tuned economic incentives and with minimal government intrusion into people's lives and business decisions. It can be imposed without burdensome regulations or restrictions. Without betting on the technological winners among future energy technologies and without putting regulations in every corner of our society, we can effectively slow global warming in a conservative's way.

26 OBSTACLES TO CLIMATE-
CHANGE POLICIES

The science and economics of global warming are clear. Unless forceful measures are taken, the planet will continue to warm. The result will be increasingly severe damage to the natural world and to vulnerable parts of human systems. Policies to slow climate change are economically simple if politically difficult. They involve raising the price of CO_2 and other greenhouse gases and harmonizing the price across countries.

How much progress have we made in implementing an effective policy? If we use carbon prices as a metric, very little. I suggested that a price of $25 per ton of CO_2 would be necessary to limit climate change to $2\frac{1}{2}°C$. Actual carbon prices at a global level are today a miniscule fraction of that—on the order of $1 per ton of CO_2.[1] The reality is that the community of nations has taken only the tiniest of steps to slow warming.

Why has the progress been so slow? David Victor, a pioneering political scientist at the University of California in San Diego, has written about how global warming policies have become caught in a special kind of gridlock in which politics, economics, myopia, and nationalism interact to block meaningful progress.[2] This final chapter analyzes some of the obstacles on the road to sensible global warming policies.

PRISONERS OF NATIONALISM

The first set of obstacles is the result of economic nationalism. National governments face a dilemma because the costs of emission reductions are national while the benefits from slowing climate change are widely dispersed around the globe. This structure of local costs and distant benefits gives strong incentives for free riding. Individual countries will benefit from local inaction and global action to abate CO_2 emissions.

This is the celebrated "prisoner's dilemma," which in this context can be better called the "nationalist dilemma." If each country seeks a strategy that maximizes its national welfare, taking other countries' policies as given, then the resulting abatement will be much smaller than if each country took global benefits into account.

It is worth spelling out the logic here because it is such an important factor in international global warming policies. Suppose that there are five identical countries and that an additional ton of CO_2 emissions does $5 worth of damage to each of the countries. Each country would, in a purely rational national calculation, reduce its emissions as long as the cost of emissions reductions was less than $5 per ton. If all countries follow this logic, the outcome is the "noncooperative equilibrium" of game theory. In this equilibrium, the overall level of abatement comes where the cost of abatement in each country would be $5 per ton.

But this is too little from a global perspective. A ton of country A's emissions does $5 of damage to country A, but it also does the same amount of damage to the four other countries. So the global damages are $25 per ton, not $5 per ton. This means that the world as a whole is abating too little. An additional ton of reductions would cost only $5, but the total benefits would be $25.

Several empirical studies have examined how the nationalist dilemma dilutes the effectiveness of global warming strategies. On the whole, they confirm that rational nationalistic behavior toward climate change would lead to a level of abatement substantially smaller than would occur with national policies that take global welfare into account. For example, I used the regional DICE model to calculate a global optimal carbon price of CO_2 in 2020. If every country considers only its own benefits in its calculations, the noncooperative globally averaged carbon price would be about one-tenth of the global optimum.

The nationalist dilemma also has implications for the implementation of agreements. Not only do countries have strong incentives to ride free by not participating or taking minimal policies, but they also have incentives to cheat if they do join strong climate-change agreements. If they hide emissions or overstate their reductions, their own economic welfare will improve even though the welfare of other countries will deteriorate. Suppose that country B has agreed to reduce its emissions to the point where the marginal costs are $25 per ton. This is a fine outcome for the world, but from country B's point of view, it has a net cost of $20 per ton. So country B has strong incentives to overstate its abatement and to pretend that it is keeping its promises.[3]

While the nationalist dilemma is an intrinsic difficulty in global warming policies, it is not fatal. Some countries have joined in cooperative agreements to overcome the tendency to underinvest in overcoming global externalities. The agreement to phase out ozone-depleting chemicals is an example where free-riding tendencies were overcome. The answer to the dilemma is to establish penalties on nonparticipants that overcome the tendency to ride free. I discussed one possible approach in Chapter 21, in which a climate treaty buttressed by trade sanctions could overcome the nationalist dilemma.

PRISONERS OF THE PRESENT

The nationalist dilemma is amplified by a second factor, the time-distant nature of the payoffs from emissions reductions. Climate-change policies require costly abatement in the near term to reduce damages in the distant future. A rough estimate, discussed in Part IV, is that the benefits of reductions come about half a century after the emissions reductions.

Figure 44 illustrates the generational trade-offs, based on the emissions limits proposed in the Copenhagen Accord.[4] It shows the net benefits for early and late periods, for three groups of countries and the

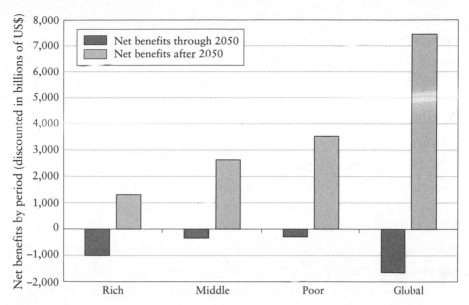

Figure 44. The temporal trade-off in climate-change policies. The bars show net benefits (equal to damages plus abatement costs, all discounted at market interest rates) for country groups for two time periods. The left solid bars are the net benefits for the first half century, while the light shaded bars are the net benefits for the balance of the period through 2200.

world. Net benefits here are the negative of costs, which include both damages and abatement costs, discounted back to 2010 at market interest rates. While these numbers are primarily illustrative because there was no specific agreement, the results are similar to those calculated for other policies. Countries are categorized as rich, middle income, and poor based on their per capita incomes. The net benefits before 2050 and the net benefits for the period 2050–2200 are compared.[5]

The left solid set of bars, all below the zero axis, shows the estimated net losses for the period 2010–2050. For example, the Copenhagen Accord has near-term net costs for rich countries of approximately $1 trillion. The global cost is about $1.5 trillion.

The second, light shaded set of bars, which are uniformly positive, shows the net impacts for the period 2050–2200, again discounted to 2010. The net benefits for the rich countries are $1.3 trillion, which does offset the first-period costs. For other groups, the benefits after 2050 are much larger than the earlier costs. Taking all countries together, the net benefits in the post-2050 period are $7.4 trillion as compared with the pre-2050 net costs of $1.6 trillion.

Some important points emerge from this discussion. To begin with, for the world as a whole, a cooperative agreement such as that underlying the Copenhagen Accord would be highly beneficial in the long run. All countries will eventually benefit. However, this is an investment with a very long-term payoff. Most countries must wait at least half a century to reap the fruits of their investment.

From a practical point of view, this raises a thorny problem in generational politics. People often resist making sacrifices for future generations. For example, should we reduce spending on health care for the elderly to provide schooling for the young? The temporal trade-offs are similar in slowing global warming. Asking present generations to shoulder large abatement costs for future generations, particularly if they're richer, is difficult to sell. The delayed payoffs reinforce the incentives of the nationalist dilemma, so the temptation is doubly high to postpone taking the costly steps to reduce emissions.

PRISONERS OF PARTISANSHIP

A third set of obstacles involves the unavoidable reality that there are losers as well as winners from an ambitious global warming policy. I have already shown that most countries will experience net costs from global warming policies over the next few decades. Some powerful groups will also be economically disadvantaged, and these costs will be largely concentrated in sectors that produce or use fossil fuels.

For example, suppose that the United States adopts emissions limits like those contained in the Copenhagen Accord or proposed by the Obama administration in 2009. According to estimates by the Department of Energy, coal use would decline by half over the next decade. There were 90,000 coal miners in 2011, so the reduced coal use might reduce employment by around 40,000 workers. The loss of 4,000 jobs per year in an economy with 130 million workers does not seem like a huge obstacle. But the coal industry has strong congressional representation and great folk songs. So a global warming policy that imposes high carbon prices and thereby reduces coal production and employment will face strong opposition.[6]

This example would be repeated in many sectors. Companies engaged in coal mining and in coal-fired generation of electricity would show declines in profits. There would be similar but quantitatively smaller impacts in industries dependent on other fossil fuels.

Table 15 provides a calculation by a modeling team of the effect of a $25 per ton of CO_2 price on costs in major industries.[7] Three industries will be heavily affected and experience more than a 10 percent rise in costs: electric utilities, cement manufacturing, and petrochemicals. The

Table 15. Impact of carbon price by industry. This table shows those industries most and least affected by carbon pricing. For each, the table shows the increase in production cost of a $25 per ton CO_2 price. Percentages reflect full input-output impacts (i.e., include indirect as well as direct costs).

Industry	Increase in production costs (%)
Most affected:	
Electric utilities	20.75
Cement manufacturing	12.50
Petrochemicals	10.50
Aluminum	6.50
Iron and steel mills	5.75
Lime and gypsum manufacturing	5.25
Fertilizer manufacturing	4.50
Paper mills	4.00
Paperboard mills	4.00
Least affected:	
Computer and electrical equipment	0.75
Other transportation equipment	0.75
Retail and wholesale trade	0.50
Information services	0.50
Business services	0.50
Finance and insurance	0.25
Real estate and rental	0.25

list also shows those industries that would be the least affected—retail and wholesale trade, real estate, and finance. The relative costs of production in these industries would be lowered by a CO_2 price, and their output and employment would tend to expand.

In democratic countries, elected representatives will face pressure to oppose measures that disadvantage their current constituents or financial contributors. Thus representatives from coal mining states and countries are particularly resistant to global warming policies that raise coal prices. This would include the United States, China, and Australia among countries, and West Virginia, Kentucky, and Wyoming among U.S. states. Similarly, countries with large oil exports such as the OPEC nations will find their incomes declining and therefore would generally oppose strong curbs on CO_2 emissions.

In countries like Britain, Sweden, and Spain, with minimal production and employment in coal-based industries, governments can support aggressive global warming policies with less fear of domestic opposition. Similarly, those countries that import most of their energy fuels will face less opposition to climate-change policies from domestic businesses.

Over the long run, strong global warming policies will probably benefit the majority of people in countries like the United States. However, industries like finance or pharmaceuticals, which would benefit slightly from a recycled carbon tax, are too busy fighting regulatory reforms to support strong climate-change policies. Therefore, a small minority from well-represented industries and their amply funded lobbying groups are able to block policies that would benefit the larger, longer-run interests of the majority—born and unborn.

PRISONERS OF ECONOMIC SELF-INTEREST

While the roadblocks of representative democracy are a fundamental part of an open society, a more pernicious obstacle arises from what Naomi Oreskes and Erik Conway call the "merchants of doubt."[8] Their argument is that scientific or pseudo-scientific advocates undermine the normal processes of science. This process differs from the democratic process, where competing interests and values jostle for votes. In the doubt-creating process, groups undermine, distort, or create facts and theories in an attempt to refute mainstream science, confuse the public, and prevent political action.

The best-documented case of doubt creation was the campaign of the cigarette companies to combat the medical evidence that cigarette smoking causes cancer. Scientific evidence on the link between smoking and cancer was documented a century ago, and the evidence piled up in the 1950s. Beginning in 1953, the largest tobacco companies launched a campaign to undermine the scientific evidence that cigarette smoking is dangerous. The most devious part of the campaign was the underwriting of researchers who would support the industry's claims. The approach was elegantly expressed by one tobacco company executive: "Doubt is our product since it is the best means of competing with the body of fact that exists in the mind of the general public. It is also the means of establishing a controversy."[9]

We find similar evidence of doubt production in the debates about global warming, although the complete story cannot be understood because of the opacity of the doubt-producing machinery. One documented example came to light when an enterprising journalist collated grants by ExxonMobil, which funneled $8 million to organizations, many of which challenged the science or economics of global warming.[10] A similar example is the "sixteen scientists" whose contrarian arguments were analyzed in Chapter 24. Very few of this group have been active in scientific research on climate-change science or economics—other than to create confusion.

One of the worrisome features of the interest group–based attacks on climate science and policies is that the stakes are much larger for global warming than for smoking. Tobacco sales in the United States are approximately $30 billion. By contrast, expenditures on all energy goods and services in the United States are around $1,000 billion.[11] A carbon tax large enough to bend the temperature curve from its current trajectory to a 2°C or 3°C maximum would have significant economic effects on many workers, businesses, and countries. Global warming is a trillion-dollar problem requiring a trillion-dollar solution, and the battle for hearts, minds, and votes will be fierce.

OVERCOMING THE OBSTACLES

The previous two chapters have analyzed the obstacles to developing a rational and effective public policy on climate change. Public opinion and a substantial wing of American politics are moving in one direction even as scientific views are moving in the other. Powerful economic forces that oppose climate-change science have muddied the water and confused the public with misleading arguments and scientific-looking claims.

This is not the first occasion when scientific findings have met strong opposition, nor will it be the last. We saw earlier how the tobacco industry became the merchants of doubt to confuse the public and block public policies on smoking.

How did the tobacco story run its course? Eventually, through tireless and patient efforts, doctors and scientists won over the public on the question of whether smoking cigarettes causes cancer. Figure 45 shows the evolution of public opinion on the question of cancer and

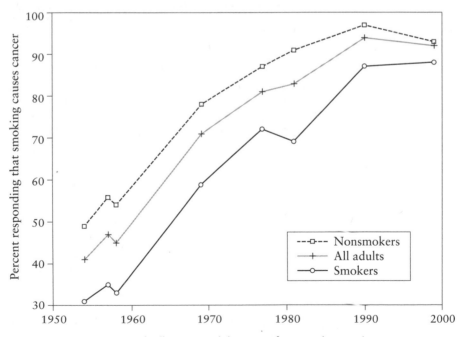

Figure 45. Americans gradually accepted the scientific view that smoking causes cancer even as the tobacco industry conducted its campaign of deception.

smoking. After a half century of education, even smokers admitted that smoking was harmful.[12]

In part to stem smoking, tobacco taxes are currently a major source of revenues for governments. High carbon taxes have a more compelling economic logic than do tobacco taxes—for the health of humans, the planet, and government budgets.

The lesson for scientists is clear. There is no substitute for clear and persistent explanations of the science along with refutations of contrarian attacks. The evidence will become increasingly clear each year, as it did with smoking. Obstructionists will find themselves as if on a melting ice floe. The political winds will eventually shift.

A FINAL VERDICT

This chapter has presented a somber but realistic discussion of the state of the debate and the obstacles to implementing efficient and effective policies to slow global warming. Governments have made little progress in implementing policies. Some of the obstacles are structural, such as the global nature of the impacts and the long lag between costly policies and ultimate benefits. Other obstacles are economic, as when merchants of doubt attempt to confuse the public to maintain their profits.

Now that we have reached the end, what would be the findings of an impartial jury? A fair verdict would find that there is clear and convincing evidence that the planet is warming; that unless strong steps are taken, the earth will experience a warming greater than it has seen for more than a half million years; that the consequences of the changes will be costly for human societies and grave for many unmanaged earth systems; and that the balance of risks indicates that immediate action should be taken to slow and eventually halt emissions of CO_2 and other greenhouse gases.

These basic findings must be qualified and constantly updated because of the uncertainties involved at all stages of the link from economic growth through emissions and climate change to impacts and policies. But the basic findings have stood the test of time, rebuttal, and multiple assessments by hundreds of natural and social scientists. There are no grounds for objective parties simply to ignore the basic results, to call them a hoax, or to argue that we need another half century before we act.

Humans are putting the planet in peril. But humans can undo what they are doing. Moreover, this can be achieved at relatively low cost if people accept the realistic threat of global warming, put in place an economic mechanism that penalizes carbon emissions, and take vigorous efforts to develop low-carbon technologies. By taking these steps, we can protect and preserve our precious planet.

NOTES

CHAPTER 1   FIRST ENCOUNTERS IN THE CLIMATE CASINO

1. These quotations are from diverse sources such as Gallup polls, a report from a conservative think tank, a report on scientific views, and a leading U.S. newspaper.

CHAPTER 2   A TALE OF TWO LAKES

1. This point is emphasized by Stephen Jay Gould in *Wonderful Life: The Burgess Shale and the Nature of History* (New York: Norton, 1990).

2. A short sketch is provided at Salt Ponds Coalition, www.saltpondscoalition.org, accessed March 27, 2013.

3. You can see a picture of the Aral Sea past and present at NASA, Earth Observatory, "Aral Sea," August 25, 2003, http://earthobservatory.nasa.gov/IOTD/view.php?id=3730.

4. For a short essay by a distinguished environmental scientist on the Aral Sea and a parallel story on Lake Chad, see Michael H. Glantz, "Lake Chad and the Aral Sea: A Sad Tale of Two Lakes," Fragilecologies, September 9, 2004, www.fragilecologies.com/archive/sep09_04.html.

CHAPTER 3   THE ECONOMIC ORIGINS OF CLIMATE CHANGE

1. Calculations by the author.

2. Data on CO_2 emissions for Figures 2 and 3 are from the Carbon Dioxide Information Analysis Center, http://cdiac.ornl.gov/, and the U.S. Energy Information Administration, www.eia.doe.gov. GDP is from the Bureau of Economic Analysis back to 1929 and by private scholars before that period, spliced together by the author.

3. Here is the simplest climate equation: $(1 - a)S = 4\varepsilon\sigma T^4$. This equation relates the temperature of the earth (T) to factors such as the solar constant (S), the reflectivity

of the earth (*a*), and some physical parameters. We can solve this equation and get a first approximation of the earth's temperature, but it misses many of the details because it has no atmosphere, ocean, or ice. You can think of climate models as adding further dimensions to this simplest equation—different layers of the atmosphere, the oceans, ice, winds, and so on. When all those are added—in a climate model—the resulting calculations will produce a set of predictions for all the variables.

4. Among the many books on climate modeling, see Paul Edwards, *A Vast Machine: Computer Models, Climate Data, and the Politics of Global Warming* (Cambridge, MA: MIT Press, 2010). An online history by Spencer Weart, "The Discovery of Global Warming," is available at American Institute of Physics, www.aip.org/history /climate/pdf/Gcm.pdf, or with hyperlinks at www.aip.org/history/climate/GCM .htm.

5. For simplicity, in the text I refer to all results as coming from the DICE model, whereas they sometimes come from different versions, as indicated in the source notes.

6. The DICE model is available at my home page at the Yale Department of Economics, which also includes instructions on how to use it: climatecasino.net or dicemodel.net.

7. For those who like equations, this is known as the Kaya identity or Kaya equation. It says that we can calculate CO_2 emissions as the product of three terms (components): population × GDP per capita × the carbon intensity of GDP:

$$CO_2 = Pop \times (GDP/Pop) \times (CO_2/GDP),$$

where CO_2 is carbon dioxide emissions, Pop is population, and GDP is real gross domestic or world product. The actual numbers are taken from the RICE 2010 model. Simple calculus will show that the logarithmic or geometric growth rate of CO_2 equals the growth rate of Pop plus the growth rate of (GDP/Pop) plus the growth rate of (CO_2/GDP). Strictly speaking, the arithmetic sum of growth rates is slightly lower than the actual number because of second-order terms, but that is negligibly different for the examples used here. The calculations are by the author.

8. I have relied on the projections of the IAMs because I find them to be the most scientific, transparent, and empirically based approaches. Many studies in the natural sciences, particularly climate models, have relied on a standardized set of projections known as the Special Report on Emissions Scenarios (SRES), which were prepared for the Intergovernmental Panel on Climate Change. See Nebojsa Nakicenovic and Rob Swart, eds., *IPCC Special Report on Emissions Scenarios* (Cambridge: Cambridge University Press, 2000), www.ipcc.ch/ipccreports/sres/emission /index.htm.

9. Figure 5 shows the results from eleven models surveyed by the EMF-22 project plus a projection from the Yale RICE-2010 model (line with circles). The EMF results are described in L. Clarke, C. Böhringer, and T. F. Rutherford, "International, U.S. and E.U. Climate Change Control Scenarios: Results from EMF 22," *Energy Eco-*

nomics 31, suppl. 2 (2009): S63–S306; detailed results were made available by Leon Clarke. The RICE and DICE model results along with references are available at dicemodel.net.

CHAPTER 4 FUTURE CLIMATE CHANGE

1. Richard Alley, *Earth: The Operators' Manual* (New York: Norton, 2011); Stephen H. Schneider, Armin Rosencranz, Michael D. Mastrandrea, and Kristin Kuntz-Duriseti, eds., *Climate Change Science and Policy* (Washington, DC: Island Press, 2010); James Hansen, *Storms of My Grandchildren: The Truth about the Coming Climate Catastrophe and Our Last Chance to Save Humanity* (London: Bloomsbury, 2009).

2. The Intergovernmental Panel on Climate Change (IPCC) has published a series of reports on climate change, mitigation, impacts, and adaptations. They were published in 1990 (First Assessment Report), 1995 (Second Assessment Report), 2001 (Third Assessment Report), and 2007 (Fourth Assessment Report). A Fifth Assessment Report is being published starting in the fall of 2013. Each assessment has three different volumes: Science, Impacts, and Mitigation. The reports are available online at www.ipcc.ch/publications_and_data/publications_and_data_reports.shtml. They are also available in hard copy, published by Cambridge University Press, Cambridge, UK. Hereafter these will be referred to by the number of the assessment and the volume, as in IPCC, Fourth Assessment Report, *Science*, p. 63.

3. Data come from the National Oceanic and Atmospheric Administration, Earth System Research Laboratory, Global Monitoring Division, "Trends in Atmospheric Carbon Dioxide," www.esrl.noaa.gov/gmd/ccgg/trends/. Data on atmospheric CO_2 are collected from many sites today, and the numbers agree closely with the Mauna Loa observations. This discussion oversimplifies the distribution of CO_2 in the different reservoirs. Additionally, this calculation omits land-use conversions over this period, but they are very poorly measured.

4. Here is an explanation for those who are interested in the details: The fraction of CO_2 emissions that remains in the atmosphere is called the "airborne fraction." Carbon-cycle models estimate that the airborne fraction declines over time because CO_2 gets absorbed in the upper ocean and then slowly diffuses through the lower oceans. In addition, some of the CO_2 is taken up by trees and plants. Estimating the time profile of the absorption is complicated because it involves chemistry, ocean dynamics, and biology. We can examine a study using a carbon-climate model designed by a team of scientists from Germany and Switzerland to give a sense of the dynamics. They used their computer model to calculate the impact over a 1,200-year period of a pulse of CO_2. Suppose there is an injection of x tons of CO_2 in year 0. Then the model calculates that 50–70 percent remains after 50 years; 35–55 percent remains after 100 years; 28–45 percent remains after 200 years; and around 15 percent remains after 1,200 years. The range for a given year depends upon the size of the CO_2 injection, with the lower number for small injections and the higher number for large ones. See G. Hoss et al., "A Nonlinear Impulse Response Model of

the Coupled Carbon Cycle-Climate System (NICCS)," *Climate Dynamics* 18 (2001): 189–202. Alternative estimates from the IPCC report are that 30–50 percent of emissions remain in the atmosphere after 100 years. The integrated economic-climate models constructed at Yale University (the DICE-RICE 2010 models) use a calibrated model in which 41 percent of an emissions pulse remains after a century.

5. A particularly useful summary is in Benjamin D. Santer, "Hearing on 'A Rational Discussion of Climate Change: The Science, the Evidence, the Response,'" House Committee on Science and Technology, November 17, 2010, http://science .house.gov/sites/republicans.science.house.gov/files/documents/hearings /111710Santer.pdf.

6. A technical note will help you understand the basic climate science and the impact of increased "radiative forcing." Solar radiation at the top of the atmosphere is calculated to be 341 watts per meter squared (W/m^2) over the entire globe. About two-thirds of the incoming radiation is absorbed by the atmosphere or earth's surface, and it is emitted back to space as long-wave (or infrared) radiation. The impact of increased concentrations of GHGs is to increase the absorption of long-wave radiation, and the measure of this increase is called the change in "radiative forcing," a measure of the impact of increased concentrations of CO_2 and other factors in altering the energy balance of the earth. This is usually calculated as a change in net radiation in the troposphere (the lowest level of the atmosphere). For example, a standard calculation is that a doubling of atmospheric CO_2 leads to the equivalent of an increase in the radiation in the troposphere of about $4 W/m^2$. When all the interactions take place, this is estimated to lead to an increase in the global average surface temperature of about 3°C. So you can think of the greenhouse effect as similar (but not equivalent) to an increase in solar radiation.

7. The curves are drawn on the basis of detailed model estimates from the IPCC's Fourth Assessment, *Science*. Model runs for the IPCC's Fifth Assessment Report suggest that the equilibrium and transient climate sensitivities of the surveyed models are virtually unchanged from the fourth report for later vintages of the same models. The range of equilibrium climate sensitivity across the eighteen models reviewed for the fifth assessment was between 2.1 and 4.7°C. I have smoothed the curves to simplify the presentation. The smoothing assumes that the distributions of the estimates are log-normal and have the same mean and dispersion as the model results. See Timothy Andrews, Jonathan M. Gregory, Mark J. Webb, and Karl E Taylor, "Forcing, Feedbacks and Climate Sensitivity in CMIP5 Coupled Atmosphere-Ocean Climate Models," *Geophysical Research Letters* 39 (2012): L09712, doi:10.1029/2012GL051607, 2012.

8. The first systematic survey by the National Academy of Sciences in 1979 produced estimates that were close to those of the most recent assessment by the IPCC. *Carbon Dioxide and Climate: A Scientific Assessment* (Washington, DC: National Academies Press, 1979).

9. The response over the medium to long term is not precisely determined because it involves many slow-feedback mechanisms, such as the melting of the large ice sheets, as well as complex systems such as ocean circulation.

10. Temperature data come from the Goddard Institute for Space Studies (GISS), the National Climatic Data Center (NCDC), and the Hadley Centre for Climate Prediction and Research.

11. The modeling assumes that all influences other than CO_2 are small at the global level in 2010 and grow slowly over the next century. The major reason for the small non-CO_2 effect is that the cooling effects of aerosols (small particles) offsets the warming effects of other gases. The quantitative impact of aerosols is a major uncertainty for warming over the near term.

12. I provide a technical note for the specialists. Although some of the EMF-22 IAMs provide temperature trajectories, they exclude short-lived GHGs or aerosols and therefore do not provide an accurate temperature projection. The runs shown in Figure 9 take the industrial CO_2 concentrations from the models. We then combine these with estimates of land-use CO_2 emissions and the radiative forcings for other GHGs from the RICE-2010 mode. We then put all these into the climate module of the RICE-2010 model. The ten models were ETSAP-TIAM, FUND, GTEM, MERGE Optimistic, MERGE Pessimistic, MESSAGE, MiniCAM-BASE, POLES, SGM, and WITCH. A full description of the models is contained in the source at L. Clarke, C. Böhringer, and T. F. Rutherford, "International, U.S. and E.U. Climate Change Control Scenarios: Results from EMF 22," *Energy Economics* 31, suppl. 2 (2009): S63–S306.

13. Most of the points are from IPCC, Fourth Assessment Report, *Science*, Chapter 8. The last point regarding aerosols is drawn from Jeff Tollison, "Climate Forecasting: A Break in the Clouds," *Nature* 485 (May 10, 2012): 164–166. The discussion of extremes is from Christopher B. Field et al., eds., *Managing the Risks of Extreme Events and Disasters to Advance Climate Change Adaptation: Special Report of the Intergovernmental Panel on Climate Change* (Cambridge: Cambridge University Press, 2012), www.ipcc-wg2.gov/SREX/.

14. A picture of the MIT roulette wheel can be found at David Chandler, "Climate Change Odds Much Worse Than Thought," MIT News, May 19, 2009, http://web.mit.edu/newsoffice/2009/roulette-0519.html.

CHAPTER 5   TIPPING POINTS IN THE CLIMATE CASINO

1. The temperature proxy is derived from the analysis of the GISP2 ice core. Data are from R. B. Alley, *GISP2 Ice Core Temperature and Accumulation Data*, IGBP PAGES/World Data Center for Paleoclimatology Data Contribution Series #2004-013, NOAA/NGDC Paleoclimatology Program, Boulder, CO, 2004, ftp://ftp.ncdc.noaa.gov/pub/data/paleo/icecore/greenland/summit/gisp2/isotopes/gisp2_temp_accum_alley2000.txt.

2. This concept is drawn from Johan Rockstrom et al., "Planetary Boundaries: Exploring the Safe Operating Space for Humanity," *Ecology and Society* 14, no. 2 (2009), www.ecologyandsociety.org/vol14/iss2/art32/.

3. Thanks to my students at Yale for helping to develop this diagram.

4. Here is a useful definition that captures the time dimension of abrupt climate change: "Technically, an abrupt climate change occurs when the climate system is

forced to cross some threshold, triggering a transition to a new state at a rate determined by the climate system itself and faster than the cause." See National Academy of Sciences, *Abrupt Climate Change: Inevitable Surprises* (Washington, DC: National Academies Press, 2002), 14. I am particularly grateful to Richard Alley for explaining many of these phenomena to me in the context of geophysical changes.

5. Dornbusch's quip is actually a profound observation about tipping points and mathematical "catastrophic systems." See Rudi Dornbusch and Stanley Fischer, "International Financial Crises," CESIFO Working Paper No. 926, Category 6: Monetary Policy and International Finance, March 2003. We can often predict that dangerous situations will occur while we cannot predict the timing of the catastrophe. This is why the canoe tips over. If the canoe's exact tipping point were easily predictable, then we would avoid it. One way of understanding this is to remember that financial crises and abrupt events are different from high tides in their intrinsic unpredictability. People often proclaim that they predicted the economic crisis of 2007–2009, but if you look carefully, you find that most of them were regularly predicting crashes that did not occur. This point was captured by Paul Samuelson's remark: "Stock markets have correctly predicted nine of the last five recessions."

6. A useful summary of the evidence is contained in Jonathan T. Overpeck et al., "Paleoclimatic Evidence for Future Ice-Sheet Instability and Rapid Sea-Level Rise," *Science* 311, no. 5768 (2006): 1747–1750. An example was the very rapid sea-level rise 14,600 years ago, when sea level rose by about 13 feet per century for a total of 50 feet. The reasons are not yet understood but might have involved the unstable West Antarctic Ice Sheet. See Pierre Deschamps et al., "Ice-Sheet Collapse and Sea-Level Rise at the Bølling Warming 14,600 Years Ago," *Nature* 483 (March 2012): 559–564.

7. See IPCC, Fourth Assessment Report, *Science*, Table 7.4, p. 535, and the surrounding discussion.

8. This argument is presented in James Hansen et al., "Target Atmospheric CO_2: Where Should Humanity Aim?" *Open Atmospheric Science Journal* 2 (2008): 217–231.

9. This discussion is based on "The Coral Reef Crisis: Scientific Justification for Critical CO_2 Threshold Levels of < 350ppm," Output of the technical working group meeting, Royal Society, London, July 6, 2009, www.carbonequity.info/PDFs/The -Coral-Reef-Crisis.pdf.

10. Timothy M. Lenton et al., "Tipping Elements in the Earth's Climate System," *Nature* 105, no. 6 (2008): 1786–1793.

11. Table N-1 gives a detailed list of tipping points and timing.

Major tipping points have been ranked by the time scale during which they are likely to occur. One important factor is the amount of warming at which the tipping point is likely to be reached. Note that the tipping may be very slow—in slow motion so to speak—rather than all at once like a canoe. The first column contains a shorthand list of the tipping points. Some have been explained earlier; others are generally self-explanatory. A more detailed description is given below. I have sorted these points from near term to long term by the time scale shown in the second column. Some tipping elements are likely to occur in the very near term, such as

Table N-1.

Tipping element	Time scale (years)	Threshold warming value	Level of concern (most concern = ***)	Concern
Arctic summer sea ice	10	+0,5–2°C	*	Amplified warming, ecosystems
Sahara/Sahel and West African monsoon	10	+3–5°C	**	Wet period
Amazon rain forest	50	+3–4°C	***	Biodiversity loss
Boreal forest	50	+3–5°C	*	Biome switch
Atlantic thermohaline circulation	100	+3–5°C	**	Regional cooling
El Niño–Southern Oscillation	100	+3–6°C	**	Drought
Greenland Ice Sheet	> 300	+1–2°C	***	Sea level +2–7 m
West Antarctic Ice Sheet	> 300	+3–5°C	***	Sea level +5 m

reduction or disappearance of most or all Arctic summer sea ice. Others are on a century time scale, such as those involving the massive Greenland and Antarctic ice sheets.

The third column is of particular interest and shows the warming values at which the tipping may occur. Note the large range of values for most tipping elements. We simply do not know the dynamics of the processes for important tipping elements like the ice sheets. The fourth column shows a qualitative assessment of the importance of each element. The number of stars indicates the level of concern caused by the passing of a tipping point. Particular attention should be given to the three-star elements.

The following is a brief description of each tipping element. Most are drawn directly from Lenton et al., "Tipping Elements," with some editing for brevity. (1) Arctic summer sea ice: disappearance of the ice in the Arctic regions in summer months. (2) Sahara/Sahel and West African monsoon: changes in the precipitation patterns in the Sahara/Sahel region may lead to greening of this region. (3) Amazon rain forest: a dieback of the Amazon rain forest, in which at least half of its current area is converted to rain-green forest, savannah, or grassland. (4) Boreal forest: a dieback of boreal (far northern coniferous) forests, in which their global area, including potential additions from northward migration of plants in a warming climate, is at least cut in half due to widespread conversion of boreal forests to open woodlands or grasslands. (5) Atlantic thermohaline circulation: a reorganization of the Atlantic meridional overturning circulation that involves a permanent shutdown of convection in the Labrador Sea and a drastic reduction in deep water overflow across the Greenland-Scotland ridge by at least .80 percent. (6) El Niño-Southern Oscillation (ENSO): a shift in the ENSO mean state toward El Niño–like conditions. (7) Greenland Ice Sheet: melting of the Greenland Ice Sheet to an alternative state that is largely ice free. (8) West Antarctic Ice Sheet: disintegration of the West Antarctic Ice Sheet to an alternative state in which West Antarctica becomes an archipelago.

This discussion is based in part on Lenton et al., "Tipping Elements." Updated and simplified in Katherine Richardson, Will Steffen, and Diana Liverman, eds., *Climate Change: Global Risks, Challenges and Decisions* (New York: Cambridge University Press, 2011), 186.

12. IPCC, Fourth Assessment Report, *Science*, p. 342 (data on ice sheets).

13. Ibid., Chapters 6 and 10.

14. A study finds three stable equilibria with 20, 60, and 100 percent of current ice volume. Alexander Robinson, Reinhard Calov, and Andrey Ganopolski, "Multi-stability and Critical Thresholds of the Greenland Ice Sheet," *Nature Climate Change* 2 (2012): 429–432.

15. Frank Pattyn, "GRANTISM: An Excel Model for Greenland and Antarctic Ice-Sheet Response to Climate Changes," *Computers and Geosciences* (2006): 316–325.

16. The slippery slope is a highly stylized example showing how a system with hysteresis behaves. "Hysteresis" means that an outcome is path dependent. For example, if you take a stick and bend it, and then let go, the final state will depend upon whether you bent it past the breaking point.

CHAPTER 6   FROM CLIMATE CHANGE TO IMPACTS

1. These are the chapter headings from IPCC, Fourth Assessment Report, *Impacts*.

2. Jared Diamond, *Collapse: How Societies Choose to Fail or Survive* (New York: Viking, 2005).

3. The emphasis in Table 2 is slightly different from the IPCC report, however, because some of the major issues identified in the IPCC report are, in fact, heavily managed and therefore seem less likely to be of long-run concern. For example, much of the work on impacts concerns agriculture, which is increasingly managed and constitutes a declining share of economic and human activities. Similarly, the emphasis on health consequences has a very static view of the health care system (see Chapter 8). Several reports also emphasize the harmful impacts of migration without considering how migration also acts as a valuable safety valve to relieve the pressures from regions that are harmed by income or environmental shocks. This list is primarily drawn from IPCC, *Climate Change 2007: Impacts, Adaptation, and Vulnerability* (Cambridge: Cambridge University Press, 2007), with particular attention to "Summary for Policymakers" and the chapter on ecosystems.

4. A detailed case argued for very low targets (about 1½°C above preindustrial levels) is made by climatologists in J. Hansen, M. Sato, R. Ruedy, P. Kharecha, et al., "Dangerous Human-Made Interference with Climate: A GISS Model Study," *Atmospheric Chemistry and Physics* 7 (2007): 2287–2312.

CHAPTER 7 THE FATE OF FARMING

1. The conclusions about economic growth and climate change are shared by all the integrated assessment models and are not just peculiar to the RICE-DICE models. Two examples illustrate the point. In the well-known *Stern Review* on the economics of climate change—generally considered very pessimistic—the average output growth over the twenty-first and twenty-second centuries was forecast to be even more rapid than shown in the Yale-DICE model. Even with the damage estimates by the *Stern Review*, average living standards would still grow by at least a factor of more than eleven over this period. See Nicholas Stern, *The Economics of Climate Change: The Stern Review* (New York: Cambridge University Press, 2007), Chapter 2. Another example is the group of models used in the EMF-22 model comparison study (see the discussion in Part I). The average of the assumed growth rates of GDP per capita over the period 2000–2100 was 1.7 percent per year. The lowest growth rate of any model for any region was 0.7 percent per year (by the MESSAGE model for the United States). For low-income countries, the average growth rate was assumed to be 2.3 percent per year.

2. The consumption and climate data come from runs of the Yale RICE-2010 model.

3. This is a good example of the power of compound interest and growth, which we will meet often in this book. You can often estimate the growth of something using the "rule of 70." This rule states that a quantity will double when it grows at x percent per year for $(70/x)$ years. So for example, if per capita output grows at 2 percent per year, it will double in 35 years. So run this forward for six 35-year periods, or 210 years, and the growth is a factor of $(2 \times 2 \times 2 \times 2 \times 2 \times 2) = 64$. The growth of a factor of 15.3 for the growth scenario over 200 years is actually 1.37 percent per year.

4. One analyst who does take this path is Herman Daly, ed., *Steady-State Economics*, 2nd ed. (Washington, DC: Island Press, 1991).

5. Justin Gillis, "A Warming Planet Struggles to Feed Itself," *New York Times*, June 4, 2011.

6. Stern, *The Economics of Climate Change*, 85–86.

7. IPCC, Fourth Assessment Report, *Impacts*, pp. 10–11.

8. See, for example, Robert Mendelsohn and Ariel Dinar, *Climate Change and Agriculture: An Economic Analysis of Global Impacts, Adaptation, and Distributional Effects* (London: Edward Elgar, 2009); and Ariel Dinar, Robert Mendelsohn, R. Hassan, and J. Benhin, *Climate Change and Agriculture in Africa: Impact Assessment and Adaptation Strategies* (London: EarthScan, 2008).

9. An excellent study of adaptation in agriculture is Norman Rosenberg, "Adaptation of Agriculture to Climate Change," *Climatic Change* 21, no. 4 (1992): 385–405.

10. Redrawn by the author based on IPCC, *Climate Change 2007: Impacts, Adaptation, and Vulnerability* (Cambridge: Cambridge University Press, 2007), p. 286.

11. We see from the figure that adaptations increase yield by about 20 percent relative to no adaptation. Other than fertilization from the increased atmospheric CO_2, what are the important adaptations? In fact, the studies usually consider a relatively limited set of adaptations. They usually do not include changing crops or using new genetic varieties, and they almost never involve shifting land to non-agricultural uses. Moreover, technological change to improve adaptation is not considered. From an economic point of view, it would be very surprising if no adaptations occurred over a period of several years, and indeed the number of adaptations assumed in most studies is on the lean side of realistic expectations. The studies are likely to underestimate the actual extent of adaptations over the coming decades in situations where farms are well managed.

12. Data come from the Bureau of Economic Analysis, Table 1.3.4, www.bea.gov, and refer to the price of value added in the farm sector relative to all GDP.

13. See IPCC, Fourth Assessment Report, *Impacts*, p. 297. At 3°C, two models showed an increase in food prices of around 15 percent; two models showed a decrease of around 10 percent; and one model showed no change.

14. The reasoning is as follows. World wheat production in 2008 was 680 million metric tons, of which about 10 million tons was from Kansas. A 10 percent decline of Kansas production is estimated to raise prices by about 0.5 percent. This would raise the prices of products with wheat by less than 0.1 percent.

15. Data for the United States come from Bureau of Economic Analysis, NIPA Table 1.3.5 (www.bea.gov). Data for country groups come from the World Bank, World Development Indicators, http://data.worldbank.org/data-catalog/world-development-indicators.

16. The calculation assumes that consumer welfare is a log-linear utility function in farm goods and nonfarm goods. The share in the utility function is calibrated using the share of gross farm product in GDP (from Bureau of Economic Analysis, NIPA Table 1.3.5). Food prices contain substantial nonfarm inputs and are a larger share. This model assumes that the price elasticity of raw food is minus one. If the elasticity is assumed to be smaller, then the size of the shock and the magnitude of the decline are proportionally larger.

CHAPTER 8 THE IMPACT ON HUMAN HEALTH

1. Here is the summary from the IPCC chapter on the subject: "Projected trends in climate change-related exposures of importance to human health will increase malnutrition and consequent disorders, including those relating to child growth and development; increase the number of people suffering from death, disease and injury from heat waves, floods, storms, fires and droughts; continue to change the range of some infectious disease vectors; have mixed effects on malaria; in some places the geographical range will contract, elsewhere the geographical range will expand and the transmission season may be changed; increase the burden of diarrhoeal diseases; increase cardio-respiratory morbidity and mortality associated with ground-level ozone; increase the number of people at risk of dengue; bring

some benefits to health, including fewer deaths from cold, although it is expected that these will be outweighed by the negative effects of rising temperatures worldwide, especially in developing countries." IPCC, Fourth Assessment Report, *Impacts*, p. 393.

2. Nicholas Stern, *The Economics of Climate Change: The Stern Review* (New York: Cambridge University Press, 2007), 89.

3. A detailed discussion of the methodology is contained in Anthony J. McMichael et al. *Climate Change and Human Health: Risks and Responses* (Geneva: World Health Organization, 2003).

4. The details of the numbers presented below are as follows: Estimates are based on the low adaptation and unrestrained emissions scenarios. The temperature assumptions in the WHO study correspond to the emissions and temperature projections for around 2050 in the economic models reviewed in Part I, so I generally identify these as impacts for 2050. A range of impacts is presented (low, mid, high), and I present the high case with some discussion of other cases. These estimates are based on 2004 population and mortality rates but assume some growth in incomes over the half century.

5. For estimates of the global burden of disease using the DALY concept, see Christopher J. L. Murray and Alan D. Lopez, *Global Health Statistics* (Cambridge, MA: Harvard School of Public Health, 1996). Data on DALYs are published by the World Health Organization and can be found at www.who.int/healthinfo/global _burden_disease/estimates_regional/en/index.html. Some scholars prefer QALYs, which are quality-adjusted life years, but public health specialists have generally focused on DALYs, partially because the "quality" aspect of health is so hard to measure.

6. Guy Hutton et al., "Cost-Effectiveness of Malaria Intermittent Preventive Treatment in Infants (IPTi) in Mozambique and the United Republic of Tanzania," *Bulletin of the World Health Organization* 87, no. 2 (2009): 123–129.

7. Author's calculations based on data from Anthony J. McMichael et al., *Climate Change and Human Health*.

8. To prepare the estimates, I took the upper-bound relative risk estimates from McMichael et al., *Climate Change and Human Health*, for each of the major sources that they derived for 2030 and applied them to the baseline mortality risk from the WHO data cited for 2004 in Anthony J. McMichael et al., *Climate Change and Human Health: Risks and Responses* (Geneva: World Health Organization, 2003). The temperature estimates came from the Yale-RICE 2010 baseline, which reaches the same temperature level in 2050 as the climate assumptions in McMichael et al., and so we have labeled these as "2050 impacts." There will be some inconsistency because that study used different assumptions about GDP growth. For each of the three diseases, we took the upper response for the "unmitigated emissions" scenario. Note that there were two estimates of health impacts. One estimate provided a zero estimate of impacts, and the second was the "midrange" estimate. The upper estimate was simply double the midrange. If instead we averaged the two source estimates, the numbers would be approximately one-half of those shown. The es-

timates for all regions are shown in Table N-2 (from the WHO study and Christopher J. L. Murray and Alan D. Lopez, *Global Health Statistics* [Cambridge, MA: Harvard School of Public Health, 1996]).

Table N-2.

Increased risk from climate change	Total	Diarrheal diseases	Malaria	Nutritional deficiencies
	Disability-adjusted life years lost per 1,000 persons			
Africa	14.91	6.99	7.13	0.80
Eastern Mediterranean	1.06	0.61	0.06	0.39
Latin America	0.26	0.24	0.03	0.00
Southeast Asia	4.53	2.34	0.02	2.18
Western Pacific	0.35	0.27	0.08	0.00
North America and western Europe	0.02	0.02	0.00	0.00
World Average	**3.09**	**1.56**	**0.85**	**0.69**

Increased risk as percentage of baseline mortality	Total	Diarrheal diseases	Malaria	Nutritional deficiencies
	Losses from climate change as % of all losses			
Africa	2.92	1.37	1.40	0.16
Eastern Mediterranean	0.61	0.35	0.04	0.22
Latin America	0.16	0.14	0.02	0.00
Southeast Asia	1.71	0.88	0.01	0.82
Western Pacific	0.23	0.18	0.05	0.00
North America and western Europe	0.01	0.01	0.00	0.00
World Average	**1.31**	**0.66**	**0.36**	**0.29**

9. The data on life expectancy are from the World Bank, World Development Indicators.

10. Calculations are by the author.

11. This estimate uses detailed regional population and income estimates and is based on the GEcon data set with population and per capita GDP at a 1° × 1° resolu-

tion. It assumes that incomes in each grid cell grow at the average of the sub-Saharan African region in the RICE-2010 model. There are 2,597 observations. The GEcon data base is available at gecon.yale.edu.

12. IPCC, Fourth Assessment Report, *Impacts*, p. 409. This is one of many statements, some of which are inconsistent.

13. Robert W. Snow and Judy A. Omumbo, "Malaria," in *Disease and Mortality in Sub-Saharan Africa*, 2nd ed., ed. D. T. Jamison et al. (Washington, DC: World Bank, 2006) Chapter 14.

14. See World Health Organization, *World Malaria Report 2011* (Geneva: WHO Press, 2011).

CHAPTER 9 PERILS FOR THE OCEANS

1. See Chapter 15. For a graph of the differences among climate models, see IPCC, Fourth Assessment Report, *Science*, p. 812, Figure 10.31. The range of estimates for thermal expansion of the oceans for scenario A1B is 14–38 cm by 2100. I suspect that the size of this range is largely due to differences in the temperature trajectories.

2. Christian Aid, *Human Tide: The Real Migration Crisis*, May 2007, www.christian aid.org.uk/images/human-tide.pdf.

3. Center for Naval Analyses, *National Security and the Threat of Climate Change* (Alexandria, VA: CNA Corporation, 2007), www.cna.org/nationalsecurity/climate/.

4. The current estimate of SLR comes from various sources. For land ice, a recent study suggests about 1.5 mm per year, while estimates of thermal expansion are about 0.5 mm per year. The comparison of RICE and IPCC scenarios is shown in Figure 16. These estimates are drawn from IPCC, Fourth Assessment Report, *Science*; Chapters 5 and 10 and are updated with current estimates. The estimate for the twenty-first century is for IPCC-SRES scenario A1B, Table 10.7, ibid., p. 820. Similar results are found for scenario B2. The range of thermal expansion for the models is from 0.12 to 0.32 meters over the century.

5. A widely cited study that shows more rapid SLR estimates is Stefan Rahmstorf, "Sea-Level Rise: A Semi-Empirical Approach to Projecting Future Sea-Level Rise," *Science* 315 (2007): 368–370. I have attempted to reestimate the equations and have found that they are statistically unreliable. The coefficient on temperature has a p value of 0.26. The forecast errors for the SLR projections over the twenty-first century are approximately ±2 meters. A discussion is contained in William D. Nordhaus, "Alternative Policies and Sea-Level Rise in the Rice-2009 Model," Cowles Foundation Discussion Paper No. 1716, August 2009. Further estimates in 2013 indicated even larger errors than the earlier estimates.

6. This phrase is the striking title of a report by a committee of the National Academy of Sciences, *Abrupt Climate Change: Inevitable Surprises* (Washington, DC: National Academies Press, 2002).

7. The RICE-2011 model projects an SLR of 0.73 meters for 2100. This is at the high end of current models but slightly below the projections in Rahmstorf, "Sea-Level Rise," n. 89.

8. These calculations are by the author, based on the Yale G-Econ database, which has developed a data set on area, population, and output for the entire world. See Yale University, "Geographically Based Economic Data (G-Econ)," http://gecon.yale.edu.

9. A description of the SLR module of the Yale RICE model is available at William Nordhaus, Yale Department of Economics, http://nordhaus.econ.yale.edu/RICE models.htm.

10. See particularly James Hansen et al., "Target Atmospheric CO_2: Where Should Humanity Aim?" *Open Atmospheric Science Journal* (2008): 217–231.

11. Calculations by the author based on the Yale G-Econ database, which has developed a data set on area, population, and output for the entire world. See Yale University, "Geographically Based Economic Data (G-Econ)."

12. The correlation between elevation and per capita income for all populated regions is −0.09. The average per capita income in red zone regions in 2000 was $6,550 while that in regions above the red zone was $6,694.

13. See World Heritage Convention, "Operational Guidelines for the Implementation of the World Heritage Convention," http://whc.unesco.org/en/guidelines.

14. The case studies can be found in UNESCO, World Heritage Convention, *Case Studies on Climate Change and World Heritage* (Paris: UNESCO World Heritage Centre, 2007), unesdoc.unesco.org/images/0015/001506/150600e.pdf.

15. For example, Andrea Bigano, Francesco Bosello, Roberto Roson, and Richard S. J. Tol, "Economy-wide Impacts of Climate Change: A Joint Analysis for Sea Level Rise and Tourism," *Mitigation and Adaptation Strategies for Global Change* 13 (2008): 765–791, projected losses in 2050 to be less than 0.1 percent of world output.

16. This important point was discovered in a series of pioneering studies by Gary Yohe and colleagues. See for example Gary Yohe et al., "The Economic Cost of Greenhouse-Induced Sea-Level Rise for Developed Property in the United States," *Climatic Change* (1996): 1573–1580.

17. The study of ocean carbonization is a new field. It was discovered almost by accident by Ken Caldeira about a decade ago, and one of the first studies was Ken Caldeira and Michael E. Wickett, "Oceanography: Anthropogenic Carbon and Ocean pH," *Nature* 425 (2003): 365. Here is a simplified explanation of the chemistry. Atmospheric CO_2 combines with ocean water to form carbonic acid (H_2CO_3), a compound that releases positive hydrogen ions into the water, thus lowering the pH (shifting toward acidity). This trend is usually balanced by the buffering effect of negative carbonate ions (CO_3^{2-}) in the water. But as more CO_2 is introduced into the system, the amounts of buffering carbonate decline. This also leads to a lower saturation state of calcium carbonate ($CaCO_3$).

18. One of the earliest studies was Richard A. Feely et al., "Impact of Anthropogenic CO_2 on the $CaCO_3$ System in the Oceans," *Science* 305 (2004): 362–366. A very readable nontechnical survey of the issue is in Scott C. Doney et al., "Ocean Acidification: The Other CO_2 Problem," *Annual Review of Marine Science* (2009): 169–192.

19. An example can be found in C. L. Sabine, R. A. Feely, R. Wanninkhof, and T. Takahashi, "The Global Ocean Carbon Cycle," *Bulletin of the American Meteorological Society* 89, no. 7 (2008): S58. A figure can be found in S. Neil Larsen, "Ocean

Acidification—Ocean in Peril," Project Groundswell, January 24, 2010, http://project groundswell.com/2010/01/24/ocean-acidification-ocean-in-peril/.

20. See Philip L. Munday et al., "Replenishment of Fish Populations Is Threatened by Ocean Acidification," *Proceedings of the National Academy of Sciences* 107, no. 29 (2010): 12930–12934. They report, "Larvae exposed to elevated CO_2 were more active and exhibited riskier behavior in natural coral-reef habitat. As a result, they had 5–9 times higher mortality from predation than current-day controls, with mortality increasing with CO_2 concentration."

CHAPTER 10 INTENSIFICATION OF HURRICANES

1. The content of this chapter draws upon William Nordhaus, "The Economics of Hurricanes and Implications of Global Warming," *Climate Change Economics* 1, no. 1 (2010). The important scientific studies are Kerry A. Emanuel, "The Dependence of Hurricane Intensity on Climate," *Nature* 326 (1987): 483–485; and Thomas R. Knutson and Robert E. Tuleya, "Impact of CO_2-Induced Warming on Simulated Hurricane Intensity and Precipitation: Sensitivity to the Choice of Climate Model and Convective Parameterization," *Journal of Climate* 17, no. 18 (2004): 3477–3495.

2. Data are by the author with estimates from National Weather Service, National Hurricane Center, archives.

3. Robert Mendelsohn, Kerry Emanuel, Shun Chonabayashi, and Laura Bakkensen, "The Impact of Climate Change on Global Tropical Cyclone Damage," *Nature, Climate Change*, published online January 15, 2012, doi: 10.1038/nclimate1357. Data provided by the authors.

4. Estimates of vulnerable capital are from Nordhaus, "The Economics of Hurricanes and Implications of Global Warming." The estimates of capital stock come from the U.S. Bureau of Economic Analysis, "National Economic Accounts" (www .bea.gov/national/index.htm#fixed). Depreciation rates come from Barbara M. Fraumeni, "The Measurement of Depreciation in the U.S. National Income and Product Accounts," *Survey of Current Business* (July 1997): 7–23, www.bea.gov/scb /pdf/NATIONAL/NIPAREL/1997/0797fr.pdf. The methodology of replacement estimates is also used by Gary Yohe et al., "The Economic Cost of Greenhouse-Induced Sea-Level Rise for Developed Property in the United States," *Climatic Change* (1996): 1573–1580.

CHAPTER 11 WILDLIFE AND SPECIES LOSS

1. Anthony D. Barnosky et al., "Has the Earth's Sixth Mass Extinction Already Arrived?" *Nature* 471 (2011): 51–57. This article has an excellent discussion and its bibliography lists important background documents.

2. M. E. J. Newman and Gunther J. Eble, "Decline in Extinction Rates and Scale Invariance in the Fossil Record," *Paleobiology* 25, no. 4 (1999, Fall): 434–439.

3. Estimates of current extinction rates vary widely. One estimate that counted the actual number recorded about 1,100 species lost since 1600, or about 3 per year. See Fraser D. M. Smith et al., "How Much Do We Know about the Current

Extinction Rate?" *Trends in Ecology and Evolution* 8, no. 10 (1993): 375–378. A theoretical calculation using a model estimated a loss of 120,000 species per year. N. Myers, "Extinction of Species," in *International Encyclopedia of the Social and Behavioral Sciences* (New York: Pergamon, 2001), 5200–5202. Finally, we can examine a detailed count in the Red List compiled by the International Union for Conservation of Nature (IUCN). From 2011 to 2012, nine species were reclassified from extinct to critically endangered or lower, while four species were reclassified from critically endangered to extinct or possibly extinct. The difference between the high and low estimates is a factor of approximately one hundred thousand. So to begin with, measures of actual extinctions are imprecise in the extreme.

4. Estimates of the threats to species are particularly uncertain given the difficulties of identifying extinctions or determining the probability of extinction. The most comprehensive estimates are provided by the International Union for Conservation of Nature (IUCN) Red List. The IUCN provides several distinct categories: extinct, extinct in the wild, critically endangered, endangered, vulnerable, and low risk.

Most analyses of extinction threats include everything from critically endangered to vulnerable. Here is a brief description of the categories. Extinct and extinct in the wild are obvious in principle but often difficult to determine, as was explained in note 3. The other definitions are complicated. "Critically endangered" is defined as meeting *any one of five criteria*, which are given in abbreviated form: (a) population reduction in recent period or near-future period by at least 80 percent; (b) extent of occurrence estimated to be less than 100 km² or extent of occupancy less than 10 km²; (c) population less than 250 mature individuals and declining; (d) population less than 50 mature individuals; (e) quantitative analysis showing the probability of extinction in the wild is at least 50 percent within ten years or three generations, whichever is the longer.

"Endangered" is similar but is met when any of five analogous quantitative criteria are met. For example, (e) is quantitative analysis showing the probability of extinction in the wild is at least 20 percent within twenty years or five generations, whichever is the longer. "Vulnerable" has similar criteria, with the fifth being the probability of extinction in the wild is at least 10 percent within 100 years. One important weakness of the classification scheme is that it considers primarily populations in the wild. So plants might be threatened in the wild but flourishing in cultivated gardens.

The IUCN in 2012 assessed a total of 63,837 species which revealed 19,817 are threatened with extinction. In this count, 3,947 were described as "critically endangered," 5,766 as "endangered," and the balance were listed as "vulnerable."

5. The figure is adapted from Anthony D. Barnosky et al., "Has the Earth's Sixth Mass Extinction Already Arrived?" *Nature* 471 (2011): 51–57. The threatened species, as determined by the International Union for Conservation of Nature, are ones listed as critically endangered, endangered, or vulnerable. The biological names for the groups (taxa) from left to right are Aves, Chondrichthyes, Decapoda, Mammalia, Scleractinia, Reptilia, Coniferopsida, and Amphibia. For reference, the numbers of

known species include mammals (5,490), birds (10,027), corals (837), and conifers (618). For some taxa, the number of known species is much smaller than the estimated numbers.

6. See Chris D. Thomas et al., "Extinction Risk from Climate Change," *Nature* (2004): 145–148.

7. An exemplary study that shows the methodology is Kent E. Carpenter et al., "One-Third of Reef-Building Corals Face Elevated Extinction Risk from Climate Change and Local Impacts," *Science* 321 (2008): 560–563.

8. This statement is often encountered, but it has no documentation and is clearly wrong.

9. David J. Newman and Gordon M. Cragg, "Natural Products as Sources of New Drugs over the 30 Years from 1981 to 2010," *Journal of Natural Products* 75, no. 3 (2012): 311–335. I have benefited from a research report prepared by Yale students: Hcsu Yang and Gang Chen, "Economic Aspects of Natural Sources of New Drugs," April 2012, unpublished, on which the paragraph is based.

10. Most of this paragraph is taken from Paul Samuelson and William Nordhaus, *Economics*, 19th ed. (New York: McGraw-Hill, 2009).

11. I am grateful to Kerry Smith for comments on an earlier draft and suggestions on how to improve the current section. A useful appraisal is National Research Council, *Valuing Ecosystem Services: Toward Better Environmental Decision-Making* (Washington, DC: National Academies Press, 2004).

12. See D. F. Layton, G. M. Brown, and M. L. Plummer, "Valuing Multiple Programs to Improve Fish Populations," prepared for Washington State Department of Ecology, April 1999, www.econ.washington.edu/user/gbrown/valmultiprog.pdf.

13. A good summary of the debate is contained in the *Journal of Economic Perspectives* 26 (2012, Fall), www.aeaweb.org/articles.php?doi=10.1257/jep.26.4. Here is a striking example of the uncertainty. After the *Exxon Valdez* oil spill in 1989, two teams of researchers were asked to provide estimates of the damages for litigation. One side generated an estimate of $4,900 million in lost economic value. Another found a damage estimate of only $3.8 million. The major difference was that the former included nonuse or externality values, while the latter did not. For a discussion, see Catherine L. Kling, Daniel J. Phaneuf, and Jinhua Zhao, "From Exxon to BP: Has Some Number Become Better Than No Number?" *Economic Perspectives* 26 (2012, Fall): 3–26.

14. Sean Nee and Robert M. May, "Extinction and the Loss of Evolutionary History," *Science* 278, no. 5338 (1997): 692–694.

15. Particularly interesting are a series of studies by Martin Weitzman, including what he calls the Noah's ark problem. This involves choosing which species to preserve. See his "Noah's Ark Problem," *Econometrica* 66 (1998): 1279–1298. For an important study on alternative metrics, see Andrew Solow, Stephen Polasky, and James Broadus, "On the Measurement of Biological Diversity," *Journal of Environmental and Economics Management* 24 (1993): 60–68. To date, there has been little success in applying these metrics in valuation work.

16. Arthur Schopenhauer, *On the Basis of Morality*, trans. E. F. J. Payne (Providence, RI: Berghahn, 1955).

CHAPTER 12 ADDING UP THE DAMAGES FROM CLIMATE CHANGE

1. The data refer to the value added by sector (which represents the total sales less purchases from other businesses). So for agriculture, this excludes purchases of fuel and fertilizer. A major statistical decision was how to partition real estate between moderately and lightly vulnerable sectors. I assume that low-lying real estate is susceptible to storms and flooding and is therefore moderately vulnerable. Using the Yale G-Econ database, I estimate that 6 percent of U.S. output and population lies below 10 meters of elevation (see Table 4), and I use that as the basis for determining the moderately affected share of real estate. Data for industrial output come from the U.S. Bureau of Economic Analysis, "Gross-Domestic-Product-by-Industry Accounts, 1947–2010," www.bea.gov/industry/gpotables/gpo_action.cfm. Spatial data are from Yale University, "Geographically Based Economic Data (G-Econ)," http://gecon.yale.edu.

2. Data are from the World Bank, *World Development Indicators*, http://data.worldbank.org/data-catalog/world-development-indicators.

3. Figure by the author drawn using data from Richard Tol, "The Economic Impact of Climate Change," *Journal of Economic Perspectives* 23, no. 2 (2009): 29–51. The estimate from the RICE-2010 model is from the author. The IPCC estimate comes from the Third Assessment Report and was cited in the Fourth Assessment Report, *Impacts*, Section 20.6.1.

4. Some studies apply "equity weights" to the estimates, so that $1 of damages in low-income regions is counted as more than $1 in high-income regions, which would generally raise the damage ratio. This will explain that point for interested readers. Suppose we have two regions, A and B. Their per capita incomes are $10,000 and $5,000. Then, to reflect equity, we might weight losses to B as twice those of region A (if the social welfare function is of the logarithmic nature, where social welfare is the log of consumption). The relative weights in the RICE-2010 model are slightly different, but the answer will make little difference for the calculation reported here. An unweighted calculation, like those shown in Figure 22, simply takes the total losses and divides by total global income. An equity-weighted calculation takes the losses for each person (or more realistically for each region) and weights that by the equity weight.

5. Table N-3 shows the incremental damage from warming (from Tol, "The Economic Impact of Climate Change"). This calculates the additional damages per degree of temperature increase. The estimates use a quadratic function fitted to Tol's estimates and extrapolated out to 4°C. Note that the data only cover the range through 3°C, so beyond that the estimate is an extrapolation. The incremental damages show the change in damages per degree change in temperature and are calculated for the increment from 1/2°C lower to 1/2°C higher than the number shown. That is, the estimate for 3°C equals the damages at 31/2°C minus the damages at 21/2°C. The figures in parentheses are the standard errors of estimates for each temperature from the least-squares regression.

Table N-3.

Temperature	Incremental damages (% of output per °C)
1	−0.2 (± 1.5)
2	2.0 (± 1.5)
3	4.2 (+ 1.5)
4	6.3 (+ 3.2)

Note: The figures in parentheses are the standard errors of the estimates for each temperature.

6. According to Penn World Table 6.3, Indian per capita real income grew by a factor of 5.9 from 1950 to 2010, while Chinese per capita income grew by a factor between 15 and 33, depending upon the measures used. See Alan Heston, Robert Summers, and Bettina Aten, "Penn World Table Version 7.1," Center for International Comparisons of Production, Income and Prices at the University of Pennsylvania, November 2012, from https://pwt.sas.upenn.edu/php_site/pwt71/pwt71_form.php.

CHAPTER 13   DEALING WITH CLIMATE CHANGE: ADAPTATION AND GEOENGINEERING

1. See William Easterling, Brian Hurd, and Joel Smith, *Coping with Global Climate Change: The Role of Adaptation in the United States*, Pew Center on Global Climate Change, 2004, http://www.pewclimate.org/docUploads/Adaptation.pdf. They write, "The literature indicates that U.S. society can on the whole adapt with either net gains or some costs if warming occurs at the lower end of the projected range of magnitude, assuming no change in climate variability and generally making optimistic assumptions about adaptation. However, with a much larger magnitude of warming, even making relatively optimistic assumptions about adaptation, many sectors would experience net losses and higher costs. The thresholds in terms of magnitudes or rates of change (including possible nonlinear responses) in climate that will pose difficulty for adaptation are uncertain. In addition, it is uncertain how much of an increase in frequency, intensity, or persistence of extreme weather events the United States can tolerate."

2. Consider what it would cost to pump enough seawater 1,000 feet up and dump it on the Antarctic ice sheet to offset projected sea-level rise. I assume that the pumps are 85 percent efficient and require 0.00369 kW per gallon per minute per foot of head. I assume that the operation requires removing 10 cm of sea level equivalent, for a total of 8×10^{17} gallons of water per year. Plugging this annual volume of sea water into the formula yields an energy demand of about 5×10^{13} kWh per year. This is about twice the current total global electricity generation and would cost approximately 10 percent of today's world GDP.

3. The first thorough discussion of geoengineering came in a National Academy of Sciences committee report in 1992 on climate change. See National Research Council, *Policy Implications of Greenhouse Warming: Mitigation, Adaptation, and the Science Base* (Washington, DC: National Academies Press, 1992). A useful, more recent discussion of different geoengineering strategies along with the distinction between solar radiation management and CO_2 removal is found in a report by the U.K. Royal Society, *Geoengineering the Climate: Science, Governance and Uncertainty*, September 2009, RS Policy document 10/09.

4. A useful set of model runs and discussion is in Katharine L. Ricke, M. Granger Morgan, and Myles R. Allen, "Regional Climate Response to Solar-Radiation Management," *Nature Geoscience* 3 (August 2010): 537–541.

5. John von Neumann, "Can We Survive Technology," *Fortune* (June 1955).

6. Geoengineering involves more than just climate science or designing clever space mirrors. The political and social aspects are emphasized in an important review, Edward A. Parson and David W. Keith, "End the Deadlock on Governance of Geoengineering Research," *Science* 339 (2013): 1278–1279, available at www.keith.seas.harvard.edu/preprints/163.Parson.Keith.DeadlockOnGovernance.p.pdf.

CHAPTER 14   SLOWING CLIMATE CHANGE BY REDUCING EMISSIONS: MITIGATION

1. The long-term projections are from the Goddard Institute for Space Studies, "Forcings in GISS Climate Model," http://data.giss.nasa.gov/modelforce/ghgases/.

2. Data come from Carbon Dioxide Information Analysis Center, "Fossil-Fuel CO_2 Emissions," http://cdiac.ornl.gov/trends/emis/meth_reg.html.

3. Prices are measured at the wholesale level for crude fuels. Emissions rates and prices are from Energy Information Administration, for 2011 from www.eia.doe .gov. Emissions are from www.eia.gov/environment/data.cfm#intl, while prices are from the Annual Energy Outlook and the associated data from www.eia.gov /forecasts/aeo/er/index.cfm.

4. The estimates in the table have been developed by the author. They are surprisingly difficult to calculate given the complexity of the interactions in the economy. The calculations start with energy consumption of the residential sector from the Energy Information Administration. I assume that CO_2 emissions are proportional to energy use, which is not strictly accurate. The estimates for air travel and automobiles are from the Energy Information Administration.

5. The information on how much CO_2 and other GHGs are contained in different goods and services has not been done by statistical agencies on a detailed basis for the United States. It involves using input-output analysis for different industries— for example, determining how much oil goes into the rubber that goes into your walking shoes, as well as how long they last. Most estimates exclude the capital inputs. If the goods are imported, then the data on CO_2 content of the imports are unavailable. The estimates in the text use CO_2 input-output tables prepared by the Department of Commerce, but they have multiple problems of interpretation. See

U.S. Department of Commerce, "U.S. Carbon Dioxide Emissions and Intensities over Time: A Detailed Accounting of Industries, Government and Households," Economics and Statistics Administration, September 20, 2010, www.esa.doc.gov/Reports/u.s.-carbon-dioxide for the background documents, especially Table A-63.

6. A good starting point is the report of a panel of the National Academy of Sciences, *Limiting the Magnitude of Future Climate Change* (Washington, DC: National Academies Press, 2010), available free at www.nap.edu. See especially the summary in Chapter 3. There are also panel reports for different sectors that provide more detail.

7. Energy Information Administration, "Levelized Cost of New Generation Resources in the Annual Energy Outlook 2011," www.eia.gov/oiaf/aeo/electricity_gen eration.html. Estimates on emissions per kilowatt hour are from the Environmental Protection Agency, www.epa.gov/cleanenergy/energy-and-you/affect/air-emissions .html.

8. These calculations were made using the Yale DICE-2012 model. Other estimates of this scenario, for five models of intermediate complexity, are found in IPCC, Fourth Assessment Report, *Science*, p. 826.

9. See *The Future of Coal: Options for a Carbon-Constrained World*, Massachusetts Institute of Technology, 2007, http://web.mit.edu/coal/The_Future_of_Coal.pdf.

10. Ibid.

11. For a technological description and several useful references, see D. Golomb et al., "Ocean Sequestration of Carbon Dioxide: Modeling the Deep Ocean Release of a Dense Emulsion of Liquid CO_2-in-Water Stabilized by Pulverized Limestone Particles," *Environmental Science and Technology* 41 (2007): 4698–4704, http://faculty .uml.edu/david_ryan/Pubs/Ocean%20Sequestration%20Golomb%20et%20al %20EST%202007.pdf.

12. Freeman Dyson, "The Question of Global Warming," *New York Review of Books* 55, no. 10 (June 12, 2008).

13. The synthetic tree has been in the "information" stage for several years. The current proposal is really an industrial chemical process that requires a massive amount of land and equipment to make a dent in CO_2 concentrations. It has yet to be proven on a large scale. The discussion of the Lachner tree is drawn from his "Air Capture and Mineral Sequestration," February 4, 2010, unpublished, available at http://science.house.gov/sites/republicans.science.house.gov/files/documents/hear ings/020410_Lackner.pdf.

14. See Ray Kurzweil, *The Singularity Is Near: When Humans Transcend Biology* (New York: Viking, 2005). Those who are skeptical should remember that computers with much less power than a cell phone filled an entire room in 1960. Kurzweil argues that thin-film solar panels will be so inexpensive that we could place them on our clothes to generate power. Additionally, we could put huge solar panels in space and beam the power back to earth by microwaves. How would Kurzweil get the materials into space? With a space elevator, described as "a thin ribbon, extending from a shipborne anchor to a counterweight well beyond geosynchronous orbit, made out of a material called carbon nanotube composite." To bring this discussion back to earth, recent work on space elevators suggests that they will be almost as expensive as space planes, on the order of $1,000–$5,000 per kg to put materials in

space, so these ideas have a long way to go down the learning curve before they can make a dent in anything.

CHAPTER 15 THE COSTS OF SLOWING CLIMATE CHANGE

1. The details of the calculation are as follows. (1) My old refrigerator uses 1,000 kWh per year, while the new one uses 500 kWh per year, so the savings are 500 kWh per year. (2) Assume that electricity generation emits 0.6 tons of CO_2 per 1,000 kWh. So my new refrigerator saves about 0.3 tons of CO_2 per year. (3) Electricity costs $0.10 per kWh, and my new refrigerator costs $1,000. My total 10-year cost (without discounting) is $1,000 for the new refrigerator less $50 per year of electricity savings, for a total cost of $500. (4) Therefore, without discounting, the cost of saving a ton of CO_2 is $500/3 = $167 per ton of CO_2. (5) Discounting complicates the story because both electricity savings and CO_2 savings are in the future. Let's consider the present value of the cost of replacing the old refrigerator. This equals $V = 1,000 - 50/(1.05) - 50/(1.05)^2 - \ldots - 50/(1.05)^9 = 595$. So in the discounted case, the cost of saving the CO_2 is $595/3 = $198 per ton of CO_2. This calculation does not discount the CO_2 reductions.

2. Calculation is by the author.

3. An important study of the impact of reducing methane and "black carbon" is in Drew Shindell et al., "Simultaneously Mitigating Near-Term Climate Change and Improving Human Health and Food Security," *Science* 335, no. 6065 (2012): 183–189. Taking all measures is estimated to reduce global mean temperature by about 1/2°C by 2070, which is the same as a set of much more costly measures to reduce CO_2 emissions. The measures proposed by the authors are as follows: control of CH_4 emissions from livestock, mainly through farm-scale anaerobic digestion of manure from cattle and pigs; diesel particle filters for on-road and off-road vehicles as part of a move to worldwide adoption of Euro 6/VI standards; ban on open burning of agricultural waste; substitution of clean-burning cookstoves using modern fuels for traditional biomass cookstoves in developing countries; extended recovery and utilization, rather than venting, of associated gas and improved control of unintended fugitive emissions from the production of oil and natural gas; and separation and treatment of biodegradable municipal waste through recycling, composting, and anaerobic digestion as well as landfill gas collection with combustion and utilization. Some of these would require extensive interventions in the activities of hundreds of millions of households, while others are more easily undertaken. (This paragraph is a partial list that is taken almost verbatim from ibid., Supporting Online Material, Table S1.)

4. The estimate compares the reference run with the no-international-offsets run. Source: See U.S. Energy Information Administration, "Energy Market and Economic Impacts of H.R. 2454, the American Clean Energy and Security Act of 2009," Report SR-OIAF/2009-05, August 4, 2009, www.eia.doe.gov/oiaf/servicerpt /hr2454/index.html.

5. Curves are derived from various sources as collated by the author. The bottom-up models are primarily from IPCC, Fourth Assessment Report, *Mitigation*, p. 77. The

top-down models are combined from the RICE-2010 model as well as results from the EMF-22 study.

6. Here is an example where bottom-up models sometimes underestimate the costs. In estimating the cost of reducing CO_2 emissions from power plants, they often assume that all power plants are new. This would lead to a big advantage for low-emissions gas plants over high-emissions coal plants. In reality, for existing capital, the generation costs for coal are lower than those of new gas plants, so the bottom-up model will find negative cost emissions reductions when in reality they do not apply to the actual capital structure of the economy.

7. Calculations have been prepared by the author using the 2010 version of the regional RICE model.

8. The EMF results are contained in Leon Clarke et al., "International Climate Policy Architectures: Overview of the EMF 22 International Scenarios," *Energy Economics* 31 (2009): S64–S81. The comparison with the RICE model is difficult because the EMF estimates include only the Kyoto gases and do not include aerosols and other influences. For this reason, the EMF calculations are likely to overestimate temperature increases.

CHAPTER 16 DISCOUNTING AND THE VALUE OF TIME

1. There is one interesting difference between economic discounting and visual perspective. The size of objects in space are inverse to the distance, while those in finance are inverse to the exponential of time. So financial perspective has a curved shape.

2. The descriptive versus prescriptive view was thoughtfully described and analyzed in the IPCC's Second Assessment Report. See Kenneth J. Arrow et al., "Intertemporal Equity, Discounting, and Economic Efficiency," in *Climate Change 1995: Economic and Social Dimensions of Climate Change*, Contribution of Working Group III to the Second Assessment Report of the Intergovernmental Panel on Climate Change, ed. J. Bruce, H. Lee, and E. Haites, 125–144 (Cambridge: Cambridge University Press, 1995).

3. One of the earliest advocates of a very low discount rate was William Cline, *The Economics of Global Warming* (Washington, DC: Institute of International Economics, 1992). Another prominent advocate of the prescriptive approach is the *Stern Review*: Nicholas Stern, *The Economics of Climate Change: The Stern Review* (New York: Cambridge University Press, 2007). These studies advocated using a combination of assumptions about economic growth and generational neutrality that led to a very low discount rate of goods. For those interested in the details of the *Stern Review*'s calculations, here is a brief summary. We assume zero population growth, constant growth in per capita consumption at rate g, and no externalities, risk, taxes, or market failures. The analysis relies on the Ramsey-Cass-Koopmans model of optimal economic growth. The model is based on two preference parameters: the pure rate of time preference (ρ) and the elasticity of the marginal utility of consumption or inequality aversion (α). The latter is a parameter describing the rate at which the marginal utility of per capita consumption declines with higher

consumption. If societal welfare is optimized, then the optimal path in long-run equilibrium is given by $r = \alpha g + \rho$, where r is the rate of return on capital. In the *Stern Review* setup, $g = 0.013$ per year and $\alpha = 1$. The pure rate of time preference is assumed to be $\rho = .001$ per year to reflect the probability of human extinction due to asteroid collisions. This leads to a real discount rate of 1.4 percent per year. The central features of the low-discount rate assumptions are a low pure rate of time preference and a low rate of inequality aversion. This approach has been adopted by the British government. See HM Treasury, *The Green Book: Appraisal and Evaluation in Central Government* (London: TSO, 2011), www.hm-treasury.gov.uk/d/green_book_complete.pdf.

4. Recall that most economic projections used in climate modeling studies assume that living standards grow rapidly over the coming decades. To make the point numerically, suppose that average consumption grows at 1½ percent per year for the next century. Then global per capita income would rise from around $10,000 to $44,000. So in comparing costs and benefits, we are comparing people who are relatively poor today with people who are relatively rich a century from now.

5. For an analysis of rates of return on alternative assets, although somewhat dated, see Arrow et al., "Intertemporal Equity, Discounting, and Economic Efficiency."

6. The first quote is from Office of Management and Budget (OMB), Circular A-94 revised, October 29, 1992, while the latter is Circular A-4, September 17, 2003. This is available on the White House web site, currently at www.whitehouse.gov/omb/circulars_a094.

7. Data are from the World Bank, *World Development Indicators*, http://databank.worldbank.org/ddp/home.do.

8. Specialists in discounting raise two further questions here. First, should discount rates be constant over time? And how should they reflect the uncertainties over the longer run? No unanimity exists about these issues, but most practitioners generally hold that the discount rate is likely to decline over time. The major reason is that most growth projections see lower population growth, and some also see slower long-run technological change. As the economy slows, more of our savings are set aside for capital deepening, which will tend to lower the return on capital. Treatment of uncertainty is more complicated and depends upon the source of risk and uncertainty. If we are uncertain about future economic growth, our plans will tend to put a larger weight on outcomes with lower discount rates, because they outweigh the paths with higher discount rates. In many modeling approaches, this would tend to reduce the average discount rate for the different scenarios. These two effects occur in the very long run—for periods of investments covering many decades or even centuries. The net impact is generally to raise the value of distant damages prevented. For a fine analysis of this subject, see Christian Gollier, *Pricing the Planet's Future: The Economics of Discounting in an Uncertain World* (Princeton, NJ: Princeton University Press, 2012).

9. Tjalling C. Koopmans, "On the Concept of Optimal Economic Growth," *Academiae Scientiarum Scripta Varia* 28, no. 1 (1965): 225–287.

CHAPTER 17 HISTORICAL PERSPECTIVES ON CLIMATE POLICY

1. See National Research Council, *Limiting the Magnitude of Future Climate Change*, America's Climate Choices series (Washington, DC: National Academies Press, 2010), http://dels.nas.edu/resources/static-assets/materials-based-on-reports/reports-in-brief/Limiting_Report_Brief_final.pdf.

2. The complete language is contained in United Nations, "United Nations Framework Convention on Climate Change," 1992, Article 2, http://unfccc.int/resource/docs/convkp/conveng.pdf.

3. See the Kyoto Protocol's initial statement of purpose, which reads, "*In pursuit* of the ultimate objective of the Convention as stated in its Article 2." See "Kyoto Protocol to the United Nations Framework Convention on Climate Change," 1997, http://unfccc.int/resource/docs/convkp/kpeng.html.

4. The statement adopted reads, "To achieve the ultimate objective of the Convention to stabilize greenhouse gas concentration in the atmosphere at a level that would prevent dangerous anthropogenic interference with the climate system, we shall, recognizing the scientific view that the increase in global temperature should be below 2 degrees Celsius, on the basis of equity and in the context of sustainable development, enhance our long-term cooperative action to combat climate change." See Copenhagen Accord, December 12, 2009, http://unfccc.int/files/meetings/cop_15/application/pdf/cop15_cph_auv.pdf.

5. See European Union, "Limiting Global Climate Change to 2 Degrees Celsius," January 10, 2007, http://europa.eu/rapid/pressReleasesAction.do?reference=MEMO/07/16; G8 Information Center, "Declaration of the Leaders: The Major Economies Forum on Energy and Climate," L'Aquila Summit, July 9, 2009, www.g8.utoronto.ca/summit/2009laquila/2009-mef.html.

6. An excellent history of the 2°C target is contained in Carlo Jaeger and Julia Jaeger, "Three Views of Two Degrees," *Climate Change Economics* 1, no. 3 (2010): 145–166.

7. National Academy of Sciences, *Limiting the Magnitude of Future Climate Change* (Washington, DC: National Academies Press, 2010).

8. The ice core data provide estimates of the temperature over Antarctica, which show an average temperature approximately 8°C lower than the present era at the last glacial maximum 20,000 years ago. There is uncertainty about the extent of global warming at the last glacial maximum. The IPCC's Fourth Assessment Report puts the warming since then at 4–7°C; IPCC, *Climate Change 2007: The Physical Science Basis* (Cambridge: Cambridge University Press, 2007), 451. A recent study of the last glacial cycle puts the difference at a little under 4°C; Jeremy D. Shakun, Peter U. Clark, Feng He, Shaun A. Marcott, Alan C. Mix, Zhengyu Liu, et al., "Global Warming Preceded by Increasing Carbon Dioxide Concentrations during the Last Deglaciation," *Nature* 484 (2012): 49–54. I take a value of 5°C as a reasonable consensus. I then transformed the Antarctic temperature into global mean temperatures assuming a scaling factor of 5/8. This is likely to get the broad sweep but will not accurately represent higher-resolution movements. I am grateful to Richard Alley for suggesting this approach.

9. Estimation of temperature before the modern period uses temperature "proxies." The most widely used proxies for the distant past are ice cores from Greenland, Antarctica, and other ice sheets. The data have been produced by several teams of scientists working for many years. A primary source is J. R. Petit et al., "Climate and Atmospheric History of the Past 420,000 Years from the Vostok Ice Core, Antarctica," *Nature* 399 (1999): 429–436. Detailed data come from Carbon Dioxide Information Analysis Center, U.S. Department of Energy, "Historical Isotopic Temperature Record from the Vostok Ice Core," http://cdiac.ornl.gov/ftp/trends/temp/vostok/vostok .1999.temp.dat.

10. William Nordhaus, "Economic Growth and Climate: The Carbon Dioxide Problem," *American Economic Review* 67 (February 1977): 341–346. The article emphasized that the target was "deeply unsatisfactory" because it did not involve any balancing of costs and benefits. However, there were at the time no estimates of the damages from global warming, so this target was a substitute for an approach that balances costs and damages.

11. German Advisory Council on Global Change, *Scenario for the Derivation of Global CO₂ Reduction Targets and Implementation Strategies*, Statement on the Occasion of the First Conference of the Parties to the Framework Convention on Climate Change in Berlin, March 1995, www.wbgu.de/wbgu_sn1995_engl.pdf.

12. IPCC, Fourth Assessment Report, *Impacts,* Technical Summary, p. 67.

CHAPTER 18   CLIMATE POLICY BY BALANCING COSTS AND BENEFITS

1. A fine exposition of cost-benefit analysis is in E. J. Mishan and Euston Quah, *Cost-Benefit Analysis*, 5th ed. (Abington, UK: Routledge, 2007).

2. Here are some additional details about how the curves were generated. I took the DICE-2012 model and estimated costs and damages for different temperature thresholds, with full participation and with limited participation. Costs and damages were then annualized and expressed as a function of annualized total income.

3. To calculate the lag, I added a pulse of emissions in 2015 to the DICE-2010 model. I then calculated the lag of damages behind emissions, which was 47 years and is rounded to 50 years.

4. The 4 percent discount rate is calculated as the long-run discount rate on goods and services. This is combined with a growth rate of the economy of 3 percent per year. See Chapter 16 for a discussion of the role of discounting.

5. The tipping cost or catastrophic damage function is written as $D/Y = .006\,(T/3.5)^{20}$. The .006 means that at $3\frac{1}{2}°C$, tipping damages are .6 percent of world income. The term $(T/3.5)$ means that the threshold is $3\frac{1}{2}°C$. The exponent 20 leads to a sharp discontinuity at 3°C.

6. The algebra here is straightforward if the result is surprising. Suppose that total cost is $C(T) = A(T) + \theta D(T)$, where C, A, D, and T are total costs, abatement, damages, and temperature in that order, and θ is an uncertain parameter. Then minimizing cost is achieved when θ is set at its expected value.

7. Report of the United Nations Conference on Environment and Development, Rio de Janeiro, June 3–14, 1992, available at www.un.org/documents/ga/conf151/aconf15126-1annex1.htm.

8. This is an important statistical point. If we look back to Table N-1, we see that the threshold for the West Antarctic Ice Sheet is 3 to 5°C. For simplicity, assume that this is a uniform distribution over this range, or that each value between 3 and 5 has an equally likely chance of being the threshold. From a probabilistic vantage point, it is no longer a threshold. Rather, there is a gradually increasing chance of having this dangerous outcome, rather than a sharp one at, say, the central value of 4°C.

CHAPTER 19   THE CENTRAL ROLE OF CARBON PRICES

1. Amber Mahone, Katie Pickrell, and Arne Olson, "CO_2 Price Forecast for WECC Reference Case," Scenario Planning Steering Group, report of Energy + Environmental Economics, May 21, 2012, www.wecc.biz/committees/BOD/TEPPC/SPSG/SPSG%20Meeting/Lists/Presentations/1/120522_CO2_Forecast_PPT_SPSG.pdf.

2. A thoughtful treatment of the ethics of climate change is contained in John Broome, *Climate Matters: Ethics in a Warming World* (New York: Norton, 2012). If you read this book and take it seriously, you will see how difficult it is to act in an ethical way in a warming world when you have substantial CO_2 emissions. Many of the ethical dilemmas raised by Broome would be removed if carbon were properly priced.

3. See Interagency Working Group, "Interagency Working Group on Social Cost of Carbon, United States Government," *Technical Support Document: Social Cost of Carbon for Regulatory Impact Analysis Under Executive Order 12866*, 2010, available at www.epa.gov/oms/climate/regulations/scc-tsd.pdf.

4. A further discussion is contained in William Nordhaus, "Estimates of the Social Cost of Carbon: Background and Results from the RICE-2011 Model," Cowles Foundation Discussion Paper No. 1826, October 2011. These papers are available at http://cowles.econ.yale.edu/P/cd/cfdpmain.htm.

5. Figure derived from various sources and collated by the author from Leon Clarke et al., "International Climate Policy Architectures: Overview of the EMF 22 International Scenarios," *Energy Economics* 31 (2009): S64–S81.

6. The experiments were constructed in terms of "radiative forcings" rather than temperature. For a description of the basics of radiative forcings, see Chapter 4, n. 6. These are the EMF-22 estimates for the scenario in which radiative forcings of long-lived greenhouse gases are limited to 3.7 W/m². The models include only long-lived forcings and exclude aerosols and other radiative forcings, so they tend to overestimate the temperature trajectory. The EMF-22 projections indicate the 3.7 W/m² scenario would correspond to about 3°C temperature increase if other forcings are ignored. If aerosols are included, however, it would be closer to 2½°C. For a discussion, see Leon Clarke et al., "International Climate Policy Architectures."

7. Impact on prices assuming that demand is unresponsive (zero price elasticity of demand) and that the supply price does not change (supply is perfectly price elastic). This is likely to overstate the price impact, particularly for heavily taxed items that are not internationally traded. Author's calculations based on 2008 U.S. consumption levels from the Energy Information Administration.

8. The table takes the consumption for a representative U.S. household and calculates the impact of a $25 per ton carbon price. Note that the impacts are much higher on carbon-intensive sectors like automotive gasoline or electricity than for information or financial services. This table excludes emissions from other sectors, such as government, and the total is therefore smaller than that in Table 6. Calculation assumes electricity generation is 50 percent from coal and 50 percent from natural gas. Air travel uses calculator from International Civil Aviation Organization, "Carbon Emissions Calculator," www2.icao.int/en/carbon offset/Pages/default.aspx. Price of flight from Expedia.com at $300 per round trip. Financial and information CO_2 intensities from Mun S. Ho, Richard Morgenstern, and Jhih-Shyang Shih, "Impact of Carbon Price Policies on U.S. Industry," Resources for the Future Working Paper, RFF DP 06-37, November 2008. All consumption data are from BEA and assume that personal consumption is 67 percent of GDP, 125 million households, assuming CO_2 intensity of consumption is equal to that of GDP.

9. Congressional Budget Office, *The 2012 Long-Term Budget Outlook,* January 2013, www.cbo.gov/publication/43907.

CHAPTER 20 CLIMATE-CHANGE POLICIES AT THE NATIONAL LEVEL

1. Figure constructed by the author from ICE Europe, https://www.theice.com/. These prices are a splice of different vintages of permits.

2. For details on the design of a carbon tax, see Gilbert E. Metcalf and David Weisbach, "The Design of a Carbon Tax," *Harvard Environmental Law Review* 33 (2009): 499–566.

3. A more detailed comparison of carbon taxes and cap-and-trade systems is contained in William Nordhaus, *A Question of Balance* (New Haven, CT: Yale University Press, 2007), Chapter 7. The contrary point of view can be found in a study by Robert Stavins, *A U.S. Cap-and-Trade System to Address Global Climate Change,* prepared for the Hamilton Project, Brookings Institution, October 2007. I have omitted some of the technical reasons, such as those relating to the linearity or nonlinearity of the cost and benefit functions, which are discussed in the publications cited here.

4. Some good places to start are Gilbert Metcalf, "A Proposal for a U.S. Carbon Tax Swap: An Equitable Tax Reform to Address Global Climate Change," Hamilton Project, Brookings Institution, November 2007, www.hamiltonproject.org/files /downloads_and_links/An_Equitable_Tax_Reform_to_Address_Global_Climate_ Change.pdf; Metcalf and Weisbach, "The Design of a Carbon Tax."

CHAPTER 21 FROM NATIONAL TO HARMONIZED INTERNATIONAL POLICIES

1. An interesting study of successes and failures is Inge Kaul, Isabelle Grunberg, and Marc Stern, eds., *Global Public Goods: International Cooperation in the 21st Century* (Oxford: Oxford University Press, 1999).

2. See particularly Scott Barrett, *Environment and Statecraft: The Strategy of Environmental Treaty-Making* (Oxford: Oxford University Press, 2003).

3. United Nations, "United Nations Framework Convention on Climate Change," 1992, http://unfccc.int/resource/docs/convkp/conveng.pdf.

4. Data largely from CDIAC, with other estimates by the author.

5. A list of meetings and their reports can be found at the website of the "United Nations Framework Convention on Climate Change," http://unfccc.int/2860.php.

6. Author's calculations based on data from World Development Indicators database, http://databank.worldbank.org/ddp/home.do.

7. The problem of corruption in quantitative systems is an important point. Quantity-type systems like cap and trade are much more susceptible to corruption than price-type regimes. An emissions trading system creates valuable assets in the form of tradable emissions permits and allocates them to countries. Limiting emissions creates a scarcity where none previously existed and is a rent-creating program. The dangers of quantity as compared to price approaches have been demonstrated frequently when quotas are compared with tariffs in international trade interventions. Calculations suggest that tens of billions of dollars of permits may be available for foreign sale under an international cap-and-trade regime. Given the history of privatizing valuable public assets at artificially low prices, it would not be surprising if the carbon market became tangled in corrupt practices, undermining the legitimacy of the process. Consider the case of Nigeria, which had annual CO_2 emissions of around 400 million tons in recent years. If Nigeria were allocated tradable allowances equal to recent emissions and could sell them for $25 per ton of CO_2, it would raise around $10 billion of hard currency annually—in a country whose nonoil exports in 2011 were only $3 billion. A carbon tax gives less room for corruption because it does not create artificial scarcities, monopolies, or rents. Tax cheating is a zero-sum game for the company and the government, while emissions evasion is a positive-sum game for the two domestic parties. With taxes, no permits are transferred to countries or leaders of countries, so they cannot be sold abroad for wine or guns. There is no new rent-seeking opportunity. Any revenues would need to be raised by taxation on domestic consumption of fuels, and a carbon tax would add absolutely nothing to the rent-producing instruments that countries have today.

8. A useful analysis of the history of verification in international environmental agreements is contained in Jesse Ausubel and David Victor, "Verification of International Environmental Agreements," *Annual Review of Energy and Environment* 17 (1992): 1–43, http://phe.rockefeller.edu/verification/.

9. An extended discussion along with a comprehensive list of treaties is in Barrett, *Environment and Statecraft*.

10. An interesting study that compares the issues of enforcement mechanisms in climate change with those in other areas with externalities is Peter Drahos, "The Intellectual Property Regime: Are There Lessons for Climate Change Negotiations?" Climate and Environmental Governance Network (Cegnet) Working Paper 09, November 2010. A review of provisions in different countries, international law, and institutions, and a case for the use of trade sanctions is in Jeffrey Frankel, "Global Environmental Policy and Global Trade Policy," John F. Kennedy School of Government, Harvard University, October 2008, RWP08-058.

CHAPTER 22 SECOND BEST AND BEYOND

1. Barack Obama, "State of the Union," February 12, 2013, available at www.whitehouse.gov/state-of-the-union-2013.

2. This discussion about taxes holds to a first approximation. Advanced economic analysis would take into account the potential distortions from taxation. The lesson from tax economics is that existing tax distortions can change the optimal climate policy substantially. Work by University of Maryland economist Lint Barrage indicates that existing tax distortions may lower the optimal carbon price by about one-third in the case where the revenues are raised by taxation or auctioning (see her "Carbon Taxes as a Part of Fiscal Policy and Market Incentives for Environmental Stewardship," Ph.D. dissertation, Yale University, May 2013). The question of how much further the optimal price should be reduced if allowances are given away is an open question, but it is clear that free allocation would further reduce the optimal carbon price even more.

3. This is taken from the regulatory analysis, *Final Regulatory Impact Analysis Corporate Average Fuel Economy for MY 2017–MY 2025 Passenger Cars and Light Trucks*, August 2012. This is available from the government at www.nhtsa.gov/static-files/rulemaking/pdf/cafe/FRIA_2017-2025.pdf. The regulatory analysis is 1,178 pages and has virtually no relationship to the popular justification by the proponents. Virtually all the benefits (around $600 billion) are private; they result from fuel savings that are greater than the incremental cost of the fuel economy improvements. Only a net total of $5 billion of the $600 billion of benefits result from externalities. Moreover, the $5 billion is the sum of positive benefits of $50 billion from CO_2 reductions and negative benefits of $45 billion from externalities such as increased congestion. If the private technology costs are compared with the CO_2 and other pollution benefits, the costs are greater than the benefits. This finding is consistent with the Resources for the Future study (see n. 4).

4. Alan J. Krupnick, Ian W. H. Parry, Margaret A. Walls, Tony Knowles, and Kristin Hayes, *Toward a New National Energy Policy: Assessing the Options* (Washington, DC: Resources for the Future, 2010), www.energypolicyoptions.org.

5. Ibid., Appendix B.

6. The policy benchmark chosen for the studies is the climate-change proposal of the Obama administration, which is similar to the bill passed by the U.S. House of

Representatives in 2009. This policy is discussed in Chapters 18 and 21 and aims at an average reduction in CO_2 emissions of 10 percent over the 2010–2030 period, with most of the reduction occurring at the end of the period.

7. National Research Council, *Effects of U.S. Tax Policy on Greenhouse Gas Emissions* (Washington, DC: National Academy Press, 2013).

8. Energy-cost myopia goes by many names. It is also called the energy efficiency gap and the energy paradox. For a skeptical view, see Hunt Allcott and Michael Greenstone, "Is There an Energy Efficiency Gap?" *Journal of Economic Perspectives* 26, no. 1 (2012): 3–28. A strong advocate of the gap is the consulting firm McKinsey, for example in *Unlocking Energy Efficiency in the U.S. Economy*, 2009, www.mckinsey .com.

9. This calculation is similar to the one used for replacing my refrigerator (see Chapter 15). For simplicity, it assumes that gasoline and diesel fuels have the same price per gallon, which has been true over the long run. It assumes a zero real discount rate for simplicity. Assuming that the real discount rate is 5 percent per year, then the discounted savings would be $3,164, but the point is basically the same. To make this a break-even deal, the real discount rate would need to be 17.3 percent per year.

10. Data on sales of diesel and gasoline cars for 2010 are found at BMW Blog, www.bmwblog.com/wp-content/uploads/2010-Diesel-Economics2.png.

11. A wonderful book that illuminates the many insights of behavioral economics is George A. Akerlof and Robert J. Shiller, *Animal Spirits: How Human Psychology Drives the Economy, and Why It Matters for Global Capitalism* (Princeton, NJ: Princeton University Press, 2009).

12. Drawn from Alan J. Krupnick et al., *Toward a New National Energy Policy*, Appendix B.

CHAPTER 23 NEW TECHNOLOGIES FOR A LOW-CARBON ECONOMY

1. *Nature*, November 29, 2012.

2. The actual rates are 5-year moving averages, assuming GDP growth averages slightly above 2 percent per year to 2050.

3. See William Nordhaus, "Designing a Friendly Space for Technological Change to Slow Global Warming," *Energy Economics* 33 (2011): 665–673. The figure is drawn from this article with changes for the present publication.

4. See n. 3 for calculations.

5. Data come from the U.S. Energy Information Administration, Annual Energy Review 2009, DOE/EIA-0384 (2009), Washington, DC, August 2010.

6. Many of the potential new technologies along with strategies to promote them are described in a special issue of *Energy Economics* 33, no. 4 (2011).

7. Estimates of dates of availability and status by the author. CCS, carbon capture and storage estimates from U.S. Energy Information Administration, "Levelized Cost of New Generation Resources in the Annual Energy Outlook 2011," www.eia .gov/forecasts/aeo/electricity_generation.html.

8. The study is reported in Leon Clarke, Page Kyle, Patrick Luckow, Marshall Wise, Walter Short, and Matthew Mowers, "10,000 Feet through 1,000 Feet: Linking an IAM (GCAM) with a Detailed U.S. Electricity Model (ReEDS)," August 6, 2009, emf.stanford.edu/files/docs/250/Clarke8-6.pdf.

9. Data are courtesy of Doug Arent of the National Renewable Energy Laboratories.

10. John Jewkes, David Sawers, and Richard Stillerman, *The Sources of Invention*, 2nd ed. (London: Macmillan, 1969).

11. Many of the ideas developed here are contained in Nordhaus, "Designing a Friendly Space."

12. The estimates for CCS come from Howard Herzog, "Scaling-Up Carbon Dioxide Capture and Storage (CCS): From Megatonnes to Gigatonnes," *Energy Economics* 33, no. 4 (2011).

13. See the fine analysis by John P. Weyant, "Accelerating the Development and Diffusion of New Energy Technologies: Beyond the 'Valley of Death,'" *Energy Economics* 33, no. 4 (2011): 674–682.

14. F. M. Scherer, *New Perspectives on Economic Growth and Technological Innovation* (Washington, DC: Brookings Institution Press, 1999), 57.

15. The program can be reviewed in its enthusiastic annual report; see Advanced Research Projects Agency-Energy, "FY 2010 Annual Report," http://arpa-e.energy.gov /sites/default/files/ARPA-E%20FY%202010%20Annual%20Report_1.pdf.

CHAPTER 24 CLIMATE SCIENCE AND ITS CRITICS

1. Ron Paul (www.foxnews.com/us/2012/01/23/republican-presidential-candi dates-on-issues, www.npr.org/2011/09/07/140071973/in-their-own-words-gop -candidates-and-science, and http://ecopolitology.org/2011/08/22/republican -presidential-candidates-on-climate-change/); James Inhofe, *The Greatest Hoax: How the Global Warming Conspiracy Threatens Your Future* (Washington, DC: WND Books, 2012); James M. Taylor, "Cap and Trade—Taxing Our Way to Bankruptcy," Heartland Institute, May 5, 2010, http://heartland.org/policy-documents/cap-and -trade-taxing-our-way-bankruptcy.

2. Andrey Illarionov, http://repub.eur.nl/res/pub/31008/; and Václav Klaus, www.climatewiki.org/wiki/Vaclav_Claus.

3. See "Climate Change," Wikipedia, http://en.wikipedia.org/wiki/Climate_ change, accessed January 28, 2011.

4. William J. Baumol and Alan S. Blinder, *Economics: Principles and Policies*, 11th ed. (Mason, OH: South-Western Cengage, 2010), 6.

5. See National Academy of Sciences, "About Our Expert Consensus Reports," http://dels.nas.edu/global/Consensus-Report.

6. *Strengthening Forensic Science in the United States: A Path Forward* (Washington, DC: National Academies Press, 2009), www.nap.edu/catalog.php?record_id=12589 #toc. If you look at the National Academies Press, www.nap.edu/, you are sure to find some very interesting recent studies.

7. National Research Council, *Climate Change Science: An Analysis of Some Key Questions* (Washington, DC: National Academies Press, 2001).

8. Committee on Stabilization Targets for Atmospheric Greenhouse Gas Concentrations, National Research Council, *Climate Stabilization Targets: Emissions, Concentrations, and Impacts over Decades to Millennia* (Washington, DC: National Academies Press, 2011).

9. IPCC, Fourth Assessment Report, *Impacts*, "Summary for Policymakers," pp. 5, 10.

10. "No Need to Panic about Global Warming," *Wall Street Journal*, January 27, 2012.

11. A useful website that contains articles with a skeptical view is Climate Change Skeptic, http://climatechangeskeptic.blogspot.com/. Many websites currently respond to contrarian views. A particularly good one is "How to Talk to a Climate Skeptic: Responses to the Most Common Skeptical Arguments on Global Warming," Grist, www.grist.org/article/series/skeptics/.

12. The present chapter is adapted from William Nordhaus, "Why the Global Warming Skeptics Are Wrong," *New York Review of Books*, March 22, 2012, and a further response, "In the Climate Casino: An Exchange," *New York Review of Books*, April 26, 2012, available at www.nybooks.com. I omit two of the arguments that are essentially rhetorical, which are that skeptical climate scientists are living under a regime of fear akin to that suffered by Soviet biologists in the Stalinist era; and that the views of mainstream climate scientists are driven primarily by the desire for financial gain. A discussion of these points is in my articles from the *New York Review of Books*.

13. For those who would like to know how statisticians approach the issue of rising temperatures, here is an example. Many climate scientists believe that CO_2-induced warming has become particularly rapid since 1980. We can use a statistical analysis to test whether the increase in global mean surface temperature was more rapid in the 1980–2011 period than during the 1880–1980 period.

A regression analysis determines that the answer is yes, the post-1980 rise in temperature was indeed faster that the historical trend. Such an analysis proceeds as follows. The series TAV_t is the average of three global temperature series from GISS, NCDC, and Hadley. We estimate a regression of the form $TAV_t = \alpha + \beta$ Year$_t + \gamma$ (Year since 1980)$_t + \varepsilon_t$. In this formulation, Year$_t$ is the year, while (Year since 1980)$_t$ is 0 up to 1980 and then (Year −1980) for years after 1980. The Greek letters α, β, and γ are coefficients, while ε_t is a residual error.

The estimated equation has a coefficient on Year of 0.0042 (*t*-statistic=12.7) and a coefficient on (Year since 1980) of 0.0135 (*t*-statistic=8.5). The interpretation is that temperatures in the 1880–1980 period were rising at 0.0042°C per year, while in the later period they were rising at 0.0135°C per year more rapidly. The *t*-statistic in parentheses indicates that the coefficient on (Year since 1980) was 8.5 times its standard error. Using standard tests for statistical significance, this large a *t*-coefficient would be obtained by chance less than one time in a million. We can use other years as break points, from 1930 to 2000, and the answer is the same: There has been a more rapid rise in global mean temperature in the most recent period than in earlier periods.

14. A technical discussion showing how to separate the human-induced changes from the background noise is contained in B. D. Santer, C. Mears, C. Doutriaux, P. Caldwell, P. J. Gleckler, T. M. L. Wigley, et al., "Separating Signal and Noise in Atmospheric Temperature Changes: The Importance of Timescale," *Journal of Geophysical Research* 116 (2011): 1–19.

15. Here is an explanation for those interested in how climate models are used to separate the effects of human-induced factors from natural forces. In numerous experiments, modelers have calculated the consistency of historical temperature observations with different factors. In these experiments, they have run their models to simulate the historical temperature trajectory from 1900 to the present both with and without CO_2 and other human-induced factors in their assumptions. More precisely, they first do one set of runs in which the calculations include only natural forces such as volcanic eruptions and changes in solar activity (a simulation "without GHGs"). They then do another set of runs including CO_2 and other greenhouse gases as well as natural forces ("with GHGs"). They then compare the two sets of runs with the actual temperature record. These experiments have consistently shown that temperature trends over the twentieth century can be explained only if accumulations of CO_2 and other greenhouse gases are included. By 2010, the simulations without GHGs underpredict the temperature increases by more than 1°C. Another interesting feature of the model runs is to show the importance of aerosols. If the influence of aerosols is excluded, the models tend to predict a temperature trajectory above the actual path. (To see a graph with the different runs and the actual temperature, see IPCC, Fourth Assessment Report, *Science*, p. 685f. A more recent set of runs with the same results is given in Olivier Boucher et al., "Climate Response to Aerosol Forcings in CMIP5," *CLIVAR Exchanges* 16, nos. 2 and 56 [May 2011]).

16. IPCC, Fourth Assessment Report, *Impacts*, p. 687.

17. Opinion of the court in *Massachusetts v. Environmental Protection Agency*, 549 U.S. 497 (2007).

18. Richard S. J. Tol, "The Economic Effects of Climate Change," *Journal of Economic Perspectives* 23, no. 2 (2009).

19. This point can be seen in a simple example, which would apply in the case of investments to slow climate change. Suppose we were thinking about two policies. Policy A has a small investment in abatement of CO_2 emissions. It costs relatively little (say $1 billion) but has substantial benefits (say $10 billion), for a net benefit of $9 billion. Now compare this with a very effective and larger investment, Policy B. This second investment costs more (say $10 billion) but has substantial benefits (say $50 billion), for a net benefit of $40 billion. B is preferable because it has higher net benefits ($40 billion for B as compared with $9 billion for A), but A has a higher benefit-cost ratio (a ratio of 10 for A as compared with 5 for B). This example shows why, in designing the most effective policies, we should look at benefits minus costs, not benefits divided by costs.

20. This is one of the central conclusions in IPCC, Fourth Assessment Report, *Science*, p. 10. The IPCC has a very precise definition here. "Likelihood . . . refers to a probabilistic assessment of some well-defined outcome having occurred or occurring in the future." The term "very likely" means ">90 percent probability."

21. Richard Feynman, *The Character of Physical Law* (Cambridge, MA: MIT Press, 1970).

CHAPTER 25 PUBLIC OPINION ON CLIMATE CHANGE

1. The science literacy questions are from National Science Foundation, *Science and Engineering Indicators, 2012*, Appendix Table 7–9, www.nsf.gov/statistics/seind12/. The questions are as follows:

Continental drift (true): "The continents on which we live have been moving their locations for millions of years and will continue to move in the future."

Heliocentric (true is Earth around Sun): "Does the Earth go around the Sun, or does the Sun go around the Earth?"

Radioactivity (false): "All radioactivity is man-made."

Antibiotics kill viruses (false): "Antibiotics kill viruses as well as bacteria."

Big bang (true): "The universe began with a huge explosion."

Evolution (true): "Human beings, as we know them today, developed from earlier species of animals."

Also see Jon Miller, "Civic Scientific Literacy: The Role of the Media in the Electronic Era," in Donald Kennedy and Geneva Overholser, eds., *Science and the Media*, 44–63 (Cambridge, MA: American Academy of Arts and Sciences, 2010). The global warming question is from Harris Interactive, "Big Drop in Those Who Believe That Global Warming Is Coming," New York, December 2, 2009, www.harrisinteractive .com/vault/Harris-Interactive-Poll-Research-Global-Warming-2009-12.pdf.

2. Miller, "Civic Science Literacy."

3. I gathered data from surveys on global warming covering the period 1997–2012 from www.pollingreport.com/enviro2.htm. (I am grateful to Jennifer Hochschild for pointing me to this source.) Here are the details of the calculations. The Harris polls are not included in the compilation from pollingreport.com, and were added to the sample for this study and to Figure 42. There were 103 observations, but we took only those from Gallup, Harris, and Pew because they had repeated surveys, which produced 67 observations. We calculated the fraction responding that they believed global warming was occurring or the analogous answers to similar questions. We then did a regression with dummies for each of the surveys (reflecting differences in the questions), estimated a kernel fit to the residuals, and added the mean. This produced the smooth line in the figure. The Harris survey shows the steepest decline from 2007 to 2011, from 71 percent to 44 percent answering yes to the question, "Do you believe the theory that increased carbon dioxide and other gases released into the atmosphere will, if unchecked, lead to global warming and an increase in average temperatures?"

4. The average number of correct answers to eleven questions was 56 percent in 1992, 60 percent in 2001, and 59 percent in 2010.

5. This paragraph is based on Allan Mazur, "Believers and Disbelievers in Evolution," *Politics and the Life Sciences* 23, no. 2 (2004): 55–61; and Darren E. Sherkat, "Religion and Scientific Literacy in the United States," *Social Science Quarterly* 92, no. 5 (2011): 1134–1150.

6. The results here are all bivariate relationships (taking two variables at a time). But they tended to hold as well in multivariate statistical analyses that used all explanatory variables. However, for those concerned about statistical methodology, it should be noted that the causality in these relationships has not been carefully controlled. Since political and religious views are in turn determined by other variables (such as parents' politics, religion, and education), we cannot make unambiguous causal statements about the determinants of scientific views.

7. See Pew Research Center, "Little Change in Opinions about Global Warming," October 10, 2010, http://people-press.org/report/669/.

8. The Gallup poll is Jeffrey M. Jones, "In U.S., Concerns about Global Warming Stable at Lower Levels," March 14, 2011, www.gallup.com/poll/146606/concerns -global-warming-stable-lower-levels.aspx. The longer-term divide is discussed in Riley E. Dunlap and Aaron M. McCright, "A Widening Gap: Republican and Democratic Views on Climate Change," *Environmental Magazine* (September–October 2008), http://earthleaders.org/projects/psf/Dunlap%20%20McCright%202008 %20A%20widening%20gap%20Environment.pdf.

9. Nearly half (47 percent) in a survey said that fossil fuels are the fossilized remains of dinosaurs. See Anthony Leiserowitz, Nicolas Smith, and Jennifer R. Marlon, *Americans' Knowledge of Climate Change* (New Haven, CT: Yale Project on Climate Change Communication, 2010), http://environment.yale.edu/climate/files /ClimateChangeKnowledge2010.pdf.

10. Zaller is a political scientist from UCLA who has written the classic study on the subject, John Zaller, *The Nature and Origins of Mass Opinion* (Cambridge: Cambridge University Press, 1992).

11. Shaun M. Tanger, Peng Zeng, Wayde Morse, and David N. Laband, "Macroeconomic Conditions in the U.S. and Congressional Voting on Environmental Policy: 1970–2008," *Ecological Economics* 70 (2011): 1109–1120. I am grateful to Shaun M. Tanger for providing the raw data. As an example of how the scorecard was constructed, the 2010 scorecard examined two votes on an amendment to overturn the EPA's endangerment finding on global warming, three energy-related fiscal measures, a lead paint regulation, and a bill to build a fence on the southern U.S. border. Note that the score does not indicate the importance of the issues in a particular year but just the voting patterns.

12. Remarks on signing annual report of Council on Environmental Quality, July 11, 1984.

13. A list of economists who favor carbon taxes as an approach is provided by Greg Mankiw, "The Pigou Club Manifesto," Greg Mankiw's Blog, October 20, 2006, http://gregmankiw.blogspot.com/2006/10/pigou-club-manifesto.html. A compendium of views can be found at "Conservatives," Carbon Tax Center, www.carbon tax.org/who-supports/conservatives/.

14. "Blinder's Carbon-Tax Plan Provokes Strong Responses," Letters, *Wall Street Journal*, February 7, 2011.

CHAPTER 26 OBSTACLES TO CLIMATE-CHANGE POLICIES

1. There is a wide range of estimates, however, as shown in Figure 55 and the accompanying discussion. The actual carbon price in 2010 is from William Nordhaus, "Economic Aspects of Global Warming in a Post-Copenhagen Environment," *Proceedings of the National Academy of Sciences (US)* 107, no. 26 (2010): 11721–11726.

2. David Victor, *Global Warming Gridlock: Creating More Effective Strategies for Protecting the Planet* (Cambridge: Cambridge University Press, 2011).

3. The estimates of the noncooperative price are from Nordhaus, "Economic Aspects of Global Warming."

4. Estimates of the net benefits are from the "Copenhagen Accord" scenario from William Nordhaus, "Economic Aspects of Global Warming in a Post-Copenhagen Environment," *Proceedings of the National Academy of Sciences (US)*, June 14, 2010.

5. My thanks to Nat Keohane, who suggested the presentation in this figure.

6. Data on employment are from the Bureau of Labor Statistics for employment at www.bls.gov/ocs/current/naics4_212100.htm. Results on coal use are from Energy Information Agency at www.eia.gov/coal/.

7. Estimates from Mun S. Ho, Richard Morgenstern, and Jhih-Shyang Shih, "Impact of Carbon Price Policies on U.S. Industry," Discussion Paper RFF DP 08-37 (Washington, DC: Resources for the Future, November 2008).

8. See Naomi Oreskes and Erik Conway, *Merchants of Doubt* (New York: Bloomsbury, 2010).

9. Brown and Williamson Tobacco Corporation, "Smoking and Health Proposal," 1969, available at Legacy Tobacco Documents Library, http://legacy.library.ucsf.edu/. There is an extensive literature on the tobacco industry's strategy for distorting the scientific record and promoting views that were favorable to smoking. See Stanton Glantz, John Slade, Lisa A. Bero, and Deborah E. Barnes, *The Cigarette Papers* (Berkeley: University of California Press, 1996); and Robert Proctor, *Cancer Wars: How Politics Shapes What We Know and Don't Know about Cancer* (New York: Basic Books, 2007).

10. Chris Mooney, "Some Like It Hot," *Mother Jones* (May–June 2005), http://motherjones.com/environment/2005/05/some-it-hot. The list is available at http://motherjones.com/politics/2005/05/put-tiger-your-think-tank. A more comprehensive list of organizations supported by ExxonMobil is at the "Organizations in Exxon Secrets Database," www.exxonsecrets.org/html/listorganizations.php.

11. Energy expenditures are at U.S. Energy Information Administration, "Annual Energy Review," August 19, 2010, www.eia.doe.gov/aer/txt/ptb0105.html. Tobacco sales exclude taxes and distribution.

12. The question asked was, "What is your opinion—do you think cigarette smoking is one of the causes of lung cancer?" Lydia Saad, "Tobacco and Smoking," Gallup, August 15, 2002, www.gallup.com/poll/9910/tobacco-smoking.aspx#4, accessed January 26, 2012.

INDEX

Abatement costs: cost-benefit analysis of, 206–212; of meeting different climate objectives, 177–180

Acidification of oceans, 113–115

Adaptive strategies: for agriculture, 84–89; for climate change, 150–152; costs of, 151; for health risks, 96–99; for hurricanes, 120–121; in managed systems, 72–73

Advanced Research Projects Agency-Energy (ARPA-E), 288–289

Aerosols and radiative forcing, 157–158

Africa, health risks for, 93–94, 96, 97–98

Aggregate cost-reduction curve, 173–176

Aggregate damage estimates, 139–141

Agriculture, 78–90; adaptation and mitigating factors for, 84–89; impact of climate change on, 82–84; management of, 71, 78, 85

AIDS epidemic, 95–96

Airborne fraction, 329–330n4

Air conditioning in India, 96

Air pollutants, greenhouse gases as, 299

Akerlof, George, xi

Albedo effect, 44, 153–154

Allowances in cap and trade, 233–235

Alternative investments, rate of return on, 187–188

Antarctic ice core samples, historical temperature variations based on, 200–201, 351n8

Antarctic ice sheet, 105

Anti-global warming policy, 309–311

Anxiety discounting, 192–193

Appliance regulation, 262

Aral Sea, 13

ARPA-E (Advanced Research Projects Agency-Energy), 288–289

Atlantic thermohaline circulation, 57–58

Atmospheric CO_2 concentrations, 4–5, 38–39, 329–330n4

Automobiles: fuel efficiency standards, 262–265; gasoline vs. diesel engine, 268

Barrage, Lint, xi, 356n2

Barrett, Scott, xi, 245

Baseline scenario, 79

Baumol, William, 294–295

Becker, Gary, 314

Becquerel, Edmond, 283

Behavioral diversity, 133

Benefits vs. costs. *See* Cost-benefit analysis

Biomass energy, 279
Biosphere: CO_2 absorption into, 38–39; in positive feedback interactions, 58
"Black carbon" reduction, 348n3
Blinder, Alan, 294–295
Border tax, 242–243, 255–256
Boskin, Michael, 314
Bottom-up models, 174–176, 349n6
Boyer, Joseph, xi
Brainard, William, xi
Bush, George W., 296

CAFE (Corporate Average Fuel Economy) standards, 263
Canada and Kyoto Protocol, 254–255
Canute (King), 113
Cap and trade: advantages and disadvantages, 239–241; allocation of, 239–240; defined, 6, 223; hybrid with carbon taxes, 241–243; international policy of, 249–250, 251; mechanism of, 233–236; similarity to carbon taxes, 237–238; volatility of, 239
Capital: migration due to hurricanes, 120–121, 341n4; productiveness of, 191
Carbon-based fuels, 4, 19–20
Carbon calculator, 226, 354n8
Carbon capture and sequestration (CCS): and carbon pricing, 242; costs of, 279, 280, 286–287; technologies for, 163–165
Carbon cycle, 29, 38, 58, 329n4
Carbon dioxide (CO_2) concentrations: atmospheric, 4–5, 38–39, 329–330n4; and climate change, 40–42; and CO_2 emissions, 37–39; growth curve for, 31–35; and human activity, 38; in ice cores, 38
Carbon dioxide (CO_2) emissions, 6, 157–168; aggregate cost-reduction curve for mitigation of, 173–176; calculator, 226, 354n8; and carbon intensity, 22–23; contrarian view

on toxicity of, 299; current technologies for mitigation, 161–165; economic growth linked to, 252–253; economic impact of, 17–18; futuristic technologies for mitigation, 165–168; and global temperature targets, 176–180; global warming linked to, 4–5; household perspective of, 160–161; mitigation costs, 169–181; projections for, 30–35; and radiative forcing, 157; sources of, 158–160; trends in, 19–23. See also Carbon dioxide (CO_2) concentrations
Carbon fertilization, 84–86
Carbon intensity: carbon footprint, 160, 226; reduction of, 162–163; of U.S. economy, 22–23, 166, 276. See also Carbon dioxide (CO_2) concentrations
Carbonization of oceans, 113–115, 340n17
Carbon prices and pricing, 6–7, 9, 220–232; actual global, 316; advantages and disadvantages, 239–241; allocation of, 239–240; conservative view of, 313–315; consumers affected by, 224; and deadweight loss, 262; defined, 220, 221–223; in developing countries, 254, 355n7; differences between methods for, 239–241; economic functions of, 222, 224–225; energy price impact of, 229–230; and environmental ethics, 225–227; and fiscal picture, 231–232; hybrid methods, 241–243; industry impact of, 321–322; innovators affected by, 225; integrated assessment models for, 228–229; international harmonization of, 252; international regime for, 250–252; and investment in low-carbon technologies, 282, 286–287; mechanisms for setting, 233–237; payers of, 223–224;

in practice, 222–223; producers affected by, 224–225; rationale for, 221–222; resistance to, 259; similarity of methods for, 237–238; social cost of carbon in, 227–228; tradable permits or taxes for raising, 223–224; trends in use of, 237; zero, 313. *See also* Cap and trade

Carbon sequestration. *See* Carbon capture and sequestration (CCS)

Centigrade (°C) scale, 37

Certainty vs. likelihood, 301–302

CFCs (chlorofluorocarbons), 171

CH_4. *See* Methane

China: and clean development mechanism, 265–266; per capita income, 145

Chlorofluorocarbons (CFCs), 171

Cicerone, Ralph, 296

Cigarette smoking, 323, 324–325

Clean Air Act, 299

Clean development mechanism, 265–266

Climate: defined, 37; sensitivity, 42–44; variability, 51–53; weather vs., 37, 74–75

Climate Casino metaphor: climate policy in, 300–301; cost-benefit analysis in, 215–217; metaphor of, 3–4, 48–49; risk premium for hazards in, 141–143; tipping points in, 5, 50–66; uncertain CO_2 trajectories in, 33–35

Climate change: as beneficial, 299–300; defined, 36–37; economics of, 6, 17–35, 147–194; ethics of, 353n2; impacts of, 10–11, 67–146; mitigation of, 147–194; projections, 36–49; science of, 4, 12–66, 294–296. *See also* Economics of climate change; Impacts of climate change; Policy-making; Science of climate change

Climate Change Skeptic (website), 359n11

Climate equation, 327–328n3

Climate science. *See* Science of climate change

Cline, William, xi, 349n3

Clinton, Bill: and global warming as political issue, 309, 310; and Kyoto Protocol, 259–260

Clouds, 44

CO_2. *See* Carbon dioxide

Coal: advanced with CCS, 279, 280; cost of reducing consumption of, 172, 173; employment from, 320–321, 322; as source of CO_2 emissions, 158–160; switching to natural gas from, 162–163; as U.S. energy source, 278, 279. *See also* Carbon-based fuels

Coastal systems and sea level rise, 104–108, 112–113

Collapse (Diamond), 72

Compound interest: and discounting, 192; and economic growth, 335n3

Computerized models, 23–28

Consensus, scientific, 294–296

Conservatives, climate change policy of, 309–311

Consumers, effect of carbon price on, 224

Consumption: defined, 185–186; today vs. tomorrow, 185–186

Contingent valuation methodology (CVM), 130–133

Contrarians, 9, 293–302. *See also* Critics

Conway, Erik, 322

Copenhagen Accord (2009), 199, 200, 247–249, 318–320

Copenhagen temperature target: and cost-benefit analysis, 218; cost of meeting, 176–181, 194; and damages from climate change, 146; and ecological damage, 203; and historical global temperature variation, 200–203; regulatory approach to, 267; scientific basis and rationales for, 200–204; and sea level rise, 105; and technology, 276;

Copenhagen temperature target (cont.) and tipping points, 204; U.S. endorsement of, 197–198; wide acceptance of, 199–200

Coral reefs, 59–60, 126

Corporate Average Fuel Economy (CAFE) standards, 263

Corruption in quantitative systems, 254, 355n7

Cost-benefit analysis, 205–219; applied to climate change, 206–212; in Climate Casino, 215–217; and contrarian view, 299–300; critiques of, 217–218; defined, 205; with discounting, 210–212; with expected value principle, 215; with limited participation, 208–212; and nationalism, 317–318; with precautionary principle, 216–217; time-distant payoffs in, 318–320; with tipping points, 212–215; with universal participation, 212

Costs: of adaptation, 151; aggregate cost-reduction curve for, 173–176; of electricity generation, 278–280; marginal, 7, 249; of meeting global temperature targets, 176–180; metric for measuring, 170; negative, 171, 175–176, 178, 271; of reducing CO_2 emissions, 171–173; of slowing climate change, 75–76, 169–181. *See also* Cost-benefit analysis; Discounting

Country participation: in cost-benefit analysis, 208–212, 218; and cost of meeting global temperature targets, 177–180; universal, 7, 177–180, 212

Critics, 9, 293–302; and policies in Climate Casino, 300–301; and scientific consensus, 294–296; and unattainable certainty, 301–302; views on global warming of, 297–300

Crop productivity, 83

Crop yields, 83

CVM (contingent valuation methodology), 130–133

DALYs (disability-adjusted life years), 92–95, 97

Damages: aggregate estimates of, 139–141; calculations of, 29; from climate change, 135–146; in cost-benefit analysis, 206–212; ecological, 203; from hurricanes, 117, 118, 119; incremental, 344–345n5

Dams and fish populations, 130–131

Deadweight (efficiency) loss, 261–262

Decarbonization: and CO_2 growth curve, 31–32; historical trend of, 276, 277; reasons for, 22–23

Democrats, climate change policy of, 309, 310, 311

Department of Energy, 286

Descriptive approach to discounting, 187, 188

Developed countries, health risks for, 94–95

Developing countries: health risks for, 93–94, 95–96, 97–98; in international agreements, 252–254

Diamond, Jared, 72

Diarrheal diseases, 92, 93–95, 97–98, 338n8

DICE model, 29–30, 32, 328nn6–7; contrarian views vs., 300; for cost of meeting global temperature targets, 177–180; for economic growth and climate change, 79–82; for estimates of aggregate damages, 139–140; for health impact, 97–98; and nationalist dilemma, 317–318; for sea level rise, 105–108; for temperature increase, 47, 201, 202

Diesel engine vs. gasoline, 268

Diffenbach, Noah, xi

Disability-adjusted life years (DALYs), 92–95, 97

Enhanced greenhouse effect, 41

Enteric fermentation, 160

Environmental ethics and carbon pricing, 225–227

Environmental migration, 102–104

Environmental shock, rebound after, 133

Equilibrium, noncooperative, 317–318

Equilibrium response, 42–44

Equity weights in social cost of carbon, 344n4

Ethanol-based fuel subsidies, 265

Ethics: and carbon pricing, 225–227; of climate change, 353n2; of discounting, 191–192

European Commission on temperature target, 199

European Union (EU) CO_2 Emissions Trading Scheme, 235–236, 244, 259, 265

Evolution and politics, 306–307

Expected value principle, 215

Externalities: approaches to, 244–246; and climate change as economic problem, 6, 17–19; of innovations and technological change, 285, 286; scientific consensus on, 294–295; and value of endangered species and ecosystems, 128–130

Extinction, 122–134; categories of, 343n4; and challenge of valuing nonmarket services, 125–126; climate change and potential for, 124–125; defined, 343n4; and genetic diversity, 133; other causes of, 128; rate of, 122–123, 124–125, 341–342nn3–4; sixth mass, 122–123; and valuation of ecosystems and species, 126–133; in the wild, 343n4. See also Endangered species

Extreme weather, 118–119. See also Hurricanes

Exxon-Mobil, 323

Fahrenheit (°F) scale, 37

Farming. See Agriculture

Fast feedback processes, 58–59

Feedback effects, 44–45, 58–59

Feldstein, Martin, 314

Feynman, Richard, 301, 303

"Fingerprints" of climate change, 41

Fiscal incentives, 260, 266

Fiscal policy and carbon taxes, 231–232

Fisheries, 115

Fish populations and dams, 130–131

Focal policy, 76–77

Food prices, 87–88

Fossil fuels. See Carbon-based fuels

Free-market solution, 313

Free rider problem, 8–9, 254–257

Fuel as source of CO_2 emissions, 158–159

Fuel efficiency standards, 262–265

Fuel switching, 162–163

Full participation (in international agreements). See Universal participation

Functional diversity, 133

Funding: for research and development, 285–286; and transition of new technology to marketplace, 287–289

Furnace regulatory policy, 262

Future climate change. See Projections

Fuzzy telescope problem, 101–102

G-8 (Group of 8) on temperature target, 199–200

Gases. See Greenhouse gases (GHGs); Natural gas

Gasoline as source of CO_2 emissions, 158–159

Gasoline engine vs. diesel, 268

Gates, Bill, 73, 98

GCAM model, 281

Generational free riding, 8

Generational tradeoffs, 318–320

Genetic diversity, 133

Impacts of climate change (cont.)
hazards, 141–143; vulnerability by
economic sector, 136–139; and
weather vs. climate, 37, 74–75; on
wildlife and species loss, 122–134
Inaction as international response to
climate change, 245–246
Incentives: for adaptation, 120; and
Aral Sea, 13; carbon price as, 150,
221, 224–225, 226, 238; effective,
6, 7; and Kyoto Protocol, 8; to
prevent free riding, 244, 254, 256,
257; for technological innovation,
166, 225, 260, 274, 283, 288
Income: and CO_2 emissions, 252–253;
in India and China, 145; and life
expectancy, 95, 97, 98; and
migration, 103
Incremental damage, 344–345n5
Indexes of scientific literacy, 303–304,
361n1
India: health risks in, 96, 97; per
capita income in, 145
Indicators of global warming, 297–298
Industrial vulnerability by economic
sector, 136–139
Innovation: effect of carbon price on,
225; nature of, 283–287
Input-output analysis, 346–347n5
Insulation, 269
Insurance premium for hazards,
141–143
Integrated assessment models (IAMs),
7, 28–30; for carbon pricing, 227,
228–229; for cost-benefit analysis,
210–212; for economic growth and
climate change, 79–82; for EMF-22
project, 32–33; of health impact,
97–98; for sea level rise, 105–108;
for temperature projections, 46–47
Integrated gasification combined cycle
with CO_2 capture, 164
Interest: determinants of, 184–185;
example of, 182–183; real vs.
nominal rates of, 183–184

Interest group-based attacks on
climate science and policy, 322–323
Intergovernmental Panel on Climate
Change (IPCC): on climate change
and agriculture, 83, 88; consensus
report of, 296, 298, 301; on ecological damage at various temperature
thresholds, 203; on estimates of
aggregate damage, 140; on future
climate change, 38, 43, 45–47; on
health impact, 98, 336n1, 338n8;
and ocean acidification, 114; on sea
level rise, 106; on species loss, 125
International climate agreements:
enforcement mechanisms for,
254–257; history of, 198–200,
246–249; obligations for rich and
poor in, 252–254; structure of,
249–250. See also Policymaking
International Institute for Applied
Systems Analysis (IIASA), 278
International Social Survey Program,
306
International Union for Conservation
of Nature (IUCN), 342–343nn3–5
Invention: effect of carbon price on,
225; nature of, 283–287
Investments: discounting applied to,
190–191; in low-carbon technologies, 286–287; rate of return on,
187–188; and transition of new
technology to marketplace,
287–289
Invisible hand of markets and global
externalities, 18–19
IPCC. See Intergovernmental Panel on
Climate Change
Irrigation systems, 85
IUCN (International Union for
Conservation of Nature),
342–343nn3–5

Jewkes, John, 284
Joint Global Change Research
Institute, 281

Kaya equation, 328n7
Keohane, Robert, xi
Kolstad, Charles, xi
Koopmans, Tjalling, xii, 193
Kurzweil, Ray, 167
Kyoto Protocol (2012): and Canada, 254–255; carbon pricing in, 251, 252; clean development mechanism in, 265; failure of, 247–249, 257; history of, 199, 246–247; limited participation in, 178, 208–209; negotiation of, 309–310; rich vs. poor countries under, 252, 253; and SO$_2$ program, 235; technology after, 275; U.S. response to, 259–260

Lackner, Klaus, 166
Laffer, Arthur, 314
L'Aquila Summit (2009), 199–200
League of Conservation Voters, 310
Liberals, climate change policy of, 309, 310, 311
Life expectancy, 95, 97–98
Likelihood vs. certainty, 301–302
Limited participation, 177–180; cost-benefit analysis with, 208–212
Living standards and climate change, 79–82
Lovejoy, Tom, xi
Low-carbon technologies, 161–168, 274–289; for agriculture, 86–87; and carbon intensity, 166–167; challenges for, 274, 276–277; estimating costs of, 171–173; funding for development of, 285–286; hurdles for, 280; investment in, 286–287; after Kyoto Protocol, 275; models of, 281–282; and nature of innovation, 283–287; promising, 277–283; subsidies for, 260, 266; transition to, 280–282; underinvestment in, 263, 267–271

Macroeconomic models, 24
Malaria, 92, 94, 98, 338n8

Malnutrition, 92, 94, 338n8
Managed systems, 5, 70–74
Mankiw, Greg, 314
Manne, Alan, xi
Marginal costs, 7, 249
Marketplace, transition of new technology to, 287–289
Market value of endangered species and ecosystems, 128–129
May, Robert, 133
Mayhew, David, xi
Medicine as managed system, 73
Mendelsohn, Robert, xi, 84
"Merchants of doubt," 322–323
Methane (CH_4): impact of reducing, 348n3; in positive feedback interactions, 58; radiation absorption by, 40; and radiative forcing, 157; released through enteric fermentation, 160
Migration: as adaptive strategy, 72; environmental, 102–104; and sea level rise, 109–110
Minimax strategy for cost-benefit analysis, 216–217
Misconceptions and public opinion, 306–311. See also Critics
Mitigation strategies: for agriculture, 84–89; costs of, 169–181; current technologies for, 161–165; future technologies for, 165–168; and health risks, 96–99; technologies for, 6, 157–168
Modeling, 23–30; building of, 27–28; components of, 25–27; computerized, 23–28; contrarian view of, 298; DICE, 29–30, 32, 328nn6–7; differing results of, 44; human-induced factors from natural forces in, 360n15; important results of, 47–48; integrated assessment, 7, 28–30; projections for, 30–35; purposes of, 28; reality vs., 25, 26–27; separating effects of human-induced factors from natural forces

Modeling (cont.)
in, 360n15; as tool for understanding, 23–28
Moral hazard, 156

Nakicenovic, Nebojsa, xi, 278
National Academy of Sciences:
endorsement of 2°C temperature target by, 197–198, 200; identification of climate change risks, 295–296; on subsidies, 266
National climate policies, 233–243;
differences between carbon pricing methods in, 239–241; harmonization of, 249–252; hybrid carbon pricing methods in, 241–243; mechanisms for setting carbon prices in, 233–237; similarity of carbon pricing methods in, 237–238
Nationalist dilemma as obstacle to climate change policies, 8, 317–318
National Renewable Energy Laboratories, 281
National Science Foundation: funding by, 286; on public opinion, 303–304
Natural forces vs. human-induced factors in climate models, 360n15
Natural gas: advanced with CCS, 279, 280; conventional combined-cycle, 279; cost of reducing consumption of, 172, 173; as source of CO_2 emissions, 158–159; switching to, 162–163, 170; as U.S. energy source, 278, 279. *See also* Carbon-based fuels
Natural greenhouse effect, 40–41
Nature on technology after Kyoto Protocol (2012), 275
Near-market value of endangered species and ecosystems, 128–129
Nee, Sean, 133
Negative costs, 171, 175–176, 178, 271
Net benefits, 300, 360n19
Netherlands, sea level rise in, 112
New York Times on climate change and agriculture, 82–83

Nigeria, CO_2 emissions in, 254, 355n7
Noah's ark problem, 343n15
No-growth scenario, 79–82
"No market failures" approach, 263
Nominal interest rates, 183–184
Noncompliance with international climate treaties, 254–257
Noncooperative equilibrium, 317–318
Non-linear reaction to stresses, 54–56
Nonmarket service valuation, 125–126
Nonregulatory approaches, 260, 265–267
Nonuse value of endangered species and ecosystems, 128–130
Nuclear power, 278–280
Nutritional deficiencies, 92, 94, 338n8

Obama, Barack: climate policy, 260, 276; fuel efficiency standards, 262; regulatory approach, 275, 309, 320
Obstacles to climate change policies, 316–326; economic self-interest as, 322–323; nationalism as, 317–318; overcoming, 324–325; partisanship as, 320–322; time-distant payoffs as, 318–320
Oceans, 100–115; acidification of, 113–115; carbonization of, 113–115, 340n17; change in currents, 57–58; CO_2 absorption into, 39; gravitational storage of CO_2 in, 165. *See also* Sea level rise (SLR)
Office of Management and Budget (OMB) on discount rates, 188–189
Oil: as source of CO_2 emissions, 158–159; as U.S. energy source, 278. *See also* Carbon-based fuels
Opportunity-cost approach to discounting, 187, 188
Oreskes, Naomi, 322

Paleocene-Eocene thermal maximum (PETM), 115
Paleoclimatic temperature extremes as target, 202
Panel of experts, 295–296

Participation in global regime: in cost-benefit analysis, 208–212, 218; and cost of meeting global temperature targets, 177–180; universal, 7, 177–180, 212

Partisan divide: closing of, 312–315; development of, 309–311; as obstacle to climate change policy, 320–322

Path dependence, 62, 63

Per capita income: in China and India, 145; distribution of emissions by, 252–253

Percentage tariff on imports from noncomplying countries, 255, 256

Permian-Triassic extinction, 122–123

Permits in cap and trade, 233–235

Personal perspective on climate change, 14–16

PETM (Paleocene-Eocene thermal maximum), 115

Petroleum: cost of reducing consumption of, 172, 173; as source of CO_2 emissions, 158–159

Pew survey on global warming (2010), 307

Photovoltaic solar energy, 279, 283–284

Pigovian tax, 313

Policymaking, 8–9, 195 289; alternative approaches to, 259–273; carbon prices in, 6–7, 9, 220–232; in Climate Casino, 300–301; cost-benefit analysis for, 205–219; critics of climate science in, 9, 293–302; and energy-cost myopia, 267–271; "focal policy," 76–77; global climate policy, 8, 244–258; historical perspectives on, 197–204; impacts of, 10–11; inefficiency of, 179; interest group-based attacks on, 322–323; international agreements on, 8, 198–200, 244–258; at national level, 233–243; nonregulatory, 265–267; obstacles

to, 316–326; overview, 7–8; politics of, 291–326; and public opinion, 306–307, 309–311; regulatory policy, 260, 262–265, 272–273; research and development in, 261; scientific basis of $2^\circ C$ target in, 200–204; and technology innovation, 9–10, 274–289

Policy module in climate models, 29

Popp, David, xi

Positive feedback interactions, 58

Postcombustion removal, 162, 163–165

Precautionary principle, cost-benefit analysis with, 216–217

Precompetitive generic enabling technologies, 287–288

Preparation as adaptive strategy, 152

Prescriptive approach to discounting, 186–187

Present value at different discount rates, 190, 191

Prevention as adaptive strategy, 152

Prices and pricing: of agricultural products, 87–88; of energy, 229–230; of food, 87–88; zero price of carbon emissions, 313. *See also* Carbon prices and pricing

Producers, effect of carbon price on, 224–225

Productive investments, 191–192

Projections: basic principles of, 30–33; carbon dioxide emissions and concentrations, 37–39, 40–42; in climate modeling, 30–35, 42–45; in climate science, 36–37; and climatic roulette wheel, 48–49; defined, 24; of temperature trends, 45–47; uncertainty about, 33–35

Public opinion, 9–10, 303–315; closing partisan divide in, 312–315; formation of, 307–309; on global warming, 304–306; and misconceptions, 306–311; and politics, 306–307, 309–311; on science, 303–304

Quantitative systems, corruption in, 254, 355n7

Radiant energy, 40–42
Radiation, 40–42
Radiative forcing, 157–158, 330n6, 353n6
R&D. *See* Research and development
Rate of return on alternative investments, 187–188
Ratio scales, 21
Reagan, Ronald, 312
Real interest rates, 183–184
Red List, 342–343nn3–4
Red zone for sea level rise, 108–111
ReEDS model, 281
Reflective particles, injection into atmosphere of, 153–154
Refrigerator, cost of energy-efficient, 170, 348n1
Regional approaches to climate change, 246
Regulatory policy, 260, 262–265, 272–273
Reilly, John, xi, 88
Reinforcing feedback interactions, 58
Religion and scientific views, 306
Renewable energy sources, 278, 280–281
Republicans, climate change policy of, 309–311
Research and development (R&D): in climate policy, 261; effect of carbon price on, 225; funding for, 285–286
Resources for the Future (RfF), 263–265
RICE model, 29, 46, 47
Richels, Richard, xi
Rio Declaration on Environment and Development (1992), 216
Risk premium for hazards, 141–143
Roemer, John, xi, 186
Rutherford, Tom, xi

Sachs, Jeffrey, xi
Salt ponds in southern New England, 12–13
Salvage therapy, 155
Samuelson, Paul, xii, 332n5
Sawers, David, 284
Scarf, Herbert, xi
Scherer, F. M., 287–288
Schultz, George, 314
Science of climate change, 4, 12–66; carbon dioxide concentrations, 37–42; carbon dioxide emissions, 19–23, 37–39; consensus in, 294–296; critics of, 9, 293–302; economic origins of, 17–35; future of, 36–49; interest group-based attacks on, 322–323; modeling of, 23–30; personal perspective on, 12–16; projections, 30–35, 42–47; public opinion on, 303–304; scientific literacy indexes, 303–304, 361n1; tipping points for, 50–66
Sea level rise (SLR), 48, 100–113; and coastal systems, 104–108, 112–113; components, 104–105; current estimates, 104, 105, 339n5; delay in, 100–101; and environmental migration, 102–104; and fuzzy telescope problem, 101–102; impacts of, 108–111; management, 73; due to melting of Greenland Ice Sheet, 64; red zone for, 108–111; retreat vs. defense from, 112–113; and world heritage sites, 111–113
Sea level rise equivalent (SLRe), 61
Services: CO_2 and other GHGs contained in, 160, 346–347n5; reduced carbon intensity of, 162
Slow feedback processes, 59
Slowing climate change, 147–194; adaptation and geoengineering for, 149–156; costs of, 75–76, 169–181; discounting and value of time for, 182–194; emission reduction for, 6, 157–168; steps to take for, 9–10

SLR. *See* Sea level rise

Smith, Adam, xi

SO$_2$ (sulfur dioxide) emissions, allowances to limit, 235

Social cost of carbon, 227–228

Solar power, 167, 279, 280, 281, 283–284, 347–348n14

Solar radiation, 40–42, 153–156, 330n6

Solow, Robert, xii

Special Report on Emissions Scenarios (SRES), 45, 328n8

Species, valuation methodology for, 126–133

Species-area relationship, 127

Species loss. *See* Endangered species; Extinction

SRES (Special Report on Emissions Scenarios), 45, 328n8

Stavins, Robert, xi, 354n3

Stern, Nicholas, xi, 186

Stern Review (2007): on discounting, 186, 349–350n3; on economics of climate change, 83, 335n1; on health impact, 91

Stillerman, Richard, 284

Stresses, non-linear reaction to, 54–56

Stringency increase over time, 7–8

Sub-Saharan Africa, health risks for, 96, 98

Subsidies: for ethanol-based fuels, 265; for "green" technology, 260, 266

Sulfur dioxide (SO$_2$) emissions, allowances to limit, 235

Supreme Court on greenhouse gases as air pollutants, 299

SUVs and fuel efficiency standards, 262

Synthetic tree, 166

Tariffs on imports from noncomplying countries, 255–256

Taxes and taxation: border, 242–243, 255–256; energy, 260; Pigovian tax, 313. *See also* Carbon prices and pricing

Technical University of Vienna, 278

Technologies, low-carbon. *See* Low-carbon technologies

Temperature: projections, 45–47, 48, 201, 202; proxies for, 200–201, 331n6; scales for, 37; statistical analysis of, 297, 359–360n13; targets, 176–180, 206–212; thresholds, 203; tolerable window of, 202–203; trends, 45, 46; variations, 200–203. *See also* Copenhagen temperature target

Temporal tradeoffs, 318–320

Thermal expansion and sea level rise, 104

Thermal solar energy, 279

Threatened species, 343n5. *See also* Endangered species

Thresholds, 50–51, 212–215

Thunderstorms, 118–119

Time-distant payoffs as obstacle to climate change policies, 318–320

Tipping points, 5, 50–66; climate change dangers of, 56–60; concept of, 53–54; cost-benefit analysis with, 212–215; defined, 53–54; Greenland Ice Sheet melting, 60–66; illustration of, 54–56; temperature targets to prevent, 204; and thresholds, 50–51; and variability of past climates, 51–53

Tobin, James, xii

Tol, Richard, xi, 139–141

Tolerable temperature window, 202–203

Top-down models, 174–176

Tornadoes, 118–119

Trade, agricultural, 88. *See also* Cap and trade

Transient response, 42–44

Trees in CO$_2$ emission reduction, 165–166, 242

Tropical storms. *See* Hurricanes

Two degree (2°) C temperature target. *See* Copenhagen temperature target